THE CONTROL AGENDA

THE CONTROL AGENDA

A History of the Strategic Arms Limitation Talks

Matthew J. Ambrose

CORNELL UNIVERSITY PRESS   ITHACA AND LONDON

First published 2018 by Cornell University Press

Printed in the United States of America

Library of Congress Cataloging-in-Publication Data
Names: Ambrose, Matthew J., author.
Title: The control agenda : a history of the Strategic Arms Limitation Talks / Matthew J. Ambrose.
Description: Ithaca : Cornell University Press, 2018. | Includes bibliographical references and index.
Identifiers: LCCN 2017028026 (print) | LCCN 2017031400 (ebook) | ISBN 9781501712012 (epub/mobi) | ISBN 9781501709371 (pdf) | ISBN 9781501713743 (cloth : alk. paper)
Subjects: LCSH: Strategic Arms Limitation Talks—History. | Strategic Arms Limitation Talks II—History. | Nuclear arms control—United States—History. | Nuclear arms control—Soviet Union—History. | United States—Foreign relations—Soviet Union. | Soviet Union—Foreign relations—United States.
Classification: LCC JZ5665 (ebook) | LCC JZ5665 .A63 2018 (print) | DDC 327.1/747—dc23
LC record available at https://lccn.loc.gov/2017028026

Cornell University Press strives to use environmentally responsible suppliers and materials to the fullest extent possible in the publishing of its books. Such materials include vegetable-based, low-VOC inks and acid-free papers that are recycled, totally chlorine-free, or partly composed of nonwood fibers. For further information, visit our website at cornellpress.cornell.edu.

For Jillian

Contents

Acknowledgments

I am indebted to a number of individuals and institutions that helped shape this book. The Harry and Lynde Bradley Foundation and The Ohio State University both provided generous support at critical junctures for research and travel expenses; without this help, this project might never have been completed. I am also grateful to the staffs of the National Archives at College Park, MD, and the Reagan, Carter, and Ford Presidential Libraries for assisting a relative newcomer to archival research. I am also grateful to the family of Paul A. Nitze for granting me permission to access Mr. Nitze's papers and to the staff of the Library of Congress for helping me navigate them.

My editor, Michael McGandy, deserves special mention for being willing to engage so thoroughly with my initial proposal and manuscript. Mr. McGandy's incisive comments and suggestions did a great deal help me improve my initial efforts and his belief in the value of the work helped inspire me to finish it.

I have benefited from excellent mentors throughout my time in academe. At Vassar College, Prof. Robert Brigham provided my first real to exposure to the history of U.S. foreign relations. He taught me many of the critical elements of historical thinking and supported my interests in arms control and intelligence studies. At Ohio State, Prof. Robert McMahon helped me hone these skills and pushed me to make bold arguments where the evidence demanded it. Also at Ohio State, Prof. Peter Hahn provided a model of professional and academic integrity; he encouraged me to strive for the highest standards of rigor and clarity.

Numerous colleagues have helped shape my thinking and arguments about many aspects of this work. I am especially grateful to Prof. David Stebenne and Prof. Jennifer Siegel of The Ohio State University; Dr. David Hadley; and Dr. Ronald Granieri, Dr. Ted Keefer, Dr. Glen Asner, and Dr. Erin Mahan of the Historical Office of the Office of the Secretary of Defense.

The views expressed in this book are the author's alone and do not necessarily reflect the views of the Government Accountability Office or the United States government.

THE CONTROL AGENDA

THE PROMISE OF CONTROL

On October 26, 1974, Secretary of State Henry Kissinger found himself in Moscow with a Soviet artillery piece pointed at him. Kissinger had been negotiating with the general secretary of the Communist Party (and de facto leader of the Soviet Union) Leonid Brezhnev and his foreign minister, Andrei Gromyko. The subject was arms control: specifically to limit so-called strategic weapons, the largest missiles and bombers that made up the bulk of both countries' nuclear arsenals. The United States and Soviet Union had signed the first Strategic Arms Limitation Treaty (known as SALT I) two years earlier but its terms were limited, both in scope and duration. Both parties hoped to negotiate a more comprehensive, permanent, follow-on agreement (commonly referred to as SALT II). By 1974, however, progress on such an agreement had come to a standstill. After Gerald Ford became president, Kissinger hoped to get negotiations back on track. Doing so required meeting with Brezhnev in his country and on his terms.

Kissinger was accustomed to dealing with Brezhnev, whose bon vivant demeanor concealed a tough, patient negotiator. But by 1974, Brezhnev's age of 67 had begun to take a toll on his mental acuity. Though still capable, he would fidget in long meetings, showing off trinkets and tchotchkes; conversations with him tended to meander. On this day, Brezhnev revealed a tabletop-sized artillery piece during the discussion and began to play with it. He claimed that it worked but that he did not know how. He alternated pointing the gun at Kissinger's aide and at the secretary of state himself. Gromyko, trying to preserve some semblance of decorum, suggested that Brezhnev point the gun at him instead of their

1

guests. Brezhnev ignored him. Instead, he produced a miniature artillery shell and loaded it into the cannon. After a few tugs at the model's lanyard, the hammer dropped. A tense moment followed, but nothing happened and the meeting continued. Ninety minutes later the gun went off with a puff of smoke and a loud bang.[1]

If Brezhnev's antics exasperated Kissinger, he did not show it. Frustration quickly became one of the defining features of the SALT negotiations. Subsequent negotiations did not change this dynamic, which remained true well after Kissinger left office. Brezhnev could easily have been expressing his own frustration and boredom with what was among the most complex and intractable issues of the day.

As foreign policy initiatives go, the Strategic Arms Limitation Talks seem to stand apart. The negotiations set many precedents for modern arms control, yet most of the terms of the SALT I and II treaties expired after a few years or never went into effect at all. Arsenals with the destructive potential the Soviet Union and United States possessed had never existed before, and attempts to stop a runaway arms race such as this were virtually unprecedented. At times the fate of the entire world seemed to hang in the balance. Though the stakes seemed high, scholars continue to debate just how much the agreements actually changed the nuclear arsenals of each superpower.

For these reasons, the SALT agreements rarely receive top billing when scholars review the history of arms control. The Intermediate-Range Nuclear Forces (INF) Treaty and the Strategic Arms Reductions Treaty (START) are better known (and better studied) for the role they played in the end of the Cold War. Given their enduring character and the drastic reductions in arms they brought, the prominence of these treaties seems justified. Their negotiating history is equally memorable, characterized by dramatic summit meetings, negotiating breakthroughs, and supposedly visionary leaders operating within a dynamic international environment.

Compared to these events, SALT was a slog. Its negotiations took place during an era of stagnation and relative (though deteriorating) international stability, its pace was often glacial, and the process itself was deeply frustrating, even traumatic, for those involved. The INF and START negotiations and the treaties they produced were very different from SALT, but this was deliberate: many of the negotiators involved bore scars from a decade of fighting over SALT issues. By the time of the 1985 summit meeting between President Ronald Reagan and General Secretary Mikhail Gorbachev, virtually every weapon under discussion had featured in SALT negotiations at some point. Some of these systems were developed explicitly in response to the terms of or trends exposed by the SALT negotiations. Both parties brought with them the ugly political baggage of over fourteen years of debates over how to shape and control the nuclear balance and which party bore more of the blame for the status quo. An entire generation of policymakers cut their teeth on these debates, arguing in a vocabulary (since faded into obscurity) of "strategic superiority," "counterforce targeting," and the "window of vulnerability."

Though the issues at play were often abstract and technical, the SALT negotiations were a human process. Specific individuals shaped the negotiations as much as any technological development. Some, like Kissinger, used the negotiations to navigate between opposing groups: on one side a restive domestic populace that was deeply dissatisfied with the arms race and on the other powerful interest groups committed to the Cold War. Some, like President Jimmy Carter, saw the opportunity to secure a legacy as a peacemaker without imposing compromises that might alienate important constituencies. Others, such as the statesman and longtime negotiator Paul Nitze, saw in the negotiations a vessel for their worst fears of a deteriorating balance of power between East and West. And some, like President Ronald Reagan, saw a deeply flawed process that was likely too compromised to achieve a positive outcome that they would rather break than bend any further. Personalities, political exigencies, and occasional human foibles all exerted profound influences on the process. The SALT negotiations' most significant legacies developed as a result of the perspectives these individuals brought to bear.

The continued engagement of senior government officials with such a recalcitrant issue had significant and wide-ranging effects. The emphasis on achieving and maintaining a balance forced policymakers to think harder than ever before about the development of nuclear weapons and strategies for using them. The political implications of nuclear parity prompted new thinking about the nature of deterrence and alliance politics. The social and political circumstances surrounding the negotiations inevitably affected them as well. The ways policymakers adapted to these conditions in their pursuit of arms control reveals important truths about how they viewed their opponents, their allies, and their domestic rivals. In this way, the *experience* of SALT—its negotiation, the debates it triggered, and its repercussions—exerted influence beyond the terms and expirations of the agreements themselves.

This influence reverberates today. Unfortunately, nuclear issues have enjoyed a resurgence in recent years, and the implications for arms control are disturbing. The U.S. Department of State alleges that the Russian Federation has conducted multiple missile tests in violation of the INF Treaty. The process of revealing these allegations has prompted complaints in Congress about the integrity of the compliance-reporting process and accusations that the Department of State has downplayed or concealed noncompliance in order to ensure Russian cooperation in other areas. When the Obama administration revealed its Joint Comprehensive Plan of Action for dealing with Iran's illicit nuclear program, widespread debates ensued about whether a better deal was possible, what role the prerogatives of Congress ought to play, and what the consequences of rejecting the plan might be.

The politics of each of these issues are rooted in debates over the SALT agreements. The role of congressional oversight, the adequacy of verification regimes, and what to do with an agreement that is widely recognized as flawed all featured regularly in arguments surrounding SALT policies. In these cases, whether they were aware of it or not, politicians and policymakers from all sides were reading from a script first written over forty years ago.

The relevance of SALT is unlikely to fade in the future. Today, all but one of the nuclear weapons states that signed the Treaty on the Non-Proliferation of Nuclear Weapons are modernizing their nuclear forces. The arsenals of the People's Republic of China and the Russian Federation have attracted significant attention, particularly as their arsenals and declaratory policies have begun to stray from long-held assumptions. The full extent of the U.S. program is yet to be determined but is routinely (and conservatively) estimated to have a life-cycle cost of over $1 trillion. In the face of these changes, long-held policies such as the ban on nuclear testing and the rejection of nuclear first use have come under question. Mutual recriminations between the powers have already begun, but a return to the cycle of bilateral negotiations typified by the SALT and START agreements seems unlikely.

The SALT negotiations took place in an era with important parallels to the present. Today, as in the 1970s, U.S. politics are characterized by a concern about the threat of "decline," a real or perceived diminution in national strength, be it military, moral, or political. Then, as today, an era of U.S. dominance was coming to end and the nation was entering an era characterized by rising great powers and a decrease in relative economic and military power. As in the 1970s, the threat of economic stagnation today looms large. These factors have given the SALT experience a new relevance for dealing with an increasingly inhospitable climate for arms control.

The Means and Ends of SALT

From 1969 to 1983, the United States and the Soviet Union engaged in a continuous set of negotiations over nuclear weapons. The Strategic Arms Limitation Talks, or SALT, lasted until 1979 and produced two finished agreements: SALT I and SALT II. The Intermediate-Range Nuclear Forces negotiation spun off from

SALT in 1980, carrying over a number of secondary issues from SALT II while still conforming to many of SALT's basic underpinnings. Negotiations grew so routine that they became divorced from whatever agreement they sought to achieve next and were instead seen as a continuous process. In this process, senior policymakers on each side formulated a policy and presented and discussed these positions at formal diplomatic exchanges. These exchanges were punctuated by intermittent summit meetings by heads of state or cabinet officials. As this cycle repeated itself, policymakers primarily thought of their task as tending to the more abstract "SALT process." Often the entire suite of issues and activities the negotiations encompassed was shortened to the term "SALT."

The agreements the SALT process produced are some of the most significant milestones of the Cold War. SALT I was widely seen as among the signal achievements of Nixon's policy of détente vis-à-vis the Soviet Union. In contrast, the failure to ratify SALT II marked the death knell of détente and a return to conflict and competition. Through this period and after, the military, political, and diplomatic influence of SALT was profound. In the United States, the development of virtually every major weapons system after 1969 was influenced in some way by the ongoing talks. The incumbent president's performance on SALT issues became a recurring theme in presidential elections.

While negotiating such ambitious and complicated accords stretched the abilities of both governments, the relatively open and decentralized character of the U.S. government presented additional challenges. Negotiating competently required publicly reconciling difficult questions of nuclear strategy, ideology, and popular politics. Even when presidential administrations attempted to keep any prospective agreement narrowly tailored, the scope and complexity of the negotiations inexorably grew. The soaring rhetoric accompanying SALT I helped raise public expectations that stepping back from Armageddon was not only possible but within reach. Elevated public expectations put additional pressure on U.S. negotiators, straining the process further and increasing the costs of failure or delay.

Though the public unquestionably helped frame and motivate negotiations over strategic arms, the SALT process was driven by elites. Indeed, it is impossible to divorce the legacies of SALT from the overall policy that gave birth to it: détente. It is a testament to SALT's thorniness that Henry Kissinger and the other framers of détente originally saw arms control as only a small piece of a larger strategy. Instead, the place of the SALT negotiations in détente grew in importance until they were at the center of that strategy, such that the rejection of SALT II signaled the end of détente itself.

The elite character of arms control is what made it so attractive to the architects of détente. Détente had powerful social underpinnings linked to public concerns, not least of which was the omnipresent threat of nuclear annihilation. After the domestic upheavals, chaos, and conflicts of the 1960s, leaders across the globe sought to shore up their positions. Student protests in the United States, the Cultural Revolution in China, and the general disorder in Europe of 1968 all contributed to a sense of internal instability among world leaders. In international affairs, the intractability of the Vietnam War, memories of the Cuban Missile Crisis, and the crushing of the Prague Spring all made clear that unlimited competition among the superpowers was unsustainable. If political leaders could not bring some stability to world affairs restive domestic populations might revolt, imposing their own blunt, potentially unfavorable limits on competition.

The policy of détente, therefore, was an effort by elite national decision makers to use foreign policy to simultaneously sate and mute the concerns of their respective populaces. National elites used diplomacy to aggrandize their roles, centralize their authority, and satisfy domestic constituencies in order to secure their positions. In nuclear affairs, SALT neatly filled this role.

During a period characterized by fractious domestic politics, declining executive power, and an increasingly toxic politics associated with nuclear weapons, arms control became one of the constitutive elements of executive authority. The SALT process became a means to its stated diplomatic ends and to the continuance of investments in nuclear technology and specific deployment policies. In its worst moments, the SALT process became a perverse symbiosis between the Soviet Union and United States in which neither party could sustain unrestrained competition but neither could they abandon the competition entirely for fear of what their domestic constituencies and foreign competitors might impose instead.

The negotiating process allowed both governments to carve out the directions they wanted their arsenals to go. The resulting agreements allowed leaders to provide assurances to their own people that these new investments were sanctioned and therefore necessary to maintain the carefully wrought balance. Thus, national elites rendered themselves indispensable while inoculating themselves against domestic backlash from continued nuclear competition. This arrangement, which reinforced leaders' control over their own domestic political processes while providing a measure of influence over their opponents', began to resemble a kind of condominium, or joint sovereignty arrangement. While this pattern did not solely define the process, the overtones of domestic condominium left SALT's ability to achieve results stunted, until a new paradigm of arms control could take its place.

The SALT process also accelerated trends in thinking about nuclear strategy, though not necessarily in ways that benefited the process. While previous U.S. administrations had dabbled in nuclear strategy, few had much stomach for its horrific details. They were content to set out general principles or to substitute budgetary principles for strategy. By inviting high-level decision makers to consider routinely how to construct and preserve a nuclear balance, the SALT process created new avenues by which different nuclear doctrines could earn consideration and become policy. In particular, the structure and principles of the SALT process may have accelerated the trend in the United States toward adopting counterforce doctrines, in stark contrast to the relatively basic model of deterrence that underpinned the earliest SALT efforts.

Near the center of these events, exerting considerable influence without ever becoming the defining figure, was Paul Nitze. Nitze was a distinguished figure in the national security world for over twenty years prior to participating in the SALT negotiations. From 1969 onward, Nitze's story is effectively the story of SALT. Nitze's relationship with arms control was often fraught and even contradictory. He had qualms from the beginning about aspects of the process. These reservations grew into full-blown opposition. But by the end of the 1980s, after nearly two decades of continuous involvement with the issue, he was widely seen as one of the most respected authorities on the subject, and one of its most prominent advocates. Much like the SALT process, Nitze's record of influence on SALT was mixed, its dénouement tinged with failure. He was in many ways one of his generation's most fervent supporters of arms control (under the right circumstances), but he was also one of SALT's fiercest and most influential critics. Whether working for or against it, Nitze helped shape the SALT process and its legacies more than almost any single individual. His story is therefore essential to understanding the process as a whole.

Verification

Verification is one of the most important and unexamined aspects of this process and indeed of the process of diplomacy and state making in general. Used in this context, verification refers to the means by which governments monitor compliance with an arms control agreement, through espionage, transparency measures, or other techniques. Unfortunately, the vast majority of information about the capabilities of governments to conduct these activities was classified (and in many cases still is). Nevertheless, verifying the terms of these agreements was a critical function of the SALT process. By forcing national security elites to confront verification questions routinely, the SALT process required a continuous reassessment of essential, even existential questions.

Verification questions were at the root of the epistemology of the national security state, forcing its members to consider what it meant to know anything about its adversaries and what standard of knowledge was required to define a threat. Attitudes about what could be verified adequately and what needed to be verified were some of the most important fault lines in debates about the nature and utility of the SALT process. As the process grew more complex and dynamic, better verification measures became necessary, but these capabilities remained so highly classified that public debates on the subject were at best highly circumscribed, further influencing how the public perceived the process.

Verification issues had dynamic effects on the negotiations. The compliance and monitoring regimes the SALT agreements authorized could only be tested after the highest-profile elements of negotiation, signing, and ratification had occurred. At first these functions occurred outside the public eye, but over time they provided a track record for policy makers to parse or criticize. Eventually arguments over whether previous agreements were verifiable took place in discussions of the merits of new agreements. Ensuring an adequate verification regime on the next agreement then became more difficult, as negotiators had to address existing track records while avoiding opening old wounds left from the compromises of previous agreements.

Too often, verification issues are treated as after-the-fact technical concerns or bad-faith objections to new agreements. This view discounts what is often the most controversial aspect of any new arms control agreement. Thus, this book will include developments in verification in the overall narrative of the SALT process.

Note on Nomenclature

Astute readers will notice that this book adheres almost exclusively to the NATO reporting names for Soviet weapons, such as the Strategic Rocket Forces. Although the opening of the Soviet archives has revealed the once-secret names for most of these systems, using the NATO names serves several purposes. Most important, the terms offer consistency. Since Soviet negotiators never revealed the internal names for these weapons, the NATO names were the de facto official terms for the purposes of arms control negotiation and were used by both sides. The highly compartmentalized nature of the Soviet system could also sometimes obfuscate the nature of the weapons to which internal labels applied. Sometimes the Soviets gave two names to a single system or labeled new missiles as "upgrades" for essentially political reasons. Because these details were so closely held, however, few members of the Soviet leadership or negotiating teams were aware of these discrepancies. While the internal labels were no doubt important within the Soviet military or design bureaus, the NATO names were both more widely understood by the negotiators and are more accessible to readers.

ARMS CONTROL: CONTEXT AND PRECEDENTS

The first meeting of the SALT talks in 1969 was the culmination of more than a decade of work through one of the most turbulent periods of the postwar era. During this time, the most important features of the nuclear competition came into focus. The leaders of both superpowers became familiar with the implications of this competition and agreed on the need for negotiated measures to curb its worst excesses. These events took place in the context of geopolitical turmoil. Beginning with the Berlin Crisis of 1961, through the Cuban Missile Crisis, the Vietnam War, and ending with the Soviet invasion of Czechoslovakia and the repression of the Prague Spring, this decade exhausted any appetite for brinksmanship among policy makers and their domestic populations. The combination of a budding strategic consensus and geopolitical turmoil left policy makers increasingly open to cooperative measures that limited the dangers of competition. By the end of the 1960s, both superpowers were actively seeking a more cooperative superpower relationship through the policy of détente, in which arms control would play a critical role.

International schemes for restricting weapons are not new. For instance, the Washington Naval Treaty of 1922 restricted naval tonnage to a set ratio among the major powers. The Geneva Protocol of 1925 banned the use of chemical weapons in war. As policies, these initiatives were of a piece with the disarmament movement, which was strongly influenced by the same Progressive Era discourse that produced the League of Nations and the Kellogg-Briand Pact. These agreements set precedents for the later arms control movement.[1]

"Arms control" came to define a specific movement in the 1950s that was formed by an intellectual union of several groups. The first such group was the nuclear disarmament movement, which grew out of criticism of the strategic bombing of cities during World War II. The second group was traditional liberals concerned that the arms race was fueling the Cold War with the Soviet Union. The third group consisted of civilian intellectuals attempting to develop credible strategies for the use of nuclear weapons. Prior to the development and popularization of the arms control concept, these groups were leery of one another. Civilian nuclear theorists responded skeptically to traditional disarmament proposals because they believed that nuclear weapons were now a permanent feature of the international system and could not be "un-invented." Traditional liberals resisted association with impolitic and radical nuclear disarmament proponents because the United States had built and used the first atomic bombs. The disarmament and liberal schools both felt disgusted by the callousness with which defense intellectuals described nuclear scenarios in "megadeaths," and both suspected that thinking too seriously about how to use nuclear weapons might cause countries to feel more comfortable using them.[2]

What nearly all of these groups could agree on, dating back to the disarmament advocates of the Progressive Era, was that arms races were dangerous and that unbridled competition in arms eventually makes war inevitable. This position had some historical basis. Before World War I, Great Britain, previously the dominant naval power in Europe, raced to stay ahead of the rising naval power of Imperial Germany. This race included several metrics, including gross tonnage, the number of ships in the fleet, and which country could build the largest single ship. The competition in naval arms became frightfully expensive over time and was a source of rising international tension. After the war, the naval arms race was commonly held to be a contributing factor in setting off the conflict. As a result, the Washington Naval Conference tried to avoid future conflicts by imposing caps on naval tonnage. The caps shrank fleets significantly and maintained the balance of power by imposing a fixed ratio between the major powers.[3]

Academics expanded on the dynamics of arms races in the decades that followed. Political scientists held that arms races were an outgrowth of the "security dilemma," according to which no country, acting alone, can feel secure without accruing enough power to make all other countries insecure. Economists used game theory to illustrate how if one party in an arms race risked losing its superior position, it might be tempted to attack preemptively while it still maintained a measure of dominance. Foreign policy thinkers combined these abstract concepts into a model wherein competition escalates until war becomes inevitable. The idealized nature of this "spiral model" prevented it from being immediately applied to real policy making. Those in government in the 1940s and 1950s, especially anticommunists and defense hawks, found more salient the experience of World War II, in which acting against Nazi Germany sooner may have averted conflict. Nevertheless, the relationship between arms races and inevitable conflict became firmly entrenched in popular culture.[4]

Limits on Testing

The issue of nuclear testing began the process of unifying these disparate groups. Open-air nuclear testing came under increasing criticism in the late 1950s, particularly due to the consequences of radioactive fallout for public health and the environment. Starting in 1958, the Soviet Union adopted a unilateral moratorium on nuclear testing, putting pressure on the other nuclear powers (the United States and United Kingdom) to do the same. The Eisenhower administration reluctantly reciprocated on a temporary basis that was conditioned on Soviet entrance into negotiations on a formal treaty banning nuclear testing.[5]

Up to that point, the Soviet practice on disarmament issues was to endorse the spirit of almost any proposal (conditioned on U.S. agreement) but then dismiss verification or enforcement concerns as narrow-minded and unnecessary. When the United States would insist on adequate measures to ensure that all parties adhered to an agreement, Soviet diplomats would excoriate the U.S. position as standing in the way of progress over picayune concerns. Hoping to avoid this dynamic, the Truman and Eisenhower administrations steered clear of commitments to disarmament in general while vaguely endorsing attempts to "regulate" arms with strategic implications.[6]

The nuclear test ban issue was the first occasion when the United States actually joined such a formal negotiation, despite the fierce opposition of the military establishment (personified by the Joint Chiefs of Staff) and the U.S. nuclear weapons complex (the agencies, bureaucrats, and national laboratories charged with developing and producing nuclear weapons). President Eisenhower and Secretary of State John Foster Dulles led the shift to a more accommodating stance. Both expressed concern that the United States would lose too much in the way of international standing if it continued testing in the face of growing public concern. Cold War paranoia ran high in the United States during this time, and the idea of negotiating with Communists (let alone endorsing a deal that required negotiators to "trust" their Soviet counterparts) remained highly controversial. The process would have to be carefully managed lest skeptical forces mobilize to overwhelm the possibility of an agreement.[7]

The talks began but predictably deadlocked over the issue of verification. Detecting nuclear tests in the air, in space, or underwater was relatively easy, but underground testing would be more difficult. International committees of scientists issued papers arguing that earthquake-detecting seismic instruments could detect almost any underground test above a relatively low threshold. Data from the most recent U.S. tests significantly complicated this picture, expanding the minimum detectable yield between four times and (theoretically) three hundred times the international committee's estimate. U.S. scientists further concluded that underground tests could be confirmed only when inspectors testing for radioactive traces of a nuclear blast could visit the site in person.[8]

Soviet negotiators fiercely disagreed with the U.S. analysis and attacked inspections proposals as an entrée to Western espionage and a violation of their sovereignty. The most that Western negotiators could extract from the Soviets was acceptance of a finite number of veto-proof inspections per year. Soviet delegates said they could determine the exact number later, but disagreements over technical data and how the inspecting agency could be organized made clear that whatever the number was, it would likely not be enough for the United States.[9]

The talks collapsed in 1960 when the Soviet Union downed a U.S. U-2 spy plane over its territory, beginning a wave of crises that spanned the next two years. President Kennedy tried to make some progress when he took office in 1961, but the Soviet Union broke the moratorium with a spate of nuclear tests at the height of the Berlin Crisis, further damaging the prospects for an agreement. Kennedy reluctantly resumed testing in kind, first underground and in limited fashion, then resuming open-air tests under pressure from the Joint Chiefs and the national laboratories.[10]

The Cuban Missile Crisis of 1962 proved to be such a harrowing enough experience that a return to negotiations seemed possible for both sides. Following a series of private overtures, both superpowers dispensed with their attempts to ban underground testing and instead restricted the agreement to underwater, atmospheric, and space-based testing. The nuclear powers met in Moscow to sign the Limited Test Ban Treaty in August 1963 and invited other countries to sign on. Dozens of countries eventually ratified the agreement.[11]

The Limited Test Ban Treaty was a triumph in many ways, but it differed significantly from later attempts at arms control. Its precedential value was clear: it showed that mutually beneficial negotiations between the superpowers were possible and that they could produce substantial results. This type of cooperation contrasted starkly with the brinksmanship of the Cuban Missile Crisis less than a year earlier.[12]

The treaty was not a complete sea change for the politics of arms control, however, and it did not lay the foundation for all future arms control efforts. By 1963, the politics of a test ban were more closely aligned with the incipient environmental movement than with the forces calling for an end to the arms race. Much of the popular commentary on a test ban focused on the health and environmental impacts of testing, most notably in the Baby Tooth Survey, which showed that measurable quantities of radioactive fallout had worked their way into children's baby teeth by way of the global milk supply. Underground testing had virtually no impact on these issues, but it did allow nuclear weapons design work to continue in a slightly more cumbersome fashion. Although the impact of the treaty on public health was significant, its impact on the strategic balance was more circumscribed.[13]

Despite the involvement of antinuclear activists and leading scientific figures in rallying support for a test ban, most scholars still argue that the U.S. transition from opposing disarmament to halting acceptance of arms control was a basically conservative one, driven by the pragmatic concerns of elites. The United States retained a clear quantitative and qualitative edge in nuclear weapons during the 1950s and 1960s. U.S. officials feared that arguments in favor of disarmament targeted unique U.S. advantages and that the concept was premised on the idea that the weapons themselves were intrinsically threatening, rather than those who were wielding them. President Eisenhower and Secretary of State John Foster Dulles ultimately agreed to join the test ban negotiations because they were directed less at eliminating nuclear arms than at regulating their uses. This distinction implied that such weapons were a normal part of the international order and were not intrinsically destabilizing but had externalities that could be addressed through negotiation.[14]

Despite Dulles and Eisenhower's tentative pursuit of arms control, a bureaucratic edifice developed to facilitate their efforts that, like many bureaucracies, proved to be more persistent than the issue that brought it into existence. In 1960, the State Department announced the opening of a new Disarmament Administration under its auspices.[15] A year later Congress and President Kennedy passed the Arms Control and Disarmament Act, which converted the Disarmament Administration into an independent agency of the executive branch, renamed the Arms Control and Disarmament Agency. Proponents of the new agency, which included President Kennedy, envisioned an independent force for arms control within the executive branch that would be able to advocate without being muzzled by diplomatic or military bureaucracies. Whether segregating the agency from the diplomatic apparatus was a help or hindrance is debatable, but as the agency grew over the next decade it became a vehicle for bringing large numbers of scientists and policy thinkers who were sympathetic to arms control into government. Establishing an independent agency also promoted the impression that arms control efforts would be an ongoing feature of foreign policy. This permanence also contributed to the impression that progress on arms control issues should be continuous. This could prove problematic during periods of tension or when negotiators deadlocked on substance.[16]

Outside of government, events in the 1960s helped reconcile many test ban proponents to the idea of arms control, such that the term became synonymous with positions held by large swaths of the political spectrum, especially among the liberal, cosmopolitan establishment. The nuclear doctrines of deterrence and its corollary, assured destruction, gained their most prominent articulation during this period. These concepts helped galvanize diffuse groups that had opposed or resisted the arms race but lacked a common platform or plan of action.

Deterrence, Damage Limitation, and Assured Destruction

Beginning in 1960 and continuing through the decade, the economist Thomas Schelling wrote a series of articles and books on the theory of conflict as it applied to nuclear weapons. Schelling's work built on that of previous nuclear theorists, particularly those associated with the Rand Corporation think tank such as Bernard Brodie. To Schelling, it was obvious that nuclear weapons could not be eliminated altogether, yet any nuclear exchange seemed certain to produce catastrophic results. From these premises, Schelling reasoned that the ideal strategy would be to develop nuclear weapons in a way that would prevent their use. Schelling argued against the use of nuclear weapons on the battlefield and any attempt to make nuclear weapons effective against enemy military targets.[17] In doing so, Schelling placed himself between two extremes of a perceived ideological spectrum. Smaller nuclear weapons experienced a brief heyday in the 1950s among disarmament advocates who hoped they would make a global cataclysm less likely. Conversely, the idea of using nuclear weapons primarily against military targets (a "counterforce" strategy) was long associated with hard-line anti-communists and military hawks.[18]

Schelling believed that instead of these strategies, the ideal nuclear posture would consist solely of massive, relatively inaccurate weapons that could only be used against cities and populations. This deliberate inadequacy would convince any opponent that these weapons would only ever be used in a retaliatory strike, since they could serve no useful role in trying to fight or win a war. Opposing nations would therefore not have to worry about the possibility of being militarily defeated in a massive, preemptive attack (a so-called first-strike scenario). Without this concern, opposing states would have less reason to engage in furious arms races in which both sides would require dominance to be assured of their own security and neither side would be able to achieve it.[19]

Schelling's formulation was counterintuitive but compelling. This version of classical nuclear deterrence turned the destructive power of nuclear weapons, once thought to be so great as to be useless, into an advantage. To be applied to the real world, however, the doctrine would also require that most research into improving nuclear weapons' accuracy, readiness, or ease of use be halted, as these would undercut the impression that nuclear weapons served only a retaliatory role. Organizations in charge of developing and maintaining such weapons might naturally object to the idea that unsophisticated weapons that had not been upgraded were inherently superior.

The doctrine of countervalue deterrence gained widespread popularity during the 1960s and provided a basis for promoting nuclear stability in what appeared to be an increasingly unstable world. It finally provided a common platform for promoting nuclear stability through negotiation and limiting the growth (or at least the threat) of nuclear weapons. As a result, it was most useful to the growing movement that was calling for negotiated arms control. While far from unanimous, the doctrine was accepted in many corners. It found widest acceptance among urban, liberal elites, most of whom were associated with the Democratic Party, and with the Republican Party's pragmatic establishment in the Northeast.[20]

The relative simplicity of the classical deterrence model meant that it was easy to promote among lay citizens but difficult to implement across a military establishment with complicated priorities. Before 1961, the ability to implement a nuclear strategy in anything more than broad details was limited: both the United States and Soviet Union had only a handful of ballistic missiles and the United States relied on fleets of bombers whose performance in an actual war would be difficult to predict and would depend on a host of factors. Intelligence was poor, and most strategic planning focused mainly on the desire not to fall too far behind in the military balance. The United States lurched from fears of a "bomber gap" or a "missile gap" and instituting large programs to counteract them (both turned out to be illusory, as the Kennedy administration soon discovered). When the arsenals of both powers turned toward ballistic missiles, it became possible to relate the size and composition of the force to specific goals. Ballistic missiles were more reliable than bombers and provided a stronger correlation between a weapon and its target. But enormous pressures to seek nuclear dominance persisted, despite the instability this might cause. Starting in 1961, Secretary of Defense Robert McNamara took responsibility for rationalizing the U.S. nuclear posture in terms of both size and doctrine. The result of these efforts included some elements of classical deterrence and also concluded that only opening negotiations with the Soviet Union on strategic weapons could ensure long-term stability.

McNamara, an economist by training, had contributed to the use of statistical methods in the bombing campaign against Japan in World War II. Following the war, he and a team of like-minded statisticians applied novel systems-engineering techniques to turn around the ailing Ford Motor Company, of which McNamara was eventually named president. When President Kennedy appointed him in 1961, McNamara saw his mission as rationalizing the hidebound Department of Defense, particularly in the area of weapons development. McNamara saw the system of acquisition as wasteful, dominated by petty interservice rivalry, and lacking a unified strategy. Even though the Kennedy administration oversaw an expansion of defense spending, McNamara was determined to make sure that these expenditures went toward sound, economical programs that suited a coherent strategy.[21]

Although in the early years of McNamara's tenure, nuclear strategy and nuclear acquisition were less connected, their convergence proved inevitable. In contrast to the Eisenhower administration's reliance on massive retaliation, mainly by strategic bombers, the Kennedy campaign's priority was flexible response. More slogan than strategy, the phrase implied ensuring that adequate forces and plans existed to give policymakers options other than launching a massive nuclear strike in the event of a crisis. To this end, the administration boosted spending on conventional forces while also reviewing the existing plans for nuclear war, which up to that point had been the exclusive preserve of the air force.[22]

What McNamara found was horrifying. The air force plan was an absurdity; it assumed that war would begin with a decision by the Soviet Union to launch an all-out assault, which U.S. nuclear forces would then preempt by delivering almost its entire nuclear arsenal. In this plan, holding back a strategic reserve was a moot point, as it only left more of the Soviet Union standing to prepare a counterattack. The air force plan made no attempt to discriminate between China and the Soviet Union and did not include a way to hold some part of U.S. forces back. It would destroy peripheral countries in the Eastern Bloc in order to eliminate a single military target.[23]

McNamara recognized the plan's many failings. It envisioned the first move by the Soviet Union as a Pearl Harbor–style surprise attack but then assumed that the United States would have enough warning to preempt it. But what if the warning signs were missed? Or what if the war started on a smaller scale in an unexpected location? In addition to these practical concerns, the plan was genocidal. Casualties in the hundreds of millions were not an unfortunate side effect but the very goal. The plan's authors had nothing to say to these objections; to them, restraint in war was the only true absurdity.[24]

Identifying these flaws was easy. Replacing them with something better proved vexing. Over the next four years, McNamara announced a series of new nuclear doctrines before realizing that each presented problems of its own. McNamara's first move was to simply introduce options and flexibility: the president should at least be able to decide which countries to make war on. In this aspect, he was somewhat successful. But introducing any further complexity proved problematic. What were legitimate targets? What level of destruction was necessary or acceptable? McNamara then announced a shift to a counterforce policy that avoided cities in the first stages of an exchange. This strategy would primarily target military installations and, to the extent possible, the nuclear weapons of the Soviet Union. By prioritizing these targets, McNamara intended to degrade the Soviets' ability to harm the United States while retaining a sufficient reserve to put Soviet population centers at risk, thus controlling escalation. The death toll from such plans was still staggering, but it was an improvement. Unfortunately, McNamara eventually realized that because it was possible for a U.S. weapon to miss or fail before reaching its target, more than one U.S. weapon would be required for each Soviet weapon. This would impose a considerable cost burden on the United States over the long run, and if the Soviets were to adopt a similar strategy it would accelerate the nuclear arms race even further.[25]

This version of counterforce was just one part of a trio of programs that sought to make it possible to fight a nuclear war and then minimize the resulting damage the enemy would still be able to inflict. Collectively these efforts formed a strategy broadly known as damage limitation.[26] In addition to counterforce targeting, damage limitation also required active civil defenses, specifically a massive federally funded fallout shelter program designed to reduce the number of casualties from a nuclear war. The third element was the pursuit of an anti-ballistic missile (ABM) system that was capable of eliminating warheads. All of these concepts proved problematic from political, economic, and strategic perspectives, and the more McNamara engaged with each, the more he and his senior advisors at the Department of Defense became convinced that they were untenable and that any feasible alternative required formal negotiations with the Soviet Union. While nuclear targeting doctrine played out behind closed doors, ABM and civil defense issues were fought out quite publicly.

Civil defense sputtered out first. Nuclear shelter programs always had dedicated boosters, especially in Congress, but once the Kennedy administration began exploring the details, the difficulty of selling such a grim program became clear. Pouring billions of dollars into building shelters would indeed save tens of millions of lives in the event of a nuclear conflict. However, the rosiest projections still showed that the United States would suffer losses of nearly an order of magnitude higher in an exchange. While the Kennedy administration supported some limited efforts early in its tenure, the Cuban Missile Crisis soured the mood of Congress and the public for doomsday preparation. The government subsequently funded only token programs and the issue became relegated to the political fringe for the remainder of the Cold War.[27]

Missile defenses proved to be a thornier issue. Research into this technology dated to the 1950s, but McNamara (and many scientists) were doubtful that the technical hurdles could be surmounted. Ballistic missiles can travel at up to 15,000 miles per hour. Designing a rocket capable of coming close would be difficult. Constructing a radar system capable of detecting and tracking and targeting thousands of potential warheads would be even more difficult. Yet when the Soviet Union debuted a supposedly functional ABM system in 1963 and China tested its first atomic weapon in 1964, pressure from Congress and the military establishment to accelerate from research to deployment increased.[28]

McNamara and the Johnson administration resisted these calls, as the administration had begun to sour on damage limitation in general. By 1964, McNamara's civilian "whiz kids" had begun to provide analyses that undermined the idea of damage limitation as a goal worth pursuing. These analyses argued that whatever the strategic wisdom of counterforce targeting, nuclear shelters, or expansive missile defense systems, each failed to make much economic sense. All the benefits that these tools conveyed to limit the damage the United States would experience (often at great cost) could be wiped out by relatively modest increases in Soviet offensive weaponry. Missile defenses cost more than ballistic missiles, shelter programs made only a marginal difference, and targeting the enemy's weapons would require permanent, sustained numerical superiority. This criticism appealed to McNamara's economics background in particular: if an investment in a system could not convey an enduring advantage, the funds were best allocated elsewhere.[29]

With these facts in mind, McNamara began promoting an alternative strategy of assured destruction. McNamara argued that the ideal nuclear force structure was one that could absorb a first strike and still be able to destroy 50 percent of Soviet industry and 30 percent of the Soviet population. His theory was that this level of damage was sufficiently unacceptable to Soviet leaders that they would never contemplate a first strike against the United States.

McNamara had no particular insight into Soviet thinking; these percentages were the point of declining marginal returns. The Department of Defense concluded that a force of about 400 nuclear weapons could achieve these damage figures. This force would strike the best targets first. What possible targets remained would rapidly become smaller and less desirable, such that an additional 400 weapons would produce only a 10 percent increase in damage.[30]

Assured destruction solved several problems. First, it provided a limiting principle that McNamara could use to resist uneconomical requests for defense spending beyond actual requirements. Over the next few years, McNamara was able to rely on assured destruction principles to impose a cap of 1,000 (from requests of up to 1,400) on the Minuteman Intercontinental Ballistic Missile

(ICBM) program, cancel a new strategic bomber, and hold off demands for an expansive missile defense system.[31] The strategy also helped reconcile the United States to the reality of changing Soviet nuclear forces.

The Soviet missile program accelerated during this period, particularly after the Cuban Missile Crisis. Before this point the Soviet military could deploy only a limited number of ICBMs, most of which were on exposed launch pads that were vulnerable to a first strike. As the 1960s wore on, Soviet ICBM deployments accelerated and the missiles were increasingly deployed from hardened silos that were resistant to nuclear blasts. These changes reduced the ability of the United States to destroy all or even the majority of Soviet systems capable of targeting the nation. At a certain point damage limitation became insufficient because the damage that was likely to occur would still be unacceptable. Assured destruction improved this situation; it limited the damage by avoiding the conflict entirely.[32]

The strategy bore many resemblances to Schelling's formulation of classical deterrence, but it was not identical. Assured destruction was a budget principle first and a strategy second. It did not provide complete guidance for the exact order and priority of targets in the official nuclear war plan. Instead, these targets were a mishmash of industrial areas, command-and-control facilities, Soviet weapons, and, eventually, population centers. The strategy did not preclude qualitative improvements to weapons either, as deterrence might. Indeed, one of the tradeoffs McNamara made in order to impose a cap on ICBMs was his agreement to support the air force's Minuteman II upgrade program that would boost accuracy in the hope of achieving a hard target capability; that is, the ability to destroy a missile in its silo.[33]

McNamara's assured destruction policy could still be derailed if the Soviet Union took steps that indicated that they did not share in the concept's premises—for example if they seemed to be pursuing a first-strike capability. Conscious of the bomber gaps and missile gaps of the previous decade, the Johnson administration resisted calls to match the Soviet Union system for system. McNamara feared that the superpowers were locked in an action-reaction cycle in which each incremental move by one country to improve its security position prompted a countermove that left both countries less secure. McNamara argued that the cycle had to be broken lest it take on a life of its own, but breaking out of tit-for-tat weapons development would not be easy without getting the Soviet Union on board with the assured destruction concept.[34]

The developing Soviet ABM system posed the greatest threat to McNamara's goals. The location of the Soviet system around Moscow proved especially worrisome. Some inferred that the fact that Soviet planners had placed the system there instead of closer to the Soviet ICBM force indicated that they did not expect to have missiles left to defend by the time they needed to use their ABM system.

Put another way, the Soviet ABM system seemed intended to thwart a retaliatory strike against a population center rather than a first strike against Soviet nuclear forces. This chain of logic led many defense hawks to believe that the Soviet leadership was pursuing a first-strike capability that they could then use to either emerge victorious from a nuclear exchange or to blackmail the United States.[35]

Anticommunists and defense hawks from both parties demanded that the United States pursue a comparable capability, lest it fall behind in the technological arms race and concede a qualitative edge to the Soviet Union. But ABM opponents argued that the weapons themselves were a threat to stability. The ability to thwart a nuclear attack weakened the credibility of an opponent's deterrent. A sufficiently powerful ABM system could support a first strike, and the development of such a system could prompt an opponent to adopt a "use it or lose it" mentality and strike before its nuclear forces became irrelevant.[36]

Though the issue of ABM systems was fraught, it held great promise. If managed properly, achieving an understanding here could break the action-reaction cycle and establish a consensus with Soviet leaders on the uses of nuclear weapons. although the Department of Defense engaged in research and development for a missile defense system, McNamara continued to fight and prevent its deployment for years, arguing that it was destabilizing and uneconomical.[37]

Under pressure, the Johnson administration began to engage the Soviet Union diplomatically on the issue of missile defenses. Following the Limited Test Ban Treaty, the superpowers had negotiated productively on small-scale multilateral arms-control agreements, such as the Outer Space Treaty, which was signed in January 1967. These efforts helped lay a foundation for future interaction on more central security issues. The Soviet response to U.S. concerns about ABMs was cool, however. The buildup in Soviet offensive forces over four years had been rapid, but they were still trying to catch up to the U.S. arsenal. From their perspective, the United States did not begin to object to missile defense until it looked like it might become a comparative advantage for the Soviet Union.[38]

U.S. overtures culminated in the June 1967 summit between Soviet premier Alexei Kosygin and President Johnson in Glassboro, New Jersey. McNamara himself attended to give presentations to the heads of state about the destabilizing effects of missile defense and to explain why negotiations to place capped offensive weapons at the center of the arsenal of each nation were necessary. The Soviet Union, which had long been on the losing side of U.S. nuclear dominance, certainly agreed that the nuclear arms race had reached unnecessary extremes. But on ABMs the Soviets would have none of it. "Defense is moral, offense is immoral!" became Kosygin's refrain. Basing one's nuclear doctrine on the ability to slaughter millions of people in a cost-effective way was a far worse thing than trying to defend oneself. Although the meeting was a landmark event, the Soviet delegation left without making any commitments to negotiating about offensive or defensive nuclear forces.[39]

With no prospect of formal talks in the near future, the Johnson administration relented and agreed to construct the Sentinel ABM system in September 1967. The People's Republic of China had tested its first hydrogen bomb just a few months earlier, providing a pretext for the U.S. claim that the strategic situation had changed. Because the system was still designed to protect cities, McNamara sold Sentinel as a "thin" defense against a Chinese attack that was not intended to be or was not capable of stopping a Soviet nuclear attack. When the army announced that Sentinel would require nuclear-tipped interceptors in the near suburbs of U.S. cities, fierce local opposition quickly brought the program's future into question.[40]

Efforts to engage the Soviet Union continued through 1968. Work on the Nuclear Non-Proliferation Treaty (NPT) through 1967 and 1968 helped create a more cooperative atmosphere between the powers. The treaty recognized both nations as nuclear great powers and worked to preserve their common interest in preventing the nuclear club from expanding. At the signing of the treaty in July 1968, President Johnson announced that the Soviet Union had agreed to meet with the United States to discuss limitations on strategic arms.[41]

In the year since Glassboro, several factors had influenced Soviet leaders to change their minds. In order to convince nonnuclear states to sign, the NPT included a commitment by the major powers to gradually reduce and eliminate their stockpiles, although the treaty did not mention timeline or specifics. The specter of a U.S. ABM system that could outpace the Soviet system likely also weighed on Soviet leaders. Importantly, the buildup in Soviet nuclear weapons had finally reached a point where they could realistically reach parity with the United States in the next few years. By the late 1960s the development of the Soviet missile program had reached breakneck speeds, deploying 200–250 new siloed ICBMs every year, with no end in sight.[42] With some form of equality with the United States in reach, there was less cause for Soviet leaders to feel as though they were entering negotiations from a position of inferiority.

The fact that Soviet leaders agreed to talks did not mean that they had come to accept assured destruction and wanted to seek a deterrence framework. Quite the opposite, in fact. Thinking about nuclear doctrine was frighteningly shallow in the decision-making circles of the Soviet Union. While there was no question that nuclear war would mean the virtual end of Soviet society, the arrangement and planned use of forces very much adhered to a damage limitation concept that centered on the idea of fighting and winning a nuclear war. Keeping up with the U.S. strategic program was a greater burden on the smaller, less productive

Soviet economy. Soviet leaders planned to take the ABM system around Moscow to the national level, but even protecting Moscow proved frightfully expensive. Following through on plans to take it national would cost so much that it would threaten other, arguably more effective programs, such as offensive missiles. What was worse, the new multiple-warhead U.S. missiles (discussed below) threatened to make the Soviet missile shield even more porous. The Politburo had not recognized the implications for stability of the balance between offense and defense, but its members saw that the ABM program's capabilities were restricted by finite resources. Negotiation to rationalize the balance between defense and offense would allow the Soviets to stay competitive with the United States much more affordably. Negotiations would also allow the Soviets to bring up uncomfortable political questions, such as the stationing of U.S. nuclear weapons in NATO countries.[43]

Conclusion

The superpowers agreed to hold the first round of talks before the end of 1968. The Johnson administration wanted to make its mark before the transition. Unfortunately, in August 1968 the Soviet Union invaded Czechoslovakia and violently extinguished the liberalizing movement that came to be known as the Prague Spring. Western outrage was considerable and the Johnson administration refused to meet as scheduled, for fear of seeming to condone the invasion. SALT would have to wait until 1969 and the incoming Nixon administration to begin in earnest.[44]

A great deal had changed in the nuclear outlook by the end of the Johnson administration, yet these changes were not as deep as they might have seemed. The prospect of nuclear arms control between the superpowers met with widespread public approval, but subsequent developments illustrated the difference between supporting a process and supporting a specific agreement. The superpowers seemed poised to accept McNamara's policy of assured destruction in the coming talks, but its impact on nuclear targeting doctrine was minimal. To the broader public, however, détente was at hand, the deterrence theories of Thomas Schelling were predominant within the U.S. government, and negotiations to ensure that the Soviet Union held similar views were about to get under way. The U.S. military still had plans for developing new nuclear weapons, and not all of them fit the mold of simplified nuclear deterrence. It also remained to be seen if a reduction in armaments could produce improvements in security and cooperation elsewhere or if the regional and ideological elements of the Cold War had been fueling the arms race, rather than the reverse.

As much as the previous decade helped set the stage for what was to come, the major events of the 1960s set few precedents about which type of weapons to negotiate over and why. Environmental concerns were the deciding factor in bringing the Limited Test Ban Treaty into being; above-ground testing had no real impact on the strategic balance. McNamara had sought to negotiate over ABMs to relieve pressure from Congress to spend money on a system that he felt was uneconomical. Given McNamara's strong views, it is unclear if he regarded negotiation as a vehicle to restrain Congress and the Joint Chiefs as much as the Soviet Union. Finally, U.S. analysts in 1968 began to wonder if a sufficiently large Soviet nuclear force would call into question the ability of the United States to meet its commitment to third countries, such as NATO members.

Analysts in 1968 began to realize just how rapidly the Soviet ICBM force was poised to grow over the next few years. Up to that point, the Soviet nuclear force had trailed the United States badly, even during the brief periods when the United States mistakenly assumed otherwise. Soviet scientists struggled with the development of a long-range strategic bomber, and the Soviets lacked the overseas bases that would make them potent. The early Soviet lead in rocket and ballistic missile technology was hamstrung by technical obstacles and they were not truly intercontinental. The Cuban Missile Crisis prompted a renewed commitment by Soviet leaders to overcome these hurdles (especially with regard to ICBMs) and to never be inferior to U.S. nuclear forces again. Whereas McNamara restrained new deployments after 1964, Soviet spending accelerated. By 1968 and 1969, the Soviet Union had the ability to add hundreds of missiles to its arsenal per year, catching up to and even exceeding the United States in only a few years. Nuclear parity between the Soviet Union and the United States would be a seismic shift in the strategic balance, one that would call into question the ability of the United States to meet its commitment to third countries, including NATO members.

SALT was founded with the intention of bringing the threat of nuclear arms and a nuclear arms race under control. Yet when the talks began in 1969, both countries still had a great deal to learn about the nature of their competition. Nuclear targeting doctrine was still relatively rudimentary. In the following years, rhetorical commitments to deterrence principles would clash with the reality of increasingly sophisticated delivery systems. Finally, despite outward appearances, the structure of the superpowers' arsenals remained starkly different.

Both parties saw SALT as one part of a broader effort to reduce Cold War tensions that was known as détente. Those who pursued a sense of control in both international and domestic politics, in large part in response to the instability of the 1960s. Once at the table, the SALT process tempted negotiators with a new means to shape the development of their nuclear arsenals, while insulating them from the political consequences of continued nuclear competition. It remained to be seen if placing curbs on nuclear arms would actually reduce conflict between the superpowers or if the nuclear arms race was a symptom of the Cold War rather than the cause. SALT was a quest for control, but the subjects and limits of that control had yet to be discovered.

NEGOTIATION: A NEW DIMENSION IN STRATEGIC COMPETITION

The Strategic Arms Limitation Treaty of 1972, or SALT I, was the first major bilateral strategic arms control treaty.[1] In many ways, it established the structural and diplomatic framework for each of the successive nuclear arms limitation treaties of the twentieth century. Unlike earlier arms control treaties, such as the Nuclear Non-Proliferation Treaty, SALT I and its successors were explicitly bilateral and remained so, involving only the United States and the Soviet Union as direct participants. Unlike their predecessors, the SALT I treaties imposed limits on the deployment of a range of weapons instead of banning particular uses of them or controlling the infrastructure for producing them.

Far from being heralded as a humanitarian triumph, SALT I received only qualified and occasionally begrudging support in the United States in some quarters. SALT I was negotiated in a far more ecumenical fashion than later treaties; the range of strategic concepts and political priorities among U.S. negotiators was broad. Because of this diversity, the Nixon administration held up the treaty as one of its main accomplishments but also felt compelled to scapegoat more dovish negotiators in an attempt to mollify outside critics. Unlike later treaties, whose negotiators benefited from the experience of the SALT I negotiations, participants had only a limited understanding of the realities of modern arms control negotiation, including its dizzying complexity, its glacial pace, and the second-order effects that resulted from previous agreements. SALT I became one of several agreements that represent the high-water mark of détente. Its completion marks the beginning of a new phase of the nuclear arms race in which restraints, negotiation, and competition combined in increasingly unpredictable ways.

Inaugurating the Era of Détente

The Nixon administration took office at a pivotal moment. The previous year, 1968, had proved deeply disturbing to the political leaders of almost every major industrial country. Antiwar protests rocked the United States, splitting and embarrassing the Democratic Party. The Tet Offensive in Vietnam established public perceptions of the war as unwinnable. A new generation of student protestors challenged the very underpinnings of the Cold War.

These forces could be felt in the shift in public attitudes about nuclear weapons over the previous fifteen years. Meaningful polling on arms control issues can be extremely difficult given their technical nature. During the Cold War, functional knowledge of the basics of nuclear weapons and different delivery systems was widespread. Yet awareness of, interest in, or detailed knowledge of specific arms control proposals tended to lag behind awareness of the weapons themselves.[2] Even when majorities of those polled seemed to favor the general idea of negotiating with the Soviet Union or restricting specific kinds of weapons, voters regularly elected candidates who supported vigorous defense spending and were skeptical of arms control initiatives. General attitudes toward nuclear weapons and the effects of nuclear war proved easier to measure. These polling results illustrated the depths of fear nuclear competition generated and the political rewards that might flow from assuaging such fear.

In short, American attitudes toward nuclear weapons vacillated between confident and comfortable acting alone to morally ambivalent and even despairing. In the 1940s, those who were polled roundly rejected the idea of a U.S. pledge not to use atomic weapons first in a conflict. During the Korean War, one poll showed that two-thirds of Americans were willing to use nuclear weapons in response to a conventional Soviet invasion of Europe. In 1956, only a few years after the Korean War and after the Soviet Union had tested a thermonuclear device of its own, this number fell to 40 percent. The Soviet Union's development of long-range bombers and ballistic missiles also heightened Americans' sense of vulnerability. By 1963, 52 percent of those who were polled rated the odds of their surviving a nuclear attack as poor.[3] While negotiations with the Soviets were not necessarily the highest priority for voters at the time (law-and-order issues and the Vietnam War tended to predominate), between 60 and 80 percent of survey respondents favored them for the purpose of limiting anti-ballistic missiles.[4]

After years in the political wilderness (a result of his narrow loss of the 1960 presidential election followed by his disastrous 1962 campaign for the California governorship), Richard Nixon reemerged on the national stage in 1968, positioning himself as a force for stability, capable of quelling domestic strife while alleviating fears of the consequences of international conflict. Nixon was known as an anticommunist: he was a former chair of the House Un-American Activities Committee and had served as President Eisenhower's vice president. However, his long career in politics enabled him to affect an "elder statesman" posture with which he could seek more flexibility in foreign policy. Nixon claimed he would be better able to prosecute the Vietnam War than the Johnson administration, while also bringing about "an honorable end" to the conflict. Nixon also promised an "era of negotiation" with the Soviet and Chinese governments after two decades of confrontation.[5] These statements formed the underpinnings for Nixon's "détente" policy. Though his foreign policy platform affected centrism, he ran to the right on social issues such as law and order and defeated his main opponent, Hubert Humphrey, by only half a million votes.

While Nixon attempted to play to the middle on foreign policy, by 1969, the Cold War consensus was breaking down. Generational changes and rifts associated with the Vietnam War presaged a long and painful period of polarization that would last to the end of the Cold War. The Nixon administration was not immune to this effect. On the issue of arms control the Nixon administration initially incorporated a diversity of views toward nuclear weapons and the purposes of arms control. Personal and ideological differences sharpened over time and recriminations began even before SALT I was complete, resulting in the scapegoating of most of the State Department officials involved and a number of others who shared a traditional "arms controller" perspective.

At the top was President Nixon. While intensely interested in an arms control agreement as a political goal, he saw the majority of arms control issues as esoteric and left most technical issues to Henry Kissinger. Nixon retained the final authority about what specific negotiating strategies were to be used and was interested in understanding Soviet actions at the negotiating table mainly as a way of decoding the overall Soviet disposition.[6] However, extended attention to complex technical issues, such as the overall composition and implications of U.S. nuclear forces, proved to be beyond Nixon. At various points in National Security Council meetings he expressed thinly veiled contempt for prevailing orthodoxies such as assured destruction and using ABM systems to protect missiles rather than cities.[7] Kissinger noted Nixon's tendency to become "glassy-eyed and irritable" during extended debates.[8] Nixon made clear that he was attending such meetings more to add a presidential veneer to the proceedings than to actually participate in them.

In less technical fora than National Security Council meetings, Nixon was capable of expressing quite compelling reasons for pursuing arms control.[9] When he was giving instructions and making decisions about negotiating strategy, Nixon evidenced a holistic view of the potential for arms control and its place in his strategic thinking. Nixon believed that continued pursuit of nuclear dominance was unsustainable politically, fiscally and geopolitically.[10] However, once Nixon's anticommunist credentials were challenged, as they were during the ratification proceedings for SALT I, he became reactive and far more combative. Thus, while the issue may have been prominent in Nixon's thinking, his substantive commitment to arms control was shallow.

National Security Advisor Henry Kissinger was perhaps the most influential figure in shaping the accords, though his overall views can be difficult to characterize. A professor of government at Harvard University, Kissinger had experienced a meteoric rise to prominence as a scholar of foreign relations. His earliest academic work focused on the ability of Prince Metternich to construct a stable balance of power in Europe following the Napoleonic Wars of the late eighteenth and early nineteenth centuries. Kissinger held up Metternich as an archetypical statesman who managed to negotiate his way to the center of European decision making even though he came from one of the weakest of the major European powers. Following the success of his 1957 book *Nuclear Weapons and Foreign Policy*, Kissinger rose to prominence as a commentator on modern foreign policy problems, particularly NATO issues and nuclear weapons.

When he was not part of the government, Kissinger seemed to have quite strongly formed views on U.S. foreign policy, but once he was in power he became harder to define clearly except by a few key concepts that influenced his decision making. Much has been made of the concept of "linkage" in Kissinger's thinking and its role in shaping Nixon administration foreign policy. In its most basic formulation, linkage sought to unify relations with the Soviet Union across a wide variety of issues, from arms control and Vietnam to trade relations and even to Jewish emigration. Ideally, positive developments in some areas would beget deliberate improvements in others. In Kissinger's view, this was simply a restatement of traditional diplomacy: positive relationships reap rewards for both parties, whereas conflict causes breakdowns in productive relationships.

In the realm of arms control, linkage was somewhat controversial, as it seems to downplay the threat of nuclear annihilation by connecting it to far more mundane issues between the superpowers. The Nixon administration initially intended to delay arms control talks until positive progress had been made on other fronts such as the Middle East and Vietnam, but key administration figures expressed an interest in arms control from their earliest interactions with Moscow.[11] Kissinger and Nixon both believed that the Soviet Union was more interested in SALT than they were and sought to delay SALT to use it as an incentive to encourage cooperation elsewhere.

Kissinger did not expect SALT to provide significant benefits to the United States by itself; for him, its value was its relationship to other issues. While preparing the U.S. position for the talks, Kissinger noted that any foreseeable SALT agreement would do little to reduce overall defense expenditures because strategic forces were only a fraction of the total defense budget.[12] A strong believer that national power grew from a variety of sources, Kissinger often treated the arms race as almost a distraction, a result of focusing too much attention on military power in efforts to avert crises and settle geopolitical conflict. Kissinger also disagreed with the idea that the arms race was a primary driver of the Cold War and so was also skeptical about the idea that political breakthroughs with the Soviet Union would ensue simply because of the completion of an agreement.[13]

Nixon seemed somewhat more sanguine about the prospect of arms control and improved relations. In one of his first letters to Secretary of State William Rogers and Secretary of Defense Melvin Laird, he wrote "I am convinced that the great issues are fundamentally interrelated. I do not mean by this to establish artificial linkages between specific elements of one or another issue or between tactical steps that we may elect to take. But I do believe that crisis or confrontation in one place and real cooperation in another cannot long be sustained simultaneously."[14] For Kissinger, arms control was primarily a means of managing the Soviets' rapid growth in strategic arms and of establishing a framework for nuclear competition that would be more manageable for both parties and would prove to be less of a hindrance to progress in other areas.[15] The difference was subtle, but real: Nixon saw SALT as a normative good, while Kissinger saw it as a way to prevent competition over nuclear weapons from interfering with his goals elsewhere.

SALT negotiations proved to be one of the least linked areas of Nixon administration foreign policy. Kissinger later admitted that in arms control, linkage was not so much a deliberate negotiating strategy as it was an attempt to negotiate specific issues with an awareness of the overall strategic picture in a way that avoided wedding the actions of adversaries to the negotiations.[16] Once the talks began, political pressures made breaking off negotiations or delaying an agreement increasingly difficult; this had the effect of further weakening linkages with world events. The head of the U.S. SALT delegation noted this possibility when the Soviet negotiators did not react to some of the most controversial U.S. actions of the period, including the mining of Haiphong harbor and the invasion of Cambodia.[17] While foreign policy issues might have been interconnected, the SALT talks seemed to take on a life of their own from an early stage.

Career civil servant and diplomat Gerard Smith was the head of the U.S. SALT delegation. Smith was an old-line Republican from the moderate Northeastern wing who headed the Arms Control and Disarmament Agency (ACDA). Nixon selected Smith for this role mainly because of his experience of working for the Atomic Energy Commission. He was an active participant in policy discussions on SALT. Smith embodied many of the conventional views of deterrence and nuclear arms control that were common among State Department and ACDA employees. Smith was one of the few top policymakers in the United States who had personally witnessed a nuclear test, an experience that had turned him into a nuclear abolitionist at heart.[18] Smith's views and his consistent desire for autonomy from Kissinger's oversight brought him into conflict with the administration as the negotiations wore on. Smith eventually resigned in disgust over the administration's treatment of the negotiators when the administration purged several other "arms controllers" in exchange for Senator Henry Jackson's support for SALT.[19]

While Smith may have opposed many categories of weapons on ethical grounds, he still understood their strategic significance and the need to negotiate within the context of nuclear strategy to effect changes. When he referred to his overall opposition to anti-ballistic missile systems, Smith would self-denigrate, calling his perspective "parochial."[20] This allowed him to maintain credibility among a group of policymakers who were far more accepting of nuclear weapons.

Smith believed that mutual vulnerability was the first step toward authentic reductions and an end to the arms race. To that end, Smith also believed that his goal in the negotiation of SALT should be to enshrine classical deterrence in the framework of the treaty, limiting any weapons that could be suitable for a first strike or that threatened mutual vulnerability. This view brought Smith into conflict with the defense establishment, particularly certain civilian strategists who were calling for the development of limited counterforce and first-strike capabilities, even if only as bargaining chips. Smith felt that such strategies were divorced from reality.[21]

Paul Nitze supported the Nixon administration with technical and strategic advice, though at a slightly lower level than Smith and Kissinger. As the primary author of NSC-68, one of the original statements of containment policy under President Truman, Nitze was a formative figure in the Cold War. This document outlined a view of the Soviet Union as expansionist and domineering, a position that required the United States to commit to military containment. Nitze later served in a variety of roles in the Kennedy and Johnson administrations. Despite his alarmist view of the Soviet Union, Nitze was a strong supporter of arms control and had developed official recommendations for a comprehensive strategic reductions scheme as early as 1964. Nitze was also instrumental in the decision to develop multiple-warhead missile technology in the 1960s.

While Nitze believed that large numbers of nuclear weapons were bad for superpower competition, he was less concerned about absolute force levels than he was about their impact on superpower relations. What Nitze most feared was a Soviet first strike. To Nitze, certain actions (such as the deployment of Soviet ABM systems around Moscow) indicated that the Soviet Union might not be locked in an arms race with the United States but was instead stuck in a defense-offense cycle.[22] In such a cycle, the Soviet Union would need to develop a weapons system that could negate and defeat the U.S. nuclear arsenal and then rely on its overwhelming conventional forces to impose its will. Although this possibility was not likely to occur for some time, Nitze believed that it could not be ignored and had to be addressed if arms control negotiations were ever to begin.

The path of Nitze, a lifelong Democrat, into the Nixon administration was unique. As the Johnson administration left office, Nitze, who found himself in private life for the first time in eight years, grew restless. When the Nixon administration made a crucial decision in 1969 to renew development of an ABM system, an uproar in Congress ensued. Grassroots organizations decried the development of ABM systems as a provocative and potentially destabilizing move that could endanger the as-yet-unscheduled arms control talks. When Nitze was in the Johnson administration, he had opposed comprehensive ABM systems that would protect the U.S. populace, but the Nixon administration had proposed a scaled-down, thin defense designed to protect U.S. ICBM silos. In addition, Nixon announced his intention to pursue arms control in a way that linked offensive and defensive systems, a key component of Nitze's 1964 proposal.[23] These changes to the planned system transformed Nitze from a lukewarm opponent to a fervent advocate for missile defense.

Nitze joined with former secretary of state Dean Acheson and prominent nuclear strategist Albert Wohlstetter to form the Committee to Maintain a Prudent Defense Policy. The group, which employed only a handful of staff and was funded mainly out of its members' pockets, provided critical support in efforts to chip away at resistance from members of Congress to authorizing the proposed ABM system. The performance of this group in private briefings and in testimony in Congress impressed many senior policy makers. When the Nixon administration extended an offer to Nitze to become the Department of Defense representative on the SALT delegation, he accepted. In addition, Senator Jackson hired Albert Wohlstetter's protégé, a young Richard Perle, to assist in his work on the Armed Services Committee. Both selections would prove fateful.[24]

The Department of Defense and Joint Chiefs of Staff (JCS) also supported arms limitation talks and even recommended against the initial delay in opening the talks that Nixon and Kissinger had proposed.[25] These groups favored the talks, but they recalled the failure of the nuclear test moratoria in the 1950s,[26] and therefore opposed unilateral actions or other diplomatic peace offerings that were not part of a formal agreement.

Both organizations' support for any future agreement was predicated on an ability to verify compliance with a very high degree of confidence. Verification of the parties' compliance with any arms control package would involve spy satellites and other forms of reconnaissance (referred to as national technical means of verification) because of the Soviet Union's history of objecting to on-site inspections. The JCS supported a limited agreement to test the reliability of national technical means of verification. Such an agreement would focus intelligence resources on a few weapons; this would make detecting violations relatively simple. This way, the JCS could guarantee the shortest possible time between the detection of violations and the resumption of U.S. weapons production.[27]

These stipulations the Department of Defense and JCS made were considerable, but one concept—parity—overcame these concerns and gave them a reason to support an agreement. The United States had not deployed any new strategic weapons since 1967. It had frozen its force levels at 1,054 ICBMs, 656 submarine-launched ballistic missiles (SLBMs), and 576 strategic bombers.[28] Despite previous protests against the "bomber gap" in the 1950s and the "missile gap" during the 1960 election, the United States had to that point maintained overwhelming superiority in most aspects of the nuclear arms race, particularly in delivery vehicles. After the Cuban missile crisis, the leaders of the Soviet Union rallied around the goal of never again finding itself at a nuclear disadvantage vis-à-vis the United States. Soviet planners engaged in a crash deployment program that significantly increased every category of delivery vehicle, particularly ICBMs. In 1965, the Soviet Union had approximately 220 ICBMs and over 100 SLBMs. By 1968, this figure had grown to over 860 ICBMs and over 120 SLBMs and was on track to exceed the United States in both ICBMs and SLBM forces by 1971.[29] As the Vietnam War raged and sentiment against defense spending ran high, most within the Department of Defense came to the conclusion that arms control ought to happen *before* parity was achieved. An early arms control agreement would lock the United States in a superior position by freezing further Soviet deployments and would prevent "unilateral arms control" through the means of budget cuts and public pressure.[30]

Advances

By the late 1960s, the nuclear arms race was about to enter a new and dangerous phase that the main participants were only vaguely aware of. Up to that point, nuclear dominance was defined for the most part in terms of numbers:

competition centered on the total number of nuclear weapons, what levels of destruction they could yield, and which side had more delivery vehicles. The primitive weapons of the time were ideally suited to a general policy of deterrence. By 1969, however, qualitative improvements were closing in on several important thresholds that could fundamentally alter a weapon's purpose and new technologies had become technically conceivable that could destabilize the strategic balance. Of these changes, three were most important to the shape of the arms race: the development of ABM systems, the development of multiple independently targetable reentry vehicles (MIRVs), and improvements in the accuracy of silo-based ICBMs.

Anti-ballistic missile systems posed the most obvious threat to deterrence. In 1963, the Soviet Union unveiled, to great fanfare, an ABM system designed to fire a highly accurate nuclear-tipped rocket into the upper atmosphere for the purpose of annihilating an enemy nuclear weapon.[31] U.S. defense planners such as Robert McNamara objected to this system, especially when they discovered that it was to be deployed first around Moscow. Protecting cities from nuclear attack reduces the deterrent value of an opponent's weapons and introduces an unnecessary element of instability. Protecting a city instead of protecting weapons implies that there would be few weapons remaining when the ABM system would need to be used. If that were not the case, the ABM system would be located in a missile field. In the worst case (though not necessarily the most likely one), protecting the capital city could suggest a first-strike posture and implied that the system would be used to foil a retaliatory second strike instead of promoting deterrence.

Deployment of the equivalent U.S. Sentinel ABM system stalled in 1968 due to public protest and the presidential elections. The Nixon administration thus faced a dilemma: hold off on development and go into the negotiations without the negotiating leverage of an ABM system or authorize the system's construction and be accused of endangering the talks by seeking new and destabilizing capabilities. Like the Soviet system, the Sentinel system protected cities, but doing so required the United States to host massive nuclear-tipped rockets in city suburbs. Although opinion polls showed that attitudes toward the ABM system had not changed much, basing nuclear weapons next to population centers prompted a storm of well-publicized protests. The strength of this reaction from typically quiescent suburban voters significantly dampened enthusiasm in Congress for the project.[32]

The Nixon administration decided that it could not back away from ABM systems entirely. It needed the leverage an active ABM program provided, but in a configuration that was more politically and strategically defensible. Thus, the Safeguard system, which was designed to protect remote ICBM fields from attack, was born. Because it protected missiles, the system could be defended as strengthening deterrence. Despite Safeguard's clear relationship to the upcoming SALT negotiations, the administration maintained the position that it was intended to thwart a Chinese missile attack. This supposedly justified its small size and likely low level of reliability.[33]

Although the Nixon administration won an early victory in securing Congressional majorities for its ABM program, it did so at great cost. The backlash against the Sentinel program had seriously frightened numerous members of Congress. Moving the interceptors out of urban areas did little to mollify those who opposed the system on strategic and cost grounds. With the Vietnam war raging, spending on new weapons programs was less popular than ever. And with SALT approaching, the system could easily be seen as a provocation. Securing an active ABM program was a critical component of the Nixon administration's SALT strategy, however, and the administration could ill afford to lose that battle. It sunk much of its early political capital into producing legislative majorities for the program. Opposition peaked in August 1969, when the administration fought back an attempt to defund the program. With the Senate deadlocked 50–50, only Vice President Spiro Agnew's tie-breaking vote prevented the program from being eliminated.[34]

In contrast to ABMs, MIRVs were far less visible to most strategists and to the public before SALT. The United States began testing MIRVs in 1964, partly as a cost-effective way to improve the destructive potential of existing missiles and partly to try to defeat Soviet ABM systems.[35] A MIRV allows a single missile to launch multiple warheads into space that can then break off, independently select their different targets, and reenter the atmosphere on a trajectory to hit these targets. Multiple reentry vehicles (perhaps with a few decoys dispersed among them) could easily overwhelm existing ABM systems. MIRVs could also select targets that were scattered geographically, dispersing the overall loss of destructive potential if a single rocket failed in the boost phase or was destroyed by an ABM. Unfortunately, because they consolidated a large number of warheads in fewer missiles, MIRVs were potentially destabilizing because they presented fewer targets to any opponent interested in a first strike.[36] Before SALT was ratified, few military planners considered MIRVs to be a serious problem. The United States was at least five years ahead of the Soviet Union in developing MIRV technology and most experts were willing to accept the potential risk of destabilization because the technology could provide a much less costly means of defeating Soviet ABM systems. With MIRVs, the United States could avoid an expensive ABM race and still maintain strategic dominance.[37] However, this position came back to haunt those in favor of aggressive MIRV deployment when it was discovered that the

Soviet Union's larger, heavier missiles had even greater MIRV potential than their U.S. counterparts.

Advances in ICBM accuracy were another destabilizing trend. These were the hardest to verify. Land-based ICBMs were housed in concrete-reinforced silos that could withstand anything less than a direct hit by another nuclear warhead. The earliest generations of these missiles were far too inaccurate to reliably hit a target as small as a silo and could practically be used only against large targets such as cities or above-ground military installations such as airfields. This level of inaccuracy rendered silo-based ICBMs "safe" from enemy attack and therefore provided a much cheaper and more efficient deterrent option than long-range bombers, which were vulnerable and labor-intensive, or SLBMs, which were less accurate and more expensive. McNamara had considered shifting to a counter-force posture before 1964, but such a stance would require permanent superiority, because it takes more than one weapon to destroy an opponent's weapon with confidence. If the Soviet Union were to also take this counterforce stance, it could accelerate the arms race even further, so McNamara froze most further deployments and improvement programs, with the exception of the MIRV program. The Soviet Union did not reciprocate this gesture, largely because its forces still lagged those of the United States. What was worse for U.S. policymakers was the Soviet Union's latest generation of missiles, particularly the SS-9, which appeared to have the potential to destroy a reinforced ICBM silo if it could strike it accurately. What had once been the safest and most effective leg of the U.S. nuclear triad suddenly faced the possibility of becoming the most vulnerable.[38]

Preparations

With Henry Kissinger at the helm of the National Security Council (NSC), that body grew to one of the main policy-making bodies in the Nixon administration. Established by the National Security Act of 1947, the NSC was a group of executive appointees (such as the national security advisor) and cabinet-level officials (such as the secretaries of state and defense). It was designed to improve policy making by bringing diplomatic and military officials into a single body and giving them the responsibility of recommending specific courses of action to the president.[39] Nixon's primary experience with the NSC was as vice president during the Eisenhower administration. He organized the NSC in his administration similarly; he presided over regular meetings presided and mediated disputes between different factions. Nixon was not Eisenhower, however: lacking the national security credentials of Eisenhower, he never had the self-confidence or credibility necessary to remain consistently engaged at all levels of NSC activity.

As a result, considerable power devolved to Kissinger to shape the proceedings of the NSC and present recommendations to the president. Furthermore, Nixon's secretive style and distrust of "the bureaucracy" gave Kissinger further leeway to make foreign policy decisions without consulting the relevant cabinet officials, such as the secretary of state.[40] Kissinger famously bypassed the cabinet and even the NSC itself on the execution of policy with the use of his covert backchannel with Soviet ambassador Anatoly Dobrynin (communications that were properly reserved for the Department of State), but the NSC remained a critical forum for coordinating and developing foreign policy simply by virtue of Kissinger's control of it and its organization, particularly at the beginning of the Nixon administration.[41]

Before a date was set for the first round of SALT talks, Nixon ordered a review of U.S. strategic policy and the relative standing of the U.S. nuclear force vis-à-vis the Soviet Union.[42] Although the review may partially have been intended as a stalling tactic (Nixon and Kissinger were reluctant to set a date too soon), but arms control talks proved politically irresistible. Kissinger blamed the early opening of arms control talks on media leaks that increased the public clamor for immediate negotiations. Kissinger blamed "the bureaucracy" for these leaks; believing they occurred because of differences with the administration about the timing of the talks.[43] Kissinger's low regard for most of the executive branch presaged his increasingly centralized management style as his tenure progressed.

The comprehensive review segued easily into an analysis of the near-term possibilities for negotiating an arms control regime with the Soviet Union and what options and limits on specific technologies would benefit the United States and still satisfy the notoriously difficult negotiators of the Soviet Union. An NSC paper detailing these issues posited a series of four possible arms control "packages" that incrementally expanded the number of systems to be limited.[44] These scenarios were then submitted to the various stakeholders on the NSC for comment and criticism. The participants assumed that the results of the analysis of these scenarios would influence the U.S. negotiating position once the talks began, despite nearly universal agreement that the United States should not submit a comprehensive proposal immediately for fear of providing an open-ended opportunity to the Soviet Union to criticize it and score propaganda points.

Notably, Ambassador Smith made waves early on by rejecting the NSC paper and its alternatives as insufficient. In a memorandum dated June 11, 1969, he recommended that a new package be included in the NSC's deliberations. Smith summarized his proposal as "Stop Where We Are" (SWWA). Its premise was simple: offer to immediately halt all new strategic weapons deployments if the Soviets would do the same. The package also required a halt to all improvement and upgrade programs that could increase the throw weight or accuracy of existing ballistic missiles. While Smith's rejection of the existing bureaucratic process did not bode well for serious consideration of his ideas, his proposal gained credibility after NSC members scrutinized it.

Smith's argument rested on the likelihood that the more comprehensive any arms limitation regime became, the easier it would be to verify. Regimes that were more comprehensive lengthened the time needed for a de jure violation to become a de facto decrease in U.S. security. This would maximize the time and the flexibility the U.S. had to respond. For example, a regime that banned the deployment of a weapon but not its testing or production would pose a risk because a weapon would have to complete all phases of development before it violated the terms of the treaty. If the violation can be declared only at the point of deployment, the party in compliance with the treaty would be disadvantaged in terms of developing its own version of the weapon. However, if the regime banned the testing, production, and deployment of a weapon, violations could be detected at a far earlier stage, giving the party in compliance with the treaty more time to consider the situation and either attempt to halt development of the weapon or withdraw from the treaty altogether.

Concerns over the lag between detection and response had been one of the JCS's main arguments for emphasizing easy verification. In addition, halting the start of the production of new strategic missiles would enshrine U.S. nuclear dominance in exchange for simply halting the only existing strategic programs the United States had: ABM (which would prove expensive and unreliable in almost all near-term scenarios) and MIRV. Because the proposal brought verification problems to their logical minimum and assured U.S. dominance, it sidestepped many of the complicated, borderline metaphysical debates that plagued the discussion of the NSC's packages.[45] In fact, once it was subjected to the standard war-gaming analysis, the SWWA proposal actually represented a net *increase* in U.S. security when compared to the expected situation in five years without an agreement, and it scored better than several of the NSC's intermediate packages. While Kissinger initially seemed disdainful of Smith's proposal, and included advising against it in a presentation of options to the president, the proposal resolved so many outstanding concerns that it could not be excluded from a process that was ostensibly designed to reconcile those differences.[46]

One particular merit SWWA had over other options was the fact that it was simple to understand. This is what drew Smith to it. One of the intrinsic difficulties of the NSC's form of policy planning was that it combined uncertainty, engineering questions, and speculation about the enemy's intentions in a process of ever-increasing complexity. While the NSC originally envisioned four packages for planning purposes, the list of objections, qualifications, and hedges designed to contain possible Soviet duplicity grew. Less than a month before the first round of SALT talks began, the number of options to be presented to the president had expanded from the original four to include options labeled I, II, III, III-A, IV, V, V-A, VI, and VII.[47] The NSC spun its wheels, attempting to hash out complicated issues by balancing concerns about security, survivability, and verifiability without any form of Soviet input. As a result, the issues the NSC was considering splintered into ever-more-granular problems instead of being resolved. Discussions of ABM limitations stalled over the issue of how to prevent a Soviet surface-to-air missile system from being surreptitiously upgraded to an ABM platform. Other completely speculative problems included what to do if the Soviets upgraded medium-range ballistic missiles by outfitting them with an additional rocket stage, bypassing any (as-yet-undefined) limitations on ICBMs.[48] Participants recognized these efforts as some of the most in-depth analysis strategic nuclear issues that had ever undertaken.,[49] Yet they did not yield anything close to a decision.

This trend did not escape Kissinger; he later noted that the early NSC reports did little to inform the initial U.S. position in the negotiations. What the initial NSC meetings did provide, however, was an institutional road map that indicated how each department and how specific constituencies viewed the possibilities of arms control and which issues would likely prove to be sticking points or require more delicate navigation through the bureaucracy.[50] It is quite possible that the experience of these initial deliberations encouraged Kissinger, for good or ill, to make expanded use of the Dobrynin backchannel as a way of bypassing the bureaucratic cacophony.

The NSC came to consensus on one significant point: a MIRV ban was likely unworkable. The subsequent failure of the SALT treaties to address the MIRV issue became a black mark on the record of SALT, but this outcome was largely determined by the decisions of the Johnson administration and was set in stone by the Nixon administration before the talks began. The NSC discussions also illustrate another implicit conclusion: that a technological approach that focused on the largest strategic systems would address the worst aspects of the nuclear arms race.

MIRVs seek to overwhelm ABM defenses cost effectively without necessitating expensive new missiles. The U.S. defense establishment had grown quite comfortable with the idea of deploying them, to the degree that the JCS credibly maintained that a ban could seriously affect the relative nuclear standing of the United States. For instance, an analysis of one of the more restrictive arms control packages performed outside the JCS argued that a ban on MIRVs and a medium-to-high ceiling on ABMs would degrade U.S. retaliatory capability to a fraction of its original potential. The report found that the United States could lose almost all of its land-based missile forces in a first strike and over 50 percent of the damage done by the United States in retaliation would come from the use of aging B-52 bombers. Without MIRVs, certain reasonable-sounding arms control options could force the United States to rely on a bomber-heavy force structure reminiscent of the 1950s despite the significant technological advancements in the interim.[51]

By 1969, considerable inertia was derailing U.S. plans to deploy MIRVs. Discussions of their limitations met with significant resistance. Much of it grew from concerns about verification: a simple ban on deploying MIRVs would be impossible to verify without on-site inspections, and even then partial disassembly of missile payloads might be necessary instead of simply observing them up close. Supporters of a ban posited that testing could be banned as well. Unfortunately, the United States had already deployed a functioning MRV in the form of the Polaris A-3 SLBM, which clustered smaller warheads around a single target without providing independent guidance. The Soviets would almost certainly demand the right to test and then deploy their own MRV missiles. Although the CIA claimed it could tell the difference between a MRV test and a MIRV test, the NSC was skeptical.[52]

Time militated against a ban on MIRV testing and deployment. By mid-1969 the United States was preparing its final round of MIRV tests. In theory, once they were completed, the United States could begin converting missiles to MIRVs without further tests. (The process itself would take longer, but subsequent tests were mainly refinements.) If the United States were to offer a dual ban on testing and deployment after fully testing its MIRV systems, the Soviets could justifiably object. Why should the Soviets agree to a ban on testing when the United States was nearly finished? Such a ban would give the United States a technological advantage, leaving the Soviet Union to begin testing from scratch in the event of a breakdown of the accord.

This timeline threw the MIRV problem into stark relief and forced several of the main NSC figures to come to conclusions about their priorities with regard to shaping U.S. security. In stark contrast to his later positions, Paul Nitze was relatively unperturbed by the possibilities of MIRVs, mainly because he proposed a method of reducing launchers that would mitigate their effects.[53] Nitze argued that the overall framework an agreement established could exclude MIRVs if it was properly balanced with regard to other systems. While he was hardly enthusiastic about MIRVs, Nitze tended to see them as interrelated with ABMs.[54] He did not see either as dangerous in themselves but saw the relationship between the two as the threat to stability. In not aggressively pursuing a MIRV ban at that time, Nitze also sought to preserve the U.S. bargaining position and have at least one offensive program where the United States was in the lead. Furthermore, Nitze thought that MIRVs lent specific short-term advantages to the United

States, particularly if the SALT accords did not halt the Soviet missile buildup before it achieved parity. Because many in the NSC believed a resulting treaty would be time limited, a short-term advantage might be worth the potential long-term liability.

Smith took the opposite approach. His primary goal was to enshrine deterrence as the main form of nuclear stability. Smith, more than anyone else on the NSC, foresaw the degree to which MIRVs could be a losing technology for the United States in the long term.[55] The United States was approximately five years ahead in MIRV technology, beyond the window most members of the NSC were willing to realistically project the consequences of an arms control agreement. While MIRVs would give the U.S. land-based ICBM force an advantage in this time frame, the new generation of Soviet "heavy" ICBMs known as the SS-9 could eliminate this margin of dominance. These missiles had throw weights of three to five times that of the standard U.S. ICBM. U.S. observers originally regarded the SS-9s as white elephants, evidence of the Soviet obsession with building bigger than the West instead of building better. However, greater throw weights meant that more warheads could be packed into each missile. If they were to be converted to MIRVs and sufficient improvements were to be made in terms of accuracy (admittedly a considerable undertaking), this fraction of the Soviet ICBM force could eventually threaten over 90 percent of the U.S. ICBM force in a first strike with a substantial reserve left over.[56]

Nitze shared Smith's concern about the larger Soviet missiles' MIRV potential, but instead of trying to ban MIRVs, he became an outspoken advocate of including limitations on the total throw weight of a missile force instead of limiting the number of delivery vehicles. Nitze continued this emphasis throughout the SALT negotiations, but to no avail. Aside from Nitze and Smith, most of the NSC saw Smith's concerns as a long-term problem that the United States could adjust to as it developed. While they were sympathetic to Nitze's emphasis on throw weight over the number of vehicles, they generally regarded it as a secondary metric to be used for analytic purposes instead of as a negotiating position.

Senator Edward Brooke of Massachusetts recognized that the United States was about to attempt one of its final MIRV tests before declaring the technology operational, and attempted to pass a resolution that would have required a unilateral moratorium on further testing until the arms control talks had been completed. The proposal was scuttled, however, because the JCS and the hawkish elements of the U.S. polity loathed the idea of a unilateral moratorium as giving away the only active offensive program the United States might use as a bargaining chip. Furthermore, the proposal could not fix the MRV/MIRV problem, and halting testing at that point still gave the United States a considerable technological advantage that the administration felt the Soviet Union was unlikely to accept. While Senator Brooke's resolution garnered considerable attention, those opposed to nuclear weapons were focusing on ABMs at the time and MIRVs became far less of a public concern after the resolution was scuttled.[57]

Eventually, Kissinger convened a special panel to address the problems of MIRVs and their viability as a target for bilateral controls. This "MIRV Panel" report gave official expression to the generally pessimistic views on what would be required to effectively ban MIRVs. The primary author of the report was the NSC representative from the Department of State's Bureau of Intelligence and Research, traditionally the least hawkish branch of the U.S. intelligence community. The report concluded that "although we probably would not be confident enough to deploy our MIRV at its present state of development in other than an assured destruction role, it might be very difficult to persuade the Soviets that we had not already achieved a hard-target capability," adding that "should they achieve development of a MIRV system prior to a ban on MIRV testing, we see little prospect of determining the extent to which MIRV's had been incorporated in deployed missiles without highly intrusive on-site inspections."[58] The NSC published the report in July 1969, well after the United States had conducted its final round of MIRV tests. While the NSC never concluded that a ban on MIRVs was unacceptable, the council tacitly adopted the stance that the genie was out of the bottle and, barring a breakthrough, it was not likely that a ban was worth pursuing.[59]

The failure to take MIRVs more seriously is disappointing, particularly in view of the prominence of the issue throughout the 1970s and 1980s, but it is not surprising. The Nixon administration was less than five months old and highly active in a number of other policy fields. Any administration that but reversed its only major strategic weapons program would face serious repercussions. Even with a high-level consensus, the effort necessary to alter the course of the ship of state in time could only be described as heroic. Furthermore, none of these efforts would have improved the chances that the Soviet Union would accept limitations on MIRVs. For any hypothetical administration faced with this issue, halting and then banning MIRVs would require high costs and high risks and, from what was known in 1969, only dubious rewards.

The NSC's implicit conclusions about the nature of the arms race sprang from a series of unexamined, albeit understandable, premises. One of the primary justifications for pursuing arms control is that it is impossible to win a nuclear arms race. There is no finish line and an industrial economy can support many thousands of weapons before exhausting itself. Such arguments treated nuclear weapons and the impact they would have as primarily technological phenomena and saw only a diminished role for geopolitics. After all, if a weapon's reach is global and its potential for damage is unlimited, what does it matter where the weapons are located?

The tenor of initial consultations with NATO allies also illustrated this perspective. The Soviet Union had long insisted that the United States draw down military assets intended for the defense of Western Europe and halt technology transfers to third parties such as France and England. It argued that these policies were destabilizing and made the Soviet Union more vulnerable to nuclear attack. The United States sought to assuage the concerns of NATO allies that the superpowers would bargain away obligations to other countries in exchange for a joint nuclear "condominium"—an agreement between the superpowers that increased their security at the expense of guarantees to allied states.[60] At no point did any of the analyzed arms control packages entertained by the NSC incorporate any such geopolitical tradeoffs. They avoided technologies that directly impacted the security of Europe, such as intermediate- and medium-range ballistic missiles, in favor of technologies that could be analyzed in an abstract, actuarial sense, such as ICBMs and ABMs.

The Nixon administration's emphasis on consultation to assuage allied concerns eventually became a substitute for considering how best to defend NATO. The need to defend Western Europe was one of the original reasons for the United States to develop and maintain nuclear dominance over the Soviet Union, and one of the primary institutions of the Cold War. During one of the final NSC preparatory meetings, the discussion briefly veered into NATO issues and the nuclear balance in Europe. Ambassador Smith interjected that while consultation with NATO allies was important, the threat to land-based systems posed by MIRV was the main issue and ought to be the focus. The discussion then turned away from NATO issues except to affirm that the United States would have to provide assurances to allies that the balance in the largest systems had been preserved.[61]

Few within the U.S. government saw the emphasis on technology over regional dynamics as a problem, and not without reason. Doing so limited the ability of the Soviet Union to require the United States to withdraw some of its nuclear forces from Western Europe, weakening the alliance. Thinking too abstractly about the nuclear balance risked discounting the areas where nuclear war was most likely to break out, by growing out of a smaller, regional conflict. One of the initial, driving forces for the U.S. pursuit of nuclear dominance was the need to defend Western Europe, but the Nixon administration was specifically designing its SALT strategy not to consider the security requirements of NATO.

Although a variety of parties would challenge the perspective of Smith and the broader NSC in the coming decades, thinking of nuclear weapons as a technology rather than a geopolitical problem remained the dominant theoretical starting point in the United States. The Soviet Union clearly disagreed with this conception. The United States resisted most of the elements of the Soviet position in this area, but it was not until well after it ratified SALT I that U.S. policymakers recognized the difficulties of reconciling nuclear parity with the geopolitics of the Cold War, such as the commitment to the nuclear defense of NATO.

Negotiations

Upon reviewing the initial options presented by the NSC, President Nixon approved the three least ambitious opening positions. These emphasized relatively low ceilings or an outright ban on ABMs, did not ban MIRVs, and instituted modest caps on delivery vehicles (excluding bombers).[62] The proposals also entertained banning certain problematic variations on these delivery vehicles, such as rail- or truck-mounted ICBMs, whose mobility made satellite tracking almost impossible. Nixon also ordered Smith not to deliver these packages to the Soviet negotiators at the opening round of the talks but instead to focus on "exploration" of the issues. He hoped that if each side discussed how it viewed the nuclear arms race, the parties could come to a better understanding without making firm commitments to specific packages that could later be used against the United States. This decision rendered moot much of the NSC's efforts to develop acceptable arms control packages, as any position put forward at the negotiations would have to reflect what the negotiators had learned about Soviet priorities.[63]

These initial discussions revealed a great deal about the Soviet Union's priorities and how it viewed the nuclear arms race (or at least how it wished to have its views be seen). Perhaps the most unexpected concern of the Soviets was the overriding attention they paid to the political and accidental possibilities of nuclear weaponry. The Soviet Union raised a number of issues and proto-proposals that sought to limit escalation and force consultation in the event of a nuclear attack by an unnamed third country (China) or to limit escalation in situations of accidental launches or subterfuge intended to force the superpowers into annihilating one another. The Sino-Soviet split clearly weighed on the Soviets' minds. Their delegation may have also seen third-party proposals as a nonthreatening starting point, as it incriminated neither party as a contributor to instability.[64] The Soviets also discussed the possibility of updating the Kremlin-to-White House "hot line" (established following the Cuban Missile Crisis) with a permanent agreement and making mutual commitments to take active steps to prevent accidental launches and to disavow dangerous "launch on warning" policies. The U.S. delegation had no substantial objections to these ideas.[65]

The Soviet Union may have decided to lead with such nontechnical issues as a way of keeping its strategic priorities obscured while gauging the scope of the U.S. interest in an agreement. If the interest was merely for show, then an agreement addressing such issues would be relatively simple to negotiate and would impose few burdens on either side's military establishments. Such agreements would also provide the necessary photo opportunities to create the impression that real progress had been made. It is equally possible, however, that these issues were among the foremost concerns of the Soviet Union. Soviet negotiators may not have seen nuclear weapons technology as destabilizing in itself but may have located the danger in their intersection with human fallibility and a specific international order.

As discussions progressed, the Soviet delegation also showed a different perspective on how to measure nuclear and strategic vulnerability. Rather than focusing on the inherent stability or instability of technologies by sorting them into categories and comparing the respective stockpiles of each side, the Soviet Union defined any weapon capable of striking Soviet soil as threatening and insisted on accounting for this vulnerability in any attempt to define parity between the superpowers. This position was highly controversial because it required the United States to reclassify its forward-based systems (FBS) and the nuclear stockpiles of both the United Kingdom and France as strategic weapons. Forward-based systems included any nuclear-capable delivery system based outside the continental United States that lacked a long-range attack function but could strike within the Soviet Union's borders. This category included land- and sea-based ground-attack aircraft capable of being mounted with tactical nuclear weapons that could reach the Soviet Union, even if the mission was only one way.[66]

Restrictions on FBS might seem symmetrical in theory, but geography imposed wildly disproportionate effects on the United States. The gross megatonnage of each of these categories was small compared to what the United States regarded as "strategic" nuclear weapons, and they were universally intended for the tactical defense of U.S. allies. While these weapons were capable of inflicting substantial damage on the Soviet Union, their contribution to any overall exchange of nuclear weapons would be miniscule given the thousands of missiles and long-range bombers capable of delivering faster, more powerful, and more accurate payloads. Under the Soviet proposals, the United States would have had to remove nuclear-armed fighter-bombers stationed in Europe while imposing no restrictions on Soviet-operated MR/IRBMs that were directed at NATO countries. The United States made clear that any limitation on FBS unacceptably abridged its ability to meet its obligations to its allies. The concerns of the Soviets were understandable; their vulnerability was real. But the United States argued that the Soviet Union's geographic disadvantages would have to be addressed by some other means of calculating strategic parity.[67]

The issue of FBS proved to be one of the least tractable issues both during and after the SALT negotiations because it challenged the very definition of "strategic arms." To the United States, which drew on its substantial experience with strategic bombing in World War II, "strategic" weapons were those intended for use against cities and economies, weapons that attacked the ability or psychological desire to wage war. The Soviet Union, which had no such history of strategic bombing, gave scant consideration to traditional conceptions of anti-civilian deterrence during the formative stages of the nuclear competition. Instead, the Soviets attempted to incorporate nuclear weapons into the combined-arms warfighting traditions that had served them so well against Nazi Germany.[68]

As a result of this experience, the Soviet Union subscribed mainly to a theory of homeland deterrence. This theory posited that most scenarios that precipitated a nuclear exchange would initially manifest as regional disputes such as a general war in Europe between NATO countries and members of the Warsaw Pact. While Soviet planners assumed that both sides would deploy tactical and theater nuclear weapons, the transition from theater use to use against either superpower's homeland was the critical escalation to a general, all-out exchange.[69] In contrast, U.S. planners took NATO obligations so seriously that they assumed that a theater use of a nuclear weapon against a West German position would trigger a nuclear response against the targets that posed the greatest threat, regardless of where they were located.[70] So intractable was this issue that the parties continued to disagree even after the treaty was concluded, even though it was not mentioned in the text of the treaty.

As the talks progressed and both parties became aware of how seriously their opposites took the negotiations, the Soviet delegation expressed interest in comprehensive controls over more technological issues. The American delegation quickly realized, much to their relief, that the top Soviet priority was limiting ABM systems. Although the Soviet delegation admitted nothing officially, it seemed that the combination of the rising cost and extreme difficulty of completing the ABM system around Moscow and the fear of a superior U.S. system such as that proposed by the Nixon administration had led to a substantial shift in Soviet thinking about ABM systems.[71] In addition, the Soviet Union agreed in principle that the parties should work on a more narrow agreement first so as to build momentum and consensus for a follow-on agreement of a more permanent nature.

While a U.S. ABM system concerned the Soviet delegation the most, the rapid Soviet buildup in offensive arms concerned the United States the most, and the U.S. delegation made clear (in tandem with Kissinger's backchannel) that they would accede to permanent limitations on ABMs in exchange for interim limitations on offensive arms. The relationship between offensive and defensive weapons became one of the most lasting legacies of the SALT negotiations and its successors. The immediate impact of this position, since the United States was more concerned with offense and the Soviet Union was more concerned with defense, was the U.S. requirement that the parties negotiate about ABMs and offensive limitations "simultaneously," to prevent one party from stonewalling after achieving everything it wanted in its area of concern. As an extension of this policy, the United States also stipulated that it would not provide final approval to any aspect of the agreement until all aspects of the agreement had been agreed upon. It is common for a nation to insist that "nothing is final until everything is final" in negotiations of this nature, but this position also reflected the U.S. perspective on the strategic arms race, which was that while some weapons were worse than others, the overall strategic balance was the overriding concern.[72]

The negotiations themselves took place over the course of several years, a glacial pace that proved to be the norm in future arms control talks. Many of the issues discussed bordered on the absurd and did not necessarily reflect the strategic outlook of the negotiating parties. Months of negotiations were consumed developing neutral language that appeared to impose a limitation on both sides but in practice reflected a single country's concern. The United States, for instance, did not want the Soviet Union to build a second large radar west of the Ural Mountains, as it would be too close to the Moscow ABM system to determine if it was an early warning radar or a covert expansion of the Moscow system in violation of the agreement. The Soviet Union would not agree to a unilateral restriction in a bilateral treaty and required the United States to craft language regarding radar coverage radii and minimum distances between the two ABM sites the agreement allowed, even though these metrics were geographically irrelevant to the United States.[73] These more granular discussions introduced the participants to the ever-increasing complexity of fashioning a strategic balance between countries with vastly different geographies, technologies, and social structures. Several discussions are worth noting, however, for the innovative way they approached the problem of complexity and exerted a lasting influence on how certain individuals, particularly Paul Nitze, viewed the possibilities of arms control in the future.

The United States had significant concerns about verification relating to the Soviet Union, particularly with regard to ABM systems. As a hedge against a potential inability to detect certain forms of cheating, the United States wished to limit ancillary systems. Frustrated by his inability to convince either delegation to consider missile throw weights in addition to the number of launchers, Nitze turned to the problem of creating effective limits on ABM radars.[74] Initially, neither party sought to control radars, since no one could articulate a series of limitations that preserved the early warning facilities that were important for deterrence. Nitze believed that radars were as important as (if not more important than) limits on the number of interceptors and launchers. Once additional missile interceptors beyond what the agreement allowed were developed past the prototype phase, they would be relatively cheap and easy to make. Radar installations, however, are fixed, expensive, and take time to construct. Effectively limiting these would prevent the Soviet Union from withdrawing from the treaty suddenly and deploying a nationwide ABM system in a short time frame, relying on radars they had already constructed.

Distinguishing an ABM radar from other phased-array radars is difficult because they all operate on the same scientific principles and are distinguishable from ABM radars only in terms of degree. Nitze understood this but believed that sufficient discussion with the Soviet delegation could produce a set of objective criteria by which ABM radars could be judged. Working in conjunction with his Soviet counterpart, Alexander Shchukin, whom Nitze viewed as a kindred spirit, Nitze crafted a formula known as the "power-aperture product" of a radar and set about arguing that it should be included in the agreement.[75] The relationship of a radar's power and aperture to its purpose is complex, but Nitze's success in developing a formula bolstered his belief that negotiated solutions were possible, but only after an extremely rigorous consideration of the political and strategic dimensions of any technology.[76]

No discussion of the SALT negotiations would be complete without mentioning the Kissinger-Dobrynin backchannel. Much has been made of Kissinger's attempt to bypass the U.S. diplomatic apparatus in the hope of achieving an agreement. Kissinger's attempts to negotiate alone with the entire upper echelons of the Soviet government required considerable self-confidence and little room for error. The effects of the backchannel on the SALT negotiations and the strategic outcomes of the treaty were primarily restricted to the issues of submarines and summit negotiations.

The potential vulnerability of the U.S. land-based missile force was one of the primary concerns of the U.S. negotiators. This force was vulnerable only to land-based missiles in the Soviet Union, not to SLBMs, which were smaller and less accurate. As a result, discussions of ICBM limits took on far greater import and received the bulk of the NSC's attention. However, the NSC never seriously considered leaving SLBMs out of an agreement. Kissinger seems to have been confused by this emphasis, and at two critical points in his discussions with Dobrynin he described arms control options that he said were acceptable to the United States that excluded any limitations on SLBMs. In a memorandum of conversation dated January 28, 1971, Kissinger reported that Dobrynin asked for a clarification of the U.S. position: "He [Dobrynin] said if he had understood me correctly, I was proposing a freeze on offensive deployments—specifically, land-based missiles—in return for a formal ABM agreement. I said that was correct."[77] In case Dobrynin had misunderstood Kissinger's implication, he posed essentially the same question again less than two weeks later: "Dobrynin then asked whether we [the United States] included land-based systems only or sea-based ones as well. I said we were prepared to do either."[78]

It is impossible to tell if Kissinger deliberately meant to convey this impression or if he simply confused the term "offensive systems" with counterforce systems. Kissinger's misdirection set back the negotiations by months at a difficult moment. According to Smith,

> We had watched with some apprehension a stream of photos showing the rapid build-up of the Soviet SLBM fleet. By early 1971 the U.S.S.R. had nearly as many submarines in operation and under construction as the United States had in operation. Geography benefited the United States, as did advanced bases, but longer-range Soviet seaborne missiles which were being developed would soon eliminate a good deal of this advantage. Knowing of our preoccupation with ICBMs, the Soviets probably hoped that the "freeze" would apply only to them—and let submarine construction run free. Their ICBM launcher construction program perhaps was already topping out.[79]

Negotiating back to the point of including SLBMs was arduous. The Soviets were highly resistant to this change and attempted to run out the clock on the negotiation of SLBM limits. When it was obvious this approach would not work, General Secretary Brezhnev gave Kissinger a letter proposing the extremely high but oddly specific levels of 950 SLBMs on board 62 submarines.[80] The U.S. negotiators were puzzled but were unlikely to get any details about where these numbers came from. Smith later claimed that "some SALT officials later noted a curious coincidence that a then current U.S. intelligence paper containing low, medium and high estimates of the Soviet strategic submarine program projected at the high end of this range a Soviet fleet in 1977 [the end of the interim agreement period] of 62 submarines with about 950 launchers."[81] Either U.S. intelligence had underestimated the Soviet capacity for deploying ballistic missile submarines (which is unlikely considering their record) or the Soviets recommended a ceiling at exactly the level they had planned to build to all along.

The problems created by the parallel negotiation of the backchannel reached their absurd apotheosis at the Moscow summit of 1972. Nixon had long expressed a desire for a presidential summit in Moscow, where he and Brezhnev could sign the SALT agreements and provide a photo opportunity around the crowning achievement of détente. Unfortunately, as often happens with summit diplomacy, the parties agreed to a date without finalizing the agreement, so the Soviets, like almost any party engaged in summit diplomacy, began dragging their feet in the hope that Nixon would intervene with concessions simply to keep the treaty on track for the summit. However, Kissinger could not resist the temptation to intervene in an effort to hasten the process, with the result that the SALT delegation was negotiating increasingly granular details in Helsinki while Kissinger was negotiating similar granular details in Moscow well into the night that the accord was meant to be signed. The process was extremely chaotic, to the point that the U.S. SALT delegation did not understand what the Kissinger group was negotiating in Moscow despite Kissinger's repeated requests for advice.[82]

So chaotic was this final round of simultaneous delegation and summit negotiation that the U.S. SALT delegates were flown in without being informed about the final terms of the agreement. Nevertheless, they were expected to speak about it in detail at a press conference in Moscow.[83] Worst of all, the requirements Kissinger negotiated on phasing out older submarines and imposing limits on modernization of existing submarines required several weeks of NSC meetings and consultations with translators to determine what, exactly, the United States had agreed to at the Moscow summit.[84] During these weeks the U.S. SALT delegates were forced to testify before Congress on the value of a treaty whose requirements the White House could not seem to get straight, resulting in a rather weak unveiling that afforded hawks such as Senator Jackson the opportunity to harp on the apparent asymmetries of the agreement. The White House later deflected this criticism by turning blame on the delegation itself, in a controversial purge of the Arms Control and Disarmament Agency.

Conclusion

The final terms of the SALT agreements included a permanent treaty banning ABM systems except in two locations per country (later reduced to one): one around the capital and one around an ICBM field of specific size and density. Both sites had limits on the number of interceptors per site that were so low that neither side availed itself of a second site. The United States eventually mothballed its Safeguard system as well. The Senate ratified the ABM Treaty by a vote of 88 to 2.

An Interim Agreement of five years' duration was also included that capped U.S. forces at 1,054 ICBMs and 656 SLBMs (with the option to increase to 710 SLBMs, a concession the Soviets made because they had a greater number of submarines). Soviet forces were capped at 1,618 ICBMs and 950 SLBMs. The Nixon administration justified the greater number of Soviet ICBMs by pointing to the greater accuracy and reliability of U.S. missiles and claiming that the lack of overseas Soviet bases meant that a smaller proportion of the Soviet SLBM allowance was on patrol in its assigned area at any given time as compared to the

United States. Although the United States had a superior bomber force that the agreement did not account for, the political optics of the agreement were troubling. The Nixon administration was forced to settle for an asymmetrical "freeze" but held out hope that the permanent, comprehensive follow-on agreement of SALT II would provide a more defensible framework.

Hawks quickly began to criticize the supposed asymmetry of the agreement. Senator Henry "Scoop" Jackson was particularly well positioned to do this. Jackson, a senator from the state of Washington, typified the pro-defense Cold Warrior Democrat for decades, even as the Democratic Party began to shift away from his hard-line stances.[85] Jackson's main point of contention was that the Interim Agreement conceded to the Soviet Union superiority in the strategic arms that posed the greatest first-strike threat to the United States and that it did not sufficiently protect the United States against the larger ICBMs the Soviet Union seemed to prefer.[86] Jackson also criticized the failure of the agreement to address the gap between total Soviet and U.S. throw weights, a line of attack that Richard Perle, Nitze's former associate, no doubt encouraged. Senator Jackson seemed to share the president's suspicions of "arms controllers" in the executive branch who regarded nuclear weapons of any kind as a greater threat to U.S. security than that of Soviet communism and as a result of these misplaced priorities failed to negotiate with the best interest of the United States in mind.[87] For a senator whose relationship with arms manufacturers had earned him the moniker "the Senator from Boeing," weapons themselves were never the problem; the Soviet Union was. In his view, no foreign policy objective could outweigh the continuing need to oppose the Soviet Union both ideologically and militarily, and unless the administration could justify the SALT agreements from this perspective, he would not support them. Many conservative and Republican hardliners agreed with this point of view, but Jackson's status as a Democrat gave him greater leeway to criticize the treaty.

The administration dismissed Jackson's criticisms as irrelevant, since they did not compare the strategic balance to what it would have been without an agreement. They felt that since the United States had no plans to expand its strategic arsenal in the near future and since Senator Jackson had not proposed any such expansion since 1969, the gap would only have grown worse without efforts to slow down the Soviet buildup. Furthermore, they saw the ban on ABM systems as a significant achievement that headed off a potentially expensive and destabilizing aspect of the arms race. In addition, they believed that the number of launchers alone did not account for U.S. advantages in strategic bombers and for the fact that U.S. missiles were more accurate and more efficient than Soviet missiles.[88] What is notable about the administration's defense of the treaty is that it made no recourse to the argument that first-strike vulnerability is irrelevant if second-strike forces such as submarines are secure. Such an argument originated from deterrence theory, but it would seem that once the Nixon administration's interest in nuclear superiority was questioned, it discarded this doctrine, which had informed much of the negotiations.

The administration noted Senator Jackson's paranoia about "arms controllers" and decided to purge these individuals from the State Department, in exchange for Jackson's support. They became scapegoats for the perceived problems of the treaty. Of the seventeen civil servants serving at the top levels of the ACDA in 1972, only three remained by 1974. The rest were fired or exiled to posts for which they were overqualified or resigned in disgust over the treatment of their colleagues. Gerard Smith stayed on long enough to oversee the first plenary session of SALT II in January 1973, then resigned. Raymond Garthoff, a SALT delegate and one of the most respected Russian experts at the State Department, was sent to the Inspector General's office to audit embassies for the next three years.[89] Though Paul Nitze was ideologically closer to Jackson than the rest of the delegation, he resigned as well, issuing a scathing public statement on his resignation.[90] Senator Jackson eventually supported the agreements but attached an (unenforceable) amendment to the Senate resolution approving the Interim Agreements that barred the president from negotiating any follow-on agreement that limited U.S. intercontinental forces to an amount less than those of the Soviet Union. If Jackson could not influence the terms of SALT I, he would at the very least issue an ultimatum over SALT II.[91]

Watergate has of course tainted many of the Nixon administration's achievements, and the legacy of SALT I has been shaped by cynicism about the scandal. The Cold War did not end in the wake of the agreements, and in some cases the superpowers came even closer to a nuclear exchange than ever before (for example, with the high-alert status the 1973 Yom Kippur War triggered). Ambassador Smith noted bitterly that the Secretary of Defense later used the terms of the Interim Agreement to accelerate qualitative improvements to U.S. strategic forces, such as the Trident submarine and the B-1 bomber and that arms control could be used perversely to justify higher defense spending in order to increase future bargaining power.[92] This outcome is not as perverse as Smith asserted, however, because Smith himself justified the agreement by arguing that the United States had no active offensive strategic programs in production, whereas the Soviets were surging ahead. The United States had limited bargaining power over the Soviet Union by Smith's own calculus.

Smith later argued that the ABM Treaty was the agreement's most important legacy, and it would be unfair to judge the whole agreement solely by the future developments the negotiators failed to prevent, such as the deployment of MIRVs on heavy Soviet missiles. This perspective ignores all of the crises and developments that could have been equally destabilizing but did not happen thanks to the agreements.[93] Raymond Garthoff argued that the treaty was oversold to a degree and that while it contributed to a relaxation of tensions, no single arms control treaty can permanently change the trajectory of relations with a country if it does not alter the underlying political tensions that required the treaty in the first place.[94]

What conditions drove the strategic arms competition with the Soviet Union? The possibilities ranged from imbalances of conventional power in Europe to the ideological incompatibility of the two nations. SALT did not and could not resolve these questions and did not seek to ask them, except to vaguely suggest the principles of "deterrence" and "parity" to manage them. The final outcome of the agreements resembled deterrence thinking. Although some who embraced non-classical deterrence, such as Nitze, could accept that it was still a net improvement, the structure of the terms spoke to the deterrence world view. Limiting ABM systems provided the mutual vulnerability necessary to maintain the balance of terror. The Soviets may have had an edge for the moment with their heavier warheads, but the United States undoubtedly could have inflicted cataclysmic damage regardless of the Soviet lead.

For some, though, a partial Soviet advantage or any force structure defined by deterrence was incompatible with the strategic obligations that defined the Cold War. Starting with nuclear diplomacy under the Truman administration and continuing through the doctrines of massive retaliation under Eisenhower and the saber rattling during the Berlin Crisis of 1961, the United States relied on the threat of nuclear force (with varying degrees of success) to compel the Soviets to acquiesce in specific realms. At no point before the 1980s did NATO have the conventional forces necessary to fight off a Soviet invasion of Western Europe. Only the threat of nuclear annihilation made NATO's foundational principle credible: that an attack on one was an attack on all.

Because the deterrence position rejects the first use of nuclear weapons, promoting stability through a steady state of nuclear parity, NATO obligations, or any threat of nuclear first use cannot fit into this equation. If the Soviet Union invaded a portion of West Germany with solely conventional forces, one could legitimately question the rationality of a decision by the U.S. president to launch an all-out nuclear assault on the Soviet Union, a course that would no doubt result in a Soviet strike against the United States in kind. This course of action would privilege the continued existence of a third party over the cost of national suicide. While the threat of such an irrational course of action was sufficient to deter any aggressive moves in the short and medium terms, irrationality was not the stuff of which stable, long-term nuclear strategy is made. This was the problem of parity: it connected military obligations that required superiority with a diplomatic framework that required equality.

The statements of public officials when the SALT agreements were ratified left the impression that deterrence was both national policy and a reflection of the structural incentives of the ABM Treaty. But the reality of nuclear policy was not that simple, and while the Soviet Union concurred that a nuclear war could not be "won" in the traditional sense, many outsiders began to question whether the Soviet Union subscribed to the countervalue, second-strike posture that U.S. thinkers argued was essential to stable deterrence.[95] These voices grew louder in the years following the treaty, and their criticisms presaged shifts in U.S. policy away from deterrence.

The SALT I agreements politicized arms control as never before. Subsequent arms limitation agreements could no longer be the product of a diverse negotiating team. After SALT I, presidents began running on and being judged by their arms control plans and achievements.[96] After the experience of the Kissinger-Dobrynin backchannel, it was clear that concentrating the power to make decisions about strategic arms in the hands of a few political appointees could prove extremely dangerous given the inevitable missteps inherent in such a complex endeavor. Deferring to "experts" was equally untenable, given what happened to the State Department's "arms controllers" when they were exposed to political scrutiny. However, these experiences suggested that politicization could promote focus on a particular strategy, allowing the execution of arms control to be the application of broadly held, politically determined doctrines. Some of these doctrines incorporated deterrence; some did not.

The shifts in policy away from deterrence are among the most significant effects of SALT I and are the source of the agreement's ambiguous legacy. Although the SALT I agreements channeled the competition over nuclear weapons into a qualitative arms race that in some ways was more stable and predictable, the problem of parity remained. How could the United States deter action against third parties with a doctrine that eschewed superiority or the ability to escalate? The cap on the number of launchers engendered a serious reconsideration of the long-maligned counterforce strategy. Because both parties now had a limited number of delivery vehicles, the pursuit of more was no longer an option. Qualitative improvements and innovative strategic concepts that might previously have been dismissed as too risky or too expensive became acceptable alternatives. Instead of building more missiles, one or both parties could find ways to add reentry vehicles to their MIRVs. Instead of targeting a missile site with multiple missiles to assure its destruction, engineers were driven to make improvements in accuracy and reliability. And instead of building more missiles to ensure that an adequate number would survive a first strike, the two powers explored alternatives to the silo concept, including missile launchers that could move by rail or by land. All of these new structural incentives militated against deterrence and made counterforce strategies possible and the numerical instability that had previously been the Achilles' heel of the counterforce strategy subsided.

The realization of the difficulties of deterrence and the adjustments to nuclear strategy that resulted took several years and were largely overshadowed by Watergate, the fall of Saigon, and the negotiation of SALT II. Those who realized these difficulties adjusted to them with varying degrees of success, but with lasting consequences.

AFTERMATH AND ADAPTATION: THE ORIGINS OF SALT II

Although SALT I, which was ratified in 1972, should have been a signature achievement for the Nixon administration, its honeymoon phase was brief. During the period from 1973 to 1976, diplomats, politicians, and policy makers gradually accommodated themselves to the fact that SALT I had been the easy part. Now grueling, dizzyingly complicated negotiations were to become a part of everyday life in Washington, but without the novelty and relatively clear objectives that had characterized SALT I. In addition, the strategic outlook did not hold still while policy makers grappled with the implications of the recent accords. Instead, SALT I controlled the quantitative arms race just as a far more complex qualitative arms revolution broke out, inaugurating a new phase of competition that developed concurrently with international efforts to control it.

From 1973 to 1976, a variety of individuals and groups came to some or all of these realizations and began to act accordingly. This process of adaptation in response to SALT in turn influenced the negotiating position and strategic posture of the United States. For some decision makers, such as Paul Nitze, the experience of the negotiations prompted a reconsideration of what makes for genuinely beneficial arms control agreements. For decision makers who were at one remove from the negotiating table, such as newly appointed secretary of defense James Schlesinger, SALT I and the ensuing negotiations crystalized a number of issues of geopolitics and political economy, prompting highly consequential reevaluations of U.S. nuclear strategy. While SALT I established the context for nuclear competition and the place of arms control in the Cold War going forward, during the crucial years that followed, the decisions made, the opportunities lost, and the bureaucratic precedents that were made festered and hardened. This is when the impact of SALT became most apparent.

SALT I and the Nuclear Outlook

The Nixon administration's basic approach to the negotiation of SALT I was shaped by a deterrence framework. Ambassador Gerard Smith, the chief negotiator for SALT I, stated that enshrining the doctrine of deterrence was one of his main objectives during the negotiations.[1] In his public statements at least, Nixon also said that SALT I's main achievement was that it restricted nuclear arms to a purely retaliatory role.[2] The terms of the accord reflect this priority.

The primary component of SALT I was the Anti-Ballistic Missile Treaty, which restricted the relatively new and untested technology of missile-based interceptors, allowing each country only two ABM sites with 100 interceptors each.[3] Limiting ABMs, intrinsically defensive weapons, deliberately increased the vulnerability of each side to a nuclear strike. Mutual vulnerability was meant to act as the foundation for future stability: neither side could win a nuclear exchange at an acceptable cost. The other main component of SALT I was the five-year Interim Agreement, which limited the United States to 1,054 ICBMs and 656 SLBMs[4] and the Soviets to 1,618 ICBMs and 950 SLBMs.[5] New silo construction was banned. Missiles could be physically upgraded or even replaced, but neither missiles nor silos could be widened beyond a certain threshold. The focus on a deterrence framework was also apparent in the negotiation of these terms, as the predominant focus was on limiting ICBMs. Limitations on SLBMs, which were regarded as less threatening and useful only for second-strike scenarios, were generally seen as a secondary priority.[6]

After 1972, a number of technological changes began to complicate the negotiation of a follow-on agreement. The most problematic of these technologies was the multiple independently targetable reentry vehicle (MIRV). These vehicles make it possible for a single missile to strike several targets simultaneously and were originally developed to overwhelm ABM systems. Under the right conditions, however, MIRV technology could provide the incentive for a first strike because it consolidates a greater number of reentry vehicles into a proportionally smaller number of targets. Destroying ICBMs before they could leave their silos could confer a disproportionate advantage.[7] MIRV technology was in its final phases of testing when the Nixon administration took office. Because this technology was one of the few strategic programs the United States had in active development in 1969 and because it was not easy to verify a missile's MIRV status, the Nixon administration allowed the program to continue and chose to focus negotiations on achieving control of ABM numbers. By late 1973, there were plans to upgrade approximately 500 Minuteman II ICBMs to their MIRV variant, the Minuteman III, which contained three reentry vehicles.[8] The Soviet Union's MIRV program had yet to leave the testing phase but was poised for rapid development and deployment.

In 1972, the Nixon administration sold the Interim Agreement to Congress despite the numerical advantages it conferred on the Soviet Union by arguing that U.S. missiles were far more accurate and that MIRVs helped make up for the disparity. Soviet missiles, however, particularly their SS-9s, had throw weights three to five times that of their U.S. counterparts. When these missiles were equipped with only a single warhead, they were considered to be only vaguely threatening; it was assumed that their greater destructive potential compensated for insufficient accuracy. When equipped with MIRVs, though, these missiles could carry as many as ten reentry vehicles. The United States had the option of equipping the remaining Minuteman II missiles in its force with MIRVs, but the fact that the Soviet Union had over 50 percent more ICBMs of much greater throw weight and destructive capacity meant that their ability to effectively deploy MIRVs was far higher.[9] MIRVs, which the United States once considered one of its few unilateral advantages, quickly became one of the highest priorities for U.S. negotiators.

Another technological development that complicated negotiations was improvements in missile accuracy. Dovetailing with MIRV technology, ICBM guidance technology rapidly improved in both countries during this period, particularly as the prospect of quantitative limitations became more likely. In the United States, the ability to reliably strike an enemy's silo and disable the missile inside (what was known as hard-target capability) became a substantial possibility. This development ran counter to the framework of deterrence, however: targeting an enemy's weapons instead of its population decreased one's vulnerability and could prove to be a tempting option for striking first. MIRV technology exacerbated this problem, by creating many more warheads without producing any new targets in the form of silos. If the Soviets could improve the accuracy of their missiles (a substantial and largely unknown variable), the MIRV variants of SS-9 missiles and its derivatives could fire two or three reentry vehicles at each of the 1,054 U.S. ICBMs with over a third of their ICBM force left in reserve.[10]

By the 1980s, this prospect became popularly known as the window of vulnerability, an idea that featured prominently in rhetoric about supposed Soviet superiority. Although few discounted the possibility of this scenario, disagreement focused on how long the Soviet Union would need to achieve the necessary accuracy. (Many also questioned its relevance to the strategic balance, since SLBMs survived in almost any scenario.) Regardless, what had once been the cheapest and most reliable leg of the nuclear triad was in danger of becoming the most vulnerable. The United States had ignored MIRV technology's dangers during the negotiation of SALT I because they would not become problematic after the five-year window of the Interim Agreement and administration officials saw MIRVs as U.S. advantages within that window.

Political Developments and Personnel Changes

During the SALT I negotiations, individuals such as Henry Kissinger played an outsized role, while the role of organizations such as the Joint Chiefs were muted after the first few rounds. In the years that followed, bureaucratic wrangling figured much more prominently as the locus of control shifted away from the negotiators and toward Washington. ACDA, the Office of the Secretary of Defense, the Joint Chiefs, and various constituencies on the National Security Council (NSC) worked to integrate the arms control process into the existing array of interests.

Considering the fact that arms control agreements intersect with the prerogatives of other agencies and branches of government, one might think ongoing negotiations would endow the State Department with increased power. In reality, the opposite occurred. State Department officials proved a convenient scapegoat for the Nixon administration when it sought to gain support from anti-communist hard-liners. In administration discussions, the State Department often took on the role of a phantom group of "arms controllers" who were willing to negotiate away any U.S. advantage in the name of an agreement[11] Even Kissinger stooped to this straw-man characterization when he was negotiating with General Secretary Brezhnev.[12]

The ACDA was particularly hard hit. Nixon's purge of 1972–1974 created an opportunity to reshape the agency. Since the purge was orchestrated to appease hard-liners, many of the new staff held significantly stronger anti-Soviet positions; some even opposed arms control. These hard-liners entered at all levels, from the new director, Fred Iklé, to a promising young weapons analyst whom Richard Perle had recommended named Paul Wolfowitz.[13] The fact that Nixon ceded control over hiring to the office of Senator Jackson was not without consequences, as the agency rapidly began to align more closely with the Joint Chiefs of Staff than with Secretary Kissinger.[14]

During the SALT II negotiations, the Nixon administration found itself politically defending and implementing SALT I while simultaneously attempting to shape the nascent SALT II. The political atmosphere created by this process had a considerable impact on the approach of various administration officials to the subject of arms control. One of the primary stumbling blocks to widespread acceptance of SALT I was its numerical asymmetry. Even if this asymmetry was irrelevant because of the greater accuracy of U.S. missiles and the U.S. supremacy in heavy bombers, the numbers looked bad to those willing to take issue with them. Anti-communists in the Senate, led by Senator Jackson, agreed to support the Interim Agreement only after attaching the "Jackson amendment," which stated that no future agreement with the Soviet Union could concede superiority to the Soviet Union. It also brought the phrase "essential equivalence" in regard to arms control into common parlance. Despite initial opposition, the Nixon administration eventually acceded to the amendment, thus shaping future negotiations before they began.[15] As a result, negotiators felt pressure to ensure that any follow-on agreement had a top-line figure that was somehow identical for both countries and that had been arrived at by lumping together vastly different systems under increasingly abstract and difficult categories. Furthermore, to ensure a politically palatable agreement, negotiators had to make certain that other metrics and statistics beyond the top-line figure, such as the number of reentry vehicles or total throw weight, could not be at extreme variance.

Instead of being mollified by the administration's concessions made to him following ratification, Senator Jackson became increasingly vocal about his opinions on arms control and U.S.-Soviet relations in general.[16] As head of the Senate Armed Services Committee, Jackson often submitted long, probing lists of questions to the administration about the impact of proposed arms control policies. The implicit threat was that Jackson would delay certain defense appropriations bills if he did not receive answers. The administration provided rote, perfunctory replies to these requests, coupled with an insistence that written questions be avoided while the terms of the prospective accord were so ill defined.[17] Jackson's status as a Democrat planning a presidential campaign likely made it easier for the administration to dismiss his concerns as bad faith. Because of this dismissive attitude the Nixon administration (and later the Ford administration) missed a rising tide of discontent with the arms control endeavor.

As with almost all other issues in this period, the Watergate scandal impacted the negotiation of SALT II. Nixon placed great emphasis on building on the momentum of the SALT I agreement by beginning the first round of SALT II before the end of 1972. Starting so soon after SALT I meant that the United States did not yet have any substantive positions to offer, but this time line also drew attention to SALT II before the Watergate disclosures had done significant damage.[18] Within months, however, the president's political capital was nearly gone and had lost face with the Soviet Union. From late 1973, Soviet negotiators were skeptical that the president could make credible assurances that any agreement he constructed would pass through Congress or receive the support of voters. As the Nixon administration's unraveling continued, these concerns turned into criticisms and even into hardened positions. This collapse forced administration allies and opponents to make plans that accommodated the fact that Nixon was compromised in the eyes of the Soviet leadership.[19]

As Nixon's influence waned, Kissinger filled much of the gap. During the SALT II negotiations, Kissinger increasingly became the sole avenue of approach to the president. He presented him with predetermined courses of action and there was little discussion of alternatives.[20] Kissinger's position became even more powerful when he was appointed secretary of state in September 1973. With no more need for backchannels, Kissinger could now make use of the entire U.S. diplomatic apparatus.

Kissinger, who had successfully positioned himself as the president's intermediary on arms control issues and had public approval ratings far higher than those of the troubled president, was more influential than ever. However, he overlooked several trends that would eat away slowly at his position as the unrivaled authority on national security policy. The purge of the ACDA meant that Kissinger was one of the most pro–arms control voices in the administration. Without a credible straw man to his left, Kissinger could no longer position himself as a disinterested arbiter between different sides. Kissinger also increasingly found himself at odds with the new secretary of defense, James Schlesinger, and with the Joint Chiefs. Kissinger was also aware that having to split his attention between SALT and events such as the fall of Saigon and the Yom Kippur War gave the rest of the executive branch bureaucracy opportunities to negatively influence any nascent arms control agreement.[21]

One of the primary ways that various elements of the Washington bureaucracy influenced the U.S. position on SALT II negotiations was through discussions of the impact of SALT I. For example, when Jackson called several ACDA officials to testify before the Armed Services Committee, Director Iklé attended to introduce the witnesses. Had Iklé been a formal witness providing testimony, his prepared remarks would have required clearance from Kissinger and the White House staff, but so-called introductory remarks traditionally did not require clearance. Though Iklé's remarks were generally reassuring, he claimed the administration had no interest in several negotiating options that Kissinger had deliberately (but quietly) left open. Kissinger and the White House staff could not publicly contradict Ikle's statements without undermining perceptions of their ability to manage foreign policy.[22]

Other factors drove the geography of decision making ever closer to Washington. The negotiation of new accords with the Soviet Union such as the Threshold Test Ban Treaty added new roles for the ACDA, compliance and monitoring agreements. These new roles meant that the agency needed a full-time director based in Washington. When Gerard Smith resigned, his responsibilities were divided between two individuals: Director Iklé, a distinguished scholar with deep connections to the foreign policy establishment, and Ambassador U. Alexis Johnson, a career diplomat. Individuals below the levels of Secretary of Defense Schlesinger and Director Iklé also became adept at undermining the SALT process in defense of narrower interests, such as specific weapons systems. Admiral Elmo Zumwalt, who was concerned about how the in-development Trident ballistic-missile submarine would fare under SALT II, provided a steady stream of secrets and privileged information about the negotiations to Senator Jackson, one of the submarines biggest Congressional advocates.[23]

The latitude of the SALT II delegation contracted significantly. At first, this was because it wasn't given instructions. As a result, the delegation's role was limited at first to simply probing the Soviet position. But even as the negotiations progressed and the outlines of an agreement began to form, opportunities for the delegation to contribute were limited. Even Paul Nitze, by 1974 the elder statesman of the delegation, could not gain permission to autonomously negotiate several side issues with his counterpart, Dr. Aleksandr Shchukin, despite the fact that this partnership had been one of the most productive pairings of the SALT I negotiations.[24]

Summit diplomacy accelerated after 1972. This meant fewer incentives to pursue actual progress at Geneva, where the SALT talks took place, since a meeting between Kissinger and Brezhnev or Nixon and Brezhnev was rarely more than a year away (usually it was only a few months). Kissinger, likely remembering the chaos that parallel negotiating teams had created during the final days of SALT I, chose to handle more at summit meetings. There were several downsides to this strategy. Soviet positions tended to harden in the months before a major summit, and the collapsing political capital of the Nixon administration gave Brezhnev little reason to be more flexible.

Negotiating Developments

Negotiations reconvened in late 1972 in Geneva. The stated goal was to develop a permanent accord as a follow-up to the Interim Agreement. The underlying assumption for the United States was that a comprehensive accord entailed adding additional strategic weapons systems, such as bombers, to the framework of an agreement while also controlling the most dangerous qualitative changes to nuclear arsenals such as MIRVs. Because the Nixon administration's push to schedule the next round of talks occurred at the height of the 1972 election, very little advance work was done before the talks began.[25] As a result, the Soviet Union controlled the agenda for much of the negotiations, in the process revealing a radically different view of what a "comprehensive" accord entailed. The nature of the Soviet proposals was unexpected and the U.S. delegation's lack of an alternative plan meant that the negotiations deadlocked almost immediately and for nearly a year.

At the beginning of SALT I, the Soviet Union had pushed for a much different definition of strategic weapons than the one that was adopted. The United States had argued that weapons with intercontinental ranges ought to be the subject of the negotiation. The Soviet Union, in contrast, argued that a weapon was strategic if it was a nuclear weapon with the ability to strike one of the two superpowers from wherever it was located.[26] The Soviet negotiators also took the Interim Agreement's freeze on ballistic missiles to mean that other weapons should be restricted before returning to additional restrictions on ICBMs and SLBMs.[27]

A comprehensive accord, according to the Soviet negotiators, entailed including all of the remaining weapons of Soviet concern in the framework of the accords with two factors in mind: equivalence in technological power and geographic concerns.[28] This meant limitations not just on bombers but also on forward-based systems (FBS), the term for tactical nuclear weapons on aircraft carriers or at airbases within range of Soviet territory. The Soviets also railed against U.S. weapons programs such as the Trident, one of the first SLBMs with MIRVs, and U.S. plans to replace the aging B-52 bomber with the B-1. Soviet negotiators argued that pursuing these programs after the Interim Agreement came into effect was a ploy to gain superiority over the Soviet Union while simultaneously negotiating an arms control agreement. When U.S. negotiators tried to compare these U.S. programs to the Soviet MIRV program and its wholesale replacement of older ICBMs with more modern and powerful missiles, the Soviets argued these were only upgrades of existing systems that were necessary to achieve parity with the already MIRV-equipped U.S. missile force.[29] The Soviets' strategy of complaining about U.S. programs was probably designed to capitalize on U.S. domestic politics, as congressional support for the B-1 and the Trident was not assured during this period. Perhaps the Soviet negotiators calculated that highlighting these programs as a stumbling block to negotiations might give domestic critics of military spending a chance to cancel these programs. As evidenced by this strategy, Soviet negotiators often waited for key congressional votes on these systems before modifying their positions.[30]

The Soviet criticism of U.S. programs was wholly unacceptable to the Nixon administration, especially in the face of Soviet advancements in ICBM technology. For the United States, limiting the number of bombers was acceptable, even inevitable. Ultimately most policy makers believed it was only a matter of agreeing on a formula of how many missiles or reentry vehicles were equivalent to a single bomber.[31] U.S. negotiators argued that they had as much right to replace B-52s with B-1s (which would not occur until after the five-year term of the

Interim Agreement) as the Soviets did to replace their SS-9s with the substantially improved SS-18s.

The issue of FBS also alarmed U.S. negotiators, to the point that they never seriously entertained the possibility of accepting it into the framework. At best, FBS from aircraft carriers or small ground-attack aircraft represented only 2 to 5 percent of the destructive potential of "central strategic systems" (the euphemism the United States increasingly used to distinguish its idea of strategic weapons from that of the Soviet Union). When compared to such systems, FBS was equivalent to a rounding error.[32] Furthermore, the United States considered these to be tactical and theater forces for tactical and theater missions: nuclear weapons *in Western Europe* were the primary means of maintaining the balance of forces with the Warsaw Pact, which greatly outnumbered NATO in conventional forces. Any arrangement limiting U.S. FBS would also impose no obligations on the Soviet Union, which had numerous nuclear weapons capable of striking Western Europe that would be unaffected by their proposal, since they could not reach the United States. To the cynical among U.S. negotiators, the Soviet position was nothing less than an attempt to drive a wedge between the United States and NATO powers by divorcing theater and strategic weapons such that the Soviets could threaten Western Europe, and they could threaten the United States, but the United States could not threaten the Soviet Union from Western Europe.

Soviet negotiators clearly understood that the issue of FBS engendered resistance, even acrimony, from the United States, particularly since they had attempted to incorporate it into SALT I and failed. Why, then, did they reopen the issue? Certainly a comprehensive accord would require incorporating new systems and both sides could be expected to advocate for definitions of the problem that served their interests. But the issue of FBS struck at the heart of the Cold War in Europe and it was clearly an issue on which the United States would not budge. What did the Soviet negotiators think they would gain? Contemporaneous observers, such as Gerard Smith, argued that the Soviets saw FBS as part of a tough opening bid that was part of their overall negotiating strategy. The Soviets may have calculated that they might eventually allow themselves to be convinced to adopt a different framework but might gain some form of compensation in response to their complaints. A similar dynamic had occurred during the SALT I negotiations regarding the number of U.S. submarine bases in Europe.[33]

Breaking the Deadlock

By late 1973 and early 1974, Kissinger had managed to turn the conversation with the Soviets away from FBS and toward MIRVs, but at a cost, as the strategic picture with respect to MIRVs grew much darker during this period. For the United States, the turning point occurred at a meeting of the Verification Panel on August 15, 1973. U.S. intelligence officials revealed to Kissinger and the NSC the scale of the Soviet MIRV program. The U.S. program for land-based MIRVs consisted of conducting updates to the Minuteman II missile and the construction of a MIRV "bus" that could hold three warheads. The Soviet land-based MIRV program, which by then was well into the testing phase, consisted of four new missile designs, with improved throw weight and accuracy and could potentially hold between four and ten warheads each. This program was far more ambitious and sophisticated than the Nixon administration predicted. Worse, even if the United States could negotiate a ban on some of these new types, the Soviet test schedule was so ambitious that testing could be completed in months, after which reversing the programs became nearly impossible.[34]

U.S. policy makers could not decipher the decision making that led to the new Soviet programs. In reality, both the SALT agreement and the Soviet bureaucracy had shaped the new programs. When Brezhnev signed the Interim Agreement in 1972, significant Soviet resources were still dedicated to strategic forces, especially ICBMs. Freezing new construction of the SS-9 and SS-11 required significant reprogramming of these funds, but the Soviet Five-Year Plan system of economic governance limited budgetary flexibility. Soviet planners decided to redirect these resources into an accelerated upgrade schedule for their ICBMs. The sudden influx of resources created a free-for-all among the highly competitive Soviet design bureaus. Arbitrating among these factions during the first round of investment proved contentious. But Brezhnev and Soviet planners were awash in oil revenue and were reaping the political benefits of détente. The Soviet leadership seems to have chosen "all of the above" rather than alienate influential interest groups. Thus, the SS-18, which could carry up to ten warheads, replaced the SS-9. The SS-17 (four warheads) and the SS-19 (six warheads) both appeared to replace the workhorse SS-11. Dmitri Ustinov, a member of the Politburo whose portfolio included oversight of defense industries, was obsessed with developing a solid-fueled ICBM similar to those of the United States. He was almost solely responsible for getting the solid-fuel, single-warhead SS-16 off the drawing board and into development.[35]

Each of these new designs proved worrisome to the United States. Although the SS-16 had not yet been tested with a MIRV payload, it launched from a truck-based transporter-erector launcher that gave it a degree of mobility that could thwart efforts to verify its numbers from space. The SS-18 was frightening because of its massive MIRV potential: it could hit nearly ten times as many targets as the SS-9. Furthermore, the SS-17 and the SS-18 were roughly the same size as the missiles they intended to replace, which meant that if no significant modifications were made to the silos that housed them, their deployment would be very difficult to track. The SS-19, in contrast, was easy to verify, but for all the wrong reasons. Its substantially larger size required expanding silos in ways that only barely qualified as permissible under the Interim Agreement.[36]

Wrestling with these developments at the 15 August 1973 Verification Panel meeting, the frustrations of the groups different members began to show. Kissinger and the NSC had been working on a new proposal for SALT II, but these developments rendered it moot, and concrete ideas on how to move forward were few. Kissinger summed up the now much more basic questions the NSC had to answer before moving forward with SALT II, asking: "(1) What is a MIRV position we can take in this world? (2) What pressures can we bring on the negotiation in terms of defense programs? (3) Assuming we can't permit a MIRV freeze, what is there left to talk about?"[37] The members of the Verification Panel and the SALT II delegation discussed what forms of limitation could mitigate the threats the new generation of missiles posed, but none of those ideas were likely to meet with Soviet approval. The meeting meandered disconcertingly following Kissinger's questions, with the participants continuing to talk past one another as they tried to determine what SALT II should accomplish.[38]

Over the next several months it became clear that silo modifications that would be detectable were likely necessary for all of the new Soviet missiles. This eased U.S. concerns about verification for the SS-17, the SS-18, and the SS-19 but did little to help U.S. officials assemble a coherent position.[39] Kissinger proposed setting a limit on the number of land-based MIRVs in the range of 400–600, with the United States allowed a slight, but measurable, numerical advantage. Hard-liners such as Schlesinger and Nitze opposed such high limits because any number of Soviet land-based MIRVs above approximately 350 was capable of endangering the entire U.S. ICBM force. If the figure of 350 could be combined with reductions in or the elimination of SS-9 and SS-18 "heavy missiles," the throw weights of MIRV forces on both sides would be roughly equal. Equalizing throw weights appealed to hard-liners, but Kissinger considered this calculation to be irrelevant because the Soviet Union would never agree to a number substantially smaller than the 550 land-based MIRVs the United States had.[40]

By June 1974, at the final Nixon-Brezhnev summit before Nixon resigned, the United States proposed a rough equalization of throw weights that would give the United States 550 ICBMs with MIRVs and the Soviets 360. Brezhnev and Gromyko found these figures both puzzling and insulting. The only asymmetry of any kind they would consider was in the overall number of MIRVs (both land-based and submarine-launched), and the broadest such proposal they would accept would give the United States 1,100 MIRVs of all types and the Soviets 1,000. Even in the Soviet proposal, the difference of 100 missiles was a bare-minimum acknowledgement of the greater MIRV potential of the Soviet missile force; it did not remotely try to remedy it.[41]

Since the August 1973 meeting of the Verification Panel, Kissinger had spent more time negotiating the U.S. position with the rest of the executive branch than he had with his Soviet counterparts. Kissinger found the positions that Secretary of Defense Schlesinger and the JCS favored to be unrealistic, and as the months passed the end of the five-year Interim Agreement became more than an abstraction. As a measure of how little the two parties' positions had come together, the June 1974 summit produced only two significant outcomes for SALT II. Kissinger and Gromyko agreed to convert SALT II from a permanent accord to one set to expire in 1985. In exchange, Kissinger hinted that a shorter-term agreement would give him more flexibility to agree to higher MIRV limits, but only if the Soviet negotiators could come down on aggregates in central systems. Kissinger likely wagered that an agreement of limited duration might ease the pressure to reverse every adverse strategic trend and free up his hand to negotiate more flexibly.[42]

What Price SALT?

Kissinger's clashes with the administration's hawks, such as Admiral Moorer, and his eventual decision to be more flexible with regard to MIRVs were the result of subtly different conceptions of the SALT process and arms control in general.

In the years that followed his tenure in government, Kissinger attempted to downplay the differences between his position and those of the administration's remaining hawks, such as Schlesinger (especially as these hawks returned to influence within the Republican Party in the 1970s and 1980s). In his memoirs, Kissinger downplayed his own agency, instead emphasizing the political forces that compelled him to seek an agreement and the costs of ignoring them:

> Large sections of American and allied opinion insisted on an effort to curb the arms race. The worst posture was to be dragged kicking and screaming into a negotiation by outside pressures; *a statesman should always seek to dominate what he cannot avoid.* And so we faced a highly practical problem in the strategic field: if the Soviets MIRV-ed all of their land-based missiles with accurate warheads, our land-based missiles would be at risk by the early part of the Eighties. SALT II seemed to me an opportunity to postpone this danger for a significant period of time. (italics added)[43]

Kissinger here adopts much of the language and precepts of the hawks, particularly with regard to the vulnerability of the U.S. ICBM force. He defends his position by saying it would have postponed the danger of a crippling first strike on U.S. ICBMs for a substantial length of time, while protecting critical weapons programs from congressional cuts. Considering these political constraints, the best course was to negotiate the agreement sooner, conceding potential advantages that were unlikely to be realized while blunting the Soviet advance.[44]

At the time, however, Kissinger expressed frustration with the hawks' position in terms that seemed to question whether he shared their outlook. At one point in a press conference, Kissinger jumped on a reporter who asked if the United States could retain its nuclear edge: "What in the name of God is strategic superiority? . . . What do you do with it?"[45] Kissinger continued to believe that an agreement was critical to his détente policy. He downplayed nuclear strategy in favor of other fundamentals in the U.S.-Soviet relationship and cited domestic political calculations as one of the main reasons for seeking a negotiated nuclear balance.

In 1973 and early 1974, as talks deadlocked and the Soviet negotiators essentially set the agenda, Nitze had ample time to consider his position. Secretary Schlesinger, sensing a kindred spirit, attempted to pull Nitze away from the negotiations in March 1974 by offering him the position of assistant secretary of defense for international security affairs, although the administration abandoned this plan when even broaching the subject with Congress elicited strong resistance. In March 1974, Senator Barry Goldwater made clear that Nitze was too closely aligned with the arms control policies of the Nixon administration to be confirmed, even though Nitze was easily one of the most hawkish members of the delegation.[46]

Nitze continued his work as a SALT II negotiator in Geneva, writing reports that were ignored and becoming increasingly vocal in his criticism of the president over the scandals of Watergate.[47] Finally, in May 1974, Nitze submitted his resignation. He then issued a blistering press release that said that Nixon was being tempted to negotiate a suboptimal agreement in order to save his foundering political career.[48]

Over the next year, Nitze expanded his critique of popular attitudes and approaches to arms control in several articles. The purpose of the arms control enterprise was, as he saw it, "first, to seek both the reality and appearance of equality, or essential equivalence, of the permitted levels of strategic arms capabilities of both sides. Second, to seek limitations which would help maintain crisis stability[49] and thus reduce the risk of nuclear war. Third, to provide a basis for reducing the arms competition."[50] He argued that if ever these objectives came into conflict with one another, crisis stability was paramount. For Nitze, while the risks of seeking equivalence at the expense of crisis stability were considerable, pursuing crisis stability at the expense of continuing the arms competition would at least provide more time and preserve the possibility of pursuing the other objectives at a later date.

Nitze also argued that the U.S. delegation approached both the SALT I and SALT II talks with these concerns in mind and that flaws in the outcomes ought to be attributed solely to decisions higher officials had made that circumvented established protocols, such as the Kissinger-Dobrynin backchannel.[51] Nitze also argued that the Soviets resisted efforts to achieve mutually beneficial arms control because they were ideologically loath to negotiate from such a position:

> Soviet doctrine has always placed heavy emphasis upon what they call the "correlation of forces." In this term, they include the aggregate of all the forces bearing upon the situation—including psychological, political, and economic factors. Soviet officials took the view that the correlation of forces had been and would continue to move in their favor.[52]

If the trends in the correlation of forces were sufficiently clear, Nitze argued, the Soviet Union would view an arms control treaty that provided equal benefits to the security of both parties as inherently inequitable. Under this argument, they would instead insist that their rising power and status ought to be reflected in the distribution of the security benefits of the treaty. Failing to do so was seen by Soviet negotiators as a request to forsake the security gains that the Soviet Union had worked so hard to achieve. In other words, providing equal benefits in a treaty and then freezing the competition was a way of preventing the Soviet Union from reaching its proper status, because it did not reflect the advantages that were supposedly accruing to the Soviet Union. Soviet positions, which Nitze regarded as allowing deeply dangerous trends in the nuclear balance to continue, would not change until Soviet perception of trends in the correlation of forces began to reverse. Nitze argued that existing U.S. policy was based on the questionable assumption that reversing negative trends in the correlation of forces was politically and materially unsustainable. Accepting that assumption and pursuing arms control anyway, as Nitze accused the Nixon administration of doing, prioritized curbing the arms race over achieving equality or crisis stability.

If arresting these trends was unachievable, was not an agreement to at least limit the buildup an improvement over no agreement at all? Nitze disagreed and recalled orders he had received during his time on the State Department's Policy Planning Staff never to edit or self-censor policy analysis to accommodate concerns about domestic political feasibility:

> [Secretary of State Acheson] wanted the Policy Planning Staff to work out its analyses and recommendations . . . without considering the

acceptability of those recommendations to congressional or public opinion. He and President Truman would very much have to take those considerations into mind and make the compromises they thought necessary . . . to build the foundations for a future more receptive climate. He didn't want those compromises made twice, once by us and secondly by them. Today the main basis for assuming that there is nothing much that can be done about a significant loss of parity and crisis stability is the judgment that congressional and public opinion will not support the measures necessary to halt present trends. But is the Executive Branch taking the steps which might lay a foundation for a more favorable climate next year and the year after?[53]

Nitze accused all levels of government of a fatalism that viewed present political constraints as inevitable and insurmountable. Despite this criticism, Nitze did not explicitly reject the utility of arms control. Instead he provided a number of alternative regimes and argued that paying close attention to the overall political situation was almost as important as the perceived feasibility of any particular proposal.

Nitze's objections, though substantive, do not completely explain the manner and timing of his departure. Nitze came to SALT with a considerable pedigree. He was a former secretary of the Navy and the author of NSC-68, one of the seminal expressions of the containment doctrine. Yet for five years he worked as a junior member of the SALT II delegation. Nitze likely justified accepting the position because he believed that the unprecedented nature of SALT I had created opportunities to have a significant impact. Yet by 1974, Nitze's independence had been consistently restricted, while individuals such as Fred Iklé, who was nearly twenty years younger than Nitze, were specifically trying to hem in his autonomy as with the rest of the delegation. Passed over for promotion, and with SALT II headed in an ominous direction, Nitze very likely calculated that June 1974 (a time just before a major summit between heads of state) was one of his last opportunities to leave before his name would be permanently associated with a treaty he had done little to shape.

The Road to Vladivostok

Nitze's timing was excellent, as the six months following his departure established the principles that would govern the eventual SALT II agreement. During this time, Kissinger finally managed to remove the millstone of equal throw weight and convince the Soviets to agree to drop their demands on FBS. The long-term costs, especially for Kissinger, were high. Kissinger's SALT strategy was increasingly lonely, though he maintained the support of his new boss, President Ford. Ford entered office under the impression that pursuing SALT II provided prudent continuity in foreign policy and sought to facilitate Kissinger's efforts.

Kissinger received little help from the Soviets. For most of 1974, Brezhnev and Gromyko did not drop their insistence on some compensation for the United States maintaining its FBS, though they were willing to at least discuss formulae and aggregates as a basis for negotiating about central systems. Despite Kissinger's best efforts, progress before October 1974 was illusory. The limits on MIRVs Brezhnev proposed (1,100 for the United States, 1,000 for the Soviet Union) were not unacceptable to the United States, but only if they also included strict sublimits on or outright bans of the SS-18, a non-starter for the Soviet Union.[54]

Soviet negotiators were even more difficult than usual. Kissinger described Brezhnev's performance in October 1974 as "defensive and amateurish." Whether this was intentional or a sign of Brezhnev's advancing age is impossible to say, but neither possibility was a good sign. According to Kissinger, "Brezhnev has stalled and his comments have been unfocused, sometimes even frivolous and uninformed. So far, they have not even been calculated to draw me out." Kissinger theorized about what the Soviet strategy might be: "If this remains the Soviet position it is clear that we are paying a price for our domestic disarray, especially the congressional irresponsibility. The Soviets may calculate . . . that Congress will not vote increases in the Defense Budget so that they risk nothing by stonewalling on SALT."[55] Perhaps recognizing that the that he had pushed the Ford administration as far as they could go, Brezhnev made several concessions before the October meeting adjourned but did nothing to indicate a change in fundamental outlook.[56]

A breakthrough, if it can be called that, occurred at the presidential summit in the eastern Soviet city of Vladivostok in November 1974. There, Ford and Brezhnev agreed to a framework for SALT II that included equal aggregates, but only at a very high level. Though neither side framed it as such, the United States effectively gave up its pursuit of limits on heavy missiles with MIRV capabilities, while the Soviets gave up their demand for compensation for FBS. The parties agreed to a limit of 2,400 ICBMs, SLBMs, and heavy bombers, of which no more than 1,320 could contain MIRVs. The costs these figures imposed were minimal: both ceilings were far above existing deployment figures. The Soviet military would have to phase out some older systems as it reached the ceiling in the 1980s, but the United States was unlikely to hit the 2,400 figure before 1985. This was more substantial than anything SALT II had yet produced, and it finally brought controls on MIRVs into the arms control apparatus.[57]

While this agreement was presented as a diplomatic triumph for President Ford and a sign of détente's ability to endure, the details of the Vladivostok Accord would prove to be Kissinger's undoing. One ancillary component of the Vladivostok negotiations was the limits it placed on missiles launched from aircraft. The United States had dabbled with launching ballistic missiles from bombers in the past but had found it impractical. It was thus willing to agree to the Soviet proposal that missiles launched from aircraft with ranges of 600–3,000 kilometers would each be treated as a single nuclear delivery vehicle in the aggregate, and banned entirely air-launched missiles with ranges greater than 3,000 kilometers. After the summit, the Soviets revealed that they understood this provision to apply to air-launched cruise missiles (ALCMs), a technology on the cusp of a revival. However, the United States (specifically, Kissinger) thought the agreement covered only anachronistic air-launched ballistic missiles.[58]

Up to that point, SALT II negotiators had gradually reduced the categories of weapons the agreement controlled, even at the cost of the agreement's impact. Once cruise missiles entered the mix, the complexity of the negotiations spiraled outward again. At first, Kissinger had been one of the few proponents of the ALCM; he hoped to develop the capability and use it as leverage against the Soviets in negotiations. Air force officials initially resisted ACLMs because, if effective, they worried ACLMs would sap support for development of the next generation of manned bomber. But after the technology entered the SALT II framework in a way that potentially made both cruise missile and bomber programs less attractive, air force leaders became resistant to controls on both.[59]

Kissinger was right that the Soviets might fear cruise missiles and want to negotiate about them, but that fact cut both ways. Once they thought cruise missiles were included in the Vladivostok Accord, they would not permit the United States to excise them without a price. Unable to backtrack, Kissinger spent the rest of 1975 trying to develop a framework that could account for the unique characteristics of cruise missiles, limiting them in the final agreement just enough to satisfy Soviet negotiators, while doing as little as possible to affect actual plans for deployment. Kissinger had to accomplish all of these tasks before the military had constructed a single cruise missile of any type or even developed a doctrine for using them.[60]

A year of frenetic bargaining passed. Kissinger was increasingly the interlocutor between the Soviets and the secretary of defense and the JCS. Finally, he produced a compromise after meeting with Brezhnev in January 1976. Kissinger, still in Moscow, reported back to President Ford and the National Security Council that he saw the potential for a reasonable compromise with the Soviets: ALCMs would no longer count as a single delivery vehicle in the aggregate; only the bomber containing them would. However, a bomber equipped with ALCMs with a range between 600 and 2,500 kilometers would count against the MIRV limit as well. Brezhnev also wanted to ban all sea- and ground-launched cruise missiles (SLCMs and GLCMs, respectively) with ranges greater than 600 kilometers, but Kissinger was prepared to meet this demand with a compromise position that would permit a certain number of naval ships to carry cruise missiles, with an overall ceiling on the number of such missiles in the fleet.

The response to these proposals in the White House was explosive. The JCS and secretary of defense had tacitly consented to Kissinger's proposals, but only provisionally and with a host of unlikely caveats.[61] Now they restated their objections at a 21 January 1976 NSC meeting convened to discuss Kissinger's report on the positive Soviet response to this proposal. Kissinger's proposal did not reflect what was agreed at Vladivostok. Bombers were the nuclear delivery vehicle with the least possible role to play in a first strike and they were the only leg of the triad against which unlimited defenses were permitted in the form of fighters and surface-to-air missiles. According to them, counting bombers as MIRVs misunderstood the nature of both. Adding insult to injury, the JCS representative from the Navy revealed that Kissinger's intricately designed proposal on SLCMs was a fantasy. Navy leaders had full knowledge of the inter-agency process that resulted in Kissinger's SLCM proposal, but never once mentioned (until that moment) that they had no plans to deploy SLCMs on ships in this fashion, and had a different set of plans they believed better suited the technology.[62]

National Security Advisor Brent Scowcroft described this meeting as "surreal." Ford, seeing the chances of a SALT II agreement before the November 1976 election slip away, reacted even more sharply. Scowcroft reported that Ford was "angrier than I have ever seen him." The president "ranted about the total inconsistency with previous Defense positions, said that [the secretary of defense and JCS chairman] could god damn well try themselves to get the extra money necessary when we failed to get a SALT agreement, and stormed out."[63] Kissinger tried to follow up on the partial compromises left on the table but could not negotiate further until the Soviets made concessions on other issues that, given the approaching election, they were loath to make.

Nuclear Reconsiderations

While the U.S. government adjusted to the SALT process, others began to adjust intellectually to the impact of SALT. Both Nitze and Kissinger expressed views about the use of nuclear weapons that were rooted in the goal of preventing conflict but rejected a narrow conception of deterrence based on countervalue, second-strike forces. The latter conception of simplistic deterrence dominated discussions of arms control, however. In contrast, Nitze and others argued that this thinking was predicated on three assumptions that were open to question: 1) that a deterrence framework could survive contact with a real-world nuclear exchange; 2) that a deterrence framework could actually sustain obligations to third parties, specifically Western Europe/NATO; and 3) that both parties believed in deterrence and reflected this in their strategies and force structures. Thus, dissatisfaction with SALT reflected dissatisfaction with the scope of and the assumptions underlying nuclear strategy. Those who were dissatisfied with the direction of arms control were pushed to explore these questions of nuclear strategy, partly in response to the security environment it helped create but also in order to construct a foundation from which SALT might be critiqued. James Schlesinger addressed the first two of the three assumptions, while the Team B experiment addressed the third.

James Schlesinger, a former RAND analyst, had been appointed as secretary of defense in 1973. Schlesinger's term in office was stormy, but he had an enduring impact on appropriations policy and nuclear strategy far beyond his dismissal in 1975. Among these legacies were National Security Decision Memorandum (NSDM)-242 and its exponent, the Schlesinger doctrine.

NSDM-242 was based on a 1969 directive to reevaluate the strategic nuclear targeting plans of the United States in the event of a nuclear war. This earlier effort had failed to achieve widespread support because the size and structure of the U.S. arsenal was in flux due to the ongoing SALT negotiations.[64] The ratification of SALT I solved this issue, and Schlesinger's interest carried the reevaluation through to completion. When the NSC revisited the project, it issued NSDM-242, directing the Department of Defense to review existing targeting doctrines. Nixon was crippled by Watergate and Kissinger was preoccupied with SALT II and foreign policy crises, so Schlesinger took the opportunity to shape the public and private understanding of the policy.[65] On the surface, the new targeting doctrines were meant to create options for the president that allowed for greater flexibility to engage in localized, limited, and selective nuclear strikes,[66] but Schlesinger's memo evinced profound disagreements with the dominant deterrence-based frameworks of nuclear strategy.

Much of what is assumed about the Schlesinger doctrine is based on the public debate that followed Schlesinger's inopportune revelation of the new policy, but these assumptions are questionable. Schlesinger told the Joint Chiefs not to use the doctrine to justify new systems, and the targeting options used only weapons available in 1974, so the theory that the Schlesinger doctrine was a ploy to increase defense spending is unlikely.[67] Schlesinger's comments after revealing the new targeting guidance gave the impression that extending deterrence to

Western Europe was one of the primary motivations behind the revisions, but this was something of a simplification for public consumption.[68]

SALT I sent the signal that parity with the Soviet Union had arrived, and this fact forced a reappraisal of how to deal with one of the most persistent problems of U.S. nuclear strategy: extending nuclear deterrence to third parties.[69] Theorists have long struggled with how to deal with regional provocations and limited attacks in a situation of mutually assured destruction, since the premise that nuclear war is uncontrollable means that any response would be tantamount to suicide. The desire for limited nuclear options, plans to use theater nuclear weapons, and strategies of de-escalation initially stemmed from these concerns. NSDM-242 was the culmination of this thinking. Schlesinger added a unique spin to these options in the form of counterforce strikes.

Secretary of Defense McNamara had briefly considered counterforce strategies in 1962 but abandoned them when it became clear that they would only accelerate the arms race, given the mathematical reality that more than one weapon is necessary to reliably destroy another weapon.[70] By capping the number of delivery vehicles and therefore the number of targets, the SALT I regime altered this calculus. Counterforce strategies held out the possibility of allowing the United States to exploit its qualitative advantages in missile accuracy and MIRV technology in order to provide added deterrence credibility to its strategic forces and extend deterrence to regions such as Western Europe and the Middle East. To Schlesinger and others, deterrence based on a world-ending response was unsustainable as a policy (hence the need for limited options). In addition, they felt that because the deterrence strategy deliberately targeted civilians, it did not address the sources of confrontation (hence the need to adopt counterforce targeting plans). Counterforce strategies had an additional benefit: they were divorced from the political connotations of the term "deterrence," particularly among those who were skeptical about the arms control process.

Many criticisms of counter-force theory are valid. Counterforce and limited nuclear options had serious, potentially catastrophic drawbacks, not least of which was that they could lower the threshold for a nuclear exchange and contribute to the idea that nuclear wars were both winnable and survivable.[71] A more immediate concern in 1974 was that these doctrines seemed to contradict assurances the United States had given to the Soviet Union about the content of U.S. nuclear strategy: that nuclear war was unwinnable and that the only legitimate purpose of nuclear weapons was to prevent their own use.[72] When called upon to defend himself, Schlesinger argued that the revised targeting guidance was still worthwhile and that it would only be on the basis of this more "rational" nuclear strategic policy that genuinely beneficial nuclear arms control agreements would be reached. The episode left a mark on Ford, however, who grew dissatisfied with Schlesinger's interference with arms control policy, his resistance to defense budget cuts, and his appalling tendency to voice support for Senator Jackson's arms control proposals against those the administration was actively defending. In November 1975, Ford requested Schlesinger's resignation.[73]

Outside the administration, defense intellectuals continued to question the conventional wisdom on nuclear strategy and arms control. Nitze's longtime associate Albert Wohlstetter kick-started this criticism, questioning the very existence of an arms-race spiral. In his article "Is There a Strategic Arms Race?" Wohlstetter placed much of the blame on the CIA for adhering to simplistic analytic assumptions in describing the nature of the Soviet nuclear build-up and of Soviet intentions.[74] Wohlstetter's criticisms intersected with a critical mass of discontent with arms control that culminated in the Team B experiment of 1976.

According to Wohlstetter, all of the CIA's estimates of the Soviet nuclear threat were based on the assumption that nuclear weapons obeyed the "traditional arms-race spiral model." This model, which was embedded in the popular conception of foreign relations, held that the ethic of preparedness against external threats leads to a consistent overestimation of enemies' abilities, the classic example being the fictitious "missile gap" of the late 1950s. Wohlstetter showed that in two out of three classes of missiles, however, the CIA consistently *under*estimated the size of the total Soviet force.[75] Attempts to avoid the arms-race spiral had in fact made the CIA's analysis less accurate and provided an easy pretext for assuming that the Soviet Union shared the same priorities with regard to nuclear weapons as the United States.

Wohlstetter's criticisms resonated with anti-communist Republicans dissatisfied with the Ford administration's foreign policy. Opponents argued that under pressure from Henry Kissinger, the CIA had been providing unjustifiably rosy views of the Soviet Union in the hope of preserving détente. A group known as the President's Foreign Intelligence Advisory Board agitated for the opportunity to investigate these claims, proposing a "competitive analysis" by a panel of outside experts that would granted the same access to information as the CIA's teams. President Ford resisted initially, but by early 1976 he was facing a tough primary challenge from Ronald Reagan. Worried about his right flank, Ford authorized the experiment. The new director of central intelligence, George H. W. Bush, authorized the project and assembled the team with the board's assistance.[76] Paul Nitze provided supervision and guidance for Team B. Most of the writing and project organization was done by Richard Pipes, a professor of Russian history at Harvard University.[77]

The ostensible goal of the Team B experiment was to give outside experts the opportunity to compose their own national intelligence estimates in three different areas: Soviet air defense capability, Soviet missile accuracy, and the Soviets' strategic intentions. The first two panels were staffed with technical experts whose findings were relatively mild, although describing greater capabilities than the CIA estimated.[78] The strategic intentions panel produced an expansive picture of Soviet plans and harshly criticized the CIA's analytical capabilities.

To call the third Team B report alarmist would be an understatement. Its analyses of specifics were considered aggressive at the time. The team wildly speculated about weapons production rates and assumed that technological breakthroughs had taken place without any evidence. These estimates have since been proven almost entirely wrong.[79]

The third report's discussion of Soviet intentions was more probing and harder to discount. At the center of its argument was a single observation: from 1970 to 1976, annual military spending in the Soviet Union had increased by large, inflation-adjusted quantities each year. According to Team B, policy makers and the CIA had missed ominous military and political trends for several reasons, including a misunderstanding of the character of Soviet military policy, a desire not to overestimate for fear of feeding an arms race, and "a habit of viewing each Soviet weapons' [sic] program, or other development, in isolation from the others."[80]

The panel, which took a more "integrative" approach to these developments, decided that the Soviet military buildup was part of the short-term strategy of the USSR to challenge the United States for strategic dominance. More important, however, was the nature of this buildup. The Soviets exhibited a preference for extremely large, multiple-warhead ICBMs. The deployment patterns of these missiles and the team's analysis of the writings of Soviet officers pointed to a critical and unexamined possibility: that the Soviet Union's nuclear forces were designed for fighting and winning nuclear wars, specifically the ability to initiate, survive, and emerge victorious from an all-out nuclear exchange.[81] In other words, the Soviet Union did not accept the doctrine of simple deterrence and its posture could easily be seen as trying to undermine it. This argument paralleled Wohlstetter's original criticism. In both cases, the CIA (and, by implication, foreign policy elites) had assumed that the Soviet Union's goals and strategies resembled those of the United States and that it would therefore react to specific developments in a similar manner. The report's conclusion suggested that it was only with an understanding of these differences in outlook that arms control agreements or changes to strategic posture ought to be considered.

Conclusion

Team B enjoyed a brief heyday in 1976–1977. The *Boston Globe* relied on a series of leaks to report on the existence and general outlook of the reports. Outraged congressional hearings soon followed on the topic of the "politicization of intelligence analysis." The Carter administration, no doubt aware that it needed to work with the CIA, also voiced disapproval.[82] One could also question how groundbreaking the report's conclusion that the Soviet Union did not believe in classical deterrence really was, as the Schlesinger doctrine showed that the United States sought an escape from classical deterrence as well.

Those who had become frustrated or disillusioned with the SALT process, such as Paul Nitze and Team B, and even those who were simply skeptical about its direction, such as James Schlesinger and Fred Iklé, formed the nucleus of a network of arms control skeptics that developed in the period 1977 to 1981. Organizations such as the Committee on the Present Danger brought together anti-communist Republicans and disillusioned anti-communist Democrats and helped develop a cadre of individuals who were prepared to challenge the underlying assumptions of the SALT process when the opportunity arose. This opportunity came with the election of Ronald Reagan in 1980, but as the next chapter will discuss, the events of the intervening four years showed that this outcome was far from preordained. Developments in the realms of arms control and electoral politics would exert decisive influence on the course of SALT negotiations.

As for the SALT process itself, the experience of the Ford administration presaged the directions SALT II would take in the Carter administration. In a fractious and chaotic domestic environment in which sharp domestic divisions were sometimes reflected even in the executive branch, arms control became one of the constitutive elements of Kissinger's power and of presidential authority. At the cost of achieving some of its stated aims, such as genuine reductions or improvements in strategic stability, SALT became a tool for arbitrating differences in domestic priorities and forcing these compromises through the different levels of government without undue cost to the president.

The severity of Ford's reaction to the duplicity of the JCS in 1976 speaks to this fact. Ford's reaction seems to imply that the services were not supposed to want the cruise missile enough to fight for it to be deployed to maximum effect because that would have decreased the chances that the program (and various other defense programs) would get through Congress. Instead they were supposed to work with the SALT II negotiating team to facilitate a new arms control agreement through which they could wring defense dollars from Congress.[83] Meanwhile, the Ford administration assured doves in Congress that additional spending on cruise missile development was a prudent investment that would face limits in the next arms control agreement.[84] When the Joint Chiefs or outside critics challenged SALT's primacy in this decision-making process, angry reactions spoke to the underlying fear of losing control.

These trends continued in the Carter administration. When it became clear that substantial limitations to or reductions in the most problematic systems were unlikely in SALT II, the tendency was for the agreement to incorporate and account for more systems, from missiles to bombers to cruise missiles. Kissinger fought this trend, arguing that minor differences in the strategic balance were nothing compared to the dangers of a world without an agreement, but he failed to manage the complexities that crept into the agreement. The Carter administration, by contrast, embraced this thematic spread. This had severe consequences for the ability of his administration to sell the resulting agreement.

"IN GOOD FAITH": CARTER'S GAMBIT

Though the SALT process could survive transitions in the executive branch when Nixon resigned, it remained to be seen how arms control would influence a competitive election and a transition between political parties. However, the 1972 election came closely on the heels of SALT I, before any coherent criticism or alternatives could develop. Far more controversial issues related to the Vietnam War, student movements, and the McGovern campaign further limited the electoral impact of SALT I. Some of the first national-level attempts to grapple with arms control electorally instead arose out of the election of 1976. In this contest, Georgia governor Jimmy Carter fashioned a unique message designed to straddle the growing divide between hawks and doves within the Democratic Party. After his victory, Carter needed to resolve the vagueness of his campaign promises and operationalize his vision for arms control while drawing support from an increasingly fractious party and population. At the same time, a formal party transition established the SALT process as a bipartisan commitment, giving the impression that strategic arms control would remain a feature of U.S.-Soviet relations for years to come.

This impression, which many in the Carter administration shared, obscured growing problems beneath the surface of U.S. and international politics. From 1976 to 1980, the SALT process achieved new heights of prestige and political import, yet few of the problems that developed in the early years of the SALT II negotiations would ever be adequately addressed. These concerns were obscured by bargaining over fractions of the total deal and the hubris that all too often characterizes new administrations convinced of their ability to outperform their predecessors.

Party transitions aside, critical continuities in the SALT process remained and accelerated. The developing SALT agreement reached new heights of complexity as negotiators attempted to impose quantitative and qualitative limitations on both existing and planned systems. High-level engagement with arms control issues promoted searching reexaminations about the role of nuclear weapons in foreign policy and of how the doctrines for their use might therefore influence foreign policy. These reconsiderations failed to search deeply enough, however, and they came too late to stop the arms control enterprise from growing in size and scope until it collapsed on itself, a result of both its own weight and the shifting fortunes of détente.

Carter's success in 1976 is attributable to several factors, perhaps the most prominent of which was Watergate. Ford never fully recovered politically from his pardon of Nixon in 1974, and confidence in national leaders reached a low ebb after the revelations of the Church Committee (an investigation into abuses by the intelligence community) and the campaign finance scandals of the Nixon White House. Carter capitalized on this discontent by creating the modern Washington outsider campaign, turning national-level experience into a liability, and implying that the capital city sullied politicians the longer they were exposed to it. Carter emphasized his evangelical roots to backstop his stance of ethical superiority. When he discussed national issues such as defense spending, Carter adopted the language of efficiency, promising to apply nonideological budget principles to the out-of-touch elitists in charge of the Pentagon. Although Carter was well within the Democratic mainstream with regard to specific policies such as campaign finance reform or reducing defense spending, he used a rhetorical framework that arrived at these positions without any of the politically toxic associations with cosmopolitan liberalism or student-radical-style McGovernism.[1]

Carter's foreign policy positions during the campaign strove to straddle the emerging divide between hawks and doves within the Democratic Party. Aggressive Cold War hawks such as Senator Henry Jackson had been getting mileage out of McGovern's 1972 defeat, pointing to it as proof of the electoral infeasibility of "peace" candidates who favored reducing tensions with the Soviet Union, reducing defense spending, and rejecting interventionism on principle. The number of true hawks within the party was dwindling, however, as evidenced by Jackson's own short-lived campaign in 1976. Much of the party (and the country) sympathized with at least a few of these principles. In the wake of Vietnam, interventionism was unpopular and the defense budget was widely seen as bloated, although cutting specific programs tended to be difficult. While many Democratic anticommunists remained, few were willing to tolerate bellicosity if it led to a perception of instability or insecurity. Although this position was in line with the basic premises of détente, détente was by then a Republican issue, indelibly associated with the realpolitik of Henry Kissinger. Carter's campaign dilemma was that neither engagement nor confrontation with the Soviet Union could prove electorally viable, The Nixon and Ford administrations presented détente as a viable middle-path, but for Carter it would be difficult to out-moderate a moderate, especially an incumbent. Any Democrat running against Gerald Ford would need a sophisticated critique of détente that was still accessible to voters.[2]

The Carter campaign succeeded largely on the strength of such a critique. He found traction by emphasizing human rights and presenting a delicate mix of approval and disapproval of the Ford administration's policies.[3] Carter did not claim that détente was bad policy or that decreasing tensions with the Soviet Union was an unworthy goal. He accepted these premises whole-heartedly but argued that Kissinger-style détente had become morally twisted in pursuit of this goal. Carter said that in pursuit of conciliation, the Ford administration had paid insufficient attention to NATO issues. By signing the Helsinki Final Act, the Ford administration had accepted and even approved of Soviet domination of Eastern Europe.[4] In the name of avoiding conflict between the superpowers, the Ford administration had paid insufficient attention to the plight of Soviet dissidents who were routinely deprived of basic human rights. Carter's position was that the Republican administration continued to overinvest in weapons, particularly nuclear weapons, without due regard for their strategic implications. He said that in addition to being unnecessary and expensive, many of these systems would not be necessary if the Ford administration had asserted itself more effectively in negotiations with the Soviet Union. Carter derided the token cuts in the Vladivostok accord because they failed to address the most dangerous aspects of the arms race, arguing instead for "real arms control."[5]

Generation Gaps

Carter's positions on détente and arms control proved appealing, and he narrowly defeated Ford in the election of 1976. As Carter and his transition team began staffing the first Democratic administration in eight years, it became clear that several trends would greatly influence the course of the administration. The first was the much-commented-upon split between hawks and doves in the Democratic Party. Despite grassroots movement in the opposite direction, the Democratic Party's intellectual and policy elite on defense issues still included numerous hawks, such as Senators Henry Jackson and Sam Nunn (D-Ga.) and prominent policy intellectuals such as Secretary of Defense Harold Brown and

National Security Advisor Zbigniew Brzezinski. Although Carter's administration also included prominent doves such as Secretary of State Cyrus Vance and ACDA director Paul Warnke, few of them had the background that would enable them to weigh in on defense issues with significant credibility. As younger individuals moved up the ranks of the Democrats' policy elite, such as Deputy Assistant Secretary of Defense for International Security Affairs Walter Slocombe, they had to carefully explain previous dalliances with dovish politics such as working with the 1972 McGovern campaign.[6]

The example of Slocombe illustrates another trend that took place when the Democratic Party retook the White House. Below the cabinet level, a new generation of policy intellectuals and functionaries assumed significant responsibility for the first time. This cohort included Anthony Lake, the new head of the Department of State's Policy Planning Committee; Leslie Gelb, the Department of State's assistant secretary for political-military affairs (an influential post for arms control issues); Slocombe; and Deputy National Security Advisor David Aaron. All of these men were born in the period 1937 to 1941 and the oldest of them had turned forty the year of Carter's inauguration. While their views often diverged, several commonalities typified this group. In contrast to their superiors, for these younger men, there was no point in their careers when some form of major arms control negotiation was not under way, and they likely felt comfortable with the idea that it had become a permanent feature of the international system. Most were too young to have personal memories of World War II and they likely could not remember a time when nuclear weapons did not exist. They ranged from doves to moderate hawks, but they shared a skepticism of aggressive hawkishness that was out of step with the post-Vietnam mood. These factors contributed to considerable friction with anticommunists outside the administration, who saw the middle layer of appointees as hopeless doves.[7]

The members of this new cohort in government believed that arms control efforts were the way of the future. By 1977, the list of treaties, fora, and bilateral consultations relating to the control and deployment of military arms seemed to be growing faster than they could be completed. Finished treaties often contained provisions for periodic review, for bodies to discuss compliance issues, and follow-on negotiations for future agreements. The period from 1977 to 1981 was in many ways the high-water mark for bureaucratic activity in arms control.

Other negotiations or issues that were under consideration and subject to consultation in 1977 included controls on naval deployments in the Indian Ocean. Limits on anti-satellite weaponry and a Comprehensive Nuclear Test Ban Treaty were also being considered. In addition, the administration had inherited the Mutual and Balanced Force Reductions talks, a complex series of negotiations to introduce regional limits on conventional arms between the Warsaw Pact and

NATO. Finally, following the public discovery of the neutron bomb, the Soviet Union pushed strongly for (and the U.S. quietly and begrudgingly consulted on) a treaty banning "radiological warfare."[8]

Nitze's reputation still carried significant weight among his fellow Democrats, and during the 1976 campaign the Carter team showed no desire to alienate him. Nitze served on the Carter campaign's foreign policy task force and the party's platform committee and he volunteered his services during the transition.[9] All of these activities occurred concurrently with Nitze's participation on Team B and in the work that led to the founding of the Committee on the Present Danger.

Nitze still struggled at times with the political ground that was shifting beneath him. During a July 1976 meeting of the Carter campaign's foreign policy advisory committee, which included Harold Brown, Cyrus Vance, and Zbigniew Brzezinski, Nitze began his statement by pointing out that he disagreed with most of the people who had spoken before him. He then stated that in his view, existing trends in strategic forces were extremely negative. An argument broke out (the meeting minutes euphemistically report that "a discussion ensued"), during which both Brown and Vance pointed out that Nitze's numbers were based on unrealistic projections and depicted a worst-case scenario for the United States and a best-case scenario for the Soviet Union. Nitze had little else to say for the rest of the meeting.[10] The message seemed clear: moderate hawks had a place in the Carter administration, but 1950s-style Red-terror alarmism would not be taken seriously.

Refusing to accept defeat, Nitze conveyed his views to the White House on several occasions when he met with Brzezinski or Carter. His message was received with polite skepticism, and as time passed it became clear that he would not receive an appointment in the administration.[11] However, Nitze still had a contract for periodic consultating with the CIA and the Pentagon during this period (somehow his participation in Team B had not put the CIA off him entirely) that allowed him to keep his security clearance and presumably stay abreast of events in the world of arms control and Soviet activities.[12]

Fresh Blood

On January 20, 1977, Chief Justice Warren Burger swore in Jimmy Carter as president. The inauguration speech was shorter than most; the president spoke primarily about domestic and symbolic issues in general terms. Carter emphasized the themes of earning trust, acting with humility, and injecting a healthy dose of humanity and morality into policy making. Though he made no mention of communism or the Soviet Union, he pledged to rein in the "massive armaments race" and contribute to the ultimate goal of eliminating nuclear weapons, and he invited "all other people" to join in that endeavor.[13] In keeping with his campaign theme of greater humility, Carter eschewed the traditional limousine ride from the Capitol to the White House after the ceremony, instead walking the established route with his wife Rosalynn.

Once in office, Carter's main task was to construct the first elected Democratic administration since 1961, drawing from networks that had lain dormant for eight years. His appointments injected new blood into the National Security Council, the Department of State, and the Department of Defense. One of his first appointments was of Cyrus Vance as secretary of state. A naval officer in World War II (like Carter), Vance had been a corporate litigator in private practice until he served in a series of positions in the Department of Defense during the Kennedy and Johnson administrations. He was deputy secretary of defense for Johnson and was a delegate to the Paris Peace talks after the Vietnam War. His change of opinion toward withdrawal from South Vietnam while he was in the Department of Defense and his experience at the peace talks provided Vance with a reputation as a political dove but a savvy negotiator. His skills as a litigator made him unusually effective in negotiating for positions with which he disagreed. This characteristic and Vance's dry, obedient style would hobble him when it came time to exercise influence in the policy-making apparatus.[14]

One of Vance's most important assets on arms control issues was Leslie H. Gelb, his assistant secretary of state for politico-military affairs. Originally a professor of government, Gelb had served in the Department of Defense in the 1960s as the director of various task forces and committees, most notably the project that produced the Pentagon Papers. After his service in the Johnson administration, Gelb turned to journalism; he was the diplomatic correspondent to the *New York Times* until 1977. The combination of Gelb's knowledge of the Department of Defense and defense issues and his deep connections to the media establishment made him a powerful force on behalf of the State Department.[15]

Carter chose Soviet expert and political scientist Zbigniew Brzezinski as national security advisor. The Polish-born Brzezinski's father was a diplomat whose family was forced into exile by the Nazi/Soviet invasion of Poland in 1939. Brzezinski often cited this experience and coming to understand the devastation Poland suffered during the war as formative experiences. In his academic career, Brzezinski helped develop the concept of totalitarianism and applied it to the Soviet Union. Naturally, Brzezinski took a dim view of the Soviet Union, seeing it as aggressive but containable (most of his early writings in fact sought to distinguish Eastern European policy from Soviet policy, arguing that more engagement with the former could help undermine Soviet control).[16]

Much has been made in analysis of the Carter administration about the dichotomy between Vance and Brzezinski in Soviet policy. Vance saw détente as negotiated, nonconfrontational, and engagement-based. Brzezinski seeking sought a more triangular approach through China that cornered the Soviet Union into making the concessions necessary for détente while at the same time he worked to keep up the pressure on nonstrategic issues such as human rights and the plight of Soviet dissidents. In the conventional telling, Carter vacillated between the two until Brzezinski's influence shut out Vance in 1979. This narrative gained traction initially because of the easy bipolarity it offered journalists. It gained further traction when it became clear that the Soviet Union's experts had adopted much the same view, going so far as to review Carter's speeches, supposedly labeling some sections "CV" and others "ZB."[17]

This perspective, like most perspectives rooted in contemporary journalistic accounts, privileges ease of understanding over accuracy. Perhaps the greatest problem with it is that it denies Carter agency. Carter was deeply engaged with the substance of national security decision making and was not afraid to overrule Vance or Brzezinski on specific points. Indeed, Carter was more hawkish on certain points than even Brzezinski, especially when he believed that the point was related to an issue of basic fairness and equity in the U.S.-Soviet relationship. Conversely, Carter had more faith in the power of negotiation and engagement to achieve short-term results than Vance likely ever did.[18]

The view of the Carter administrations key advisors as bipolar also assumes that the administration's shift in policy over time to a more hawkish stance is attributable to a bureaucratic turf war that was slowly lost. This is incomplete; geopolitical events also played a role in this shift, such as the Soviets' involvement in Yemen and Africa and their invasion of Afghanistan. In fact, the Carter administration's collective understanding of the Soviet Union and what it wanted was a moving target throughout its term as a result of the Soviet Union's growing interventionism.

When he became national security advisor, Brzezinski faced several choices about how to organize and manage the National Security Council staff. Brzezinski and Henry Kissinger had been academic rivals before politics became their main pursuit (though as rivalries go, it had grown quite one-sided by the time Kissinger left academia), and much of the Carter campaign's foreign policy criticisms had centered on Kissinger's outsized role as national security advisor.[19] Yet alienating NSC staffers (many of whom owed the current state of their careers to Kissinger) out of a desire to prove that the "Kissinger era" was over would have been costly in terms of quickly building a functioning team.

Instead, Brzezinski elevated a number of NSC staffers from the Kissinger era (who usually came from bureaucratic rather than political backgrounds) and

integrated himself into its leadership using these staffers as a bridge. Most notable among these was David L. Aaron, a former foreign service officer and an
ACDA veteran who was well-versed on NATO issues and nuclear issues. He was
one of the few people associated with the SALT delegation who had survived the
1972 purge. In fact, he was promoted to the NSC as one of Kissinger's aides. He
left the NSC in 1974 to work in the office of Senator Walter Mondale (D-Minn.).
Aaron's work for Kissinger was notable, but in truth he was far more hawkish
than Kissinger (or, as would become apparent, Brzezinski).[20]

Carter chose Harold Brown as secretary of defense. Brown had a PhD in
physics. In his early career, he had worked as a research scientist in the nuclear
laboratories of the United States. Although he was a gifted physicist, Brown distinguished himself in the management of these organizations, rising to director
of defense research and engineering in 1961 and secretary of the air force in 1965.
Brown had a reputation as a moderate hawk. At his core, Brown was a technolo-
gist and manager, and as a result his approach to most issues, particularly the B-1
bomber, the neutron bomb, and arms control, had less to do with an assessment
of the Soviet Union's character than with a cost-benefit analysis related to the
factors he knew well, such as budgets and technology risk.[21]

Brown's principal advisor on SALT was Walter Slocombe, a 36-year-old
former Supreme Court clerk whose Ivy League and Rhodes scholar credentials
permitted apparently seamless career transitions between judicial and national
security affairs. Slocombe ably served the transition team and wrote several
papers on arms control that impressed Brown, despite Slocombe's previous dal-
liance with the McGovern campaign. Slocombe's title, principal deputy assistant
secretary of defense for international security affairs, belied the importance of
his position and the fact that his office rapidly became a nexus for almost all of
the interests in the Department of Defense that were touched by SALT issues.[22]

These nominations all proved relatively unobjectionable. As a result, Carter
was largely blindsided by the controversy that arose in response to his pick for
director of the Arms Control and Disarmament Agency, Paul C. Warnke. Warnke
was a partner at the law firm Covington & Burling, where he had worked under
Dean Acheson for several years. In 1967, President Johnson had appointed
Warnke general counsel of the Department of Defense and then assistant secretary of defense for international security affairs. After leaving the Department of
Defense, Warnke gained a reputation as a vocal critic of the nuclear arms race and
a supporter of arms control. Warnke had been a leading advisor to the George
McGovern campaign, though unlike more junior members of the administration
he felt no need to apologize for it.[23] What perhaps guaranteed the controversy
around his nomination was a *Foreign Policy* article he wrote in 1975 about the
nature of the strategic arms competition in a world of overkill. In it, Warnke

argued for a unilateral six-month delay in the development of the Trident submarine and the B-1 bomber to induce "reciprocal restraint" from the Soviet Union. The only victory the arms race could offer, he said, was the privilege of being the first to quit. Warnke titled the piece "Apes on a Treadmill."[24]

The directorship of the ACDA was not technically a cabinet post. The director's statutory responsibility was to act as the "principal advisor" to the president and the secretary of state. Though subordinate to the secretary of state, the position still conveyed significant access to the president, especially as the issue of arms control came to assume a more central role in U.S. political life.[25] Warnke's nomination ignited a firestorm of criticism from traditional hawks, anti-communists, and the emerging conservative movement.

Warnke was not solely responsible for the fact that his nomination turned into a major confrontation. Conservative and anti-communist forces that had lain dormant for years were increasingly dissatisfied with détente and conciliatory approaches to the Soviet Union. These forces were ready for a fight after the election of 1976 and eager for a chance to reassert themselves. Warnke's record presented an attractive target: high-profile enough to be notable but lacking the same degree of establishment respectability Vance presented. What made things worse for Warnke was that the Senate Armed Services Committee, which was stacked with a bipartisan majority of hawks, took an interest in his nomination. Hearings on Warnke's nomination gave outside critics a platform for airing their views and harshly criticizing Warnke's positions. Many of these were members of the Committee on the Present Danger.[26]

In the eyes of hawks, Warnke's real crime was not the substance of his positions, but the perceived glibness with which he expressed them. Warnke's writings when he was out of government had been so full-throated that they could easily be read as contemptuous of those who disagreed with him. Hurt feelings made a poor basis for policy discussions, and the criticism of Warnke quickly grew overheated and personal. Paul Nitze's testimony before the Senate referred to Warnke's positions as "asinine," then used an escalating series of adjectives to describe the danger they represented. Similarly frothy denunciations came from Senators Jackson and Nunn, Eugene Rostow, and others.[27]

Nitze's testimony must have stung. Warnke had been the assistant secretary of defense for international security affairs, one of the most influential positions in the Department of Defense, when Nitze had held the number two position of deputy secretary of defense in the late 1960s. The two had worked closely and well together on a number of issues. They had even put together some of the earliest hypothetical proposals for acceptable arms control agreements. Both were Ivy League elites from the Northeast and both had once worked under Dean Acheson—a critical personal connection for advancing their careers in government.[28] They shared several personality traits: both had a combative style of argumentation, both loved vigorous debate, and both exhibited a high degree of self-assurance during policy disputes. The fight over Warnke's nomination showed just how much space had developed between traditional anticommunists and liberal arms controllers in the intervening years, and these personality traits ensured the disagreement was especially brutal.

The nomination fight produced much noise but little change in immediate outcomes. Warnke's nomination made it to the floor, where it passed with 70 votes. Warnke's nomination to be head of the SALT II delegation (Carter and the Democrats in general had wanted to reunify the two posts for some time) received a less encouraging 58 votes. The disparity in these two confirmation votes should have raised alarms within the administration, but there is no evidence that they were taken as instructive of anything but a temporary spasm of opposition from unhappy anticommunists.

The disparity makes a certain amount of sense. It is easy to see how a senator could want a dove who was critical of nuclear weapons to lead the Arms Control and Disarmament Agency but might feel uncomfortable making that person the face of the U.S. government in direct negotiations. But even the vote for the director position only exceeded the two-thirds majority necessary to ratify a treaty by three votes, and the head-of-delegation vote fell far short of this mark. It had been presumed for some time that SALT II was leading to a treaty, yet the person who was ostensibly in charge of shaping these agreements proved to be a polarizing figure rather than a unifying one. After Warnke's dual appointments, a chill fell over Nitze's relations with the Carter administration.[29]

What to Do about Vladivostok

Almost immediately after they took office, these appointees threw themselves into the task of formulating a SALT policy based on the vestiges of the process left over from the Ford administration. The Vladivostok accord both attracted and repelled many members of the Carter administration. As a product of Kissinger's diplomacy, it was to be rejected according to Carter's campaign dictates because it was too conservative and protected all the wrong interests. As a package that had made significant progress toward an agreement however, it was attractive; it had the potential to lead to a quicker, simpler victory than one that came from going back to the drawing board. This victory could then act as a springboard to future agreements that came closer to Carter's vision of "real arms control."

Since the two sides had reached the agreement at Vladivostok in 1974, neither side had fully agreed to the reservations and conditions the other side sought to impose. The accord called for a ceiling of 2,400 ICBMs, SLBMs, and heavy bomb-ers and a sublimit of 1,320 on vehicles with MIRV. Negotiations over the next two years became hung up on several issues, the thorniest being the treatment of cruise missiles, particularly when they were launched from heavy bombers.[30]

Perhaps the most important post-Vladivostok accomplishment was a com-promise Kissinger organized in January 1976 whereby the Soviets agreed to some form of constraint on their controversial Backfire bomber if the United States would agree to include heavy bombers armed with cruise missiles (defined as those with a range of 600 to 2,500 kilometers) in the 1,320 MIRV limit. It would be wrong to say that the United States "agreed" to this, however, as the rest of Ford's national security team resoundingly rejected the compromise when they learned of it.[31] In typical style, the Soviets pretended to forget that they had agreed to constraints on the Backfire bomber in the intervening year. Instead, the Soviets increasingly referred to the MIRV classification of heavy bombers based on the elegance of the analogy to MIRV missiles, and claimed that attempts to revise the understanding were in fact attempts to reopen the issue.[32]

The problems with the Vladivostok agreement did not end there. The levels agreed to at Vladivostok were actually higher than existing U.S. levels and only reduced future deployments of Soviet systems. Also significant was the fact that the accord had nothing to say about heavy ballistic missiles such as the SS-9 and its successor, the SS-18. As a result, the throw-weight asymmetry between the U.S. and Soviet missile force was projected to increase even more. Although the United States had more reentry vehicles than the Soviets, if the Soviet MIRV program was allowed to run to completion, it would surge past the U.S. level in the mid-1980s. If improvements could be made to the accuracy of Soviet reentry vehicles, these trends could create serious problems for strategic stability that had long been the primary concern of arms control skeptics.[33] Even with the com-promise on air-launched cruise missiles, Soviet negotiators continued to insist on banning all other forms of cruise missiles with a range of more than 600 kilo-meters. This distance was significant because it was the shortest distance between the West German and Soviet borders, meaning that the limitation would prevent the United States from striking the Soviet Union with such missiles. The military services in particular opposed such limitations because weapons at that range were not considered strategic and never had been. Cruise missile development was also at a stage that seemed quite promising for nuclear and conventional applications. The United States' NATO allies also found the prospect of controls on ground-launched cruise missiles troubling, as in theory they could weaken extended deterrence, especially in the face of the Soviet Union's aggressive mod-ernization of its own intermediate-range nuclear forces.[34]

Opinions on specific aspects of the Vladivostok accord varied within the administration. Brown and Brzezinski loathed the idea of categorizing bombers equipped with cruise missiles as MIRVs and saw that provision as Kissinger's most negative legacy and the most dangerous compromise in SALT. Bombers, after all, were not first-strike weapons. They were too slow, and there was no limit on the amount of air defenses the Soviet Union could deploy to stop them before they reached their targets (although their "throw weight" exceeded that of almost any missile). The United States had sought limitations on MIRVs because of their rapid time to target and the sharp limitations on defenses against them; these factors made MIRVs especially destabilizing in ways that bombers were not. The fact that the United States had a far larger heavy bomber force also made this compromise seem one-sided, even if the Soviets kept their promise to permit limits on the Backfire. Brown and Brzezinski also wanted to limit heavy missiles, even if at a level higher than the few hundred Schlesinger and Nitze had argued was the threshold beyond which the level was moot.[35]

Brown and Brzezinski also saw reductions as the clearest path to a more stable strategic equilibrium, but the factors they wanted to control, such as throw weight and heavy missiles, would have ensured an imbalance in terms of which side reduced how much. Both saw the Backfire as an important political issue and were willing to fight for constraints on it but did not believe the bomber to be of strategic significance in an actual nuclear exchange.

As negotiations progressed, Brown was especially willing to go to bat to protect the cruise missile in almost all its forms.[36] Brown's zeal seemed rooted in his technological outlook: he sought to protect a system in development with significant strategic impacts that would cost much less than systems like the B-1 (which he had played a role in canceling) and the Trident submarine. Since in his view, the cruise missile lacked any obvious destabilizing characteristics, he felt its merits were obvious.

Vance was more dovish but also more pragmatic. He expressed the view that the Vladivostok ceilings were too high and agreed with Warnke in principle that there were some U.S. systems which the Soviet Union found uniquely threatening that could be sacrificed or delayed if it meant getting an agreement, such as the cruise missile. But Vance was cautious by nature and saw the Vladivostok framework as nearing completion. This factor was a significant selling point, and deviations from its framework could still alarm the Soviet leadership and diminish hopes for a completed deal. During the earliest stages of the Carter administration, Vance seemed to prefer to tinker with the Vladivostok framework just enough to remove its roughest edges (for both sides) and to bring it into effect quickly so the administration would have enough time left to negotiate another agreement that reflected its preferences.[37]

If Vance was the Carter administration's dovish ego, Warnke was its id. Less than two days after his surprisingly narrow confirmation vote, Warnke appeared at a meeting of the NSC and advocated canceling or deferring indefinitely the entire cruise missile program and offering it as a bargaining chip to the Soviets in the name of a more ambitious deal that could be quickly realized.[38] The cruise missile clearly frightened the Soviets deeply, yet it was in its infancy and little money had been sunk into it. Such an offer could motivate the Soviets to make a similar trade on MIRV verification rules or another similar issue.

This approach did not take Warnke very far, even in that meeting, which according to one report fell silent for a moment before dismissing the idea and moving on.[39] Even Vance, who was sympathetic to the idea of cruise missile limitations, did little to speak up for Warnke, who took a more pragmatic tack after that. This exchange may have been something of a wake-up call for Warnke. The arms control movement had long sought to impose constraints or bans on new weapons at the outset, before they developed a drive and rationale of their own. Such was the logic behind the arms control impact statements Congress required for all new weapons systems during this period: weapons development was a continuous process, and at any moment weapon designers could hatch the next destabilizing system, requiring a swift response. Vance and Warnke expressed this view with respect to cruise missiles in a memo to Carter. They argued for expansive limits on cruise missiles and noted that the window of opportunity could close quickly as the technology matured. But the reaction to Warnke's statement at the NSC meeting showed that while Carter may have had his sympathies with this school of thought, it was to be one perspective among many. Warnke subsequently used more pragmatic strategies in his efforts to keep up momentum and achieve an early agreement. When Vance endorsed most of the Vladivostok approach for the sake of moving on to the next agreement quickly, Warnke quickly followed.[40]

Carter's views on Vladivostok defied characterization to some extent. The president knew that he opposed what it represented because it included compromises and back-room dealings that were not fully vetted or transparent. Some of those compromises failed to achieve progress toward a more stable, safer world, while others traded on U.S. security without adequate reciprocity from the Soviet Union. Carter was sure that the aggregate numbers were too high. He absolutely insisted that agreed aggregates constitute real reductions from current levels, not cuts from planned levels. During the campaign Carter had authorized backchannel assurances to Brezhnev that if he were to be elected, he would move quickly to approve an agreement on the basis of Vladivostok and would be willing to compromise on any outstanding issues. Subsequent events illustrate the shallowness of these assurances. Although Carter wanted to move quickly, he did not think moving faster required compromises on issues of principle. In practice, this meant that Carter was willing to move as quickly as the Soviets were willing to compromise, which was not much faster than before.[41]

At the same time, Carter could often be sold on individual aspects of the Vladivostok approach with only minor changes. In these cases, or when he was evaluating a package with several such elements, Carter would note that the difference lay in the fact that linkages between specific items had been removed and the negotiation could then proceed based on a common understanding of the merits of specific provisions. Carter distrusted the idea of tit-for-tat bargaining on sensitive but ostensibly unrelated issues. Some degree of compromise was obviously inevitable, but Carter saw the ability to "[wipe] the slate clean" of these connections as a step toward his vision of a more transparent and defensible SALT process.[42]

Carter voiced his views about Vladivostok in NSC meetings and through the internal planning process, but his conception of the arms control process in general became most clear in his initial interactions with Ambassador Dobrynin and his direct correspondence with General Secretary Brezhnev. Carter believed that arms control was a process of argumentation and reasoning, in which dialogue about strategic problems interspersed with shows of good faith could generate consensus about strategic problems. This last point was related to a criticism Carter extended to both the previous administration and the Soviet leadership, whom he believed needed to be both invited and challenged to abandon their pretenses and begin serious negotiations "in good faith." Carter's use of this phrase implied both candor and reciprocity. He was prepared to insist on a more open approach from the Soviet Union, one that was more honest about its capabilities and less propagandistic in expressing Soviet concerns. Carter also believed, based on his (fairly accurate) understanding of Kissinger's approach to negotiations, that the Soviets needed to be more responsive, even proactive, in the bargaining process. No longer would Foreign Minister Gromyko's style, which had earned him the moniker "Mr. Nyet," be acceptable to the United States, leaving it to flail about, issuing proposal after proposal until something stuck. "Good faith" meant participating in a more honest and more evenly balanced exchange of ideas.[43]

As demanding as this "good faith" approach may have seemed, Carter also believed that the best way to provoke a change in Soviet behavior was to demonstrate this approach himself. Carter used it in initial meetings with Ambassador Dobrynin, when he shared his almost fantastical belief that if negotiations could commence on this footing, the parties could agree to reductions in the current agreement to aggregates as low as 1,500, that inconvenient issues such as the cruise missile and the Backfire bomber could be jettisoned in favor of negotiating based on areas of consensus, and that the world could turn to a new era in the history of nuclear weapons.[44]

Carter's correspondence with Brezhnev was less substantive but more tone deaf. The initial exchanges of letters were intended to lay the groundwork for the next major SALT meeting of either the delegation in Geneva or of more senior leaders. The letters may in fact have had the opposite effect of raising alarms in the Soviet leaders' minds about the Carter administration's intentions. As Raymond Garthoff and others have noted, the 1974 Vladivostok accord was extremely costly for the Soviet leadership. (A Soviet negotiator told Paul Warnke that Brezhnev had had to "spill political blood" to gain his government's assent.)[45] Ramming the accord past the Soviet military in particular may have left lasting scars at a time when Soviet generals likely foresaw continued steady growth in their budgets and capabilities.[46]

In these letters, Carter vaguely but explicitly criticized the accords, even as his administration prepared fallback options that deviated only in numbers, not in structure. This language was consistent with his campaign rhetoric, but it ignored the basic psychological truth that paying a high, even grievous price for a given thing makes it more dear to the possessor, not less. Brezhnev and the senior Soviet leadership had bet heavily on the Vladivostok accords. They saw arguments that they should back away from them, even rhetorically, as a threat or an invitation to self-immolate. The Carter administration strategy of pushing the Soviets out of their comfort zone and urging them to begin negotiating seriously and in "good faith" came across as effrontery and was met with increasing belligerence. The exchanges became so snippy that before the first major summit letters from both parties included multiple digressions criticizing the other's "tone."[47]

Opening Bids

The deteriorating Carter-Brezhnev correspondence seemed to do little to alter the administration's policy planning. Carter made clear from the earliest phase of the transition that he sought a resumption of high-level SALT talks at the earliest practicable date, preferably March or April 1977. In early February, Carter instructed his NSC task force on SALT issues (the Special Coordinating Committee, not to be confused with the Standing Consultative Commission created by the ABM Treaty, both of which were abbreviated as SCC) to produce a comprehensive history of the negotiations to date and a range of packages and an analysis of their implications for presentation at the bargaining table.

Unusually for SALT, the U.S. government met its deadline; Cyrus Vance made a high-profile trip to Moscow on March 27–30, 1977. Staff-level efforts were particularly prodigious. They produced three options, all of which used Vladivostok as a point of reference, by introducing additional restrictions ("Vladivostok Plus"), adding fewer restrictions ("Vladivostok Minus"), or adhering closely to the existing framework (known as the "Basic Option" but sometimes derisively called "As If Ford Had Won").[48]

The Department of State favored the Basic Option. This proposal seemed tailored to gain quick acceptance from the Soviets. It abandoned any real constraints on the Backfire and kept the 2,400/1,320 figures. ALCM-equipped bombers would count against the limit of 1,320 MIRVs, but with a formula that was much more generous to the United States. This proposal found few supporters, in part because of the supposedly lopsided nature of the concessions. Vladivostok Minus deferred the twin questions of Backfire and the cruise missile to a future negotiation in which U.S. officials would commit to discussing numerous other issues that were attractive to the Soviets as an inducement. As it was further developed, this proposal became known simply as "deferral." This proposal technically agreed to even less than the previous administration had secured in the draft text of the treaty without adding anything. For what it promised in expedience, this proposal lacked in ambition, and it had few supporters. The Pentagon favored Vladivostok Plus, which included small but significant reductions from the original aggregates and limitations on the Backfire. The JCS envisioned counting the Backfire as a strategic weapon under the aggregates and making few concessions, while the Office of the Secretary of Defense proposed pairing the Backfire with the ground-launched cruise missile, another ambiguous system, and proposing to jointly include or exclude them from the aggregate. This proposal also envisioned a tradeoff between Soviet heavy missiles and U.S. heavy bombers equipped with ALCMs, likely in a category separate from the limit of 1,320 MIRVs.[49]

Unsurprisingly, as these plans developed they incorporated more features and more tradeoffs, growing more complex, though not unmanageably so. In an enterprising moment, Walter Slocombe designed a flow chart illustrating the basic features of the three options and basic questions each option raised. Though it was appreciated within the middle ranks of the bureaucracy, its reception among the administration's most influential figures was poor. Carter, Brzezinski, Brown, and Aaron all seemed to dislike the "Slocombe Triptych" and the options it represented. They felt that the chart overcomplicated three unambitious plans. This harsh and dismissive assessment of the NSC staff's work boded ill, as these principals seemed averse to taking the time to completely understand the previous administration's work, even as they thought they could surpass it.[50]

As preparations for the summit continued, several new ideas and changes to the Vladivostok framework were introduced. Significant debates took place about issues such as limitations on the ranges of various kinds of cruise missile and attempts to control the quantitative and qualitative aspects of the arms race, both of which were strongly influenced by the ideas of Harold Brown.

Up to this point, the tentative agreement limited the range of ALCMs to between 600 and 2,500 kilometers. These ranges sought to reduce the capacity of bombers to strike dozens of targets in the interior of the Soviet Union from a distance (their "penetration capability"). Shorter-range limits lengthened the amount of time bombers were subject to the vast Soviet air defense system, thus limiting the damage they could do. Cruise missiles were harder to detect and intercept, so the smaller their range the less damage they could do. Soviet negotiators valued both limits for geographic reasons. As the rough distance between West Germany and the Soviet border, the limit of 600 kilometers would confine non-heavy bombers to a theater role with respect to cruise missiles, while a ban on ranges greater than 2,500 kilometers would prevent fleets of bombers from launching missiles from outside Soviet airspace or with only minimal exposure to the Soviet air defense system.[51]

With respect to sea- and ground-launched cruise missiles, however, the Soviets had insisted on a much more restrictive ban on ranges above 600 kilometers in all cases. Damage limitation motivated this demand. Restricting GLCMs to that range would prevent them from striking the Soviet Union from anywhere in Western Europe. The Soviets already had a 600-kilometer submarine-launched cruise missile in active use, but the majority of the U.S. population was located within 600 kilometers of the coastline. To bring a comparable percentage of the Soviet population under threat would require a U.S. submarine-launched cruise missile with a range of more than 1,500 kilometers.[52]

The difference between an ALCM and a GLCM when they were disconnected from their launchers was difficult to discern. Thus, differences in the limitations between platforms could introduce serious problems in terms of verification and negotiations. Vance and Warnke recognized this problem early on and proposed splitting the difference by imposing a blanket limitation of 1,500 kilometers on all cruise missiles. Only the second-generation ALCM, which was several years off, could exceed this range anyway, so agreeing to it would have no impact on existing plans. The proposal had enough merit that Brzezinski, the Joint Chiefs, and others were cautiously receptive. Brown and the Office of the Secretary of Defense, however, objected to this idea, arguing that the range limitation on ALCMs was too low, placing it, in Brown's words, "at the steep part of the target coverage curve"[53] for a potential nuclear exchange.

Why there was so much interest in banning a system that did not yet have a commonly understood use? As Brzezinski wrote to Carter in March 1977, "There is a wide range of views on acceptable cruise missile limitations. This in part reflects our inability at this time to define unique military requirements for long-range cruise missiles other than ALCMs on heavy bombers."[54] This statement had disturbing implications for where arms control and the SALT process were headed. The purpose of SALT was to restrain and roll back the arms race. How could either side determine that cruise missiles were driving the arms race (and therefore worthy of inclusion in SALT) if no one knew yet what they could do or how effective they would be? A ban at that point might have been easier to verify, but why did cruise missiles come under scrutiny at all given the uncertainties? Thematic sprawl of this sort plagued SALT II and the inability to link its terms to improvements in the strategic balance often served to muddy later debates over treaty ratification.

Brown injected another new idea into the SALT dynamic. Much of the concern about the nuclear arms race in recent years had been related to qualitative improvements rather than with large increases in the number of weapons. The Soviet Union had not been building new silos; instead, they were upgrading missiles in their silos. Furthermore, the vulnerability of U.S. Minuteman ICBMs was as much a question of Soviet accuracy as it was of Soviet numbers. These trends were at least partly the result of the fact that the strategic competition had shifted from quantity to quality after SALT I. Brown argued that SALT II therefore ought to move to restrict such improvements. First he proposed limiting the number and type of missile tests that could be conducted annually. The scope of qualitative improvements would thus be bounded by the ability to gain confidence that new components or techniques could work reliably. If the limit could be set low enough, even the earliest estimates of Minuteman vulnerability could be postponed for years. The idea of qualitative limitations quickly caught on and various other proposals came to the fore, such as limiting upgrades in missile systems or banning the deployment of new types of missiles, in effect giving up the planned Missile-Experimental (MX) in exchange for the Soviets' agreement to halt their program of upgrading SS-17s, SS-18s, and SS-19s.[55]

In these early months those outside the administration sought to influence the Carter administration's plans for SALT II. In fact, after one of Senator Henry Jackson's first official visits to the Carter White House, he sent the president a 23-page memo on the subject of SALT that was almost certainly written by Richard Perle. Carter graciously accepted it and promised to read it and circulate it among his staff. The memo ranged widely in its discussion of SALT issues from the abstract to the granular and was an important portent of the positions

Jackson and fellow hawks would take with respect to the developing SALT II agreement.[56]

While the memo was mostly boilerplate, in its own hyperventilating way, represented an emerging consensus on several strategic issues, and its broad strokes may have emboldened the tetrad of Brown, Brzezinski, Aaron, and Carter.[57] The memo questioned "clichéd" declarations about a "spiraling arms race" and claimed that the sense of urgency pervading the negotiations was unnecessary. It noted that the U.S. strategic forces budget had declined in real dollars by 8 percent between 1961 and 1976, while Soviet spending had surged after 1964. It also argued that the scope of SALT was growing beyond bilateral issues and was beginning to touch issues important to allies of the United States, particularly NATO members, such as intermediate-range missiles, requiring closer consultation before agreeing to anything with the Soviets. Jackson believed that cruise missiles had such substantial conventional capabilities that they ought to be shared and fully used in the defense of Europe. Their decisively theater-range nature did not rule them out as a point of negotiation for SALT II, but a distinction between them and truly strategic systems was warranted.

The memo also insisted on getting the Soviet's SS-19 classified as a heavy missile. By traditional definitions, this characterization was more than a stretch (the SS-19 was not far from the MX in many of its performance characteristics), but this point reflected a growing consensus that the SS-19 could very well represent a greater threat to strategic stability than the existing Soviet behemoth, the SS-18. If that were the case, this fact would render the heavy ballistic missile category moot and would amplify the need for broad reductions to narrow the throw-weight gap between the Soviet Union and the United States. Finally, the memo advised Carter not to be afraid of delays brought on by taking the time to negotiate an agreement outside the confines of the Vladivostok formula.[58]

One critical point in the memo that went almost unnoticed concerned verification. The memo insisted that rules and procedures for verification ought never be bargained or linked with aspects of the treaty dealing with the numbers and capabilities of specific weapons. Kissinger had already dabbled with this tactic, but as part of a package that was developed late in the Ford administration and could not gain the approval of the executive branch. In this memo Jackson tried to alert the Carter administration to what would become a prominent critique of their approach to arms control and the SALT II treaty during debates over ratification. Jackson and others argued that the terms of arms control treaties ought to be mutually beneficial, thus giving both parties incentive to preserve them and giving both sides a stake in assuring compliance. Attempting to gain an advantage by holding concessions hostage to adequate verification runs counter to this perspective and suggests instead that one party seeks to gain an advantage. The

Carter administration paid little heed to this warning and comingled substance and verification issues at several points in the coming years, setting the stage for debates that would shape the politics of verification into the present day.[59]

The administration's reaction to the memo was mixed. Especially for the younger and more dovish in the administration, Jackson's brand of anticommunism smacked of 1950s alarmism. According to Strobe Talbott, Warnke called the study a "first-class polemic," while long-time NSC staffer William Hyland noted that opting for a longer time to agreement would actually mean the United States would remain longer under the Interim Agreement from SALT I that he so loathed. Carter's reaction was more positive than most, however, and insisted on providing a response to Jackson's staff.[60] Jackson's arguments that substantial reductions could be negotiated and should not be bound by the flawed work of the Ford administration may have emboldened the members of the Carter administration who wanted to push for more in their opening bid in Moscow.[61]

A "Comprehensive" Approach

As preparations continued, the three main options became more refined. The deferral option looked increasingly less realistic, so planners tried to develop looser, more temporary constraints on Backfire and cruise missiles, creating a spectrum of options between deferral and the basic Vladivostok agreement. Some of the more aggressive aspects of the reductions proposal, such as counting Backfire as a full strategic weapon, were dropped or gradually forgotten. Carter also insisted in some of his first Special Coordinating Committee meetings that he wanted to explore reductions to levels as low as 1,500 total delivery vehicles. Although this option was included in subsequent analysis, it failed to spark much interest.[62]

The meetings to discuss these plans developed ever more subtle and complicated options but provided little sense of how to present them to the Soviets. Carter attempted to remedy this problem on Saturday, March 12. That morning, Brzezinski called a special "principals only" meeting of the SCC, inviting only Brown, Aaron, Vance, Warnke, Director of Central Intelligence Stansfield Turner, and the chair of the Joint Chiefs. Unusually, Brzezinski led the participants to the cabinet room, where they found Vice President Mondale and a flannel-shirt-clad President Carter. In a relaxed discussion, Carter voiced dissatisfaction with the NSC's staff work thus far, describing it as hidebound and intellectually lazy and expressing a desire for something fundamentally different. Brown took the opportunity to reiterate, with David Aaron, the idea of qualitative limitations, arguing that such a program would do a great deal to forestall the vulnerability of the Minuteman force, an attractive legacy for a president looking to make his mark. Brzezinski then said that a program of substantial cuts (more than the Vladivostok Plus option but less than Carter's barely serious proposal of 1,500 total delivery systems) would work synergistically with this goal. While an agreement along the lines of Vladivostok might increase Soviet confidence in the SALT process, reductions and limits on modernization would provide far more concrete benefits for U.S. security interests. Carter agreed and ordered the that a proposal be drafted along the lines just described. This would be the preferred U.S. approach. Thus was born the "comprehensive" proposal in a meeting whose existence was known of only in rumors for the next several years and with minimal staff involvement or review. This act inaugurated a trend in the preparations for the March 1977 Moscow summit in which the Carter administration unwittingly dabbled in the secrecy and top-down management style of Kissinger.[63]

The initial job of fleshing out the comprehensive proposal fell to NSC veteran William Hyland, but it bore the marks of Brown, Brzezinski, and Aaron. The comprehensive proposal came to resemble its name, incorporating most of the new ideas for controls that had been proposed in the SCC meeting. The proposal called for top-level aggregates of between 2,000 and 1,800, MIRV levels (excluding ALCM-equipped heavy bombers) of between 1,200 and 1,100, a reduction in Soviet heavy ICBMs, a freeze in the deployment of existing ICBMs, limits on qualitative improvements, annual limits on missile testing, and a ban on the deployment and testing of new types of ICBMs. In practical terms, this provision would freeze the deployment of the latest generation of Soviet ICBMs at a level at or below 550 (the number of Minuteman IIIs the United States possessed) and freeze the deployment of the heavy SS-18 below 150. In exchange for agreeing to this regime, the United States would exclude the Backfire from the Soviet aggregates and accept general assurances on the production rate and capabilities of that bomber.[64]

A proposal that boldfaced some chance of failure, and Vance and Warnke repeatedly reminded the SCC of the need for credible fallback options. The package would almost certainly be rejected and bargained down to something less revolutionary. They worried that the wider the gap between proposal and compromise, the more the administration invited accusations of weakness and retreat from hard-liners. Their point held little sway, and the SCC instead developed a minimalist fallback option. The minimalist fallback position was a variation on the deferral scheme; it proposed very loose or no constraints on Backfire and cruise missiles and a token reduction in the aggregate from 2,400 to 2,300. Carter authorized Vance to present an intermediate reductions proposal if this plan should also be rejected, but he required Vance to call to consult with the administration first.[65]

The distance between these positions illustrates the degree to which the Carter administration was at cross-purposes with itself. The comprehensive proposal was substantial, to be sure, and traded time and negotiability for potential impact. A tactic of this nature required a fallback that made the opposite tradeoff, which deferral did not do. Administration officials, especially Carter and Brzezinski, believed that a simpler agreement—that is, one that covered fewer systems with less complicated formulae—could be negotiated more quickly. Deferral failed this criterion, however, because the Soviets had made clear for years that they saw the cruise missile as one of the gravest threats to their security and would not consent to an agreement that did not include it. Furthermore, the Soviets had also made clear for years that they would not consider any linkage (or even discussion) of the Backfire with anything in SALT because it was not a strategic system.[66] The deferral strategy was based on the assumption that the Soviets wanted a quick, easy agreement more than they wanted to have their primary concerns addressed. In determining its approach to SALT, the Carter administration spent a great deal of time establishing what they wanted from the Soviets but generally failed to anticipate the Soviet response.

This secretive approach came at a cost. On March 20, 1977, Leslie Gelb attended a NATO meeting to provide assurances that the United States did not plan to change course significantly from where SALT II already was. This incongruity between what the administration was planning and what Gelb said at the NATO meeting embarrassed Gelb and created tensions within the NATO alliance about the Carter administration's seriousness. In Washington, Vance decided to provide a preview only a few days before he left for Moscow. This contrasted with Kissinger's practice of giving Ambassador Dobrynin a preview of the U.S. position a few weeks before a summit and likely contributed to the senior Soviet leadership's apprehension about the upcoming meeting.[67]

Only a few days before the summit, the administration suddenly changed tactics and began to openly discuss the details of each proposal and how they related to each other. Beginning with a speech before the United Nations and in press conferences over the week before the summit, Carter talked about both the comprehensive package and deferral and even implied that further fallback options existed when he stated "if we are disappointed . . . then we'll try to modify our stance," virtually assuring the Soviets that if they rejected both options at the approaching summit, more options would be forthcoming.[68]

These moves unsettled the Soviet leadership, especially given its known propensity for paranoia.[69] But there were signs that the Moscow summit was going to go badly even without the bumbled rollout and awkward public relations strategy. The administration's opening proposals focused more on the scope of an agreement than on the likelihood of being able to produce quick results.

The increasingly argumentative tone of Carter and Brezhnev's correspondence should have indicated that the Soviet leadership was not just committed
to the Vladivostok accord, but that that they took an expansive view of the Vladivostok framework. It was clear from the correspondence that the Soviets were
holding fast to everything that proceeded from the 1974 accords up to Kissinger's
last summit meeting in January 1976. Any plan presented as a change in direction
from the dominant trajectory, even if the Carter administration insisted it was
consistent with the original Vladivostok agreement of 1974, would represent an
unacceptable loss of face for the Soviets.[70]

Much of this antagonism was evident on the first day of the summit. Brezhnev's
public statements in the weeks leading up to the summit had indicated that the
Carter administration's human rights policies had rattled Soviet leaders. In
Brezhnev's first meeting with Vance, the Soviet leader harangued the secretary
of state with the point that criticisms of Soviet internal affairs violated the spirit
of détente. Foreign Minister Gromyko's opening statement at the first working
session insisted that the SALT process had a history captured in its negotiating
record and that both sides needed to respect and be bound by that history instead
of abandoning it on a whim. This statement sounded to some like a preemptive
refusal of the comprehensive proposal.[71]

What few concessions the Soviets made at the summit were overshadowed by
the tone and granularity of the issues on which there was movement. The Soviets
ruled out the comprehensive proposal, in particular the idea that they should
give up a substantial portion of their heavy ballistic missile force. The Soviets
claimed that Kissinger had agreed at Vladivostok that the United States would
drop their proposals about the Soviets' heavy ballistic missile force in exchange
for the Soviets dropping their proposals for eliminating the U.S. forward-based
systems. Brezhnev and Gromyko both argued that with its attempt to regulate
heavy ballistic missiles, the U.S. proposal had opened Pandora's Box and that now
the United States would have to negotiate on its FBS as well. In a brief construc-
tive moment, Gromyko said that some progress could be made on the basis of
reductions to 2,200 total delivery vehicles, but only if the cruise missile was specifically brought into the agreement and the Backfire remained unconstrained,
rehashing the Soviet government's January 1976 proposal.[72]

Once the Soviets indicated their unwillingness to negotiate on the basis of
the comprehensive proposal and their insistence that Vladivostok was the baseline for negotiations, Vance was stuck. His instructions required the Soviets to
negotiate on the basis of the comprehensive option, but the Soviet counteroffer
included cruise missiles and specifically excluded the Backfire. This ruled out
using the fallback deferral position Vance had hoped to pitch. The instructions
Vance had received also prohibited even mentioning the third, intermediate U.S.

position unless Soviet negotiators accepted key parts of the comprehensive package, an ironic outcome considering this proposal was actually closer to the Soviet counterproposal for reductions to 2,200 total delivery vehicles. Trying to find an opening so he could offer his position, Vance floated the idea that deferral could be interpreted as consistent with the Vladivostok accords. Brezhnev, unprepared or unwilling (his deteriorating condition made either possible) to consider that proposal, reiterated his threat to reopen the FBS issue and indicated that he thought it was time for the meeting to draw to a close.[73]

As much as acrimony seemed to dominate the proceedings, neither side wished to be seen as uncommitted, so the parties cobbled together enough small-bore initiatives to declare victory and return home. They agreed to convene task forces on a comprehensive nuclear test ban, Indian Ocean issues, and missile test notifications. Vance also secured an agreement that they would assign to the SALT delegations in Geneva a number of midlevel issues related to definitions, verification rules, and other technical matters. The role of the delegation shrank after 1972, which critics highlighted as a measure of Kissinger's overcentralization. Trusting the delegates to accomplish more on their own and relying less on summitry to advance the negotiations was a priority of Vance, Warnke and others, and the Soviet leadership was amenable.[74]

While the public relations strategy going into the summit had problems, the strategy coming out of the summit was worse. Vance's instinct for transparency served him ill. Instead of giving the media a terse, vague statement as would be typical for statements about unproductive diplomatic meetings, Vance decided to admit that the talks had been a bust. He told the media that the Soviets had rejected both proposals yet had "provided nothing new on their side." Vance went on to describe in greater detail the nature of the U.S. proposals without providing exact figures. Vance tried to end his statement on a high note by claiming that overall relations remained strong, but his meaning was clear: the United States was serious about arms control, and if the Soviet Union wanted to be taken seriously as well, they would have to convince both Carter and the U.S. public.[75]

Vance's statement triggered alarm among Soviet leaders. From the Soviet perspective, negotiating privately behind closed doors *was* the way to deal "honestly" with one another. The Soviets could not see the value of mixing negotiation with propaganda in an image war that seemed designed to force one side into concessions they did not want to make. From their perspective, trying to use the media to sway the policies of the opposite side signaled a desire to deny the fundamental rights of autonomy and state sovereignty that the Soviets believed were at the heart of détente. That said, Soviet leaders had never been above using the U.S. political process to gain an edge. For example, Vance thought it likely that

Brezhnev was trying to throw his weight around with a new and inexperienced administration in his reporting cable on the status of the summit talks.[76]

Carter did not take the news about how the talks had gone well. While he was pleased that the talks would continue, Carter provided a preview of what failing to negotiate "in good faith" meant to him, saying, "Obviously, if we feel at the conclusion of the discussions that the Soviets are not acting in good faith, then I would be forced to consider a much more deep commitment to the development and deployment of additional weapons." Carter also insisted that "this is a good and fair proposal," citing "unanimous agreement among the key Members of Congress, the State Department, my own staff, the Secretary of Defense, the Joint Chiefs." This was an exaggeration at best, considering how few of those listed had any role in or knowledge of the proposal. Carter's implicit threats about strategic systems were more bluster at that point, as decisions about canceling the B-1 bomber and the decision not to deploy the neutron bomb were months away. On this issue, as with others, Carter was more ready to make demands from on high than he was to deal with the fact that such pronouncements seemed to inflame the Soviets.[77]

And inflamed they were. Before Vance's plane had returned to Washington, Gromyko had taken several unprecedented measures in response to what he saw as a concerted public relations campaign to bully the Soviet Union into making concessions. Whereas Vance and Carter's statements contained the usual positive caveats about the relationship between them, Gromyko held nothing back. The foreign minister described the comprehensive proposal as "cheap and shady" and accused the United States of seeking the dreaded "unilateral advantages." Gromyko then publicly reiterated the threat he had delivered to Vance: if the United States persisted in seeking deep reductions or cuts in the heavy missile force, the Soviet Union would demand liquidation of U.S. bases in Europe and control over all platforms capable of carrying nuclear weapons, including FBS. Finally, Gromyko released the exact numbers in the Carter administration's proposal, something never before given directly to the media while an agreement was still under negotiation. Gromyko likely believed that when the U.S. public saw the numbers, they would side with his argument that it was the U.S. administration that was playing games and spinning fantasies with its unrealistic proposals.[78]

Conclusion

The fallout from the summit was considerable. While some hawks such as Senator Jackson were pleased to see the administration rejecting the Vladivostok approach and staying tough in the face of Soviet intransigence, the sniping, backbiting, and feeling of genuine surprise at the outcome left many hawks hesitant to associate themselves with the performance. For most other observers, the Moscow summit was something between a poor showing for a rookie administration and a debacle. As recriminations began, NSC staffers concluded that the main culprit was Vance, who had bumbled the public rollout of the comprehensive option and had inflamed the Soviets so much that they refused to give it an honest hearing. Carter consoled himself that the comprehensive proposal was just too "radical" for the hidebound Soviet bureaucracy. Vance's defenders at Foggy Bottom argued that he had had an unrealistic proposal foisted on him, a wish list of NSC priorities that had been developed as if the Soviets had no say.[79]

The most obvious impact of the summit was to make clear that there would be no quick agreement, if there had ever been a possibility of such a thing. Also clear was that any future agreement would have to provide sufficient cover for the Soviet leaders to argue that the results of negotiations had grown out of the achievements of Vladivostok.

It would be wrong to assume that nothing good came out of the summit, however. Indeed, the overwhelmingly negative assessments from inside and outside the administration were often colored by the same biases that had influenced administration planning: people confused timing with progress and speed with efficacy. The administration had decided against getting an agreement quickly in favor of the comprehensive approach. But the scope and surprise of the delays caused by the summit clouded positive signs that took more time to evidence themselves.

Delegating more substantive details to the negotiating delegations at Geneva, for instance, helped speed along the agreement and in fact likely strengthened the connection between the Soviet delegates and the Soviet policy apparatus, negating the main argument against doing so. The summit also established a critical precedent that, despite Soviet protestations, SALT was still subject to electoral consequences. Finally, the months that followed the summit showed that Carter had indeed achieved his objective of forcing the Soviets to be more active participants in the negotiations on a substantive level. Unfortunately, as the Soviet negotiators took up this more active approach, it was clear one of their main motivations was the concern that the U.S. government did not know what it was doing.[80]

The state of Soviet leadership in the late 1970s limited just how pro-active Soviet negotiators could be. After the March summit, Brezhnev's health deteriorated further. He withdrew from face-to-face negotiations and did not return until the last details of the agreement had to be finalized in1979.[81] Brezhnev's declining capacities contributed to the rapidly ossifying tendencies of the Soviet apparat. In the absence of strong central leadership, the different bureaucracies retreated into the defense of their interests. Furthermore, with the exception of a brief period in 1979, the oil boom of the early 1970s was coming to an end, as were double-digit increases in defense expenditures each year.[82] Lacking a strong central leader or the fruits of an expanding economy with which to smooth over disputes, Politburo decision making on SALT II devolved into a defense of institutional interests.[83] Major compromises could be expected only after a prolonged period, when it became clear that continued refusal would threaten the SALT process, and with it the détente framework that had been so critical for their careers.

Subsequent recriminations provided few conclusions about *how* the summit went wrong. There is a common tendency among new presidential administrations exhibited by many Carter administration officials. Many of these officials seemed to think that a majority of U.S. voters had provided a necessary validation of their worldview. Flush with electoral success and assured of the rightness of their position, administration figures threw themselves into SALT convinced that since a majority of voters agreed with their assessment that SALT could be done better and faster, it must therefore be true. Honest internal assessments can be difficult in such an environment.

While popular mandates could distort perceptions of the possible, frequent elections also undercut the idea of path dependence in foreign policy. It is a bitter truth that, even if one is dissatisfied with the direction of a protracted negotiation, or thinks they could have done better, they may not have the opportunity to change that direction, or reshape the agreement to reflect what they would have done better at the outset. After the Moscow summit the Carter administration found itself with the worst of both worlds: it had come out strongly against the Vladivostok accord yet had been forced to craft an agreement based on that agreement, at least in broad strokes. A bit of cynicism about campaign promises would have gone a long way toward setting the administration up for a faster resolution of SALT II, leaving time and political capital to at least attempt a SALT III agreement. All of these factors presaged the dilemma Ronald Reagan faced in 1981 when deciding whether to abide by the SALT II agreement he had run against.

The comprehensive proposal reflected two parallel drives within the administration. In tone, it accommodated Brzezinski's desire to use SALT to challenge the Soviet Union and thus learn something about their intentions. In substance, it reflected Brown's short list of technological and strategic imperatives: protect the cruise missile, control qualitative improvements, and postpone Minuteman vulnerability. Unfortunately, none of these goals was a point of consensus among administration figures, and for good reason. Had they done more to seek this consensus, they might have realized the drawbacks of their strategy. Instead, they presented their preferences under the Carter-approved guise of "real arms control." This episode illustrates what would become a main feature of SALT during the Carter administration: the propensity to subsume conflicts into the planning and negotiating process instead of developing a clear consensus about the United States' nuclear requirements, the nature of the strategic arms race, and what could be done using the foreign policy tools available.

"THINKING OUT LOUD":
THE STRUGGLE WITH SPRAWL

After the Moscow summit, the Carter administration's approach to SALT II became more serious, more collaborative, and more routine. It also came to resemble more closely the approach Ford and Kissinger had taken. As the next several years would show, Carter's early efforts in SALT II were the aberration and the remainder of his term was the norm. The SALT process' defining characteristics and pressures remained, now reasserting themselves against a chastened administration. As they recognized their mistakes and accepted generally lowered expectations about the process, Carter administration officials were able to make some progress toward an agreement in the months after summit.

The administration was still playing catch-up, however. It was trying to develop a framework that could recapture the momentum SALT II had before Carter arrived in office. Both parties needed to settle crucial details that had not yet been resolved or even addressed during substantive negotiations, such as verification and counting rules. The impact of these issues on the strategic balance could be significant.

As the contours of a final agreement grew clear, various constituencies in the Soviet Union and in the U.S. government to become even more insistent that their priorities for the next arms control negotiation be unconstrained. For the Carter administration, SALT II negotiations fell into a routine that allowed the process to proceed on its own logic without being fully integrated into broader foreign policy goals. Outside events blindsided the parties, greatly complicating the prospects for an agreement. In addition, the inability of both governments to decide what détente and SALT required of each other fueled tensions that affected not only the negotiations but hastened the return to unbridled competition.

Managing Expectations

While Carter administration officials were reluctant to accept blame for the outcome of the March summit, they clearly realized the enormity of the task of salvaging the faltering negotiations. They resolved almost immediately to lower expectations about the next Vance-Gromyko meeting in May. In addition, they made increasing use of two new, lower-profile channels to the Soviet Union: the Warnke-led SALT II delegation that was soon to reconvene in Geneva and Anatoly Dobrynin, longtime Soviet ambassador to the United States.

Dobrynin's close relationship with Henry Kissinger put Carter officials off initially. Soon after the election, Carter administration officials observed Dobrynin's habit of not taking notes during important exchanges. The ambassador's age and avuncular demeanor caused Vance and Brzezinski to worry they could not rely upon him to transmit proposals to the Soviet leadership accurately. Their experience with Dobrynin in the first few months quickly disabused them of these ideas.[1]

Over the next several months, the combination of a more flexible and proactive attitude from the Carter administration (and to a lesser extent from Soviet negotiators) and this multi-channel approach yielded some positive results without falling into the trap of inflating public expectations. When this approach began to bear fruit, members of the Carter administration (with the possible exception of Vance) became overconfident. Several times over the next several years, administration figures wrongly concluded that they were on the verge of an agreement.[2]

Administration principals met on April 7 to discuss how to limit damage from the summit. Over the next month, Carter, Brzezinski, and Vance worked with Dobrynin in successive meetings that set the parameters of what could be done in SALT II and generated a consensus about which issues had to be included and which could be excluded or deferred. Carter and Brzezinski sounded out Dobrynin on the Soviet position and potential areas of flexibility, then Vance began a series of private sessions with the ambassador in which he offered to "think out loud" about potential aspects of an agreement and the best path forward. He then invited Dobrynin to comment on which approaches sounded feasible in his estimation and which would be likely to ignite Soviet opposition. Dobrynin could then provide an official response or give Gromyko the chance to "think out loud" at his next meeting with Vance in May, where Middle East issues had top billing and therefore arms control expectations were restrained.[3] These discussions introduced the critical idea of SALT II as an agreement with several phases.

Of all of the administration principals, President Carter seemed the least chastened. As the administration tried to develop plans and proposals for consulting with Dobrynin and then Gromyko in May, Carter bristled against the notion that his comprehensive proposal was likely to be heavily revised or abandoned. Trying to avoid this outcome, Carter suggested converting SALT II into a two-year agreement that would capture most of the proposed limitations (including those on cruise missiles) but whose duration would give the Soviets incentive to negotiate a more comprehensive SALT III quickly.[4]

Administration principals disagreed about which restrictions would go into which agreement, but Vance pitched his own version to Dobrynin first. Together with Warnke he proposed a two-year agreement that included a broad set of limits on various systems in addition to the Vladivostok limits on delivery vehicles and MIRVs (2,400 and 1,320, respectively). The Vladivostok ceilings would persist through 1985, but the remainder of the treaty, which covered all limitations on cruise missiles, all limitations on heavy ICBMs, all qualitative limits, and all limitations on the Backfire, would expire after two years unless the parties could reach an agreement on SALT III. SALT III would proceed on the basis of the explicit commitments enumerated in SALT II to substantial reductions in aggregates and total MIRVs. This scheme was the inverse of deferral: instead of postponing the most controversial issues and securing reductions up front, it agreed to most of these limitations and held them hostage to a speedy resolution of the follow-on reductions effort (with the unspoken expectation among many in the U.S. government that the least popular of these limitations would likely expire).[5]

In an earlier meeting, Dobrynin had vaguely suggested the Soviet Union might entertain additional reductions when negotiations resumed and if the Vladivostok numbers were the official baseline for the agreement. He backtracked in the face of Vance's new proposal. Dobrynin now claimed that he only meant that if a SALT III agreement was concluded during the duration of SALT II, it could include reductions from the original 2,400/1,320 figures, but SALT II would not pre-commit the parties to a different set of ceilings in subsequent negotiations. Dobrynin proposed a variation on this concept, however. He suggested a "declaration of a set of principles" that would govern SALT III but would not be binding.[6]

When Vance met with Gromyko in Geneva on May 18–20, 1977, he opened with the same, informal, "thinking-out-loud" approach he had used with Dobrynin. Gromyko opened by talking about the comprehensive proposal's many failings and why the Americans' quest for "unilateral advantage" was responsible for the current state of the negotiations. Vance then made the same pitch he had made to Dobrynin. Over the next several days, Gromyko expressed skepticism and suspicions about complexity of the U.S. position. The purpose of the SALT II talks had always been to seek a single agreement, and for Gromyko, there was no reason to change that goal. However, he was willing to incorporate some shorter-term restrictions in the broader SALT II agreement in a protocol to the treaty. Gromyko had no specific objection to a Statement of Principles, so long as the core of the agreement remained the Vladivostok framework. On the surface, this formulation did not seem to contradict the original Vance-Warnke guidance. Over time, however, it would erode the idea of SALT III as a rapid follow-on with a very specific end state. SALT II and the Vladivostok framework would grow to fill the gap left by the shrinking SALT III.[7]

Gromyko was less accommodating about the substance of the U.S. proposals. While "on the whole," the proposal was still "to the one-sided benefit of the United States," he acknowledged that the differences between the parties had narrowed. Whereas the comprehensive proposal had been unacceptable and barely worth considering, this time Gromyko said that he and his colleagues had "carefully considered" Vance's presentation before rejecting it. Gromyko's concluding remarks—the substance of which was that a great deal of negotiation remained—seemed to signal that the Soviets were prepared to negotiate on the basis of this revised proposal.[8]

The administration saw the meeting as a middling success. Vance and Gromyko set another meeting for September 1977, this time in Washington. The Geneva delegations immediately began negotiating about issues such as a common database of strategic systems and missile test notifications and the U.S. delegation began probing for more information about Soviet positions and areas of flexibility. Meanwhile, the Carter administration attempted to flesh out more detailed positions and identify which aspects of Soviet forces they wanted to control and how to link them to issues on which they were willing to compromise. Having worked almost continuously on SALT issues across two summits and almost five months, administration principals agreed to wait for the Soviets to make a proposal. For some, like Vance, choosing to wait was expedient, as other responsibilities weighed on him. For others, especially Carter, waiting for a Soviet counterproposal was more personal, and Carter held on to it for longer as the Soviets failed to be forthcoming. Carter's commitment to "good faith" efforts left him feeling entitled to movement on the Soviet side.[9]

Unfortunately for the administration, the primary issues of substance, air-launched cruise missiles and heavy missiles, were also topics about which the Soviets had well-defined views and the ability to defend them by drawing on negotiating history. Because of this, waiting was not likely to prompt changes in the Soviet position. A May 1977 CIA assessment said as much but ran into opposition at the NSC. Of the assessment, William Hyland of the NSC staff derisively commented, "It simply says that the Soviet position is the Soviet position, and nothing more can be expected, except for some minor tuning."[10]

In the meantime, staff work on variations and details of the new concept continued. Initially, the U.S. preoccupation with Soviet heavy missiles continued, particularly as it related to the potential vulnerability of the Minuteman force. One modification to the U.S. position that proved popular with NSC staff was to link the limit on 250 bombers equipped with ALCMs to an identical limit on Soviet heavy ICBMs (instead of the Backfire). Since neither side had any real equivalent to the other's system, this proposal seemed like a way to consolidate two systems that were most contentious and had the highest throw weight.[11]

Between May and September, the Carter administration realized that the aggregate ceiling was far less important than getting control of MIRVs. Andrew Marshall, the director of the Pentagon's Office of Net Assessment, issued several studies during this period that complicated the connection between heavy missiles and Minuteman vulnerability. Marshall was able to convince a variety of officials, from Harold Brown to Vance's own chief Sovietologist, Marshall Shullman, that the SS-19, which used an SS-11 silo that had been deepened and widened to the maximum extent SALT I allowed, posed an equal if not greater threat than the SS-18 heavy ICBM. Outside observers such as Richard Perle supported this view.[12]

By the September meeting, Carter administration officials were convinced that MIRV ICBMs were the primary metric by which strategic stability might be measured. Discussion of plans and packages gradually moved toward creating sublimits within the agreement, either a maximum number of MIRV ICBMs or a lower total MIRV aggregate. Oddly enough, the threat of the SS-19 may have made negotiators' job easier. By making less meaningful the distinction between heavy missiles (which the Soviets said Kissinger had permanently conceded to them) and light missiles, the U.S. position could reasonably shift to the total number of MIRV ICBMs, a metric that was less likely to aggravate the Soviets. On the other hand, the United States had only 550 Minuteman III MIRV ICBMs, slightly more than half the total ICBM force. The Soviet program nearly had this many already, and work underway in the Soviet Union indicated that their program aimed for between 800 and 900 total MIRV ICBMs.[13]

Very few aspects of the U.S. proposal would have any impact on U.S. programs. For instance, to meet the 2,200 limit on total delivery systems, the United States would have to destroy a few mothballed bombers up front and later eliminate some first-generation Titan ICBMs and Polaris SLBMs as new Trident submarines came online in the 1980s. A 2,500-kilometer limit on air-launched cruise missiles would have no impact on the first-generation ALCM-A, which was limited to 1,500 kilometers. The ALCM-B, which would not come online until the early 1980s, would need only minor modifications to bring its range down from 2,800 kilometers. The NSC staff made note of these minor impacts before the May meeting, but it was clear they considered the fact that the plan entailed only minimal changes to U.S. forces a point in the plan's favor.[14]

In August 1977, Vance and Warnke used made this same point when arguing that the United States should stop waiting for the Soviets and take the initiative in the negotiations. They argued that the strategic military differences between most of the options under consideration were negligible, amounting to only 50 or 100 Soviet missiles in most cases. Writing to President Carter, Vance and Warnke identified several packages under consideration and noted that they would do almost nothing to address the threat to Minuteman. They argued that this addressing this specific threat should not be the sine qua non of the treaty, however, as a completed agreement on any of the terms under consideration would establish a precedent for real reductions. A successful SALT II would thus set the stage for significant reductions in SALT III that could address the Minuteman vulnerability problem. Vance and Warnke highlighted their basic point that "the stability represented by a SALT II agreement is as important to arms control as the content of the likely agreement itself."[15]

When Gromyko came to Washington in September, the Carter administration shifted the substance of the debate from comprehensive packages to specific systems controlled by the treaty, relating them to each other in terms of desirability and negotiability. While this added some flexibility to the give and take, it also indulged the Carter administration's propensity for seeking a separate numerical sublimit for every system of concern instead of trying to relate them to the strategic balance. The U.S. objective was to convince the Soviets to accept a reduction in the aggregate total of 2,400 ICBMs, SLBMs, and heavy bombers, as the Vladivostok accord specified, to 2,160 by 1980. The Soviet proposal was for a reduction to 2,250 by the same period closer to the end of the treaty (but a fallback position of 2,200 had been established as acceptable). The U.S. position also sought to reduce the total number of MIRV systems from 1,320 to 1,200, to be achieved by 1980. Finally, the position envisioned possible sublimits and a linking of schemes for heavy missiles (220 in most positions), ALCM bombers (250 or 220), and MIRV ICBMs (750 or 800, depending on verification and counting rules).[16]

The results of the Gromyko visit in September were impressive. They were commonly described in the media as a breakthrough and even engendered confidence that the treaty might be concluded within the year.[17] The first major sign of progress came when Gromyko explicitly expressed Soviet willingness to agree to a MIRV ICBM limit of 820 if the United States would agree to count each

ALCM bomber as one MIRV. Gromyko also provided private assurances about the range of the Backfire and promised not to increase its production rate or to equip it with capabilities that might enable it to perform strategic strikes on the United States. However, he did not include explicit production figures or a signed statement and he did not include geographic constraints in his proposed agreements. Thus, Gromyko came nowhere near the maximalist positions of the JCS and Carter. However, those who were less concerned with the Backfire in general considered this statement to be quite promising and wagered (correctly) that it was likely about 90 percent of what the Soviets would be willing to give.[18]

In his meetings with Gromyko over the next several days, Carter represented himself well on the issues. By the end of the visit, agreement had been struck on the exact framework the final treaty would reflect and most differences were limited to somewhat narrow disagreements on exact sublimits. The United States held fast to its 2,160 aggregate, the Soviets to their 2,250; the United States to its limit of 1,200 total MIRVs, the Soviets to 1,250. The United States conceded its willingness to accept a limit of 820 MIRV ICBMs, contingent on satisfactory resolution of the remaining aggregates and agreement about verification and counting rules. It also offered to include in the treaty a requirement that cruise missiles with ranges above 600 kilometers be deployed only on heavy bombers and to keep the limits on GLCMs and SLCMs with ranges above 600 kilometers and on the 2,500 kilometer range limit on all ALCMs in the three-year protocol.[19]

Once Gromyko accepted the possibility of a ceiling of 820 on MIRV ICBMs, Carter felt comfortable enough to make a compromise offer his staff had developed. MIRV ICBMs were the most threatening type of weapon under consideration in the ceiling of 1,320 on all MIRVs. MIRV SLBMs at that time lacked counterforce capability and round-the-clock availability. They were smaller than other missiles, they had a shorter range, and they were generally less threatening. The Soviets wanted to include heavy bombers with ALCMs in the 1,320 figure as well, and while the United States had yet to agree to this, they were also clearly less threatening than MIRV ICBMs. Thus the sublimit on MIRV ICBMs had downgraded the importance of the 1,320 ceiling on MIRVs, and Carter was willing to make some concessions within that category.

Carter said that the United States would concede to the Soviets the right to heavy missiles, and would include heavy bombers armed with ALCMs as MIRVs in the 1,320 sublimit, but only if the Soviets agree to an additional sublimit of 1,200 on MIRV ICBMs and SLBMs. Special counting rules would apply to these categories, however. Either party could build up to 120 ALCM-equipped heavy bombers that would apply to the 1,320 ceiling. Any such bombers above this level, however, would count against the 1,200 ceiling on actual MIRVs. Neither party would be permitted build more than 1200 MIRVs by building fewer

ALCM-equipped heavy bombers. The logic underpinning the U.S. proposal was nakedly partisan: if the United States wanted to build fewer MIRVs and more bombers (as was likely), they could do so. If the Soviet Union desired a force with more MIRVs and fewer bombers (as they would have in the absence of this proposal), they could not. Carter administration officials felt that Gromyko would go along with the proposal, as long as it was presented neutrally, because it preserved the 1,320 figure associated with the original Vladivostok accord (1200 MIRVs plus 120 ALCM-equipped heavy bombers). It also restored the January 1976 compromise offered by Henry Kissinger that counted ALCM-equipped heavy bombers as MIRVs, although the Carter version did so on terms more favorable to the United States. In both cases, the proposal gave a significant opportunity to Soviet negotiators to save face and claim a victory against the Carter administration's "SALT revisionism."[20]

Gromyko seemed vaguely receptive to the formula Carter presented, if not the exact argument he used to get there, but he would consider it only if the MIRV subceiling were at least 1,250, not 1,200. Carter stood firm and allowed the difference in position to remain after Gromyko's departure. However, administration principals thought they had discovered the key to a winning formula.[21]

The Soviets eventually agreed to the 1,200 limit on MIRVs in exchange for the U.S. acceptance of an aggregate total of 2,250 for the Soviets. Carter administration figures congratulated themselves on their ability to resolve this issue. Unfortunately, as with so many other aspects of SALT II, the administration failed to realize the degree to which they left themselves open to later criticism. They never seemed to consider how to explain this compromise to the public or those charged with ratifying the agreement. In choosing this approach, the Carter administration seemed to forget that it had conceded a principle, that ALCM-equipped heavy bombers were equivalent to MIRVs, that it had previously argued was repugnant and intolerable. These criticisms also generalized to the emerging treaty framework. When the breakthrough framework of around 2,200 aggregates, 1,320 MIRVs/ALCMs, around 1,200 actual MIRVs (and ALCM bombers above 120), and 820 MIRV-equipped ICBMs became public knowledge, public commentators questioned the need for such a complex framework, especially in light of what the public knew about the tripartite structure of protocol, treaty, and statement of principles. More than one commentator compared the emerging framework to a Russian *matryoshka* doll, in which one figure opens up to reveal a smaller figure, which contains another figure, and so on.[22]

Nevertheless, the Carter administration had succeeded in its quest to find an alternative to the inherited Vladivostok framework. Their enthusiasm was short lived. Negotiations decelerated, rather than accelerated, in the months that followed. The shared definitions and verification protocols that the agreement required proved so complex that trying to reach consensus seemed to re-litigate the original compromises. While the parties' positions grew closer on the principle of cruise missile limitations, agreeing to definitions and verification policies and even alliance politics hindered progress to a treaty. As various constituencies within the Soviet Union and the U.S. government came to a better understanding of what the final agreement would control, they became even more defensive about their priorities going into the next arms control negotiation.

Gray Areas

In its first year, the Carter administration contended with a host of issues other than SALT. These issues intersected with the treaty in different ways, sometimes by further straining relations within the administration or with potential allies, sometimes by establishing the technological and diplomatic context in which SALT occurred, and sometimes by contributing to difficulties with defining détente. The increasing thematic sprawl of SALT also intersected with new and controversial weapon systems, such as enhanced radiation warheads (ERWs) and intermediate-range missiles, which were increasingly lumped together with borderline strategic systems like the Backfire under the rubric of "gray area" systems. In some cases, these issues were purely strategic; in others, their significance was their impact on Carter's political standing and his ability to defend his record in 1980. The increasing interconnectedness of these issues and how the Carter administration tried to deal with them reveals a great deal about how and why SALT II developed as it did during this period.

One important administration initiative that proved unexpectedly costly in terms of political capital was the Panama Canal treaty. The United States had controlled the Panama Canal Zone, which had been a U.S. enclave not subject to Panamanian sovereignty since 1903, saw this as a serious point of contention in bilateral and regional relations. Carter and those on the left of the Democratic Party viewed the status quo as a millstone around the neck of the United States, an uncomfortable legacy of an era with weak norms regarding respect for the sovereignty of smaller states. Carter made the quick negotiation of a new Panama Canal treaty one of his highest priorities from his inauguration.[23] The Panamanian government proved a willing negotiating partner, and in the resulting agreement, the United States promised to relinquish control of the canal by 1999 and eliminate the much-loathed canal zone, replacing it with a jointly administered arrangement from which the United States would also withdraw by 1999.[24]

Why was the Panama Canal treaty important to SALT? For one, it was never widely popular. Gathering enough votes in the Senate to ratify it proved costly to the administration in goodwill and political capital. Opponents of the treaty were able to call on simple and powerful arguments that clearly resonated with large numbers of people. As Ronald Reagan was fond of saying, "We built it, we paid for it, it's ours."[25] Carter's rejoinder to this charge was both more abstract and more obscure; he argued that strictly legalistic notions of property rights cannot adequately describe the 1903 treaty and that reforming governance of the canal zone would place U.S. policy in the region on firmer moral footing and demonstrate a commitment to equity that would increase U.S. influence in Latin America rather than decrease it.[26]

The administration should have taken its experience with the treaty as a sign that the politics of treaty ratification are significantly different from the politics of conventional legislation. Public polling, which consistently showed a majority or a plurality against the Panama Canal treaty, indicated that the more Americans learned about the agreement, the more likely they were to support it. But because the legal status of the Panama Canal was a relatively niche issue far from the day-to-day concerns of most voters, public information campaigns were unlikely to move the needle very much. Though Carter administration officials did make some public appeals, once they were outside office, they admitted that their main strategy for ratification relied on changing the votes of individual senators.[27]

The bare success of this strategy (the agreement passed by 68–32 votes, only 1 vote more than the two-thirds minimum) failed to prompt a broader realization that if the administration did not learn how to better tailor its treaties to public opinion or to better influence the public's views, the next treaty might not fare so well. Gregory Treverton, an NSC staffer with ties to Capitol Hill, warned of this possibility as early as 1978. Treverton wrote to Brzezinski (by way of William Hyland) that a number of moderate Republican senators had expressed concern that once they had voted for the Panama Canal treaty, they would be unable to make another unpopular vote on a treaty within the same term and that the terms of SALT II might need to be modified to assure ratification.[28]

Another critical moment for the Carter administration came in June 1977 when the president announced his decision to cancel the B-1 bomber. A long-range, supersonic penetration bomber still in the development phase, the B-1 represented a major leap in performance over the B-52. It incorporated "radar minimization" techniques that presaged stealth technology. The program was also hugely expensive and was plagued with cost overruns without even being close to production. The cost per plane had risen from $40 million in 1970 to over $100 million in 1977. These rapid price increases had turned the B-1 into a perfect symbol for Defense Department waste and overspending. During the campaign, Carter repeatedly criticized Pentagon spending, citing the B-1 among other programs, and promised to cut defense spending overall. In June of 1977,

Carter had yet to cut almost anything substantial from the Defense budget and the B-1's problems seemed to have increased. The B-1 was a logical target for a significant cut.[29]

Carter explained his decision primarily in terms of budgets, costs, and benefits. According to Carter, the B-1 bomber simply cost too much yet provided too little in the way of capability. Instead of funding the bomber, Carter announced a far less expensive plan to refurbish the B-52 and equip many of them with long-range ALCMs designed to overwhelm Soviet air defenses. Commentators have noted that Carter was nearly "enamored" of the cruise missile and its promise in terms of cost and capability. His decision about the B-1 likely increased his commitment to the cruise missile over the next three years.[30]

Allies received the decision well and largely concurred with it, and the support of Secretary of Defense Harold Brown muted criticism from within the Pentagon. Anticommunist hawks in Congress and the emerging anti-détente cohort led by Nitze, however, savaged the administration for the decision. Criticisms centered on accusations that Carter had failed to think strategically. The B-1 bomber and the cruise missile were not binary choices, they argued; one could be armed with the other, creating a far more capable platform. The Soviets also seemed to agree on the formidableness of both systems, especially together, prompting accusations that the administration was not only "soft on defense" but was also engaged in "unilateral arms control" by depriving itself of an effective bargaining chip before the United States had the chance to play it.[31]

Carter's reasons went beyond the cruise missile, however. When the 1980 election revived criticism of the decision, anonymous administration allies leaked information to the press that Carter's decision was also informed by the knowledge that the stealthy advanced technology bomber (later the B-2) was only about a decade behind the B-1 in the research and development cycle. Had Carter been more able to talk about the advanced technology bomber program and its potential to operate in Soviet airspace almost unfettered, the cancellation of the B-1 might have seemed even more justified, those sources argued. In order to quell speculation and create a "firebreak" against further leaks around the highly classified program, Harold Brown held a press conference confirming the existence of the program and said that it indeed featured "a device" that could defeat Russian radar. The disclosures only stoked outside criticism, however, as critics accused the Carter administration of sacrificing a vital national security secret for the sake of political expedience.[32]

This was not the only time controversy emerged about classified information. Following reports of the breakthrough framework in September 1977, congressional committees requested classified briefings in order to get exact details as to what the administration had agreed. Secretary of State Cyrus Vance delivered

most of the briefings in this case. These briefings proved somewhat contentious, although as is the case with many congressional inquiries they tended to
devolve into complaints over process and allegations that the administration was
withholding documents instead of explicitly taking issue with the substance of
Vance's reporting. The most vocal criticism came, predictably, from Senator Jackson, and, later, through Richard Perle, who took issue with the decision to abandon serious reductions in Soviet heavy missiles. Although Jackson was the first
to sound the alarm about the threat the SS-19 posed, it was not clear what they
would have done any differently, and the issue went dormant. In November 1977,
shortly after the briefings concluded, Paul Nitze held one of his quarterly press
conferences on behalf of the Committee on the Present Danger. This conference,
however, was different from his usual presentation. Though usually specific, this
press conference surpassed all Nitze's previous press events. He recounted exact
numbers, specific details about U.S. negotiating positions and Soviet counterof-
fers, and information about the sequence of events at the negotiating table over
the previous ten months, and offered his opinion about why these were almost
universally bad. Never before had such detail about the nascent SALT II agreement been presented to the public.[33]

Strenuous objections and accusations of foul play followed. Those in the
room naturally had to wonder if this information was classified and if Nitze was
deliberately revealing it. If it was not secret, how could Nitze know it when none
of their usual sources had the same information? Carter administration officials,
including Harold Brown and the president, believed that Nitze had abused the
access to information his position as a part-time consultant with the CIA gave
him, though both seemed to agree that there was little to be done about it without
making the situation worse.[34]

Carter administration allies, either independently or with the support of the
executive branch, attempted to investigate. Senator George McGovern (D-S.D.)
wrote to Nitze's employer asking if he had access to information relating to arms
control negotiations as part of his consulting job and what protocols they used to
prevent their employees from going rogue in this way. The employer responded
that while Nitze had worked on several studies that touched broadly on arms
control, at no time did his consulting work give him access to information about
negotiating positions in SALT II. Fearing for his reputation, Nitze released a
detailed report pointing out that every piece of supposedly privileged information had a citation to open reporting. (He never explained how he distinguished
accurate public reporting from numerous conflicting reports.) Nitze and others,
such as the *Wall Street Journal* editorial page, pointed out that almost every one
of those stories had been leaked by administration officials hoping to make the
Carter administration look good and that administration allies did not become

concerned about leaks until someone critical of the administration aggregated that information and presented it in an unflattering light. Nitze mailed a copy of his report to virtually every major foreign policy figure in Washington.[35]

After this incident, the Carter administration was highly sensitive to leaks in ways that question assertions of discontinuity with the Kissinger days. While the administration was more open about the SALT process than previous administrations had been, it was open only on its own terms and at its own initiative. The Carter administration, like many administrations, became accustomed to the power over information and secrecy the modern national security state made possible. While Congress could exercise its oversight powers, it did so primarily at the sufferance of the executive branch, and its ability to go public with unflattering information was limited by what the Carter administration provided and the willingness of members of Congress to betray the confidence of the executive. When the Carter administration was presented with detailed public criticisms, it tended to focus on how information got out or to question the motives of the sources instead of noting a rising tide of discontent with détente and the impact it could have on SALT II.[36]

Another gray-area system that returned to haunt Carter involved the enhanced radiation warhead, more popularly known as the neutron bomb. On June 6, 1977, journalist Walter Pincus of the *Washington Post*, citing an obscure line item in the budget and some glib testimony in Congress, reported that the warhead design was complete and that production had commenced. The warhead was being fitted to eight-inch artillery shells and the short-range Lance missile. These two systems confirmed suspicions that the weapon was meant for NATO's front lines. The article triggered a firestorm of controversy that lasted nearly a year, touching nerves across the political spectrum and rippling through the Atlantic alliance.[37]

The ERW remains one of the most controversial weapons of the twentieth century. During and after the debate about it, the cultural power of the "neutron bomb" seemed to grow to almost mythical status, capable of annihilating all life in an area while leaving inanimate objects intact. Because it destroyed lives but not property, critics called it "the ultimate capitalist weapon."[38] Unfortunately, as public interest grew, the overheated debate about the weapon became less informative.

The ERW was first and foremost a tactical weapon. Little is known from the unclassified literature about its design,[39] but its effects and the factors that drove its development are well known. In the 1970s, the Soviet Union deployed a new generation of tactical and theater nuclear forces of higher quality and in greater numbers than ever before. Many in Western Europe questioned whether NATO could maintain local nuclear dominance much longer or if, in the age of parity, the U.S. deterrent might grow disconnected from European issues. For decades

NATO made up for its conventional inferiority with the threat of nuclear weapons, but the tactical weapons in Europe were too old and too overpowered. The yields of Europe's nuclear weapons were high in part because tanks, the mainstay of the Warsaw Pact's forces, are resistant to the blast and heat effects of nuclear weapons. In order to use tactical weapons against them effectively, it is necessary to increase yields to a point that they destroy everything in and around the battlefield for miles.[40] Overpowered tactical weapons threatened to deter their own use, potentially giving Warsaw Pact countries an incentive to take non-nuclear risks.

The ERW avoided this problem with highly penetrating neutron radiation. In sufficient quantities, neutron radiation could penetrate a tank's armor and kill the operators inside. To achieve enhanced neutron radiation, scientists had made structural changes to traditional warheads, reducing their blast and heat effects while increasing their neutron output tenfold. The result was an approximately one kiloton weapon with a conventional blast radius (against unarmored targets) of less than 600 meters. But it released enough neutron radiation to kill 90 percent of tank crews at 900 meters.[41]

Radiation poisoning ranks among the grisliest and most painful ways to die in modern warfare, and the enhanced radiation warhead's use indisputable constituted a first-use of nuclear weapon. Questions remained about the ERW's efficacy, particularly as Soviet tanks became better armored and more resistant to radiation.[42] In 1977 and 1978, instead of addressing these problems, the debate devolved into an acrimonious back and forth over nuclear first principles.

The Carter administration entered this toxic atmosphere in the summer of 1977. Within two months after Pincus published his *Washington Post* article, 73 percent of Americans had heard of the neutron bomb; within a year, this figure had risen to 89 percent.[43] Despite the volume of media coverage, only about one-third of Americans knew enough to form an opinion about the weapon. This third split evenly between support and opposition.[44] The issue disproportionately motivated anti-nuclear activists, however. One month after the Pincus story appeared, Senator Mark Hatfield (R-Ore.) introduced an amendment to strip the original line item from the budget. The administration successfully mobilized to stop the amendment, but Carter hesitated to make a public decision about production.[45]

The weapon was even less popular in Western Europe. In March 1978, Dutch peace activists organized a 50,000-person protest and presented a petition in opposition to the neutron bomb to their Parliament with over one million signatures. The Dutch Parliament passed a formal resolution of opposition to the weapon's production days later.[46] In West Germany, where later polls showed opposition to the neutron bomb at nearly 70 percent,[47] Chancellor Helmut Schmidt faced an uprising within both his coalition and his Socialist Party. What had begun as a debate about the ethics of an exotic new weapon and its role in the nuclear architecture transformed into an alliance problem.

Schmidt, threatened by the left wing of his party, wanted the United States to make a unilateral decision to produce the weapon and would not accept it in his territory unless other NATO countries would also do so. The Carter administration did not want to take the heat for producing the weapon unless it could couch the decision in one taken on behalf of NATO. Schmidt proposed that the United States link ERW production to a reduction in the number Soviet tanks or to some other regional arms control issue while at the same time working on a position on deployment. The Carter administration was receptive to connecting it to a Soviet system but also wanted to be able to conclusively close the issue.[48]

Turning the ERW production decision into an alliance issue bought the Carter administration some time, but it would not go away. Throughout 1977, Carter fought additional attempts from Congress to defund the program. Soviet statements made sure that the ERW never faded from public view. They decried the threat of "a new arms race" and claimed that the issue could threaten SALT II. By January 1978 the administration had an alliance package ready: production would commence, but in the two years before ERWs would be ready for deployment, the United States would negotiate with the Soviet Union, offering to forego deployment if the Soviets would agree not to deploy their SS-20 intermediate-range missile, the most forbidding component of the new generation of Soviet theater nuclear forces. This plan would be announced as part of a joint allied statement in which the rest of the alliance would commit to accepting the weapons if negotiations failed to produce anything.[49] The proposed statement combined specific commitments at the alliance level to deploy the weapon only if arms control talks failed. Countries such as the Netherlands and Belgium that had tenuous pronuclear majorities were ready to make private assurances that under the correct circumstances they would accept the weapon onto their territory.[50]

NATO seemed on the brink of a consensus in March 1978. But at the last minute, Carter, who had not followed the exact details of the deal as it had taken shape in the preceding months, objected. The president summoned Brown, Vance, and Brzezinski to his home in Georgia, where he stated his basic objection to approving the production of a weapon that no other country had specifically requested. To Carter, bearing the political cost of authorizing production without being able to deflect some of the responsibility to NATO seemed unfair. Carter's advisors were blindsided and unanimously advised against stipulating that NATO countries request the ERW because it would sacrifice the administration's accumulated goodwill, trust, and political capital within the alliance. When Helmut Schmidt was informed of the president's objection, he held fast to his position, as his political calculus had not changed.[51]

Left with few options, Carter punted. On April 7, 1978, he announced he would neither cancel nor approve production but would instead "defer" it, freezing the program in its current state and retaining the ability to produce the weapon at a later date. Even the usually deferential Vance had difficulty defending the president's actions in his memoir:

> Up to the point of the March 18 memorandum [enumerating the NATO statement and decision], the president had followed the unanimous advice of all his senior advisers, had signed all the letters and checked all the right boxes on the decision memoranda. But evidently in his mind, all these actions had been steps in a consultative process, not a final commitment to a particular outcome. . . . At that moment [seeing the memorandum], I can only surmise that the president's innermost self rebelled and he rejected the logic of the previous six months of arduous negotiations within the alliance.[52]

Brzezinski largely agreed with Vance's analysis of Carter's position. He believed that Carter could not get past the sense that paying the political price for production was "unfair." The fallout within NATO was considerable and the decision was not well-received in the United States.[53] Repairing damaged relationships within the alliance occupied the remainder of the Carter administration.

The ERW affair repercussions were considerable. First, it proved an abortive but instructive dry run for the NATO dual-track decision of 1979 (discussed in the next chapter). Carter's advisors subsequently paid much closer attention to modernization issues related to theater nuclear forces. They also realized that public dissatisfaction with nuclear weapons and savvy Soviet propaganda could seriously hobble attempts to maintain NATO as a nuclear alliance.[54] Less than two months later, in June 1978, Carter issued PRM-38, a presidential memorandum that directed the NSC to develop options for increasing theater nuclear force capabilities within NATO and possible ways to include such forces in future arms control negotiations.[55] After ERW, the style of the European nuclear balance (that is, its political and public ramifications), aligned with its military and strategic substance, and it became increasingly clear that only a combined diplomatic-military strategy could maintain the alliance's nuclear credibility and strategic stability in the long term.

Ultimately, the Pershing II and Tomahawk GLCM probably fit this purpose better than the ERW could, but unfortunately for NATO, the mishandling of the ERW decision made the task of preserving the alliance through such an ordeal more difficult. In addition, it was difficult to organize a new consensus on theater nuclear forces immediately after blowing up the previous one. The episode likely gave the Soviets the false impression that they had more leverage over NATO than they really did. Indeed, considering the Soviet perspective, the ERW debate of 1977–78 strongly resembles, at a smaller scale, Soviet attempts to derail the deployment of the Pershing II and Tomahawk missiles to NATO in 1983: exploiting political discontent and nuclear fears, threatening the progress of broader arms control initiatives, and trying to drive wedges between NATO members.

The ERW episode, Soviet advances in less-than-strategic nuclear warfare, and NATO plans for theater nuclear forces modernization all contributed to shifts in the shape of the nuclear balance that were occurring at the global and regional levels in the 1970s. Though the Carter administration's work to address gray-area systems took place out of the public view, it speaks to the mutability of the nuclear outlook in this period. This mutability was belied by the stability SALT purported to provide.

The deployment of the SS-20 was a watershed event in the development of Soviet nuclear forces. Most Soviet intermediate-range missiles predated the SS-9 and SS-11 ICBM force. These missiles, such as the SS-4 and SS-5, were lumbering and vulnerable, though not to be discounted entirely. Since the late 1960s, U.S. intelligence analysts had realized that the design and location of some SS-11 fields indicated an intention to mitigate deficiencies in Soviet first-generation theater nuclear forces. In other words, a significant portion of the Soviet ICBM force, which the United States believed had been designed to be directed against itself, was in fact designed to support "peripheral missions" that would strike targets on the far edges of Europe and in China. This role is usually covered by medium- and intermediate-range missiles, but the fact that the Soviets had invested in making SS-11s to cover such missions suggests that they had very low confidence in these first-generation missiles.[56]

This aspect of the SS-11's mission certainly explained why the Soviets were so concerned with "third parties" throughout the first SALT negotiations and why they believed that the raw number of missiles they had did not adequately represent the weakness of their strategic position. When the Soviets modernized their theater nuclear forces and introduced the new generation of MIRV ICBMs in the mid-1970s, this set the stage for a significant shift in the nuclear balance. Whereas the Soviet force of stunted and inaccurate SS-11s had previously been split across several missions, the formidable SS-19s and SS-17s that replaced them were clearly capable of a more specific mission and were targeted almost exclusively at the United States.

So-called peripheral and regional missions did not disappear, so how did the Soviets plan to perform these missions after removing them from their central strategic forces? The answer came in the form of the SS-20 intermediate-range missile, a quantum leap in quality and power over the first Soviet missiles. Its range was substantially higher than its predecessors, and it could be deployed on a truck-like transporter-erector-launcher. It had a MIRV final stage that was capable of delivering three 150-kiloton warheads. When U.S. observers considered the SS-20 in light of the split missions of the SS-11, some wondered if each SS-20 that appeared in Europe or on the border with China indicated that an SS-11 or one of its successors had been taken off a regional mission and was pointed at the United States. If SALT had achieved parity when the SS-11's job was split, what did it mean when its successor's job was consolidated to target the United States almost exclusively?[57]

Such a formulation overstated the strategic situation in the late 1970s. The Soviets likely never completely abandoned regional missions for their central strategic forces, and certainly the United States continued to upgrade its strategic forces during the 1970s. But that planners and intelligence officials had to consider such possibilities helps explain why changes in attitudes toward détente in 1979–1980 received less resistance from within the U.S. government than might have been expected. However, the question remains why the Soviets built so many SS-20s beyond what they had previously seemed to think was necessary for their in-theater forces. Several theories exist, but the most likely reason for the rapid buildup and deployment of the SS-20 was the appointment of Dmitri Ustinov as minister of defense in 1976. Ustinov's appointment was a departure from the longtime practice of appointing generals as minister of defense. He was an engineer with deep ties to the Soviet design bureaus responsible for research and development. When he was appointed, he had been a member of the Politburo for more than a decade and was a member of the highly influential Defense Council. He was known as a skillful bureaucratic infighter.[58]

As an engineer rather than a soldier, Ustinov was often more responsive to the desires of the Soviet research and development apparatus than the Soviet General Staff was. Ustinov was obsessed with building solid-fueled missiles to compete with the United States, such as the SS-16, but this design's third (intercontinental) stage proved to be fatally flawed. The SS-20 was little more than the first two stages of the SS-16, however, was extremely promising. Its range, payload, and mobility made for a formidable weapon. When the Politburo cancelled the SS-16, an increase in the production of SS-20s may have been Ustinov's consolation prize.[59]

Verification and Compliance

In addition to determining exact force levels, negotiators also had to work out regimes for verifying them. Whereas an open-ended reliance on the phrase "national technical means" was sufficient for SALT I, the complexity and duration of SALT II meant that both sides had to commit to an explicit understanding of terms that previously only used in a general sense, such as "national technical means" and "deliberate concealment." These debates became more numerous and intense as force levels became settled. It might have been expected that verification issues would cause some delays, as the parties could agree only on how to measure specific systems after agreeing on which systems to limit. But the scope and intensity of the debate about verification shows that other forces were at play. At that point, the concept of treaty verification was still fluid and its relationship to similar activities such as espionage and sovereignty issues was unclear. Within the U.S. government, the bureaucratic politics of verification were still handled on an ad hoc, issue-by-issue basis. Between the superpowers, *how* to negotiate verification protocols and what standards of knowledge they required had yet to be resolved. The roots of the basic concept and the modern politics and practice of treaty verification can be traced to the provisions of SALT II.

In contrast to the pattern of establishing force levels before beginning to talk about verification, the U.S. government usually focused on the question of verification while it developed its negotiating positions. MIRV verification was the issue policy makers grappled the longest with. Part of the reason SALT I failed to address MIRVs was the concern that the difference between a single-warhead and a MIRV-equipped missile was not observable inside a silo without on-site inspections. This idea was a virtual nonstarter. As frightening as the new generation of Soviet ICBMs was to the U.S. government, its exact characteristics actually helped ensure some measure of verifiability, so long as both sides could agree to certain parameters.[60]

The Nixon and Ford administrations developed several schemes to verify and distinguish among MIRV missiles, but they were limited by the fact that the new Soviet missiles were not widely deployed. Over time, they discovered that Soviet MIRV missiles were routinized and detectable, a fact that eliminated many of the "hard cases" both administrations had been developing rules to prevent. Eventually the United States staked out a position that stated that once either side tested a MIRV-equipped missile, all subsequent missiles of that type would count as deployed MIRVs. The Soviets eventually accepted this position, but only after attaching demands for U.S. concessions on verification and other rules that the United States refused to accept. Despite the failure to reach agreement, the Soviets had admitted such a principle could be acceptable.[61]

The critical feature for distinguishing which missiles had MIRV capabilities was silo modification. If the Soviets developed a MIRV that could fit on an SS-11, the process of removing the old reentry vehicle and replacing it with the new one would be relatively short and might not be detected by satellite. However, the Soviet Union designed new *missiles* to go with its new reentry vehicles. These missiles were in most cases wider (and sometimes longer) than the ones they intended to replace. They often incorporated improvements in targeting and command and control that required extensive (and detectable) modifications to existing silos. Oftentimes the silo would have to be widened before it could accept the new missile. These activities created a window through which MIRV verification rules could be applied: if every missile tested with MIRVs required significant modifications to a silo, the United States could keep much closer track of just how many MIRV-equipped ICBMs the Soviets had deployed.[62]

The Soviet contribution to these and other verification discussions illustrated the gulf between how the two sides conceived of verification. They resisted the idea that once a missile had been tested with MIRV, all missiles of that type would count as MIRV, because SS-17s and SS-18s had single-warhead variants they had already deployed. Such a rule would turn these missiles into a dead weight loss or require expensive replacements. But the Soviets also believed that a principle was at stake. Whenever the U.S. side tried to argue for specific rules on counting systems or imposing collateral constraints on how MIRVs could be deployed, the Soviets pointed to the language of SALT I as adequate and not in need of improvement. SALT I prohibited "deliberate concealment measures that impede verification by national technical means." This was a negative prohibition. From the Soviet perspective, the United States could count MIRVs however it wanted. As long as the Soviets did not deliberately impede U.S. efforts to verify the treaty, they had fulfilled their obligations. But a rule that would force them to make changes to their otherwise-compliant planned deployments just to meet verification requirements made the Soviets react as if they thought the United States wanted its homework done for it.[63]

Whenever the United States suggested potential rules for verification, the Soviets treated them like any other part of the negotiation and would only move from their position in exchange for concessions, usually with regard to force levels. The Carter administration resisted such efforts, in large part because it believed that its proposals were not self-interested but mutually beneficial. Carter officials could not categorically refuse to bargain about verification issues, though. They did not foresee that the idea of verification, and its post-negotiation corollary, compliance, were fast becoming issues of principle for many SALT-watchers, especially in Congress.[64]

Though Senator Jackson's paper had issued cryptic warnings about increasing concerns about verification issues, the administration was not forced to come to terms with the sensitivity of the issue until December 1977, when former secretary of defense Melvin Laird published an essay in *Reader's Digest* entitled "Arms Control: The Russians Are Cheating!" Laird laid out the case that the Soviets had engaged in repeated violations of both the ABM treaty and the Interim Agreement. Laird claimed that the Ford administration had been so enamored of arms control that it refused to admit these violations for fear of endangering SALT II. Laird's case was far from a "slam dunk" did not make a completely compelling case; many of his charges involved obscure radar configurations or perpetuations of the myth that the SS-19 violated SALT I's prohibition on upgrading light ICBMs to heavy status.[65] However, the article triggered renewed interest in compliance issues in Congress, particularly in light of Laird's argument that it was unwise to rely solely on those who negotiated treaties to also report on implementation.

Carter administration officials tried to respond to this sudden interest with some success. Classified briefings on the state of the negotiations cleared the air somewhat, but they also created some problems, such as leaks or greater chances for hurt feelings among members of Congress. For instance, when Vance justified dropping restrictions on heavy ICBMs by pointing to the SS-19, he gave the impression that a comprehensive assessment had concluded that the SS-19 had equal or greater counterforce potential. Congress requested the assessment, which did not exist. Instead of admitting that these conclusions about the SS-19 came about through a diffuse series of disconnected reports and briefings by a handful of minor officials, Secretary Brown instructed Walter Slocombe to write a one-page memo that read more like a declaration than an objective analysis. When the memo was the extent of the documentation Members of Congress received, a number of them were understandably displeased.[66]

Following the publication of Laird's article, Vance and Warnke commissioned reports on compliance with existing treaties and verification capabilities for the SALT II treaty. Because Laird had raised the issue of compliance so publicly, the debate had to be conducted at two levels, both unclassified and classified. Both the Pentagon and the intelligence community were hesitant to report on almost anything publicly for fear of revealing the extent and limitations of U.S. national technical means. The reports also faced resistance from the Department of Defense, some of whose officials objected to the implication that the consultations resolved any misunderstandings and that there had therefore never been any violations. While the issues involved might seem minor, they argued, many were quite ambiguous and were not suitable for definitive pronouncements. There was no reason to believe that the Soviet Union had been unaware of what their actions entailed it was always possible they might be f systematically testing the boundaries of the agreement. These officials feared that adopting a conciliatory tone in the first few years might establish a precedent of comity that would be difficult to break from in the event of more significant transgressions. Officials throughout the government worried that the unclassified version of the report might not make a strong enough case for compliance, as the most powerful national technical means systems (and therefore those most able to prove or disprove allegations of noncompliance) are usually the most classified.[67]

The compliance and verification reports arrived in Congress and quieted concerns that the legislative branch was being left out of the loop, even though SALT's most fervent critics and defenders both saw what they wanted in them. Administration officials failed to realize how limited their ability to conduct an open debate on verification was, however. Vance and Warnke were adamant that national technical means capabilities would have to be better known to the public in the future if SALT II were to pass, but these capabilities were controlled by the civilian and defense intelligence agencies, which did not see treaty verification or openness about their capabilities as their primary mission. The reports also had limited impact on public opinion. According to a March 1978 poll, two-thirds of the public (including 61 percent of Democrats) did not believe the Soviet Union could be trusted to live up to a SALT II agreement. To their credit, Carter administration officials took the unprecedented step of declassifying the fact that satellite imagery was one of the primary tools of national technical means, especially with regard to SALT I, but this process was intense and time consuming.[68] As SALT II grew more complex, questions were asked about verification capabilities beyond satellite and the Carter administration was limited in its ability to answer.

These episodes illustrate the unsettled nature of the verification concept in this period. Even as the politics of verification began to fall into a more predictable pattern, important outliers remained. The military and the Department of Defense, which approached the issue from the framework of strategic surprise and the fog of war, ordinarily advocated for the strictest possible verification standards, yet with many issues related to SALT II, their positions could be either strict or flexible, depending on their stake in the process. With certain issues such as the definition of a cruise missile's range or whether the numbers of both conventional and nuclear cruise missiles should be limited, they were quite flexible in a self-interested direction. Much of this effect is attributable to the influence of Secretary of Defense Harold Brown, who embodied this duality, especially when it came to cruise missiles. Where he saw a potential problem with verifying an issue that was important to the department, he could articulate enduring, neutral principles of verification that remain in use to this day. But when he saw a threat to a program he believed in, he would unhesitatingly argue for verification principles that served U.S. interests.[69]

Obstacles and Impositions

The autumn and winter after the September 1977 meeting were largely unproductive. Progress did not halt entirely, however. After the United States and the Soviet Union struck an agreement on rough aggregates, a handful of issues dominated the remainder of the negotiations. The primary issues included defining the limitations on cruise missiles, establishing a policy for verifying compliance with those limits, establishing the duration of and exceptions to a ban on new types of land-based ICBMs, determining the extent of the assurances the Soviets would give on the Backfire bomber, and settling disputes over the permissibility of telemetry encryption during missile tests. Three major top-level diplomatic exchanges occurred through mid-1978, in April, May, and July. While the parties reached agreement on a number of outstanding issues over these months, events external to the negotiations and protracted bargaining increasingly strained and slowed the negotiations.

The Soviet- and Cuban-backed Ethiopian army's invasion of Somalia in early 1978 injected further tension into the U.S.-Soviet relationship. Soviet adventurism in the Horn of Africa prompted the Carter administration to make the first of several internal reassessments of its Soviet policy. These reassessments usually boiled down to whether and how to address the issue of linkage. With each iteration, the Carter administration insisted on a balance between competition and cooperation in détente. It admitted that destabilizing or irresponsible Soviet activities threatened this framework, but that on the most important issues of concern, of which SALT II was virtually the only such issue by 1978 and 1979, cooperation was essential and a return to competition was to be avoided at all costs.[70]

In February 1978, SALT began to gain steam again, although from the outside it appeared to do so in an atmosphere of contention. Brezhnev lamented the lack of progress on SALT in a speech in February, touching off a minor back-and-forth between Soviet and U.S. spokesmen in which each side blamed the other for delays and insisted on their own side's readiness to move forward.[71]

In April 1978, Vance traveled to Moscow. The trip was moderately productive. One compromise stood out. Gromyko relatively quickly offered Soviet acceptance of the 1,200 MIRV figure (their previous position had been 1,250) if the United States would accept the aggregate figure of 2,250 (the U.S. position had been 2,160). U.S. officials had already concluded that the MIRV limit was more important than the aggregate, and such a clean trade-off from the Soviets was a rarity. Although he did not have authorization to accept the deal at the time, Vance reacted favorably and correctly estimated that Gromyko's compromise would find a receptive audience in Washington.[72]

The other outcome of the April meeting was made especially important in the aftermath of Carter's decision on the enhanced radiation warhead earlier that month. Since September 1977, the Soviets had pushed for a "nontransfer" provision to the protocol that would apply to GLCMs and SLCMs. The ABM Treaty had a similar provision that banned the transfer of ABMs or knowledge essential to their construction to third parties. In line with their overriding fear of cruise missiles, the Soviets wanted to ensure that this technology stayed out of the hands of third parties, by which they almost always meant West Germany.[73]

Even before Carter's handling of the ERW decision placed NATO on edge, such provisions were controversial. The Soviet proposal applied to both nuclear and conventional cruise missiles. Harold Brown insisted that conventional cruise missiles had enormous military potential against the Warsaw pact and that their sophistication and relative cheapness made them excellent candidates for strengthening the NATO alliance. Brown had no shortage of plans for the cruise missile, and NATO featured in most of them.[74]

The Soviet fear of Germans with cruise missiles had deep historical roots. But much like the question of forward-based systems, the strategic impact of such scenarios was minimal compared to that of central strategic systems. Vance's task was clear: get the Soviets to articulate a strategic (rather than a historical) reason why non-transfer was important, then craft a different, narrower rule to address that concern. Doing so would allow Soviet negotiators to save face while preserving the option of joint NATO deployments.[75]

Vance deftly used this strategy in April, when he convinced Gromyko to agree to a new principle of "non-circumvention." When pressed, the Soviets could not articulate many strategic impacts for the cruise missile that were not also true of forward-based systems. GLCMs in German hands could strike Soviet territory (as was the case with many NATO fighter-bombers) but were too slow to pose a first-strike threat. The most legitimate threat was that cruise missiles could be used in numbers great enough to overwhelm the Soviet Union as part of a coordinated attack. Vance proposed an alternate provision whereby the powers committed not to "circumvent" the treaty through third countries. This language left open the possibility of transfer, so long as the number of transfers was low enough that it would not materially impact the strategic balance. In a world of overkill and many thousands of strategic warheads this would not be difficult. The wording of the provision was such that Soviet leaders could argue that they had foreclosed the possibility that the United States would arm West Germany with enough cruise missiles to achieve dominance outside the terms of SALT II. The United States could credibly argue that the provision would not interfere with U.S. plans for NATO, which focused on the regional balance.[76]

While the April meeting achieved some results, the May and July meetings illustrated the deteriorating trends in the negotiation of SALT II. They were not unproductive, but the tone of these exchanges had clearly begun to deteriorate. Outside events also began to intrude, such as Brzezinski's visit to China in May and U.S. statements on the Soviet's trial of dissident Anatoly Shcharansky in July. Progress during these few months was so halting that even in their public statements, the parties to the negotiations seemed unable to identify any significant new areas of consensus.[77]

The most prominent example of this halting progress was the issue of a ban on new types of ICBMs. The Soviets managed to signal what position they might find acceptable in the end by rejecting all others at length. In the March 1977 comprehensive proposal, the United States had offered to forgo the MX (the U.S. answer to the SS-19, it was big and was loaded with MIRVs but was not "heavy") in exchange for major cuts to the Soviet heavy ICBM force. When the Soviets rejected both this proposal and proposed annual limits on the number of flight tests, the window during which the military services and Congress would accept cancellation of the MX closed. In May 1977, the United States reconsidered its attempts to achieve qualitative limits by proposing a ban on new types of ICBMs. The United States submitted several variations, each structured to only slightly inconvenience the timetable of the MX. The Soviets responded favorably to these proposals but added variants that banned new missiles with MIRVs but not new single-warhead missiles, of which they had at least one in development.[78]

Over the next year, the parties parried with different schemes for limiting new types, the United States trying to establish a precedent without delaying the MX timetable and the Soviets trying to maximize the impact of their proposals on the MX as the cost of establishing that precedent. Finally, in July 1978, Gromyko, who had already proposed several schemes that were not acceptable to U.S. negotiators, tipped his hand. He pointedly asked if the United States would be willing to accept a ban on deployment, but not testing, for the duration of the treaty, with an exception for one missile, with or without MIRV capability, per side. Vance did not immediately answer but interpreted the question as a signal about where the United States ought to direct its efforts. However, the "precedent" this proposal set was worrisome: it wrote a limit into a treaty, but only on the condition that it contain exceptions for all of the systems the parties already wanted.[79]

These meetings went nowhere on the remaining three issues of cruise missile definitions, the Backfire bomber, and the encryption of missile telemetry, and little was accomplished until the end of 1978. The first two of these issues illustrated the problems of "gray area" systems, as each new distinction created another dimension about which to negotiate and plan to verify. Each of these issues also intersected with deeply held beliefs within specific U.S. and Soviet constituencies. These issues were not always quantifiable, which made negotiating to a middle ground more difficult. In each of these cases the United States also overextended itself initially, then persisted in its position until it had resolved almost every other issue, repeatedly rejecting compromises.

In late 1977, Harold Brown began to insist that SALT II make a distinction between conventional cruise missiles and nuclear cruise missiles. Brown feared that the treaty could end up controlling conventional GLCMs in Europe and anti-ship SLCMs and wanted to carve out an exception for them, as they could not alter the strategic balance. Brown also wanted the right to mount long-range (600–2,500 kilometer) conventional cruise missiles on planes other than heavy bombers because they were not technically strategic weapons. Brown's demands effectively doubled the task of the negotiators, however, as now the United States needed to have a position on whether to limit the nuclear and conventional type of each cruise missile, from each platform, and at each range.[80]

So complex did the dozen or so possible categories of cruise missiles under negotiation become by late 1978 that the Soviet Union began to offer compromises to reduce the number of cruise missile classes, even though it had insisted on controlling cruise missiles in the first place. Among other things, Soviet negotiators dropped their insistence on an upward limit of 2,500 kilometers for ALCMs during the treaty period in return for concessions in other areas. The ALCM issue was at the root of the original misunderstandings of the Vladivostok accord, but the Soviets seemed to have lost patience. They could do so with some confidence, as at most the United States could only exceed this figure by 200–300 kilometers by 1985. Still, given all the emphasis Brezhnev and others placed on the need to negotiate based on the Vladivostok accord, this was a significant reversal.[81]

When the parties struck a loose agreement about which types and ranges of cruise missile would be controlled, they discovered that their interpretations of the term "range" varied greatly. The Soviets explained that when they defined a GLCM as having a range of 600 kilometers, they meant that the missile could move under its own power for no more than 600 kilometers in a straight line and that they further defined the range of a cruise missile as the maximum length it had ever traveled in a test environment. After some prodding from U.S. negotiators, the Soviets acknowledged that some allowance could be made for a small reserve that would make up for differences in fuel consumption caused by air pressure or weather conditions. Considering that one of the breakthrough technologies for the modern cruise missile was its ability to hug the earth with terrain-mapping radar, the Soviets were even willing to fall back to a position that allowed for the missiles' climbs and dives, thus defining range "as the crow flies."[82]

Unusually, the Soviet position was the most verifiable and was appealing in its simplicity. It also mirrored the position of the State Department and the Arms Control and Disarmament Agency. Harold Brown and the Joint Chiefs of Staff, however, vehemently disagreed. In addition to flying at very low altitudes, modern cruise missiles were designed to fly on a pre-programmed course that could take them around and between dangerous areas where they were likely to be detected. Because the missile was not meant to travel in a straight line, the distance it was likely to fly would almost always exceed the straight-line distance to its target. Brown convinced Carter that the U.S. position needed to have a coefficient for each class that would translate the range of its likely targets into its "maximum system operational range." These coefficients had to be explicit in the treaty to prevent accusations that United States was trying to subvert them after the fact. Brown's position had some merit, but as with the comprehensive proposal, his specific figures seemed unreasonable on their face. Brown argued that a 600-kilometer cruise missile actually needed a 120 percent range allowance to be militarily useful against targets up to 600 kilometers away—that is, an odometer range of 1,320 kilometers. Only slightly less unrealistic was Brown's demand for a 40 percent allowance for 2,500-kilometer cruise missiles, or an odometer range of 3,500 kilometers.[83]

Not surprisingly, the Soviets found these figures laughable and accused the United States of trying to subvert an existing agreement to gain a unilateral advantage. Damage limitation continued to be the main driver of the Soviet position; in this case, their position was designed to limit the ability of cruise missiles in Europe to strike the Soviet Union. But the Soviets were on better negotiating ground: their position was both more verifiable (a rarity)and closer to the spirit of the rough agreement on a framework than was Brown's proposals. Had Brown's definitions been clear from the start, the United States might have had a more defensible position, but the United States produced exact figures long after agreeing to the basic framework in 1977. Verifying these limits would also have been more difficult, although Brown and the Joint Chiefs had managed to convince Carter and Brzezinski that since only the United States would likely have these weapons during the protocol and for most of the treaty, worrying about verification was the Soviets' job.[84]

On the issues of conventional versus nuclear cruise missiles and the definitions of their ranges, the U.S. position was late in coming out and abandoned the Department of Defense's long-established preference for proposals with the strictest degree of verifiability. Why was the Department of Defense suddenly so willing to embrace ornate, difficult-to-verify controls and content to leave verification standards to the Soviets? The specific influence of Harold Brown is undeniable, as he tended not to approach SALT issues from a precedential or warfighting perspective, but on a weapon-by-weapon basis. The rest of the Defense Department likely supported Brown because they felt that the same standard was being imposed on them with the treatment of the Backfire bomber.

In the case of the Backfire bomber, the United States wanted not just assurances but also constraints, and it wanted them written down. For the Joint Chiefs and the Pentagon bureaucracy, the decision not to treat the Backfire as a strategic weapon was an open wound. Backfire zealots, to whom Carter was sympathetic, wanted controls on where the bomber could be stationed, commitments never to equip it for in-air refueling, and detailed disclosures about the exact range of the bomber under specific conditions when it was carrying a specific load.[85] But the Soviets made clear that relatively vague assurances were the most the Carter administration was ever likely to get, and only outside the SALT II agreement. They might provide a statement on the total number of bombers or the rate of production, but detailed mission profiles were out of the question. When they were pressed for details, the Soviets made clear that they owed the United States nothing in terms of information about nonstrategic bombers and that it was the job of the United States to come to its own conclusions about the Backfire. The Soviets argued that they had no verification obligations for systems that were not included in the treaty. But to the defense establishment, the decision not to include the Backfire was political. It did not change the fact that the bomber *could* have a strategic impact, and therefore the range and capabilities were intrinsically related to the ability to verify the strategic balance in the agreement.[86]

The cruise missile had a far smaller range than the Backfire, yet was included in the agreement. Over the course of 1978 these two issues became enmeshed emotionally and strategically among certain members of the Carter administration. Carter himself drew an explicit connection between the U.S. position on defining the range of a cruise missile and getting better information on the capabilities of the Backfire. Members of the Joint Chiefs argued that if the Soviets wanted to leave questions about the Backfire to the intelligence capabilities of the United States, they ought at least have to live with a fuzzier concept of the range of U.S. cruise missiles.[87]

Unfortunately, the United States had already agreed to exclude the Backfire in the SALT II aggregates and to include limitations on cruise missiles. This made the U.S. position on both of these issues weak over the long term but just defensible enough to postpone a resolution. By November 1978, Brzezinski's faith in Brown's arguments about the cruise missile had begun to wither in the face of Brown's distrust of the Soviet Union. With the help of Vice President Walter Mondale, Brzezinski developed an illustrative scenario. If the treaty permitted conventional long-range cruise missiles to be deployed on nonstrategic aircraft, how long would it be before an unconstrained cruise missile appeared on a Backfire? In that situation, how could the United States know that the missile was conventional? When Mondale and Brzezinski brought this possibility to Brown's attention, he reluctantly agreed to drop his insistence that conventional ALCMs be unconstrained, and together they convinced Carter of the wisdom of this point. This episode illustrates just how shallow the demands for limitations that were only thinly verifiable were. Brown and others subsequently backed away from their insistence on many of the problematic range allowances on cruise missiles, but the lesson was hard-learned: two years had elapsed.[88]

One of the most contentious issues of this late stage of the negotiations was also the most technical and the most difficult to discuss openly: the encryption of telemetry from missile tests. Whenever a ballistic missile was test fired, its designers would outfit many components with sensors capable of broadcasting the activity and status of those parts. Testers then assembled these broadcasts, called telemetry. In the event of a test failure, they could use this information to determine where the failure occurred. This information was understandably sensitive, but if it could be captured with national technical means, it could also yield crucial information about the capabilities of a missile under development. For decades, the United States was able to ring the Soviet Union with listening posts and powerful radar whose primary purpose was to monitor these missile tests and intercept telemetry. These test-monitoring activities, a combination of signals intelligence and measurement and signature intelligence, were among the most highly classified intelligence activities of the United States and provided a level of monitoring capability the Soviets could not match.[89]

Beginning in the 1970s, the Soviet Union began to encrypt some of these telemetry signals so that anyone listening in without the key could not immediately decipher the data. Widespread encryption began with the new generation of Soviet missiles and the number of signals being encrypted per test increased through 1978. The defense establishment and intelligence community reacted with alarm. The United States had dominated the area of measurement and signature intelligence for so long that the specter of losing this edge just as a new generation of Soviet missiles came online deeply concerned many officials.

Under SALT I, telemetry was largely an intelligence problem rather than a verification problem: monitoring missile tests was secondary to counting silos. SALT II changed this calculus. Recalling Soviet claims that the SS-18 was only an upgrade and not a new missile, the United States sought to backstop limits on new types of missiles with a secondary limitation: that the most important metrics of range, thrust, and other variables would not increase or decrease by more than 5 percent within the treaty period. This rule was a critical component of Brown's efforts to introduce meaningful qualitative limitations into SALT, but it greatly increased the task of verification. Whether these factors had changed could not be assessed unless it was possible to observe a missile in flight. And while U.S. intelligence could determine a great deal about a missile by monitoring it passively with radar, few felt that they could verify the 5 percent limit without some telemetry intercepts.

The United States' measurement and signature intelligence capabilities were so highly classified that it was often difficult to broach the subject. For years, the U.S. government forbade its negotiators from even using the word "telemetry," lest the Soviets infer the extent of U.S. capabilities. Initially, the United States tried an oblique approach; it insisted that SALT II explicitly define "national tech-nical means" and thus clarify which types of monitoring were protected from "deliberate concealment." Baffled Soviet negotiators reluctantly cooperated, but the resulting text was inadequate.[90] The issue proved to be one of the least trac-table throughout the entire Carter administration. More than the issues of cruise missiles and the Backfire, the disagreement over telemetry crystallized the par-ties' different concepts of verification.

The draft language prohibited "deliberate concealment measures that impede verification by national technical means."[91] From the U.S. perspective, this defi-nition referred to a set of surveillance technologies that moved out of the realm of espionage, and which both sides agreed not to obstruct. Encrypting telemetry was unprecedented and frustrated a decades-old technique. The United States argued that encryption thus constituted deliberate concealment.

The Soviet perspective viewed national technical means not as a set of sys-tems but as a passive commitment to allow verification. The Soviets argued that the United States could verify the terms of the treaty by means other than intercepting telemetry. Indeed, the Soviets had done so all along, as U.S. telem-etry practices did not encrypt the data but transmitted it at very low power to a highly directional antenna in the area. Intercepting such transmissions is virtu-ally impossible. Telemetry interception could also be used for purposes that went beyond verification, including military planning. Soviet negotiators argued that as long as some combination of systems could show they were in compliance, they had no obligation to expose themselves to U.S. spying techniques. To give away more information than was necessary was not "verification," it was doing the United States' job for them, or worse, granting the United States a "unilateral advantage."[92]

The U.S. measurement and signature intelligence system was so entrenched that it was difficult for defense and intelligence officials to approach missile telemetry without a sense of entitlement. The director of central intelligence, Stansfield Turner, was consistently concerned that SALT II might not be verifi-able if the Soviets were able to encrypt all telemetry. Hawks outside the adminis-tration also insisted that encryption ought to be banned outright. In addition, as congressional oversight of SALT issues increased, encryption became an issue for moderates, such as Senator John Glenn (D-Ohio), who began to express concern about the issue.[93]

In 1977, Warnke extracted a concession from the Soviets about telemetry. They conceded that *some* telemetric data was critical for verification and that each side was entitled to *some* data so they could verify compliance with the treaty. This language made it unlikely that full, across-the-board encryption would be sustained under a treaty. But the Soviets remained cagey; they claimed they could not conceive of a situation in which missile telemetry was the sine qua non of verification. If the United States were to reveal such an example, it would also reveal the extent of U.S. capabilities, something the intelligence community vigorously opposed. Perhaps sensing this reticence, the Soviet military conducted a series of tests in 1978, each encrypting more information than the previous one. The Carter administration believed this was an attempt to "smoke out" the power of the U.S. measurement and signature intelligence enterprise and at the same time set a precedent for acceptable levels of encryption. Each test alarmed intelligence officials, further convincing them of the need to ban encryption and hardening their resistance to the idea of revealing anything.[94]

Once the 5 percent limit on qualitative improvements was established in late 1977, the CIA firmed up its position, maintaining that encryption ought to be completely banned. Vance and Warnke argued that the Soviets would never agree to such terms. According to them, the only hope was to include a statement in the treaty that was ambiguous enough that the Soviets could maintain that they had not given up everything of value in telemetric data but specific enough to give the United States sufficient basis to raise encryption as a compliance issue if it became a problem. Brown and Brzezinski did not expect to get a total ban, but a vague statement was not enough for them. They wanted more explicit descriptions of what was permissible and impermissible. As had been the case with the Backfire issue, Brown and Brzezinski did not want barely sufficient assurances designed to let the Soviets save face. They wanted specifics so that if the United States ever had to raise a verification issue, it would not have to engage in a protracted interpretive debate but could point to a smoking gun. The U.S. position on encryption hardened significantly in 1978, while Soviet negotiators came to believe explicit assurances would create a de facto ban.[95]

Breaking out of the Rut

It was not until the fall of 1978 that Carter administration officials realized that existing approaches endangered possibility that the SALT II agreement could be completed in a timely fashion. The midterm elections of 1978, in which anticommunist candidates won several tough races, made it clear that the tide of anti-Soviet sentiment was rising. Groups such as the Committee on the Present Danger became nationally recognized, if strident, voices on arms control issues. Vance and Carter both began to realize that it was easy to criticize, but difficult to defend an agreement still in negotiation. The longer the agreement took, the more opportunities its opponents would have to attack it, while the administration's detailed rebuttal would have to wait for the final text.[96]

Most of the remaining issues related to cruise missiles, whose politics grew increasingly knotty. The first step towards untangling the mess came in September 1978, when Gromyko offered a compromise: in exchange for accepting the Soviets' strict definition of a 600-kilometer range for GLCMs and SLCMs, he would be willing to eliminate the upper limit of 2,500 kilometers for ALCMs. The limits on GLCMs and SLCMs extended only through the end of the protocol, whereas the limits on ALCMs were in place for the duration of the treaty. The Department of Defense already had plans for ALCMs with ranges greater than 2,500 kilometers, and a blank check to pursue them was an attractive offer which the Carter administration accepted.[97]

Following on this concession, Vance signaled that the United States was willing to split the difference on the U.S. and Soviet demands for a limit on the number of warheads per missile (a quality known as "fractionation") and a limit on the number of ALCMs per bomber. Gromyko abruptly left the United States without responding to these proposals. Gromyko and the Politburo may have sensed that the United States was becoming eager for an agreement. While the Soviets could be coaxed into showing flexibility at the margins, their negotiating strategy still rested on the idea of squeezing as many concessions out of the final stage as possible, which meant halting the momentum.[98]

Vance flew to Moscow a month later. When he arrived, he was dumbstruck as Gromyko actually began walking back the Soviet position on a number of issues on which their differences narrowed. As part of the push for qualitative limitations, the United States wanted to cap the number of RVs per missile at the greatest number with which the missile had been tested prior to signing the treaty. Gromyko offered the United States a choice between an across-the-board numerical limit that interfered with plans to mount ten warheads on the MX, or one that permitted the Soviets to increase the number of warheads on their SS-17s and SS-19s substantially. On other issues, such as a limit on the number of ALCMs per bomber, the United States and the Soviets were able to move their positions closer together but were still not yet in agreement. Regarding telemetry encryption, Gromyko not only walked back the Soviet position but undercut a recent message a senior Soviet diplomat who was sitting next to him had sent only days before.[99]

Vance and Warnke argued there was a connection between encryption and Soviet dissatisfaction with the issue of conventional versus nuclear cruise missiles. But Warnke left government in November 1978, quietly, with little fanfare. The Carter administration's dove bloc grew a little smaller and less experienced after Warnke's departure. Fortunately, Brzezinski and Mondale's vision of a Backfire armed with long-range cruise missiles convinced Carter that with respect to ALCMs, it was preferable to make no distinction between nuclear and conventional cruise missiles. Vance framed the switch as a concession in a meeting with Dobrynin in November 1978 and expressed hope that on other verification issues (i.e., encryption) the Soviets would reciprocate by showing some flexibility.[100]

In late 1978, U.S. expectations ran high. The slogan of "SALT by Christmas" was a bitter irony since it had first been trotted out the previous year, but from November to the December 21st meeting between Vance and Gromyko there were promising signs, including the possibility of a Carter/Brezhnev summit to sign the agreement by January 15th. Carter authorized the concession on nuclear versus conventional ALCMs, hoping to trigger a cascade of compromises on outstanding issues. Abandoning that distinction permitted the United States to accept the strict definition of cruise missile range for all cruise missiles, not just GLCMS and SLCMs. The Soviets also came around on missile fractionation, accepting a limit that froze the number of SS-17s and SS-19s while permitting the U.S. MX to have up to ten warheads.[101] While not a cascade, this was progress.

The Soviets had not completely changed tactics, but for every attempt they made to swing for the fences, they signaled a willingness to agree to a U.S. position. The most critical such concession came at the December 21st summit meeting, when Gromyko offered his own "agreed understanding" on encryption. Instead of agreeing that encryption was impermissible whenever it impeded verification, Gromyko offered a positive formulation, authorizing encryption so long as it did not impede. While this proposal was not perfect from the U.S. standpoint, Vance realized that this concession meant the Soviets had accepted the basic premise of the U.S. position. Vance ordered ACDA's chief technical advisor, James Timbie, to write up a compromise statement that could meet the requirements of both sides. Timbie quickly complied and Vance sent the text to Washington for approval.[102]

Here the talks hit a snag. Only days before the December 21st, 1978 meeting, the Soviets had tested a missile with a level of encryption that had been witnessed only once before (in July of that year). This enraged CIA director Stansfield Turner, who was angry that the administration had abandoned its efforts to ban encryption. Vance had obliquely mentioned the July test as crossing the line of acceptable encryption and Gromyko had obliquely acknowledged the point. These references were no longer enough for Turner, who wanted confirmation of a real-world example of a violation. Brzezinski, trying to placate Turner, instructed Vance to raise the July test with Gromyko again and highlight it as violating the agreed language. He told Vance to rely on the technique of "non-contradiction"—that is, delivering the message without requiring a Soviet response but informing them that a failure to object would be interpreted as an assent.[103]

Vance strongly disagreed, on both tactical and substantive grounds. How was non-contradiction preferable to the vague assurances already given on the subject? Reopening the issue had the potential to threaten what had otherwise been a productive meeting and might foreclose the possibility of a mid-January presidential summit. Vance demanded that the orders come from Carter, who had already retired to Georgia and had not been involved in developing the compromise. Different time zones meant that Brzezinski had to call a testy Carter late at night at his family home. After hearing Brzezinski's summary, Carter affirmed his decision.[104]

Vance delivered the message at what was supposed to be a wrap-up meeting the next day. Gromyko's reaction was not a contradiction, per se, but he hardly allowed the U.S. statement to go unanswered. Returning to his classic dyspeptic form, Gromyko refused to accept anything, saying that the new U.S. position could be used as a pretext to try to ban all encryption in the future. Later, when Vance broached the subject of a presidential summit to sign the agreement, Gromyko made clear that a date could be set only when *all* of the outstanding issues had been resolved. This included obscure issues such as a ban on cruise missiles with multiple warheads (a Soviet hobbyhorse), and a definition of reconnaissance drones that distinguished them from cruise missiles.[105] Insisting on resolving such minutiae before a summit was irregular. Some administration officials speculated that Brezhnev's failing health was part of the problem. In contrast to the SALT I summit of 1972, when Brezhnev had engaged in hours of difficult negotiation with Nixon and Kissinger, the Politburo may have wanted to finalize as much as possible before calling in Brezhnev.[106] Regardless, the promise of "SALT by Christmas" proved twice a lie.

Crawl to the Finish

Another possible reason that Gromyko rejected an early signing summit was that U.S. plans for a January 15th summit had leaked in tandem with plans for Deng Xiaoping to visit the United States later that same month to formalize relations between the People's Republic of China and the United States. Having their summit overshadowed so quickly understandably might have rankled the Soviets. In addition, by holding the finalization of SALT II in suspense, the Soviets likely sought to restrain U.S.-Chinese rhetoric about a common enemy, in which Brzezinski and Deng had previously dabbled. When Deng's China invaded Vietnam, a Soviet ally, in February 1979, the Soviets accused the United States of foreknowledge if not tacit approval of the attack. What the Soviets intended as a temporary suspense became much longer as the Carter administration came to realize the impact of the Deng visit.[107] Linkage found its way back into the SALT debate, but from an unexpected angle.

Carter administration officials expressed slightly more willingness to compromise in the months that followed, but in many areas they saw their approach fail repeatedly before they would consider alternatives. On encryption, the United States still demanded assurances based on specific tests. Twice more the administration tried to force the issue, with identical results. Turner demanded a ban, Brzezinski and Brown developed a compromise based on specifics and non-contradiction, Vance objected, and Soviet negotiators forcefully rejected it.[108]

The issue was resolved in late March, when a team of second-echelon administration appointees, allegedly tired of Turner's obstruction, drafted a letter from Carter to Brezhnev. The letter dropped any mention of specific tests and simply reiterated that *some* telemetry could, and had, impeded verification. Brown, Brzezinski, and Turner objected to this position, but Brezhnev had just rejected a letter that met their standards, so they had few alternatives. These three drafted an informal "note" for delivery to Dobrynin with the official letter. The note mentioned the specific tests and an assurance (which Vance inserted) that the United States would not argue that the treaty disallowed encryption entirely. The Soviet response said that the existing record of communication had resolved the issue satisfactorily.[109]

Gradually, grindingly, glacially, the parties compromised on the remaining issues. They compromised on qualitative limitations, allowing decreases of more than 5 percent in some cases (the blanket 5 percent figure apparently threatened a closely held Soviet test practice of weighing down missiles to shorten their trajectory).[110] Soviet negotiators originally demanded a limit on the average number of cruise missiles per heavy bomber of twenty, which the United States countered with thirty-five. In late 1978, the parties came to 25 and 30, respectively, and in December they proposed 27 and 28. By January 1979, Dobrynin had offered to accept the U.S. figure of 28 in exchange for relatively minor assurances regarding the number of cruise missiles to be mounted on existing heavy bombers.

While complex issues dominated 1978, minutiae dominated 1979. The Soviets wanted the United States to remove tents placed over missile silos to protect maintenance workers in the winter, arguing that they were a "deliberate concealment." The United States wanted the Soviet Union to stop claiming falsely that it could not distinguish between Minuteman II silos undergoing renovations and the more modern Minuteman III. It seemed absurd that these issues would take up weeks or months and dozens of meetings between Vance and Dobrynin, but the Soviets' insistence that essentially every aspect of SALT II be resolved before establishing a date for a signing summit necessitated it. On May 7, 1979, Vance and Dobrynin dispensed with the last of these points and agreed to hold a summit at the earliest practical date.[111]

Conclusion

On June 18, 1979, in Vienna, Carter and Brezhnev signed and exchanged the instruments of the SALT II Treaty. The parties had been negotiating for six and a half years. Neither party negotiated much of consequence during the meeting, but Carter ably solicited the understandings and commitments he needed and provided the unilateral statements and interpretations that backstopped the act of signing it. While doing their version of the same, Soviet representatives asserted that under international law, the treaty would not take effect until it had been ratified by both parties. Carter questioned this assertion, asking why they would not abide by the tradition that signatories have some obligations before ratifying, but his counterparts did not answer him.[112]

The terms of the treaty began with an aggregate of 2,400 strategic nuclear delivery vehicles, of which no more than 1,320 could be MIRV-equipped missiles or heavy bombers equipped with cruise missiles with a range of more than 600 kilometers (but with no upper limit on their range). The first 120 ALCM-equipped heavy bombers were excluded from the MIRV aggregate. After an agreed period to permit dismantlement, the aggregate would decline to 2,250 delivery vehicles, of which no more than 1,200 could have MIRVs, of which no more than 820 could be land-based ICBMs. Deployment of new heavy missiles was banned, which meant that the Soviet Union retained their 308 heavy missiles but the United States forfeited the ability to build the same. Each party was entitled to test and deploy one new type of ICBM during the treaty period, with or without MIRV, though this made little difference for the United States as Carter had already decided, for budgetary reasons, to delay the MX until after 1985. Neither party could equip a missile with more reentry vehicles than the maximum number with which the missile had already been tested (with a few exceptions), and the average number of cruise missiles per heavy bomber could not exceed twenty-eight. The treaty did not mention telemetry, but the negotiating record and "agreed understandings" appended to the document clarified the treatment of encryption according to the general understanding reached in March 1979.[113]

The protocol to the treaty was a paltry thing compared to what it had contained under the original proposal. Originally intended to last three years, it took effect on the date the treaty entered into force and expired on December 31, 1981, roughly two and a half years from the date of signature. The protocol banned, for its duration, the deployment of mobile ICBMs and the deployment or launch testing of GLCMs and SLCMs with a range greater than 600 kilometers. It also banned the testing or deployment of air-to-surface ballistic missiles. The Statement of Principles for SALT III remained but contained little more than a commitment to continue as they had been, seeking to improve strategic stability through verifiable limitations.[114]

On the issue of the Backfire bomber, the Soviets offered the following statement for the record:

> The Soviet side informs the U.S. side that the Soviet Tu–22M airplane called Backfire in the USA, is a medium-range bomber and that it does not intend to give this airplane the capability of operating at intercontinental distances. In this connection, the Soviet side states that it will not increase the radius of action of this airplane in such a way as to enable it to strike targets on the territory of the USA. Nor does it intend to give it such a capability in any other manner, including by in-flight refueling. At the same time, the Soviet side states that it will not increase the production rate of this airplane as compared to the present rate.[115]

Through "non-contradiction," Brezhnev tacitly confirmed the Backfire production rate as thirty per year. Where U.S. negotiators were able to extract more specific figures from the Soviets such as range, they were either contradictory or at variance with U.S. estimates.[116] U.S. officials realized that if they received too many specifics that were clearly wrong, that would call the rest of Brezhnev's statement of assurances into question. Years of efforts to get serious constraints on the Backfire had come to naught.

The Senate still had to ratify the treaty in an atmosphere of rising discontent with détente and Soviet foreign policy. The Carter administration, finally able to begin the work of answering its critics in earnest, of course argued that while the treaty was not perfect, it was a momentous step toward relieving the world of the fear of nuclear war.[117] Yet the practical impact of the treaty was unusual. Its ceilings were such that only the Soviet Union would dismantle anything to avoid the ceilings. (The United States had accelerated the retirement schedule for a few older bombers and submarines.) For all of the treaty's specificity regarding cruise missiles ranges, platforms, and warheads, none of its limitations impacted U.S. programs.

While there is something surreal about negotiating so fervently for an agreement that will not materially impact any weapons program, the vast majority of the stipulations required by Harold Brown, the defense establishment, NATO, or the Joint Chiefs focused on the precedential value of these limitations. Concerns about setting precedents were not unfounded. The protocol was originally designed to create an incentive to negotiate a successor to SALT II; its provisions were set to expire relatively soon as an inducement to negotiate quickly enough to lock them in. Entities with long institutional memories, such as the Joint Chiefs of Staff, may have looked past the modern era of SALT to the unilateral test ban moratoria of the late 1950s and early 1960s. These groups feared that when the protocol expired, the Soviets would mount a propaganda campaign to extend it without any Soviet concessions in exchange or that they would let it expire and cause significant damage to the U.S. public image and freedom of action. In such an event, the United States would have the worst of both worlds, losing both an initial technological lead and losing political and diplomatic capital when the limitations expired.[118]

Despite assurances from Carter that the protocol would not be extended *in toto* without equal or greater concessions, Soviet negotiators continued to place protocol extension first on their agenda for SALT III. Indeed, considering that the GLCMs and SLCMs the protocol limited were closely related to NATO issues, it is not difficult to imagine a Soviet pressure campaign designed to drive a wedge between alliance members and extend the protocol.[119] The Soviets had pioneered such a campaign against the neutron bomb. While the provisions of the protocol might seem secondary to those of the treaty proper, it is worth recalling Gromyko's September 1978 concession: he would allow an increase in the range of ALCMs if that meant that GLCMs in Europe would be less powerful. In the Vladivostok agreement of 1974, ALCMs were among the Soviets' highest priorities, as indicated by the counting rules for MIRV-equipped ALCMs, but by 1978, they had taken a back seat to the threat of GLCMs stationed throughout NATO.

But the protocol was dated from the treaty's entry into force; if the treaty was not ratified, the protocol would never take effect (unlike the treaty itself, to which, as Carter noted, signatories customarily still had obligations). Ratification was the first step to knowing the treaty's true impact, and ratification was a herculean task in itself. It is necessary to explore the context within which the ratification debate occurred in order to understand the treaty. As the next chapter will explore, the arms control process continued to influence policy issues throughout the government, particularly nuclear strategy, NATO policy, and defense spending. Furthermore, 1979 and 1980 were the turning point for the electoral importance of arms control, becoming a signpost for where one stood on détente and the future of the Cold War.

"SUMMARY—BLEAK": THE UNRAVELING OF DETENTE

The public statements at the time of the signing of SALT II were optimistic. Ratification seemed a relatively minor concern, and while neither side seemed to think that the age of nuclear competition had ended, Carter and Brezhnev spoke positively about the future of the SALT process.[1] However, over the next eighteen months, a succession of domestic and international events transformed the ratification process into a punishing gauntlet. Events such as the fall of the shah of Iran and the Soviet invasion of Afghanistan intersected with issues related to SALT and drew upon the administration's political capital. Many of the trends that made SALT so vulnerable had been simmering below the surface of the Carter administration as much as a year before the agreement was signed. SALT's growing complexity and thematic drift influenced a number of administration initiatives from 1978 onward, including NATO politics, nuclear strategy, and defense budgets. As these initiatives gathered steam through the remainder of the Carter administration, SALT II was negatively influenced by the impact of international events and election-year politics.

When he returned from the Vienna Summit, Carter drove from the airport to the Capitol Building to address a joint session of Congress and a national television audience. Although the summit had ostensibly been a triumph, Carter's remarks were measured. He described the SALT II agreement as the latest step in a process of coming to terms with nuclear arms that every president since Harry Truman had contributed to. But Carter made clear that the arms competition and arms control efforts would both continue even if the treaty were to be ratified. "With or without SALT II," Carter said, the United States would still have to "modernize and strengthen our own strategic forces." SALT II made "this task [strategic modernization] easier, surer, and less expensive," and a ratified SALT II treaty was "the absolutely indispensable precondition for moving on to much deeper and more significant cuts under SALT III."[2]

Carter described the need to ratify the treaty in stark terms. He described the possibility of a world with no SALT II agreement. Without SALT, the Soviets could deploy so many warheads that no land-based deterrent could ever be safe. Without SALT's verification provisions, the Soviets could make the leap to encrypting all of their missile test data. Carter stated that "it would be the height of irresponsibility to ignore" the consequences of a failure to ratify. Framing the ratification decision as he did would make it as difficult as possible for critics of the agreement to vote against ratification when the time came.[3]

Carter's swift submission of the treaty to the Senate could do little to change the normal pace of that institution. Hearings take time to arrange and the traditional August summer recess was quickly approaching. The ratification debate played out in many news cycles during the slow season for political reporting. Three separate committees had to consider the treaty and submit their reports to the Senate for review and approval: the Senate Committee on Foreign Relations, the Senate Committee on Armed Services, and the Senate Select Committee on Intelligence. Three debates characterized the ratification phase: about the agreement's diplomatic impact, about its military significance, and about its verifiability.[4]

Congress Weighs In

Carter administration officials expected ratification to be a tough sell in Congress and were prepared to shepherd the agreement through the process rather than leave it to the Senate's leadership. The administration hired several experienced Washington hands to help coordinate its efforts, including Lloyd Cutler, a DC lawyer in private practice who had deep informal ties in the government and across party lines. While the administration did try to develop a foundation of support in the public with a coordinated media campaign, its strategy for getting the treaty through committee relied mainly on lobbying individual senators and defeating "killer amendments." These amendments, instead of clarifying or interpreting elements of the treaty, sought to substantively alter provisions such that it would have to be taken back to the Soviets for renegotiation and re-signing. Hawkish critics of SALT II threatened to add a number of such amendments.[5]

Despite their format, in which the committees solicit outside testimony, congressional hearings serve the arguably more important role of allowing members of Congress to sound out their positions in response to the administration's testimony. This was evident at the hearings for SALT II ratification. As the Senate Foreign Relations Committee hearings began, Secretary of State Vance presented the administration's view first. In his testimony, Vance presented the usual arguments for SALT: it was important to U.S. allies, it would impose more limitations on Soviet behavior than on the United States, and it would curb the costly and unsustainable arms race. Later, Secretary of Defense Brown assured the committee that unrestrained competition was not in the defense interests of the United States and would threaten deterrence, whereas the SALT II treaty would strengthen deterrence and make U.S. objectives more achievable.

Administration officials received a relatively warm welcome and were treated politely and deferentially by both critics and boosters on the committee. The sternest criticism in the early days of the hearings came from well-known doves. Senators George McGovern and Edmund Muskie both pointedly criticized the treaty for failing to achieve more substantial reductions. As criticism of the treaty increased, critics such as McGovern began to backtrack, concerned that the choice would not be between an imperfect SALT II and a better SALT III but between SALT II and no treaty at all.[6]

Minority Leader Howard Baker was a pivotal voice on the committee but kept his options open to start. Addressing the committee's witnesses, Baker said, "I would like to begin . . . by agreeing with you. The question really is whether we are better off with or without this treaty. I accept that formulation. . . . In my mind, it is not a question of whether I support or whether this committee supports a treaty. It is a question of whether we support this treaty." While refusing to position himself in opposition to the entire SALT process, Baker also sought to increase his flexibility by lowering the stakes of the ratification debate: "We are not here to decide whether the world is going to be faced with nuclear holocaust. We are here to determine whether this treaty better serves the purpose of diminishing that prospect." Baker's subsequent questions were not encouraging: they focused entirely on the imbalance between the Soviet Union and United States in ICBM throw weight.[7]

Next came the administration's supporters. The previous three SALT heads of delegation, Paul Warnke, U. Alexis Johnson, and Gerard Smith, all testified in favor of the treaty and spoke in favor of the process that produced it. Representatives from the Federation of American Scientists, one of the original supporters of nuclear arms control dating back to the 1950s, also endorsed the treaty as a critical step in eliminating the threat of nuclear catastrophe that the federation had so memorably illustrated with its Doomsday Clock. With a few exceptions among conservative publications, this testimony was well received in the media and was treated as an unsurprising recitation of "common sense."[8]

As the critics of SALT II began to testify, however, their arguments received increasing attention. They also became increasingly focused; what had previously been relatively diffuse, uncoordinated criticism began to center on several points. Nitze led the charge. In his testimony, he explained that his main objection to the treaty was that it did not halt the overall negative trends in the strategic balance. Despite the requirement that the Soviets eliminate some strategic systems, Soviet forces would still increase qualitatively and quantitatively from 1979 to 1985. Nitze believed that the superpowers were at rough parity in 1979 but that after that a gap would form that favored the Soviets. In a break with many of SALT II's later critics, Nitze downplayed the question of verifiability, even though many centrist observers such as Senator John Glenn still considered it an open question. Some treaty supporters such as Senator Joseph Biden (D-Del.) tried to use Nitze's points on verification to respond to other critics, but Nitze's argument was anything but a mark in the treaty's favor. Nitze had argued that the treaty would be verifiable only if it guaranteed that cheating on a scale that would alter the strategic balance in a militarily significant way would be detected. While Nitze did not believe that SALT II necessarily met that standard, he argued that the increase in capabilities already allowed under the treaty meant that any cheating the Soviets might contemplate was not likely worth the effort, as there was a very good chance that the changes the treaty permitted would alter the strategic balance in a militarily significant way in the Soviet Union's favor. Nitze's point was that the aggregates were too high and that they too permissive toward the Soviet program.[9]

While Nitze's testimony raised alarms in some quarters, numerous senators wondered how significant his concerns really were. The trends might be bad, but would they not be worse without the agreement? And the treaty did not stop the United States from developing its primary system for addressing the imbalance, the MX. When he addressed these concerns, Nitze brought out his main objection to the treaty and to the entire SALT process. Nitze argued that ratifying the treaty could undercut perceptions of the severity of the coming gap, sapping political support from the programs that were needed to maintain the balance going forward. He also argued that ratifying the treaty would also effectively ratify the strategic gap as it would exist in 1985, meaning that at the end of the treaty the United States would have very little leverage with which to effect reductions. As for the MX, Nitze said, the Carter administration had already delayed the program and the majority of operational missiles to be procured would not come online until *after* 1985, a fact that he felt made the treaty's language about the MX mostly moot.[10]

The most glaring flaw in the treaty, according to Nitze, was that it failed to obtain explicit Soviet acceptance of the concept that the planned system of sheltering mobile MXs did not constitute deliberate concealment. Under this plan, missiles would move periodically between one of a number of empty shelters as a strategy for confusing an opponent about where each missile was. Nitze was responsible for one of the earliest versions of this concept, and he was not alone in thinking that it was the only way to protect land-based missiles once silos became vulnerable. Negotiators had tried to get the Soviets to accept a reference to the permissibility of this practice in the treaty text, but as was the case with so many verification issues, vague compromise language was the best they could do. Of course, the administration might have fought harder had the system not been so hugely expensive and had the "shell game" strategy almost any institutional support outside the Department of Defense. However, Nitze refused to accept the treaty's language because he felt that it gave the Soviets a pretext for threatening to abrogate the agreement at any time in the missile's development, potentially even holding the agreement itself hostage to the basing scheme's cancellation.[11]

Nitze's tough but reputable image and the substance of his testimony ensured a fairly civil hearing from most senators. Lieutenant General Edward Rowny proved a far more controversial figure who lacked Nitze's subtlety. In his career, Rowny had been associated with hard-line figures such as Admiral Elmo Zumwalt and Senator Jackson. Since 1971, Rowny had been the representative from the Joint Chiefs of Staff to the SALT delegation, where he proved to be a somewhat alienating figure who zealously advocated for the interests of the Joint Chiefs, especially regarding the Backfire and heavy missiles. Unlike Nitze, who abandoned SALT II relatively early, Rowny did not resign until the agreement was essentially complete in May 1979. Carter administration deputies and outside observers suspected Rowny of being a consistent leaker of unflattering information to SALT critics (a good reason for staying on the delegation so long after his main priorities seemed to have been forgotten). Rowny's testimony was met with considerable skepticism and with questions about his conduct and his integrity. These questions bore traces of Lloyd Cutler's influence.[12]

Unfortunately for the administration, questions about his integrity did not stop Rowny from becoming one of the most sweeping and visible critics of the SALT II agreement. He became closely associated with the argument that the Soviets had simply outnegotiated Carter. In his testimony, Rowny presented a detailed (and slanted) list of the opening positions and priorities the Carter administration had taken to the negotiations, including strict limits on the Backfire bomber, strategically significant reductions, and stricter controls on heavy missiles. One by one, Rowny claimed, the administration had backed away from these positions while making unilateral moves that weakened the United States at the negotiating table, such as cancelling the B-1 bomber. To veterans of SALT negotiations, Rowny's tactic of remaining a disgruntled insider only to attack the process long after he found the outcome unacceptable was risible.[13]

To the media, however, Rowny was a source of new, albeit slanted, information. Rowny's arguments gained some currency and were more rhetorically useful than Nitze's combination of abstract arguments about strategic trends and criticism of seemingly small-bore issues in the treaty text. As attention shifted from the Foreign Relations Committee to Armed Services, where hawks made up a greater proportion of both parties' representatives, these specific issues might have gained greater prominence, but the actions of a few centrist senators, with a small boost from the Carter administration, managed to change the narrative in its favor by focusing on defense budgets.[14]

The Senate Committee on Armed Services hearings began two weeks after the hearings of the Senate Committee on Foreign Relations. Brown delivered an extended version of his initial testimony. SALT II would not end the strategic competition, but it could establish a framework for a more stable form of competition. In order to maintain the balance within the parameters of the agreement, the United States would have to make a number of investments in its own capabilities so it could remain competitive. To that end, the administration had already submitted a defense budget with a 3 percent increase in real spending, a substantial amount in the context of high inflation and stagnant economic growth.[15]

Senator Jackson, eager for his chance in the spotlight, adopted a pugilistic tone that fell mostly flat. While he effectively articulated his view of the threat Soviet nuclear forces posed, Jackson's skills as a cross-examiner were lackluster. In his first opportunity to speak, Jackson spent most of his time discussing the Jackson amendment to SALT I, which required any follow-on accord to provide for "equality" in strategic forces. In Jackson's version of the legislative history, was so specific it required equality in *all* of the primary metrics for measuring strategic forces, including ICBM throw-weight. Jackson went on to list several areas of inequality, but the thrust of his comments was that the provisions of the treaty failed to comply with ambiguously worded legislation. that ratification of the treaty would implicitly repeal.[16]

The laconic testimony of the Joint Chiefs proved to be an important bellwether. The Chairman of the Joint Chiefs, Air Force General David Jones, attracted attention when he referred to the agreement as "modest but useful," a phrase the press found appealingly pithy. Jones argued, with the concurrence of the other Joint Chiefs, that SALT II was only one half of a defense plan that would adequately meet the challenges of the coming decade and that a sustained commitment to modernizing a number of strategic and nonstrategic programs was necessary to preserve deterrence. Senator John Glenn of the Foreign Relations Committee asked if Jones's assessment was not "damning with faint praise," a charge Jones denied but did not expand on. Later, Senator Jackson questioned whether the Joint Chiefs endorsed the treaty simply because they wanted to stay on their boss' good side. Impugning the integrity of a uniformed member of the military backfired, and the rest of the committee rushed to the defense of the Joint Chiefs in order to avoid being associated with Jackson's gaffe.[17]

Even Henry Kissinger supported the Carter administration's plans for defense spending. Kissinger's appearances before the Foreign Relations and Armed Services committees showed him at his wiliest and most media savvy, frustrating several senators with his oblique and vague answers. As one of the progenitors of SALT II, he could hardly disclaim the treaty entirely, but he expressed ambivalence about how the treaty would operate in the context of current geopolitical, military, and domestic trends. Although Kissinger advised senators against attempting to amend or renegotiate the treaty, he could support ratification only if there was an "understanding" between the executive and legislative branches that sustained increases in defense expenditures were necessary to arrest the negative trends in the strategic balance. Kissinger's conclusions sounded especially dark, coming from the ostensible father of détente:

> The course I propose will make SALT II far from the turn in the arms race many of us hoped for when the negotiations were inaugurated. But too much time has been lost, too many weapons systems have been unilaterally abandoned. . . . The geopolitical balance has been too severely strained . . . for SALT to be much more than a base from which, one can hope, a new and serious effort at equitable arms reduction can be made. Concrete steps to rectify the global balance are urgently required. In this context a ratified SALT II Treaty can play a useful role as a signpost to continuing negotiations, as a beacon illuminating the path to genuine coexistence and detente, and as a means to contain current tensions. But SALT must contribute to the world's security, not insecurity.[18]

Perhaps more than the administration did, Kissinger seemed to understand that public feelings against the Soviet Union were hardening. Even if these attitudes had yet to turn against arms control, they might do so in the future, and Kissinger seemed to be seeking to insulate his own legacy from that possibility.

One of the most influential members on the Senate Armed Services Committee, Senator Sam Nunn (D-Ga.), would act decisively to change the discussion regarding defense spending. Nunn maintained a low profile the first two days of hearings, quizzing Brown mostly on minor issues such as selective service and accounting for inflation in budget planning. But on the third day, Nunn announced to the committee that he would vote for SALT II, but only if it was tied to substantial increases in defense spending beyond what the Carter administration had already promised. Nunn was vague about specifics, and in subsequent days his demands ranged from $7 billion that year to a total of $20 billion over the next five years. Carter, blindsided by Nunn's announcement, first said that he would not buy votes for SALT II with defense dollars, although he did not directly claim that Nunn had proposed that. Administration officials then anonymously told reporters that the Pentagon's programs were fully funded and that Nunn would struggle to find places to spend the extra $7 billion. Nunn had little patience for the administration's arguments and quickly came up with a list of five strategic programs whose production the Pentagon could substantially accelerate with additional funds, each of which had the potential to make a difference in the strategic balance.[19]

The witness testimony portion of the hearings ended in August, followed by the summer recess. At the time, conventional wisdom indicated that the treaty was headed for narrow ratification. The criticisms that had been aired in the hearings may have stung, but they lacked a break-out moment that threatened to derail the entire process. Rowny presented the concerns of critics in an op-ed piece that argued that the focus on defense budgets distracted from a discussion of SALT II's merits. Despite the best efforts of individuals such as Senator Jackson and the Committee on the Present Danger, their work had yet to show much impact. Only after a series of unforeseen circumstances intervened did these criticisms start to gain traction in the waning months of 1979.[20]

Between July and October, a parallel debate had developed about the verifiability of treaty. While the Senate Armed Services and Foreign Relations Committees had touched on the issue, the debate took place within the Senate Select Committee on Intelligence, which drafted a report on the question of whether the treaty was adequately verifiable and what commitments were necessary to ensure that it would remain so. Although recent debates over verification and compliance meant that this report would be closely scrutinized, subsequent events complicated its reception.

First came the September 1979 "discovery" of a Soviet combat brigade in Cuba. Growing Soviet assertiveness in the Third World preoccupied many Carter administration officials by 1979, and after the success of the Sandinista movement in Nicaragua, Brzezinski requested a comprehensive review of evidence of Soviet activities in Latin America. In 1979, low-level intelligence officials learned that Soviet personnel in Cuba (whose presence had long been assumed but was little discussed) were organized as a brigade. This fact became distorted as it was reported up the chain of command, such that policy makers viewed the brigade as a new and unexpected revelation. When the discovery became public, it contributed to a narrative of rising Soviet aggressiveness in 1979 and raised new concerns about the practical and political viability of SALT II.[21]

In a measure of how interconnected SALT had become with other issues, the fall of Reza Pahlavi, the shah of Iran, complicated the Senate Intelligence Committee's work. The Iranian Revolution of 1979 disrupted a number of U.S. government intelligence activities. After the shah fled, the media reported that the United States had abandoned a number of powerful radar installations and listening posts scattered through the north and east of Iran. One of the primary purposes of these posts was to monitor missile tests from the test range in Baikonur, Kazakh, SSR. In view of the SALT agreement's limitations on qualitative upgrades, it was critical that these tests be properly observed. When administration officials were asked about the impact on treaty verification of the loss of these facilities, they initially stated that it was possible to acquire this information through other means, but they either would not provide details or said that bringing alternative systems online would take time.[22]

Publicly, the Carter administration claimed that it would remedy the deficiency by getting permission from Turkey to fly high-altitude U-2 surveillance flights along the Turkish border with the Soviet Union. The Turkish government entertained the idea for several months before deciding it would only host such activities if the Soviet Union consented to them, which the Soviet Union refused. In his testimony before the Senate Intelligence Committee, Brown could only say that U-2s in Turkey were also not necessary for treaty verification, even though that was the administration's first choice. Brown stated that planned, classified activities would fill the gap.[23] It is likely that the main means of replacing this knowledge was a highly secretive agreement between Carter and Deng Xiaoping to build a listening post inside China. Such an arrangement would have been highly sensitive and more vulnerable to shifts in local and global politics than even posts in Iran, and whether such installations could last until 1985 was questionable. Considering that they would also take several years to build, it is also questionable whether the administration had other ways of collecting this intelligence in 1979.[24]

Treaty opponents and independent-minded senators (especially Senator Glenn, who had over the past three years positioned himself as the leading Senate expert on verification) would not take the administration at its word. But open discussion of the full scope and capabilities of the U.S. measurement and signatures intelligence and signals intelligence apparatus was impossible. Instead, the Intelligence Committee assembled a detailed, classified report that fully addressed these issues and then released a much more circumspect unclassified version.

The report proved to be somewhat cryptic. The unclassified introduction to the classified report was only seven pages long, five of which related to the proper role of congressional oversight, the historical record of SALT I, and various miscellany. The last two pages dealt with SALT II. Discussing the thorniest aspects of the treaty, the committee wrote, "in general, these qualitative limitations present some problems but most can, on balance, be monitored with high to moderate confidence. There are some provisions of the Treaty which can be monitored with only a low level of confidence." The committee referred to practices (both permitted and forbidden) the Soviet Union could adopt that could "greatly complicate" verification but left open whether they expected the Soviets to implement any of them. Telemetry encryption was undoubtedly among these practices, but the language implies a wider array of concerns.[25]

On balance, the report concluded that the United States could verify a broader range of activities with the treaty than without it. Even so, the report expressed a high degree of uncertainty:

> The Treaty permits measures short of 'deliberate concealment' which could impede monitoring, and does not indicate what types of collection systems are to be considered national technical means. In the absence of the SALT II Treaty, however, the Soviets would be free to take more sweeping measures, such as unrestrained concealment and deception, which could make monitoring these strategic forces still more difficult.

Much like those who advocated for greater defense spending to preserve the strategic balance, the committee concluded that sustained, multiyear commitments were necessary to develop the intelligence capabilities the United States needed to monitor compliance with the treaty.[26]

The report's muted conclusions provided a sufficient basis for most members to go forward with consideration of the treaty on the assumption that adequate verification was assured. What the report could not do was put doubters' arguments to rest. Instead, the report pushed the unclassified version of the debate into the realm of interpretation. Doubters and treaty critics took issue not with the committee's logic, but with the assumption that the United States did not need stricter assurances on issues such as deliberate concealment and encryption. Because the report did not provide an authoritative response to these concerns, verification questions (which were often captured by the phrase "can we trust the Russians?") continued to suffuse the debate, providing a degree of uncertainty that proved corrosive to the public case for SALT II.[27]

Shortly after the Intelligence Committee report emerged, the Foreign Relations Committee began work on the final markup that would form the basis for the motion to ratify in the full Senate. Markup would prove a major test of the administration's influence in the ratification process, as those engaged in that process sought to manage the various understandings, stipulations, and "killer" amendments that preceded the final vote. Senator Baker and (to a lesser extent) Senator Richard Stone (D-Fla.) were the greatest advocates of killer amendments, and isolating them was essential. The changes Baker proposed varied; they either required the Soviets to destroy all 308 heavy ICBMs or to grant the United States a reciprocal right to an equal number of heavy ICBMs. Baker also proposed an amendment to require all Backfire bombers to count as strategic weapons. Despite the furor over the Soviet brigade in Cuba and dissatisfaction with many of the treaty's individual provisions, the committee voted down each of the killer amendments.[28]

A number of substantial amendments did pass, however. When the markup came to a vote, a 4,000-word "resolution of ratification" accompanied the treaty's text that contained dozens of understandings, reservations, and declarations, most of which were nonbinding. Seven amendments necessitated that the Soviet Union be formally notified, and two required Soviet acquiescence. Senator Glenn added language to the resolution that elevated Brezhnev's oral assurances on the Backfire bomber to treaty status. The other amendment that required Soviet assent stated that the various "agreed statements" and "common understandings" that accompanied the signing of the formal treaty instrument would have the same force as the treaty itself. Though it was reluctant, the administration promised it would accept these amendments and said that they would not likely prevent the Soviets from ratifying. The Carter administration's flexible stance on these issues, particularly regarding the Backfire, was probably intended to preempt further changes to the treaty when it came before the full Senate.[29]

On November 9th, the committee voted 9–6 in favor of approving the markup and submitting it to the full Senate. Baker and Stone voted against the treaty, as did John Glenn, who conditioned his support on improvements in the U.S. intelligence apparatus. Edward Zorinsky (D-Neb.) voted in favor of the markup but made clear that he would be supporting more "killer" amendments on the Senate floor. The treaty gained a majority, but not the two-thirds needed in the full Senate, an ominous sign. Lloyd Cutler called the outcome of the vote "a disappointment."[30]

Unraveling

The Carter administration's shift from the triumph of signing the agreement to its emphasis on using SALT II in tandem with bolstered military capabilities seemed sudden. Were these simply the pound of flesh the military and intelligence agencies (and their interlocutors in Congress) demanded in exchange for supporting a treaty of mixed effect and middling import? If so, the Carter administration was certainly quick to offer it (nearly preemptive, in fact). Much has been made of the Carter administration's shift from "dove" to "hawk" over time, but the reality of that transformation was more complicated and owed a great deal to events that contributed to an increasingly unsettling international picture.

Harold Brown is an underappreciated figure in the project of influencing the shift toward defense spending. While the Vance and Brzezinski camps debated the nature of the Soviet Union, Brown focused on intrinsic justifications for his programs, using an analytical style that appealed to Carter as an engineer and slipped past any reflexive resistance to anything that could threaten détente. Thus, Brown was able to advance his agenda without getting involved in the bureaucratic fights that outsiders tended to focus on.

In particular, Brown came to question the sustainability of the U.S. defense posture. Although the Vietnam War years had been characterized by high levels of defense spending, this spending was primarily operational. Most dollars were spent to replace or maintain equipment on the battlefield or to support it when it arrived. The 1973 transition to the all-volunteer force meant that a greater portion of the defense budget went to personnel costs, which are very similar to operations and maintenance costs, in that they are investments in current capabilities rather than future ones.[31]

During the same period, the Soviet defense budget swelled but the Soviet military spent little on operations (and even less on maintenance), while conscription kept personnel costs down. Thus, a far greater proportion of Soviet defense spending went to research and development costs and modernization. These areas all represented spending on future capabilities during a period when this was among the lower priorities of the United States. Brown's director of net assessment, Andrew Marshal, was instrumental in showing how disparities in this "investment balance" compounded over time and would require substantial increases each year to catch up to Soviet levels of investment. The argument that spending needed to be re-targeted to research and development and modernization appealed to Carter and resonated with defense hawks such as Senator Nunn.[32]

Another aspect of the changing climate was NATO's efforts to modernize its theater nuclear forces. Carter's mishandling of the neutron bomb had rattled NATO allies and undermined the confidence that many NATO government leaders, such as Helmut Schmidt, had placed in Carter. Meanwhile, Soviet SS-20 deployments accelerated. To his credit, Carter immediately set to work to develop a new NATO consensus around modernizing theater nuclear forces. Carter outlined this policy in Presidential Review Memorandum 38 in June 1978. Unlike the case with the neutron bomb, this time U.S. and NATO systems would be linked specifically to their equivalents in the Warsaw Pact in terms of both escalation and the potential for arms control. Some obstacles to consensus remained: West Germany refused to carry the entire burden, and delicate coalition governments and domestic politics limited additional basing options. Because of the explosive domestic implications of theater nuclear forces, especially the opposition that would greet their physical arrival, extensive consultations were necessary to develop consensus. The tone these consultations set did a great deal to influence public perceptions that détente was in trouble: here was NATO seriously considering one of the most significant escalations in its nuclear posture since the first ballistic missiles arrived in Western Europe in the 1950s.[33]

The dire atmosphere of these consultations should not be taken as evidence that Vance's influence was waning. Vance took the lead in forging a consensus that allowed time and diplomatic space for arms control negotiations to work before the NATO escalation occurred without undermining the credibility of the commitment to deploy. In December 1979, NATO announced its now-famous "dual-track" decision; the NATO ministers concluded that the "overall interest of the Alliance would best be served by pursuing two parallel and complementary approaches of theater nuclear forces modernization and arms control." This plan called for the eventual deployment of 108 Pershing II intermediate-range ballistic missiles and 464 ground-launched cruise missiles (neither of which would be ready for several years). At the same time, the NATO ministers unanimously endorsed the U.S. decision to pursue control of theater nuclear forces with the Soviet Union and vowed to do everything possible to support such negotiations in the hope of preventing a regional arms race.[34]

While the decision could have marked a transition to an age where any major shift in military strategy required consideration of its diplomatic and arms control implications, popular media took it as a sign of deteriorating East-West relations. Much of this perception likely came from the fact that the announcement came after SALT II had been removed from the Senate calendar. In response, the media focused on the potential for escalation instead of on negotiation.

By the time Vance testified before the Senate, a trickle of resignations of dovish members of the administration had begun that continued through 1980. The exodus began in December 1978 with the sudden departure of Paul Warnke just before the final Vance-Gromyko summit of the year. Although there has never been any indication that Warnke was forced out, resigned in protest, or was asked to leave because of the bad press his name might bring to the agreement, Even so, Warnke certainly could not have believed his influence was on the rise when he left.[35] Vance's top SALT advisor and coordinator, Leslie Gelb, left in June 1979, at a time when his counterparts, David Aaron and Walter Slocombe, were being promoted. This process culminated with Vance's resignation in April 1980, in protest over Carter's decision to mount a rescue of U.S. hostages held in Iran.

Countervailing—Counterforce

In the area of nuclear strategy, Brown and the Department of Defense did manage nearly runaway success with little influence from the rest of the executive branch. Throughout the Carter administration years, the Department of Defense and the National Security Council conducted a number of studies that grew more specific over time. This sequence began in 1977, with Presidential Review Memorandum 10 (PRM 10), which ordered a comprehensive net assessment of U.S. strategy and capabilities.[36] Many within the Carter administration arrived in office wondering if many of the shibboleths of nuclear weapons might be ripe for reconsideration, given that Carter had already achieved some success by criticizing the dominant approach to arms control. After some initial inquiries on the subject, Brzezinski delegated oversight of the studies to Brown, Slocombe, and Colonel William Odom of the NSC. He did not appoint any representatives from the Department of State.[37]

The effort PRM 10 envisioned fractured into more specific tasks over time, but the initial wave of guidance that arose from it gained articulation in Presidential Directive 18 (PD 18), titled "U.S. National Strategy." While it is still mostly classified, this directive concluded by ordering the Defense Department to undertake a review of U.S. nuclear targeting policy. The recommendations of the Nuclear Targeting Policy Review Panel were then enshrined in Presidential Directive 59, "Nuclear Weapons Employment Policy," issued on July 25, 1980. When aspects of this directive leaked, a minor uproar ensued, as it as it seemed to directly contradict the basis for classical deterrence.[38]

Presidential Directive 59 supplanted National Security Decision Memorandum 242 as the definitive guidance for nuclear planning. NSDM 242 focused on limited and regional nuclear options and emphasized counterforce possibilities and controlling regional escalation. In contrast, PD 59 sought to flesh out the entire spectrum of possibilities and emphasized two principles: endurance and flexibility.[39] The plan called for serious improvements and hardening of command, control, communications, and intelligence networks, including the ability to launch land-based ICBMs while an active exchange was under way and the ability to rapidly retarget ICBMs based on various attack criteria.[40] The new plans also emphasized a shift to an explicit counterforce posture for the first wave of nuclear attacks and a related shift that emphasized targeting Soviet control, communications, and intelligence networks, up to and including Soviet leadership.[41] In many ways PD 59 extended existing Department of Defense initiatives to nuclear forces, especially those that sought to model the U.S. posture explicitly in response to that of the Soviet Union, a so-called countervailing strategy.[42]

During the Carter administration, particularly during the first few years of leaner Defense Department budgets, Brown emphasized architectural innovation instead of focusing on procuring new systems. Architectural innovation sought to invest in the connections between existing forces helping them to fight more effectively instead of the far more expensive attempts to completely re-outfit the armed forces. Thus, Defense Department investments in general went into better communication links, improved reconnaissance capabilities, and precision munitions. With respect to conventional forces, these innovations laid the groundwork for the "revolution in military affairs" recognized a decade later.[43]

Extending these improvements to nuclear forces followed logically from this concept, as better communications capabilities would be necessary if leaders had to indicate which of many attack plans were about to be launched (an example of greater flexibility). Reinforcing these links would improve endurance by increasing the number of links (and therefore the number of operational weapons) that would continue functioning after an attack. The plans also called for a complicated "launch under attack" option, in large part because it would allow the U.S. military to employ a greater number of ICBMs during the initial exchange, making the best use of this leg of the triad while it waited for the MX to be deployed. Even specific attack options focused on how to maximize the utility of existing weapons in a resource-constrained environment.[44]

These investments also had a strategic dimension. The search for countervailing strategies was a response to a theme that had been steadily developing through the late 1970s: the belief that Soviet military and political leaders did not think like their counterparts in the United States, that they made different choices, procured different weapons, and planned to deploy them in a different manner. Brown later specifically cited the Team B experiment when he described the trend in strategic thinking to which PD 59 reacted.[45] In the late 1970s, evidence came to light, based on Soviet ICBM deployment patterns, that an early strategy for the Soviet program was to target U.S. command and control systems and that the Soviets had detected potential vulnerabilities of their own in terms of command and control.[46] Further analysis indicated that the Soviet Union had spent enormous amounts of money on systems and infrastructure to protect national-level leaders in the chain of command. The United States might play on this paranoia by making an explicit commitment to targeting leaders. That might force the Soviets to spend a disproportionate amount of their limited defense funds on protecting their leaders instead of expanding their offensive capabilities.

Those who developed these plans of course thought they were reasonable, but as PD 59 developed and became public knowledge, it was heavily criticized. So complete was the exclusion of the Department of State from the process that Secretary of State Edmund Muskie did not know of its existence until he read about it in the newspapers in August 1980. Some employees of the Department of State and the Arms Control and Disarmament Agency had apparently been involved earlier in the process, but Brzezinski had gradually cut them out, it seems, following the principle that operational planning was too much an exclusive Department of Defense responsibility to brook any interference for non-operational reasons.[47]

The directive's attempt to couch its strategic choices as a shift to a "warfighting" strategy that only reflected Soviet beliefs in the same strategy came in for serious questioning. Marshall Shulman, the Department of State's top Soviet expert, accused the Department of Defense of placing too much stock in Soviet military journals and of missing the essential point that the Soviet *civilian* leadership still believed that a nuclear war was unwinnable. According to others within the Department of State and ACDA, the directive was full of assumptions about the nature of a nuclear exchange that did not hold up under scrutiny. Launch under attack (and the even more classified launch-on-warning option) required a reliance on imperfect systems, which raised the possibility of a false positive that a limited attack could be misinterpreted as a disabling first strike. In addition, any attempts at a limited U.S. attack were necessarily constrained by the weakness of the Soviet system of damage assessment, which would assuredly overestimate the scale of any strike. Finally, a focus on targeting leaders might render the Soviet military a runaway train that no one could stop.[48]

When news of the directive leaked in August 1980, supporters of arms control predictably objected, claiming that years of policy assurances to allies, to U.S. voters, and to Soviet leaders were being undermined by a single cabinet agency with insufficient oversight. Soviet leaders expressed alarm over their perception that the United States was seeking "dominance," a principle SALT I repudiated and one that was contrary to the spirit of détente. Domestic supporters of arms control such as the Federation of American Scientists also voiced some of these and the more traditional counterarguments, the foremost of which was that planning for nuclear war was a form of self-deception because no nuclear exchange was controllable and because attempts to make them so only sought to make the unthinkable thinkable and therefore more likely.[49]

From a bureaucratic perspective, PD 59 looks like an example of defense planners run amok. Carter's decision to sign the directive after a process that so thoroughly limited the ability of interagency stakeholders to rein in the Department of Defense was a mistake. As a result, the planners' more aspirational goals threatened to outrun essential elements of the nuclear force posture as it actually stood. Indeed, even the Joint Chiefs of Staff questioned whether the planning guidance the directive outlined threatened to outstrip the actual capabilities of the command structures of the U.S. ICBM force.[50] While not all of the criticisms from the State Department and the ACDA were valid, their involvement in the process would have produced a more stable and sustainable set of policy priorities that could have been more effectively communicated. Instead, even the more sensible and mundane elements of PD 59 were threatened by the Department of Defense's botched rollout.

The PD 59 episode illustrates the increasing isolation and repetitious nature of the arguments of the supporters of arms control. The controversy failed to resonate with voters and only a few news reporters had the background to speak to the issue. But the directive was the product of a department that was in many ways deeply skeptical of the arms control enterprise and increasingly resentful of its influence on their agendas and priorities.

From the completion of the SALT I accords in 1972, critics outside and inside the Defense Department had been refining their arguments in response to the conventional wisdom about nuclear weapons and arms control. While Nitze had developed a relatively robust critique of the SALT process, the Defense Department managed to create in PD 59 a sophisticated alternative to the strict countervalue strikes of classical deterrence. New understandings of the strategic arms competition, improvements in nuclear weapons and delivery vehicles, and a decade of consultations with Soviet negotiators facilitated this new understanding.

Despite the wealth of new data and arguments, the views of individuals such as Paul Warnke, Jeremy Stone of the Federation of American Scientists, and Edmund Muskie had changed little from the debates of the early 1960s, when Robert McNamara first articulated the doctrine of mutual assured destruction. These arguments developed in response to a military establishment dominated by parochial service interests.[51] By 1979, a vastly more centralized Department of Defense mounted an assault on the shibboleths of the nuclear competition. In the face of the Department of Defense's challenge, the proponents of classical deterrence referred back, often condescendingly, to the same arguments they had developed in very different circumstances. This disconnect may partly explain why, in 1979, SALT's most fervent supporters failed to gain political support even though the public was broadly sympathetic to treaties that reduced or controlled nuclear armaments.

Linkage Resurgent

Once reported out of committee, the odds that the SALT II treaty would be ratified were not great, as evidenced by the final committee vote, but they were still good enough that the administration saw fit to try to convince Congress to ratify, hoping to achieve a narrow passage. The events of December 1979 changed that calculus, throwing the ratification proceedings into an uncertain state that persisted until the treaty expired in 1985.

Throughout 1978 and 1979, as series of coups and countercoups rocked Afghanistan. In 1979, as a brutal, incompetent Marxist government on the brink of being overthrown, the situation deteriorated into chaos. Soviet diplomatic involvement escalated until December 24, when the Soviet 40th Army crossed the Afghan border for the purpose of propping up the failing government against a rising tide of violence. Despite early military successes by the Soviets, the situation in Afghanistan devolved into a protracted guerrilla war. For months, the Carter administration had closely watched the situation in Afghanistan, but the full-on invasion by the Soviet Union took the administration completely by surprise.[52] Among the first priorities of each of the administration principals, including Brown and Brzezinski, was to isolate these events from the SALT II agreement. After negotiators had worked so hard to bring the agreement to this point, the consensus seemed inescapable: if SALT II was in the U.S. interest on its own terms, linking (and potentially threatening) one of the administration's primary foreign policy achievements to Soviet behavior at this point would be self-defeating in terms of both geopolitics and election politics.[53] Yet the Soviet invasion of Afghanistan so rocked popular perceptions of the Soviet Union's nature that it was virtual certainty that SALT II would be defeated if it was put to a vote.

From the beginning, the Carter administration struggled with the concept of linkage. While the idea that events are interconnected and synergistic was not new, the term carried a great deal of baggage from its associations with Henry Kissinger and had since acquired coercive connotations. Instead of developing a clear sense of how desirable and undesirable occurrences were related, the Carter administration tended to identify a few key areas as strategic priorities and seek to insulate them from other events or activities as much as possible. Openly discussing the Soviets' human rights failures was among these priorities; arms control was the highest priority. As this approach became more clearly associated with the Carter administration, critics had increasingly sought to oppose it by bringing up issues that ought to be held out as either carrots or sticks against Soviet activity. The administration had ignored this strategy for the most part.[54]

The invasion of Afghanistan swept this calculus away. As much as Carter administration officials did not want SALT to be linked to the issue (or almost any issue at that point), they were hostage to public opinion and congressional opinion. SALT became linked against the administration's will. Worse, the administration was placed in a bind: the more severely it reacted to the invasion, the more conspicuous continuing to pursue ratification would become giving critics an additional basis on which to oppose it. But if administration officials toned down their response to preserve SALT, they would leave themselves open to charges of being "soft on communism" in an election year and of prioritizing their own foreign policy legacy over the national interest.

Initially, the Carter administration opted for a relatively stronger reaction to show that it took the invasion seriously. An early misstep by Carter illustrated the perils of this strategy. While briefing the press on a phone call between himself and Brezhnev shortly after the invasion began, Carter expressed his bewilderment that Brezhnev would brazenly lie to him and deny that his forces had entered Afghanistan. Carter's statement instead came off as naïve, as though lying was not a standard part of the Soviet (and often the U.S.) foreign policy repertoire. SALT critics asked the logical question: if the president had just discovered that Soviets would lie when it suited them, how can he be sure that they could be trusted to adhere to SALT?[55] The issue was more symbolic than substantive: Carter's statement was a gaffe and he had dealt with Soviet half-truths before. But the episode demonstrated that the Carter administration could only excoriate the invasion so much before calling the basis for any cooperation into question.

Bowing to reality and political necessity, on January 3, 1980, Carter asked Senate Majority Leader Robert Byrd (D-W.Va.), to remove the ratification vote from the Senate calendar until the climate improved. Senator Byrd, aware of the treaty's dismal odds at that point, agreed. The administration sold this decision in part by arguing that removing a vote from the calendar did not actually withdraw the treaty from consideration. This deferred the vote until a more auspicious climate developed for ratification, ideally during the same session.[56]

Although the administration gave up hope of ratifying SALT II in the near future, its deliberations became increasingly disconnected from the political realities taking shape and from the complications posed by the fact that the treaty had been signed for six months and had yet to be ratified. Putting together a package of sanctions on the Soviet Union and strategizing about how to respond to the prolonged imprisonment of U.S. hostages in Iran consumed much of the first half of 1980. As Ronald Reagan led a coalition of conservatives and anti-communists that threatened to make serious inroads with Democrats, Carter remained committed to the treaty if only as a means of differentiating himself from Reagan. When the National Security Council finally met in June to consider how to pursue ratification, no member could see any path to a vote that could take place before the election.[57]

An air of unreality permeated these discussions. Because of the structure of the treaty, a delay in ratification could cause nearly as many complications as a complete failure to ratify. The dismantlement schedule, which only applied to the Soviets, required reductions to begin by December 30, 1980 All required systems were to be rendered visibly inoperable by June 30, 1981, and be completely disassembled and destroyed by December 31, 1981. If the treaty was not ratified in 1980, the Soviets could justifiably claim they could not meet the schedule of the treaty and insist on renegotiating it. Furthermore, the protocol to the treaty, whose provisions mostly applied to U.S. systems, also expired on December 31, 1981. The Soviet leadership could easily insist on an extension of the protocol because of the delay and could ask for adjustments to the dismantling schedule. Because Carter had promised in the clearest terms not to consent to an extension of the protocol unless the Soviets made significant concessions, reopening negotiations would put him in a difficult position. Even worse, the Senate Foreign Relations Committee report expired after December 31, 1980. After that, another round of hearings, markups, and pitched battles against amendments would take place.[58] Carter's national security team refused to take these issues seriously. They concluded that ratification of SALT II during the period when Carter might be a lame duck was not feasible and refused to consider almost any changes that became necessary due to the delay in ratification.[59]

Administration activity waned as the presidential election took center stage. Polls through much of October indicated that Carter had a tenuous lead. On October 28, Roger Molander, a member of the NSC, provided one of the rosier assessments of SALT II's chances. He argued that a reelected Carter would have a mandate to ratify the treaty thanks to the fact that SALT had been a primary issue of the campaign. Though the Senate was likely to become more conservative in the meantime, its new members were likely to be open to rational arguments in favor of ratification.[60] Carter met Reagan in a televised debate that evening, after which the polls inverted. On Election Day, Reagan won by a substantial margin.

Realignment

SALT II was a substantial, though not decisive, issue during the 1980 election season. Carter contended with a moribund economy, high inflation, the Iranian hostage crisis, and an electorate that was less and less receptive to the economic interventions of American liberalism. In addition, the discovery of Soviet ground forces in Cuba and the Soviet invasion of Afghanistan had greatly decreased public trust in the leadership of the Soviet Union at a critical moment. The Carter administration's failure to convince Congress to ratify SALT II seems attributable to a run of exquisitely bad timing.

An examination of how the parties discussed SALT II and arms control during the 1980 election reveals a somewhat more complex picture. Reagan used some of Nitze's arguments to the effect that the absolute force levels were too high and called for a program of deep mutual reductions. Reagan was more likely to use tropes from Rowny's line of criticism, however. He claimed that the way Carter had negotiated the accord was flawed and unverifiable and that the process needed to be rethought. Reagan's most stinging criticisms tended to focus on issues once removed from SALT. Reagan and his surrogates repeatedly raised the examples of the B-1 bomber, the neutron bomb, and the delay of the MX program as "unilateral concessions," opportunities for effective bargaining lost for lack of foresight. Reagan argued that his main issue with the SALT negotiations was that the Soviets supposedly lacked a fear that, if these talks failed, they would face a return to an arms race and that this limited the bargaining leverage of the United States.[61]

Perhaps SALT's real weakness, and the reason its fortunes tracked so closely with those of détente was that the process begun in 1969 no longer sought to limit a specific, narrow, class of weapons but had spread to cover a wide range of activities and systems. Reagan's criticism showed that protracted arms control negotiations had managed to infect processes of decision making that were ostensibly only tangentially related to the actual negotiations.

The modern arms control movement originated with the ideas that the nuclear arms race existed as a parallel to the Cold War and that its ends and means were driven primarily by the technologies themselves.[62] The arms control movement concluded that when the power of these weapons grew to a certain point, they were effectively useless because their destructive potential could not be rationally related to any achievable policy objective except to deter their own use. This theory grew and spread in large part because the doctrines for how, when, and against what targets to use nuclear weapons were underdeveloped until initiatives such as NSDM 242 and PD 59 brought them up to a comparable level of sophistication. If this formulation were true, then SALT II ought not to have experienced the thematic sprawl that it did, NATO allies should not have been concerned about the treaty's treatment of cruise missiles, and Reagan would have seen little cause to discuss the funding of specific weapon systems as they related to arms control.

The SALT experience demonstrated that nuclear weapons intersected with geopolitical conflicts in terms of great power competition and the tractability of the issues at stake. This fact did not necessarily make nuclear weapons militarily useful, but it made their existence rationally relatable to other issues in the international realm. Arms control, as the Carter administration pursued it (and to a lesser extent as the Nixon and Ford administrations pursued it), could not alter this calculus. Unless arms control could address underlying conflicts such as the division of Europe, there was a limit to what it could accomplish. Because there was a limit on how much negotiations could control vertically (that is, in terms of the raw numbers of weapons), the direction of the negotiations spread out horizontally until it touched on so many issues that it was essentially a vehicle for controlling outcomes across the policy spectrum. In this aspect, SALT worked much like détente: it was a vehicle for using foreign policy to aggrandize central leadership figures and strengthen their hand to deal with fractious and demanding domestic populations. This strategy worked in the case of arms control, but it could do so only as long as leaders could rely on the threat of an unrestricted arms race and nuclear apocalypse as a way of making forced compromises palatable. SALT II was not ratified because these forced compromises reflected a status quo that was increasingly unacceptable to key constituencies and to the public at large. A young Madeleine Albright may have put it best in January 1980. In a lengthy memo for the NSC, she summed up the outlook for ratifying SALT II with one word: "bleak."[63]

Looking at the SALT II agreement through this lens, Reagan's criticisms during the campaign were somewhat at variance with his policies immediately after he was elected. While Reagan did his best to threaten the Soviets with a new arms race, criticizing Carter for not turning each of his decisions into a negotiable point at a SALT summit would seem to take the trend toward using SALT to effect a domestic condominium to the extreme. Reagan in office took the opposite tack: he restricted the scope of negotiations to those that were narrowly tailored to a geopolitical problem (such as theater nuclear forces) or focused on strictly defined metrics that underpinned his administration's idea of strategic stability.

Cast-Off SALT

While the legacies of SALT endured, what can be said of SALT II? Vance and Brzezinski remained committed to the agreement and later argued that it should have been ratified.[64] Most subsequent observers tended to agree that the treaty's framework was preferable to what could have happened in the absence of any agreement, though not all shared this view. Raymond Garthoff argued that the merits of the treaty were clear, as evidenced by Reagan's later decision to abide by its terms. But Garthoff also argued that SALT should never have become the center of any policy of conciliation, as "military détente did, indeed, depend upon political détente." Any agreement privileging the former over the later would be vulnerable to sudden shifts in the political environment, as happened in SALT II.[65] Other historians are more vociferous in their criticism of the arguments arrayed against the agreement. Pavel Podvig has extensively documented how the "window of vulnerability" that would arrive with advances in Soviet missile accuracy now appears never to have occurred and was unlikely to have occurred until at least a decade later than originally predicted.[66] Anne Hessing Kahn has argued that the failure of SALT II was the culmination of a campaign by "conservatives" to use specious arguments and raw political clout to sink the entire policy of détente.[67]

The most fervent defenses of SALT II focus primarily on the unjust criticisms leveled against it. This pattern obscures a trend toward the middle in assessments of the treaty. Excluding contemporaneous accounts such as Strobe Talbott's,[68] one is hard pressed to find significant enthusiasm for the pact. As the campaign rhetoric faded and the ratification fight receded from memory, Nitze himself later tried to scale back his criticisms.[69] Assessing the treaty on its merits seems more likely to produce a consensus that SALT II was a quite modest agreement in its impact that had significant flaws. The terms of the treaty did little to alter the direction of nuclear weapons development, and while it established a precedent for reductions, even these were quite modest and concentrated on the oldest and least useful Soviet systems. In the absence of a protracted negotiation, it is questionable whether these older systems would have been retained anyway. While restraining qualitative improvements was a ground-breaking achievement, injecting the machinery of verification and compliance into such a fine-tuned assessment would likely have placed great strains on those systems, elevating minor interpretive differences to major political conflicts. Even if these disputes fell below the threshold of militarily significant verification problems, the disputes themselves would likely have proven corrosive in debates about the trustworthiness and reliability of the Soviet Union. Finally, the agreed-to limits in the treaty suffered from inequalities in other metrics. In particular, they preserved a three-to-one advantage in Soviet missile throw weight that, after accuracy, would make the greatest difference in the outcome of a strategic exchange.

Conclusion

SALT II ultimately fell victim to events. In the absence of the blows to détente and to Carter's political standing from September 1979 onward, the Senate would likely have (very) narrowly ratified the treaty, though at the cost of exhausting all of Carter's remaining political capital. Because SALT II's critics on the Committee on the Present Danger and elsewhere would likely not have been able to block ratification on the strength of their criticisms alone, they injected into the public discourse a credible negative assessment of the treaty that would resurface once events took a turn for the worse. Consistently ambivalent takes on the treaty after 1980, even by its erstwhile critics, illustrate both the lack of a full-proof case against the agreement and its underlying weaknesses.

Conclusions about the Carter administration's negotiating record share this ambivalence. The administration's opening bid clearly overshot what was achievable, wasting time and goodwill. The administration's attempts to reset expectations, encourage greater reciprocity from the Soviets, and be more transparent about its position and priorities were worthy goals. Unfortunately, the administration lacked the courage of its convictions, and the Soviet backlash against these efforts caused a hasty retreat. The Carter administration was willing to endorse these values, but not if they endangered the negotiation at hand. However, even though Carter backed away from these goals, they all became features of later negotiations and seemed, in the long run, to contribute to positive outcomes.

SALT did not die with détente. By 1981, the ideas and values of numerous policymakers across the ideological spectrum were shaped indelibly by the SALT process. Vestiges of SALT's diplomatic apparatus also remained, soon to be commanded by those who had so fiercely criticized (some would even say sabotaged) it. Negotiations on theater nuclear forces (soon to become intermediate-range nuclear forces, or INF) continued as planned. It would be a mistake to posit discontinuity between the Carter and Reagan administrations, as Carter and his subordinates ranked the modernization of theater nuclear forces and negotiations on the subject among their highest priorities from 1977. Now the question was whether those who had done so much to oppose the agreement during the SALT II debate could effectively steer its withering apparatus under the same, or even worsening, conditions. Could they navigate between threat and compromise better than the "arms controllers"? Was that even possible? The Soviets had a say as well, and it remained to be seen if, after the rebuff of SALT II, they would be amenable to the arms control goals and methods the Reagan administration chose to pursue.

INF: THE LAST GASP OF SALT

Ronald Reagan's supporters believed that his election to the presidency in 1980 was a revolution. From economic issues to social policy, Reagan represented a decisive turn against the trends the dominant political order had overseen through the 1960s and 1970s. Reagan supporters believed that he would also usher in a new era in national security affairs. The new administration touted ambitious plans for strategic modernization that would close the supposed gap between U.S. and Soviet forces. Reagan promised a departure from the processes that had produced SALT II and took a new approach to negotiations for subsequent agreements with the Soviets.[1]

Important legacies of the previous era remained, however, and could not be so casually disregarded. The vestiges and legacies of the SALT process exerted a powerful influence on the administration, constraining and influencing its decision making. At a minimum, the Reagan administration had to decide what to do with the SALT II treaty, considering how the disposition of this agreement impacted its plans for modernization and future accords. The NATO alliance continued to move to deploy deeply controversial intermediate-range nuclear missiles, while a U.S./NATO offer to negotiate on these systems was still outstanding. NATO's unanimous "dual-track decision" of 1979 had established the policy of pursuing both the deployment and negotiation "tracks" with these new weapons. Whatever administration officials thought of the dual-track decision, they knew that upsetting the delicate compromises that had produced it could strain the NATO alliance at a time when fears of nuclear devastation were higher than ever. SALT was not dead. It wasn't even past.

Without détente, nuclear arms control took on a more ominous tone; a fact that most of the Reagan administration failed to apprehend fully. The combination of the new administration's drive to challenge and reshape preconceptions about nuclear arms control and the unique issue of intermediate-range nuclear forces in Europe brought the Cold War to its hottest point since the Cuban missile crisis. In the period 1981 to 1983, INF became a vessel for debates reaching back to 1969 about what constituted a strategic weapon, stationing nuclear weapons in third countries (so-called forward-based systems (FBS)), and how to handle the various "gray area" weapons that had bedeviled previous administrations. Intermediate-range nuclear forces issues were relevant to all of these topics, and before long both the Soviet and U.S. governments came to realize that an effective INF agreement was an essential precondition for a new agreement on major strategic systems. All of the political, strategic, and domestic forces that had driven the parties into the SALT process in the first place remained, but now forced to pass through the increasingly treacherous terrain of INF.

The INF issue raised many of the most controversial and recurrent themes of the SALT process. INFs, which meant mostly missiles, grew out of the concept of theater nuclear forces, which incorporated both missiles and fighter-bombers with unusually long ranges, such as the Soviets' Tupolev Tu-22M Backfire and the United States' FB-111 Aardvark. The INF category, in turn, had grown out of SALT I–era debates over forward-based systems that were nuclear but not intercontinental and were stationed in third countries but in range of the Soviet Union. The deployment of intermediate-range nuclear forces also intersected with evolving concepts of nuclear strategy, of geopolitics, and the propaganda war for the heart of Western Europe. To the Reagan administration, these issues were too important to let them fade into a muddle of compromise. Instead of trying to contain, or sidestep the essential questions that forward-based systems and intermediate-range nuclear forces raised, the Reagan administration poured increasing amounts of diplomatic and political capital into it. Before the Reagan administration, issues relating to theater nuclear forces and intermediate-range nuclear forces were in the "gray area." They were secondary, an annoying distraction from the main issue of strategic systems. The Reagan administration oversaw the transformation of INF issues from a sideshow to the main event. Instead of seeking a quick, pragmatic (but potentially flawed) compromise, the administration turned INF negotiations into a pitched battle. Until talks collapsed in 1983, the INF negotiations were SALT's loudest echo and a defining challenge for the Reagan administration.

Anticommunists Agonistes

Reagan criticized Carter's record on arms control from several angles. He argued that negotiations were inherently flawed if the Soviets did not fear an arms race as the alternative, that Carter was too quick to compromise for the sake of an agreement, that the treaty was unverifiable, and the agreement's ceilings were too high, making the likelihood of future reductions more remote.[2] These arguments resonated with conservatives (and some anti-communist Democrats) because of concerns that extended beyond arms control. A centerpiece of Reagan's campaign narrative was the need to turn around the perception that the nation was in decline that permeated U.S. culture in the late 1970s. Many on the right were increasingly asking if the sense of decline was a psychological phenomenon, a passing funk, or if it was rooted in real social and economic trends that could lead to a permanent reduction in U.S. status and moral power.

The rise of détente had cast many committed anticommunists into a political wilderness. For years, they had wondered if their status was permanent. Why was the United States so unwilling to stand up to Soviet power? Was détente a stabilizing policy that made competition more sustainable or was it a product of a society that had grown lazy and lethargic from a long period of peace and prosperity? As they observed the younger generation, many such anticommunists wondered why they had invested so much energy in criticizing the moral failings of U.S. society, from civil rights to foreign policy, while governments in the Eastern Bloc oppressed millions of people. Such criticisms struck them as a kind of moral solipsism that permitted relentless self-criticism but did not make any effort to maintain perspective on the many, supposedly more serious, forms of evil in the world. The fact that such self-criticism led to a retreat from difficult commitments such as increasing defense spending or producing and deploying nuclear weapons validated anticommunists' sense that the United States was sleepwalking its way into a junior geopolitical status.[3] Such criticisms might have seemed out of place when compared to Reagan's optimistic tone, but both spoke to the same underlying fears. Reagan ran on a platform that flatly declared that decline was not inevitable, but it was up to his highest appointees to prove him right or face the possibility that the nation had passed the point of no return.

Such questioning might seem like the dour hand wringing of an opposition fearful of losing political relevance, but even after Reagan's election some version of these concerns remained prominent in the world views of many of his senior administration officials. Paul Nitze, a special advisor to Reagan and the secretary of state on arms control, had always been alternately fascinated and repulsed by the work of Oswald Spengler, a German philosopher who posited that every civilization inevitably entered a spiral of decline and collapse.[4] Eugene Rostow, who

Reagan appointed as head of the ACDA, routinely compared the situation of the late 1970s to his own interpretation of the period immediately before World War I, when democratic powers failed to maintain sufficient engagement with adverse trends on the European continent to avert a catastrophe.[5] Richard Perle, an assistant secretary of defense, bluntly blamed the arms control movement for contributing to the nation's decline, arguing that bilateral arms control agreements lulled citizens into a false sense of security.[6] Conservative writers often compared the United States and the Soviet Union to Athens and Sparta, drawing parallels between maritime and land powers, and between democracies and authoritarian states. These comparisons always ended asking whether the United States awaited the fate of Athens.[7] Europe was nearly written off in these arguments. Many wondered if accommodating the Soviet Union heralded the "Finlandization" of the United States[8] or if NATO risked contracting "Hollanditis,"[9] an acute allergy to hosting nuclear weapons. These concerns raised a valid question: how long could a democracy sustain a Cold War before its people grew tired of it and demanded the benefits of peace?

This apprehensive world view helps explain why so many in the Reagan administration, when witnessing the strains that public opposition to INF deployments placed on allied governments, came to believe that it was even more important for the United States to complete the deployments. INF issues became the crucible in which the democracies' ability to make the terrible choice to arm themselves for a twilight struggle would be affirmed or lost forever.

"Getting Tough"

Not everyone in the top echelons of the Reagan administration's national security team was concerned about the eschatology of democratic civilizations. Reagan's most senior advisors and cabinet officials reflected the many facets of the conservative coalition. Reagan's appointments cut across backgrounds, ideologies, and even political parties. Old-line conservatives rubbed shoulders with moderate establishment figures, "neoconservatives" from academe, and disaffected Democrats. Over time, tensions would develop between Reagan's oldest colleagues (who were mainly from California and had little national-level experience), Washington veterans with establishment leanings, and new arrivals to the government scene from ideologically conservative circles within academe and journalism.

Reflecting the dictum that "personnel is policy,"[10] Reagan made the necessary appointments to fill out his national security team but was negligent about managing workflow, refereeing disputes, or replacing ineffective figures quickly.

Because of this "hands-off" management style, the first eighteen months of the administration were uncommonly contentious and chaotic and produced little in the way of concrete arms control policy. Executive branch rhetoric, which was no better coordinated, filled the much of the policy void, influencing perceptions of the administration during a crucial period. Ill-advised and cavalier comments about the Soviet Union and nuclear war became a recurring theme for the administration, made worse by Reagan's often fuzzy recall of details from his briefings on key issues. In some cases, this rhetoric seemed intended to placate Reagan's conservative base, as if to reassure its members that his electoral victory and life in Washington had not changed his world view. But the channels he used to offer these reassurances were not well controlled, and Reagan's messages gave the impression to left-leaning U.S. and Western European audiences that Reagan was an ideological warmonger who was convinced that diplomacy was useless and that nuclear war was winnable. When the administration finally began to articulate its arms control goals and policies, it faced considerable skepticism, as these goals seemed far more ambitious and expansive than would have been expected from an administration responsible for so much bellicose rhetoric. One reporter exemplified this skepticism by sarcastically asking if the administration had been composed of "secret doves" from the start.[11]

Secretary of State Alexander Haig was one of the primary figures who attempted to assert dominance over foreign policy in Reagan's first year in office. Haig had been military assistant to Henry Kissinger during Nixon's first term. From here Haig bounced between White House and Joint Chiefs of Staff positions until he was appointed Nixon's chief of staff at the height of the Watergate scandals. As president Ford appointed Haig supreme allied commander of NATO forces in Europe. After he retired in 1979, the Carter administration's National Security Council routinely solicited his input.[12]

Haig was a moderate on foreign policy and took to the role of secretary of state, with its emphasis on conciliation and negotiation, with alacrity. Over time he found himself increasingly at odds with the Department of Defense's civilian leadership on issues related to arms control and negotiating with the Soviet Union. Haig did not mourn the death of détente and famously even revoked Ambassador Dobrynin's Department of State parking privileges.[13] However, Haig's idea of the interval between striking a "get tough" posture and then striking a deal was far shorter than that of most of his peers in the administration.

Haig had difficulty translating his prestige into influence, however. When he was challenged, Haig too often descended into bluster and empty assertions of authority. He seemed unwilling to accept that many members of the Department of Defense and the National Security Council might simply refuse to submit to his policy lead without knowing that Haig had the president's backing.[14] Over time, Haig's bluster became impotent posturing, as best exemplified by his constitutional foibles when he asserted that "I am in control here"[15] when Reagan underwent surgery to remove an assassin's bullet. In addition, Haig was too conventional a figure in an administration that saw itself as breaking decisively from the past. Transcripts of NSC meetings show that Haig had difficulty connecting with Reagan and the rest of the council, not because of lack of ability but because of differences in ideological vocabularies and world views. Ultimately Haig chose to resign in June 1982.

Haig's worst clashes occurred with one of the administration's defining figures, Secretary of Defense Caspar Weinberger. During Reagan's first term, Weinberger was probably the single most effective official in the executive branch, to the frustration of members of other agencies and departments. Weinberger entered Reagan's orbit in the 1960s, shortly after Reagan's rise to prominence in the California Republican Party. For a short while, he served as director of the Office of Management and Budget under President Nixon. Weinberger was reputed to be an able and budget-conscious administrator. His lack of defense experience led many to believe that the Reagan campaign's promised arms buildup would prove to be a more modest affair.[16]

Instead, the reverse occurred. Weinberger proved to be one of the most ruthless and successful bureaucratic actors of the late twentieth century. A lawyer by trade, Weinberger zealously defended almost every program and expenditure of the Department of Defense. He became notorious for staking out absolutist positions early in a policy process and doggedly refusing to back down. This was his approach to arms control policy. On nuclear issues, Weinberger's greatest concern was modernizing the strategic triad of ICBMs, SLBMs and strategic bombers, and he opposed any policy that might endanger one of the three legs. While he never claimed to oppose arms control categorically, he fervently believed that the Soviet Union had a significant edge over U.S. strategic forces, and that truly mutually beneficial arrangements between the two superpowers would not be possible until after U.S. modernization had a chance to run its course.[17]

The mandate of Richard Perle, Weinberger's assistant secretary of defense for global strategic affairs, included arms control and nuclear weapons issues. After the election of 1980, Perle moved from the legislative branch to the executive branch, where he became Weinberger's key advisor on arms control issues. Perle was one of the most disliked people in the Reagan administration, on all sides. His main strategy with respect to arms control policy was to obstruct, delay, and obfuscate. When he was forced to formulate a coherent policy or negotiating position, Perle did so with little or no regard for the probability that it would lead to an actual agreement. Whereas most Reagan administration officials denied it and some only vaguely implied it, Perle was one of the only members to openly

say that he opposed arms control on principle and that he would, at least theoretically, support maximalist positions specifically because they decreased the
probability of an agreement.[18]

Perle's professional style was shaped by his career as a Senate staffer. Perle's
main response almost any arms control initiative or policy as it moved through
the interagency process was to order studies, criticize new ideas without offering
alternatives, and generally insist that the development of a good idea was not
reason enough to allow the administration to be "stampeded" into adopting it
without extensive consideration at lower levels first. Perle was also good at elevating minor policy disputes to issues of principle that could brook no compromise.
While Perle was almost never personally disagreeable, such tactics engendered
considerable antipathy over the years.[19]

For an administration whose members were so divided about the wisdom of
arms control, the appointment of the director of the Arms Control and Disarmament Agency could easily prove contentious. Reagan could not put an out-and-
out hawk like Weinberger in such a position without cementing the impression
that he was uninterested in arms control. Instead, Reagan appointed a high-profile
Democrat whose ideas on arms control loosely aligned with his own. Reagan
selected Eugene Rostow, a former dean of Yale Law School whom he had met
through the Committee on the Present Danger. Rostow was both hawkish and
substantively pro-arms control, though he, like Reagan, opposed SALT II.[20]

As was the case with Haig, Rostow's personality proved to be more of an
obstacle to his influence than his politics. Rostow tried to assert a right to direct
access to the president and claimed to be the senior arms-control policy-making
official by statute. He was rudely shot down on both counts. Control of the president's schedule remained closely guarded, and Rostow was reminded that he was
subordinate to the secretary of state and subject to the secretary's authorities.
Rostow's demeanor also grated on many colleagues. His tone was often professorial and condescending, even to superiors. Even so, Rostow remained one of the
highest-placed Democrats in the administration and was an essential conduit for
the group of arms control intellectuals, such as Paul Nitze, who did not want to
see the idea abandoned entirely but believed it could be done better.[21]

First Moves

The Reagan administration immediately was forced to formulate Soviet policy on many fronts. In December 1981, the Polish government began a crack-
down against Solidarity movement activists that worried many observers, who
wondered if the world would experience a repeat of the 1968 Soviet invasion

of Czechoslovakia. The Soviet Union was waging an increasingly brutal war in Afghanistan that showed no signs of ending. Whether the Reagan administration would comply with or withdraw from SALT II remained an open question. A single round of Theater Nuclear Forces talks had taken place during Carter's lame duck period that committed the United States to the negotiation for the moment, though no date was set for resumption. Many of Reagan's senior advisors wanted to more vigorously apply export controls to the Soviets, an issue that was complicated by Soviet plans to build an oil pipeline from Siberia into Europe and by politically sensitive deals to sell U.S. grain to the Soviets that were in the works in 1981. Another tension in U.S.-Soviet relations was Reagan's decision to focus on the human rights of Soviet citizens, especially religious and political dissidents. Whether concerns about human rights were expressed primarily publicly or privately, consistent attention to the issue introduced another destabilizing factor into the relationship.

It is easy to see how arms control could have gotten lost in such a cacophony of issues, especially for a new and unorganized administration with ambivalent feelings on the subject. Unlike Carter, who inherited a set of negotiations in progress, no such platform existed that would compel the administration to focus on arms control. The Carter administration's single round of talks on theater nuclear forces had not established common terms of reference or expressed a U.S. position. Soviet and U.S. negotiators still insisted on using different terms to refer to the meeting itself.[22]

The most immediate question on nuclear arms control was whether to ratify SALT II. The State Department adhered to a standard line on unratified treaties: that neither party could take actions that "deliberately undercut" the terms of the agreement. Speaking for the anti-SALT II crowd within the administration, Secretary of the Navy John Lehman went off script in March 1981, saying that he had no objection to U.S. withdrawal from SALT II or SALT I. Richard Burt, a former New York Times reporter who had recently been appointed as assistant secretary of state for political-military affairs, was in the process of providing assurances to NATO allies about the new administration. When he heard about Lehman's remarks, he sent a cable to every NATO outpost saying that the remarks were unauthorized and the existing commitment not to undercut remained pending an administration review.[23]

Burt had no more right to pronounce on the matter than Lehman did, but he had the advantage that he was arguing in favor of the status quo. The protracted review period helped shape the eventual choice not to change the policy at all. In one instance, Caspar Weinberger wanted to cease providing treaty-required notifications of missile tests. Secretary Haig objected, arguing that doing so without a public statement would be provocative and that a decision not to comply ought at least to wait until the Department of Defense had completed its formal review of U.S. nuclear requirements. Weinberger had already used this review to delay administration consideration of positions on arms control negotiations, a fact that limited his ability to discount Haig's argument. Haig's view won out. The administration continued to issue notifications of missile tests, thus complying with SALT II from an early stage of Reagan's tenure. The longer this state of affairs dragged on without an alternative, the more attractive a decision not to ratify or to withdraw from the treaty became. Such a move would require no expenditure of political capital, it would avoid activating the protocol before it expired at the end of 1981, and the possibility that it would disrupt operational practice was small.[24]

Burt's last word was de facto policy until Reagan addressed the issue in 1982. In the interim, Reagan's criticism of SALT II moved away from fear, uncertainty, and doubt about its verifiability, and or arguments that it was a raw deal. Reagan began to argue that the agreement did nothing to stop the massive increase in Soviet warheads that would result as the Soviet MIRV program ran its course. SALT II, in Reagan's telling, went after the wrong categories in establishing limits and had set them far too high. He argued that ratifying SALT II would legitimize an arms control framework that was unacceptable, setting a precedent for a model he was specifically trying to change. Reagan announced an "interim restraint" policy in May 1982, saying that the United States would adhere to the agreement to the extent that it could verify the Soviet Union was doing the same, a policy he rearticulated every year until the accord expired in 1985.[25]

Contemporary commentators and historians have criticized Reagan's decision. These critics' main charge was hypocrisy. If, as Reagan had argued in the 1980 presidential campaign, SALT II was such a bad agreement, why did he choose to comply with it? In 1986, Reagan actually did abandon the framework, to great controversy, citing a litany of supposed Soviet violations of the agreement. That year was also the first in which the U.S. military had the opportunity to exceed agreed-upon limits. This suggests that a certain amount of pragmatism underpinned Reagan's decision.[26]

Keeping SALT II in a liminal state still had advantages. It put upper bounds on the arms race that Reagan threatened to inflict during the campaign, lending a near-term predictability to the strategic balance that could only be good for stability. Doing so gave the administration time to develop a more robust consensus about how to approach strategic arms negotiations. In view of the experience of Jimmy Carter vis-à-vis the Vladivostok Accord, foreign policy officials are sometimes better served by accepting path dependency instead of wiping away settled agreements in search of an alternative. Abandoning SALT II completely in 1981, especially when the United States had so few systems to deploy that exceeded its limits, would have imposed significant political costs with only marginal strategic gains.

The number of Soviet issues facing the administration in its first year tempted many officials to attempt to coercively link them to arms control. Secretary of State Haig considered postponing a meeting of the SALT forum dedicated to discussing compliance issues, claiming that holding back on this might afford opportunities to use the meeting as leverage in the future.[27] Weinberger also made several public statements that connected Soviet activities in Eastern Bloc countries, especially Poland, to the U.S. position on Theater Nuclear Forces talks, since Soviet aggressiveness on the continent had an impact on U.S. security requirements. The vocabulary of linkage proved hard to abandon, even among those who deeply distrusted Kissinger. The backlash from such statements was severe, however, both in the popular media and from Soviet outlets. This contributed to the narrative that Reagan was obstinate and insincere in his desire to negotiate on nuclear arms.[28]

Administration appointees eventually backed off such rhetoric, coming eventually came into sync with much of the permanent national security bureaucracy about how to approach SALT. Midlevel interagency panels had already met on the issue, and a broad consensus emerged from these that included a range of people from hawkish Richard Perle to moderate ACDA advisor James Timbie. That consensus was that linking SALT to other issues in 1981 would prove counterproductive because it would raise the profile of both issues and inflate the expectations of the U.S. public. Because the issue of arms control could not address the underlying reasons for conflict, a policy of slow-walking SALT for a time would align public expectations with probable outcomes. At the same time, the interagency panel also noted that public pressures in NATO meant that, at a minimum, the administration could not ignore the issue of arms control without threatening more serious consequences.[29]

As evidenced by the protracted debate on U.S. export controls and economic sanctions placed on the Soviet Union, the vocabulary of linkage and the impulse to coercion never completely disappeared. The administration settled into a pattern of asserting that Soviet bad behavior could not help but threaten progress in other areas without promising specific actions in response. One of Caspar Weinberger's signature contributions to arms control policy was his insistence that the United States pursue only negotiating options that were in its immediate interest. Emphasizing this point from an early stage placed the United States in a better position to continue negotiating even in moments of crisis, such as the KAL 007 incident (discussed below).In an important way, the Reagan administration's hawks helped pave the way for the first post-linkage presidency.

From Theater to Intermediate-Range

Both tracks of the dual-track decision had their skeptics and detractors in the new administration in 1981. The decision was, after all, was a Carter policy, and the Reagan administration (and Reagan himself) were very interested in over-turning Carter administration decisions. The resurrection of the B-1 bomber and the production of the neutron bomb are two examples of this zeal for revers-ing course when it came to Carter's legacy.

Much like SALT II, however, there was a difference between opposing a Carter-era decision at the time it was made and reversing it some years later. Alexander Haig, for instance, questioned the dual-track decision at the time it was made on the ground that attaching arms control to the deployment elevated public expec-tations of and fears about what he saw as routine modernization that should have been uncontroversial. Before Reagan's election, Paul Nitze made clear he did not believe a genuine equality in the European nuclear balance could be negotiated because of the nature of NATO's politics and geography, yet he also recognized that Western European demands for arms control had to be accommodated. Richard Perle believed that arms control was responsible for the entire situation, arguing that the Soviet Union had designed the SS-20 specifically in response to SALT. So great was Perle's antipathy toward both tracks of the decision that in 1983 he argued (briefly) that the deployment track itself should be abandoned before it began, lest the approaching deadline create pressure to sign an inequi-table arms control.[30]

The TNF/INF negotiations existed in an awkward state in 1981. Technically, the Statement of Principles for SALT III section of the SALT II treaty included a commitment to negotiate about forward-based systems and gray-area systems, but ignoring the Statement of Principles was easy enough without deliberately undercutting the agreement. The single meeting of the TNF talks under Carter was related in that it was concerned with largely similar systems, but the meet-ing clearly proceeded more directly from the dual-track decision than from the specifics of SALT II. The meeting still occurred in Geneva, however, the home of the SALT II negotiations, and featured many of the same negotiators from the Carter administration.

As members of the Reagan administration began studying the term "theater nuclear forces," it quickly became unfashionable. Originally, the term had encap-sulated a range of concerns about Soviet systems such as SS-20s and the Back-fire bomber. NATO allies expressed misgivings about this name, however, as the word "theater" implied the issue was weapons in a specific region, in this case Europe. But these allies wished to strengthen the connection between the U.S. nuclear umbrella and nuclear forces in the field, whereas theater nuclear forces negotiations sounded likely to weaken this connection. The United States also had numerous ground-attack planes in Europe that the Soviets could easily claim ought to be considered "TNF-range" (though they all fell far short of the Backfire). The alarm the Department of Defense, especially the JCS, expressed took negotiations over airplanes off the table. The term intermediate-range applied more specifically to missiles, the primary U.S. concern. This term kept discussions more focused on the SS-20 and reoriented the debate toward a class of weapons defined by their range rather than by their location in the European theater of operations.[31]

For a time, Reagan administration officials debated whether the existing structure of the TNF talks was too similar to the structure the SALT process had created or if they could divorce it from negotiations about central strategic systems. This debate reached an absurd peak when Haig and Deputy Secretary of Defense Frank Carlucci engaged in a protracted debate at an NSC meeting over whether the INF talks would take place in the "framework" of SALT negotiations or in the "context" of SALT.[32] The Reagan administration gradually realized that INF issues' relationship to NATO was more important than their relationship to negotiations about central strategic systems. This proved to be the decisive factor in decision making.

From early 1981 until the administration announced its position in November, a complex debate took place within the executive branch and with the increasingly stressed strained coalition governments of Western European allies. Presaging the mass protests in favor of a nuclear freeze in 1982 and 1983 in the United States, in 1981, demonstrations across Western Europe protested against the superpowers turning Europe into a nuclear chessboard. The government of Helmut Schmidt in West Germany and the government of the Netherlands remained shaky as the left wings of their social democratic parties peeled away from the governing coalitions in the face of these protests. Schmidt made increasing demands that some sort of progress take place on INF negotiations. Reflecting pressures on their government at the time, German diplomats and defense attachés began floating the idea of negotiating positions designed to preempt the deployment of U.S. missiles to Germany, or to even scrap the entire deployment across Europe.[33]

These proposals alarmed the Reagan administration. Because of technical and geographic limitations, Germany was the keystone of NATO's deployment plan. The Soviet Union's SS-20, with a 5,000-kilometer range and three MIRV warheads per missile, was a technological success. No single weapon in the U.S. arsenal could match it, so the 576 U.S. missiles in the planned deployment had to be spread across two systems to roughly match the SS-20's capabilities. The Pershing II ballistic missile was an upgraded version of the Pershing IA, a short-range nuclear missile the United States had deployed in Germany for some time. The upgrade improved its range to well inside intermediate range but nowhere near 5,000 kilometers. As a result, the only place in Europe from which Pershing IIs could strike non-artic Soviet territory was West Germany, and even then they could not reach the most sensitive targets, such as Moscow.[34] In addition, the Pershing II had only a single warhead, meaning the 108 such missiles in West Germany could only cover 108 targets, whereas the over 225 SS-20s that were deployed through the Western Soviet Union could strike over 675 targets, enough to strike every NATO military facility of any significance and every major population center in Western Europe with warheads to spare.[35]

Ballistic missiles had shorter flight times than cruise missiles. Both the SS-20 and the Pershing II could strike targets in less than fifteen minutes, a period shorter than either side's early warning systems could accommodate. By the time the great mass of NATO or Warsaw Pact military forces could realize they were under attack, the warheads would be moments from detonating. This quality was tremendously destabilizing (it was the main point of contention during the Cuban missile crisis). If West Germany voted not to approve the U.S. missile deployments, however, NATO would lose this capability.[36] At the same time, West German politicians adamantly insisted that their constituents would never accept a deployment of only Pershing IIs (and thus deployment only in West Germany). They claimed that while West German voters were prepared to show solidarity with NATO, they were not willing to be its patsy.

The Pershing II could match the SS-20 in time to target, but not in range or number of warheads. These were both critical factors in terms of strategy and negotiating leverage. The Tomahawk ground-launched cruise missile (GLCM) filled this gap. Efforts to develop a self-navigating, low-flying missile of extended range had begun in the mid-1970s. The Tomahawk that was the result could reach targets in the Soviet Union from military bases as far away as England. Each Tomahawk deployed as part of a batch of four with an accompanying mobile launcher. When deployed, each of these launch units would have one missile in the launch tube and three additional missiles on a truck close by. The downside to the Tomahawk missile was its speed: the missile flew long distances at subsonic speeds, which meant that it would take hours to strike the Soviet Union. Making a virtue of necessity, U.S. officials argued that this made the U.S. deployment more moral that Soviet missile deployments, as cruise missiles could only serve a retaliatory role and could not be used in a first strike. Soviet negotiators never conceded this point. They argued that because the Tomahawk could fly under most radar screens, it had the ability to strike undetected, even hours after launch. However, later Soviet positions indicated that they regarded the Pershing II as the far more threatening system.[37]

West German suggestions that no NATO missile deployments at all might be the ideal outcome seeped into administration rhetoric over the following months, until a unique formulation of the idea became official policy in the form of the "zero option." How a person arrived at the zero option depended on their opinion of the dual-track decision and which track they preferred. For Richard Burt, the entire INF issue was "an elaborate exercise in alliance politics,"[38] and his statements reflected that priority. The Department of State's public statements and press releases emphasized achieving equal numbers of missiles at the lowest negotiable level, including zero. Haig endorsed this language, seeing it as an important sop to prevailing public opinion in Europe that cancelling missile deployments was seen as a negotiable outcome.[39] Maintaining this possibility rhetorically would keep public opinion from interfering with the deployment schedule, which was essential to ensuring that the threat of the new missiles remained credible. Leveraging future NATO deployments against existing Soviet weapons would not be easy, but keeping public opinion sated and denying the Soviet Union any propaganda inroads held out the best chance of reaching an agreement before or coincident with the deployment.

As a rhetorical position, Haig and Burt's language might seem cynical, but it is important to remember that they had inherited the dual-track approach and that neither had supported that approach in 1979. Both preferred to treat nuclear modernization as something routine and uncontroversial. To them, making the connection with the SS-20 may have made it more possible to negotiate over the missiles' numbers and deployment pattern. Such a connection required drawing public attention to the SS-20 and emphasizing the threat it posed, fueling fears among Western European publics of turning their countries into a nuclear battlefield. Haig and Burt concluded that such public concerns ultimately weakened NATO's ability to modernize its deterrent. Since the dual-track approach had already made this connection and fueled these fears, though, it was best to accommodate public opinion with an opening bid of zero and meet public demands for an agreement in order to get the NATO deployments out of the way and enable NATO to move on to other issues that did not threaten to tear the alliance apart.[40]

Richard Perle disagreed with the zero option but still endorsed it as an opening position. To make his case, Perle cited Department of Defense studies on different combinations of mobile intermediate-range nuclear missiles in Europe. Because NATO only had between 250 and 300 military installations worth targeting, even moderate levels of SS-20s in Europe posed a threat of annihilation that would be nearly impossible to counteract. To Perle, any level of SS-20s in Europe higher than 100 and the resulting 300 warheads those missiles would carry posed an unacceptable security risk. An agreement that sanctioned substantially higher levels (the Department of State envisioned several hundred more on both sides) would prove doubly dangerous because it would give the U.S. and West European publics the misleading impression that they were now more secure.

Perle also argued (presciently, much to the frustration of his critics) that the number of SS-20s was so far in excess of the Soviets' targeting needs that it was likely they would propose cuts of their own, perhaps with a number that was higher than that the State Department was proposing but as part of a lopsided package. Doing so would put the United States in the unenviable position of arguing that it was in favor substantial cuts, but not *those* cuts. Offers between 576 and 0 would invariably become complicated as questions of balance and geography came into play. The only way to avoid this kind of one-upmanship was to preempt it, and the only number the Soviets could not undercut was zero. Thus, Perle argued that the U.S. position should be that the United States would abandon its deployment plans if the Soviets eliminated all of their SS-20s and, as a corollary, that zero was the only negotiating outcome the United States would accept before the deployment deadline.[41] A classic example of Perle's thinking, his argument was based on a somewhat logical reading of the strategic outlook that he then took to its simple but elegant extreme.

Weinberger and much of the National Security Council enthusiastically supported Perle's proposal, but Haig strongly objected. Haig complained to Reagan that the position gave him no flexibility and nowhere for the negotiations to go. A negotiating position based on this sort of absolutism might win a few news cycles and temporarily satisfy European public opinion that the Americans were not warmongers, but the Soviets would never agree to eliminate or even severely reduce an entire class of weapons based on a hypothetical threat from missiles NATO had yet to deploy.[42]

While the administration sought to come to a decision about its opening position, a parallel debate was taking place about timing and the exact nature of the forces under negotiation. After the administration completed a host of time-consuming studies required by Weinberger and his deputies, the administration agreed to aim for talks before the end of the year but avoided a hard date. Haig would then confirm this time frame and the specific elements the superpowers would discuss in a meeting with Foreign Minister Gromyko at the United Nations in September.[43]

The Haig-Gromyko meetings proved somewhat chilly. The two men traded barbs and each side probed the others' position. The uncharacteristically brief statement that was released following the meetings spoke to the limited areas of agreement the conversation produced. The discussions presaged the disagreements that would divide the parties for the next two years. Gromyko agreed to resume the talks at Geneva before the end of the year, and both men expressed

willingness to resume "without preconditions." There was no exact U.S. position yet, but Haig communicated some general principles, specifically that any
numerical limits would be global in scope, mutually applicable, and equal in
number. This latter point the United States referred to generally as the principle
of equality.[44]

Gromyko did not argue against these points in detail, but he laid out some
of the Soviet Union's primary goals, which centered on their principle of "equal
security." By this Gromyko meant that a final agreement would have to account
for differences in geography and alliances and thus provide an equally secure
environment for both countries. He explained that any ensuing agreement would
thus have to incorporate, implicitly or explicitly, the nuclear forces of the United
Kingdom and France. These forces totaled around 160 missiles, and including
them in an agreement was an absolute nonstarter for the United States. The
U.S. side also rejected Soviet attempts to control U.S. forward-based systems in
Europe (this was implied by the Soviets' mention of security requirements based
on differing geography). Gromyko made clear, as his government had done for
two years, that it would not sanction any deployment of NATO missiles and that
it regarded their deployment as a provocative act and an escalation meant to tip
the military balance in Europe away from its relatively equal state and toward the
United States. Eleven years after the opening of the first SALT negotiations, these
basic differences between the U.S. and Soviet concepts of nuclear threat not only
persisted, but had grown more pronounced.[45]

As the Reagan administration's planning continued into the fall, two choices
emerged: zero only, in which the United States would propose that the only
means of preventing the deployment was a complete withdrawal and dismantling of all SS-20s and the vintage SS-4s and SS-5s they were meant to replace;
and zero plus, which hewed closely to the original State Department line that
the United States sought zero as an ideal outcome but was willing to entertain
"serious" Soviet counterproposals that included significant reductions to equal,
global levels greater than zero.[46]

When the National Security Council met in November of 1981, Weinberger enthusiastically promoted zero only, arguing that a splashy presidential
announcement of the policy would have a serious impact on European public opinion. The JCS lukewarmly went along, having recently been warned by
Perle not to undercut the secretary in NSC meetings. The NSC staff also favored
the zero-only approach, arguing that zero plus too closely resembled the failed
Carter approach of developing a serious proposal and then undercutting itself
by developing fallbacks. Rostow and the ACDA technically favored zero plus, but
when he discussed it at the meeting, Rostow articulated a much tougher vision
of zero plus in which the acceptability of middle-ground outcomes were barely

mentioned and were left to the Soviets to try to develop fairly; the United States would not actively facilitate their development. Reagan seemed somewhat receptive to Rostow's formulation at first but disagreed that it was actually closer to zero plus than zero only, which he seemed to assume implicitly carried many of Rostow's caveats. These positions left Haig struggling in favor of zero plus. Though the meeting itself was technically not meant to be decisive, the president's preference was clear and Haig had lost.[47]

On November 18, 1981, Reagan delivered prepared remarks to the National Press Club in which he set out his administration's vision for the East-West military balance and the place of arms control within it. Reagan then unveiled the final version of the zero-only option, using a series of charts to back up his assertions. In 1974, when the Soviet Union did not have any SS-20s, the Soviets asserted that they had achieved basic parity in theater and central strategic nuclear forces.[48] By 1981, the Soviet Union had deployed over 225 SS-20s with 675 warheads, while NATO forces remained static. Yet the Soviet Union still claimed that parity existed and that any NATO missiles would upset Europe's delicate military balance. Reagan asserted he would cancel the deployment of Pershing IIs and Tomahawk missiles if the Soviets dismantled all of their SS-20s, SS-4s, and SS-5s, but he also said that when the U.S. delegation arrived in Geneva to commence talks at the end of the month, "we intend to negotiate in good faith and go to Geneva willing to listen to and consider the proposals of our Soviet counterparts."[49]

The initial reaction to the Reagan's announcement both in the United States and Western Europe was positive, but it would remain so only if the administration continued to demonstrate seriousness in engaging in the arms control process.[50] Choosing the leader for the U.S. delegation to Geneva proved an opportunity to signal just that. Haig originally wanted to appoint a career foreign service officer to the post, someone he could expect to trust and control, but Eugene Rostow disagreed. Having just returned from a tour of European capitals to bolster the administration's line that it took both tracks of the dual-track proposal seriously, Rostow argued that the position called for a senior, experienced statesman who would command credibility at home while providing reassurance to NATO's governments. Rostow recommended Paul Nitze and Reagan agreed, overruling Haig. For the first time since 1974, Nitze rejoined government full time, now as head of the INF delegation to Geneva.[51]

Budgets, Compliance, and Doctrine

The Reagan administration made a number of other defense policy decisions in its first year, many of which revisited or overturned Carter policies. These decisions were not always coordinated with events in the realm of arms control, although at times this was by design. Many in the administration resented the sprawling influence of arms control, preferring to address the issue only after attending to U.S. security needs. The decisions the Reagan administration made increased concern in both the United States and Western Europe that it did not take nuclear war seriously. This gave a significant boost to the nuclear freeze movement and to opponents in Congress of the president's strategic modernization program.

Two of the administration's most notable reversals of Carter-era policies involved the neutron bomb and the B-1 bomber. On August 9, 1981, a spokesperson announced Reagan's decision to commence production and stockpiling of the artillery and short-range rocket neutron bomb warheads. These warhead stockpiles would remain in the United States and would be deployed to Europe only in the event of a crisis. The announcement prompted surprise and alarm among NATO allies, who had hoped the issue had been buried for good. As nascent European peace movements decried Reagan's decision, the administration fired back with public statements arguing that those criticizing the neutron bomb, a 1 kiloton device, and not the SS-20, which had three 450-kiloton warheads, had become mouthpieces for Soviet propaganda.[52] Reagan's first defense budget also backed the revival of an upgraded B-1 bomber, a decision that was popular among the military hawks, but did nothing to alleviate well-known production problems and a high likelihood of cost overruns. In addition, in the four years since the Carter administration had canceled the B-1, the Advanced Technology Bomber program, which eventually led to the B-2 Spirit, had continued apace and was just over a decade away from completion. Reviving the B-1 thus came at great expense but narrowed the capability gap created by aging B-52s by only about five years.[53]

Reagan's first defense budget reversed a Carter policy in another way, in this case in the name of affordability. During the 1980 campaign Reagan had sworn to support the MX ICBM that had become so central to maintaining a land-based deterrent. Once Reagan was in in office, appointees throughout the Department of Defense emphasized the approaching "window of vulnerability," the point at which increases in the accuracy of Soviet ICBM would make a disabling first strike against the Minuteman force feasible. Instead of supporting expensive schemes that moved missiles from silo to silo in an attempt to conceal their location, as Carter and Harold Brown had, Reagan chose, at Weinberger's suggestion, a "dense pack" of fixed MX silos.[54]

The theory underlying this strategy was that when many missiles were close together, the Soviets would find it difficult to target all of them at once because their warheads would blow each other up before they could hit their targets, a process known as "fratricide." Using a "dense pack" and relying on fratricide was admittedly less survivable than previous proposals, but it had several factors to commend it, each of which indicated the dawning awareness of the Reagan administration that its plans for strategic modernization faced growing head-winds even by the end of 1981.[55]

Congress had never been enthusiastic about the cost of the various proposed basing schemes for the MX and the public opposition and opportunities for civil disobedience they generated. But by the end of 1981 this lack of enthusiasm had blossomed into full-blown opposition to the missile itself, a much bigger prob-lem for an administration that was intent on modernizing each leg of the strate-gic triad and that needed something to compete with the larger Soviet SS-19 and SS-18 missiles. In May of 1981, the Church of Jesus Christ of Latter-day Saints issued a statement opposing the shell-game basing scheme and forwarded cop-ies to members of Congress in Utah and Nevada, where the majority of these bases were to be built. Public opinion in those states, which had previously been roughly split, had swung sharply to opposition; 76 percent of the public in these two states were opposed to the plan. Influential members of Congress also voiced their opposition, including Senator Paul Laxalt (R-Nev.), a close friend of Reagan, and various environmental and anti-nuclear activist groups. While the admin-istration was usually loath to accommodate critics in Congress and the nuclear freeze movement, it knew when one of its critical programs was in danger. Thus, the administration proposed "dense pack" in its budget request in addition to its request for the restoration of funding for the B-1.[56]

The landscape for verification and compliance also changed during this period. Reagan repeated traditional conservative arguments that the Soviet Union had to be held to account with regard to compliance and monitoring, but members of his administration ran the gamut about what degree of Soviet com-pliance was required. Hard-liners inside and outside the administration argued that the Soviet Union ought not be "rewarded" with a new agreement if it could not hold itself to existing ones. They also argued that new agreements ought at least to feature much tougher verification regimes, including on-site inspections. At a minimum, the United States ought not self-censor in its discussions of Soviet compliance out of a fear of endangering relations; during negotiations the Soviet Union ought to have to explain its potential violations repeatedly before it could address its own concerns.[57]

Demands that new agreements feature on-site inspections raised concerns that such requirements would virtually preclude any new agreement. Soviet negotiators had vigorously opposed such provisions in the past. But the range of verification activities had already begun to expand when confidence-building measures were established by the Helsinki Final Act of 1976. The act permitted teams of military observers from NATO and the Warsaw Pact to periodically witness the military exercises of the other side. However, the Soviets had difficulty implementing confidence-building measures in full accordance with the agreement. Neither Carter nor Reagan allowed this to pass unremarked. But the fact that such measures existed showed that by 1981, inspections had already begun to be the norm and would continue to expand. Indeed, by 1982, before the rise of Gorbachev, Soviet diplomats routinely admitted in interviews that new agreements likely would require some new paradigm of verification using methods that went beyond national technical means.[58]

The Reagan administration had difficulty focusing on compliance and verification issues in its first term, perhaps because the odds of an agreement never rose to a level sufficient to make the chaotic interagency system work out its differences proactively. The National Security Council did not establish a verification working group until the final months of 1982, long after negotiations on the START and INF treaties had begun. Congressional pressure provided the main impetus for paying any attention to compliance issues, especially pressure from the conservative wing of the Republican Party as represented by Jesse Helms (N.C.). In response to requests from these members of Congress, the Reagan administration issued a series of annual reports on Soviet compliance. While these reports were mostly classified, they did not make allegations of actual violations. The best they could do was repeat a number of dubious claims, such as that the SS-19 was a heavy missile as defined by SALT I, that a particular surface-to-air missile system had been tested in an ABM mode (a violation of the ABM Treaty), and that various instances of telemetry encryption were still highly problematic but not overtly prohibited.[59]

This tone changed in 1983 with the discovery of the Krasnoyarsk radar complex in Siberia, which supposedly was an early-warning system. The station's power and its orientation appeared to be direct violations of the collateral restraints on radars agreed to in the ABM Treaty. By the time this issue gained traction, the INF and START talks had already broken up, so there was never an opportunity during Reagan's first term to include it in the U.S. negotiating strategy. Compliance issues came to prominence again in 1985 and 1986, as the SALT II agreement was about to expire. Administration hard-liners such as Perle and Weinberger did not embrace the issues of verification and compliance until negotiations seemed more likely to produce an agreement, but their ability to obstruct or delay those negotiations had diminished by the second Reagan term.[60] As a result, for its first four years the administration was mostly split between hard-liners who were rhetorically committed to on-site inspections, and moderates who were looking for quicker paths to agreement that involved a wider degree of unverifiability than the previous SALT agreements had considered.

Perhaps the most significant example of the Reagan administration's desire to undo out-do, or over-do Carter's main legacies was in the realm of nuclear doctrine. One outgrowth of the bevy of assessments and requirement studies the Department of Defense conducted as part of its top-to-bottom review of nuclear weapons policy was National Security Decision Directive (NSDD) 13, "Nuclear Weapons Employment Policy." This directive replaced the guidance in PD 59. It revised and expanded its requirements to a degree that called into question whether the Department of Defense retained any commitment to deterrence.[61]

Much of the motivation for NSDD 13 seemed to originate from mid-level policymakers, with its recommendations flowing up to the executive branch and down to planners at Strategic Air Command. Studies that had been released in the early 1980s showed that serious deficiencies existed in the command-and-control infrastructure of U.S. nuclear forces.[62] Early drafts of these reports had influenced PD 59 in its efforts to harden this infrastructure and thus deny the Soviet Union the ability to disrupt or prevent a nuclear attack by attacking the U.S. forces' de facto nervous system. This effort fit well within the countervailing framework that guided PD 59, as it built upon evidence that the Soviet Union already intended to target these assets to make up for its qualitative disadvantages. PD-59 had ordered U.S. nuclear forces to target the Soviets' command-and-control infrastructure to deny them such an ability. By 1981, these studies showed that the deficiencies of the U.S. system were in many cases far worse than had originally been believed. Harold Brown's goal with these studies was to optimally apply limited defense resources to offset Soviet strengths and target their weaknesses. The Reagan administration's goals were more expansive. The central goal of NSDD-13 was still to deny the Soviet Union the capacity to win a nuclear war, but the idea of making deterrence work with essentially equivalent forces fell by the wayside.[63]

In the years since Team B had asserted that Soviet nuclear doctrine differed from that of the United States, with potentially catastrophic consequences, the intelligence and defense communities had come to share this view to some degree or another. Under the influence of Weinberger's team, however, U.S. policy came to the brink of abandoning deterrence. NSDD 13 asserted that U.S. forces needed to be capable of denying the Soviet Union any conceivable political or military objective in a nuclear attack. It also said that the United States had to be able to wage nuclear war "successfully" and dominate the Soviet Union at every level of conflict, with the result that any nuclear exchange would end on terms that were favorable to the United States. The document concluded with veiled references to civil defense and potentially even to missile defense, at first using the argument that they bolster deterrence but then claiming that they would make it easier to survive and prevail in a nuclear exchange.[64]

Like any major declaration of policy, NSDD 13 was a consensus document. It is possible to interpret the final document as designed to promote deterrence and make nuclear war unlikely by ensuring that the U.S. capacity to wage war, regardless of the level of the exchange, could survive the next-lowest exchange. But the language veers toward the goal of dominance and achieving victory in a way that ultimately promoted confusion among senior members of the Reagan administration and fear among the general public as snippets leaked out. By the end of 1981, both Weinberger and Reagan had made damaging gaffes, likely informed in part by their readings or misreadings of NSDD 13, regarding the idea that nuclear wars could be limited in scope or duration or that they could be "won."[65] Outlandish statements by lower-level appointees about issues such as civil defense and replacing the doctrine of deterrence with a doctrine of "compellance" based on nuclear dominance further plagued the administration. Just at the moment when Reagan and his cohorts were trying to assure the U.S. and Western European publics that they took nuclear weapons and arms control seriously, such statements did serious, lasting damage to their credibility and galvanized opposition forces such as the nuclear freeze movement.[66]

A Different Shade of SALT

On November 30, 1981, Nitze and a U.S. team met with a Soviet in Geneva for the first negotiations toward a treaty on intermediate-range nuclear forces. Nitze worked with the Soviet head of delegation to improve operating procedures and remove small issues that would only distract from the larger issues. Instead of negotiating a start and end date for each session, thus activating a form of brinksmanship in which each party waited for the other to request a break, the delegations met for eight weeks at a time, with eight-week intervals at home. From the outset, Nitze made clear that the United States desired a substantive agreement; he was not there to mark time or solely to win propaganda points. Nitze also relished the opportunity to keep the Soviet negotiators on the defensive about the political implications of their military deployments. For Nitze, the negotiations offered best of both worlds: a chance to be the one to hold the Soviets to account rhetorically and at the same time work toward positive negotiating outcomes.[67]

The Politburo's pick for Nitze's counterpart gave some indication of how seriously the Soviets took the negotiations: Ambassador Yuli Kvitsinsky was a widely respected member of the Soviet diplomatic corps; his appointment a demonstration of Soviet seriousness. Kvitsinsky had served as deputy chief of the Soviet mission in Bonn for the previous three years. Appointing someone with deep knowledge of the West German political scene was a sign of the Soviet Union's grasp of the geopolitical importance of exchanges at the bargaining table. Nitze found it more agreeable to work with Kvitsinsky than with most Soviet delegates he had encountered in the past, though the relationship was still occasionally rocky. Kvitsinsky made no secret of his ambitions, and was aware of how far he had risen in the Foreign Ministry and how far he might yet reach. Like many Soviet diplomats, he was prone to periodic polemical outbursts, but Nitze was able to work past these harangues, especially when they met in private.[68]

When Nitze found his counterpart too ideological for productive discussion, he was often able to connect better with the military representatives on the Soviet delegation, who seemed embarrassed by their colleagues' propagandizing. In particular, Nikolai Detinov earned Nitze's respect for his clear understanding of the relative balance of forces in Europe and his off-the-record admissions that many Soviet talking points on the definition of a medium-range system were nonsense.[69] Detinov was, in fact, more than a military liaison; he was also a member of the "little five" decision-making body within the Politburo, a deputies' group of the Politburo convened to perform technical analyses and make recommendations on Soviet arms control proposals to the "big five" senior members of the Soviet government. Kvitsinsky's implied political connections and Detinov's role in Soviet decision making meant that the Soviet delegation again had a much shorter line of communication to the Politburo than the U.S. delegates did to the White House.[70]

From the start, the Soviet delegation made clear how its half of the propaganda war would be fought: by expanding the accounting of medium-range systems, offering a freeze or even significant reductions, and bringing U.K. and French nuclear forces into the all with the goal of shutting the United States out of Europe. All of these ideas were based on the premise that the Soviets could force the United States to cancel its planned deployment of missiles in NATO countries. The Soviets were trying to squeeze out U.S. forward-based systems once and for all.[71]

Soviet negotiators argued that if all of the theater-range weapons arrayed across Europe were accounted for, including both missiles and nuclear-capable aircraft with similar ranges as missiles in this class had, then the U.K., U.S., and French nuclear forces outnumbered those of the Soviet Union by several multiples. To make this argument, Kvitsinsky cited dubious figures for aircraft range that included nearly all of the tactical air forces of the United States, including the F-15 Eagle, the F-4 Phantom, and the FB-111 Aardvark. Despite the West's numerical advantage, Kvitsinsky first repeated what General Secretary Brezhnev had offered only a few weeks before the first round of talks began: the Soviets would freeze the deployment of all medium-range systems until a comprehensive agreement was reached. Given that the Soviet military was then deploying the SS-20 at a rate of two per week, the proposed freeze implied a genuine sacrifice.[72]

Kvitsinsky also offered an alternative that seemed even more dramatic than the deployment freeze: both the Soviets and the United States, the United Kingdom, and France would reduce the weapons that were "threatening Europe" to approximately 300 per side. This proposal required the Soviets to remove hundreds of missile and air units and went a long way toward demonstrating Soviet seriousness. The genius of the position was that the United Kingdom and France had about 250 nuclear delivery vehicles total, including bombers and missiles, all of which the Soviets included in their calculations. If the United States accepted this proposal, it would have to reduce its already-limited presence in Europe to a paltry fifty systems of any kind, while the Soviet Union would only have to withdraw the great bulk of its mobile SS-20s and Backfires behind the Ural mountains in order to meet its obligations.[73]

The reductions proposal was even more lop-sided on closer inspection. The Soviets' initial deployments of the SS-20 replaced retiring SS-4s and SS-5s on a roughly one-to-one basis. Around 1979, after the deployment of SS-20s became controversial and the prospect of negotiating on these systems became certain, the Soviets accelerated the deployment and halted the decommissioning of SS-4s and SS-5s. This was likely a deliberate move to temporarily pad their force figures, giving them a margin to negotiate away at minimal cost to themselves.[74] Any reductions under this proposed scheme would likely have come almost exclusively from SS-4s and SS-5s.

Nitze's instructions were to remain mum on the issue of aircraft; the JCS adamantly insisted that they should not be included in an agreement on intermediate-range weapons and feared that even discussing the concept might generate pressure to include them. The instructions did give Nitze some latitude (though not as much as his minders in Washington believed) to dispute Soviet mischaracterizations, so he wasted no time in dissecting the Soviet position.[75] He pointed out that the Soviet numbers did not add up: the Soviet statistics used global figures for the number of U.S. medium-range aircraft but counted only Soviet aircraft that had been deployed to the European theater. Nitze also argued that it was problematic to compare the ranges of ballistic missiles, cruise missiles, and aircraft. Aircraft are designed for a return trip, while missiles are not. Aircraft flight profiles are also far more versatile, which makes it more difficult to establish an authoritative range figure. A variety of factors such as altitude, speed, armaments, and even humidity affect an aircraft's exact range. Most important, Nitze emphasized that aircraft were vulnerable to unrestricted air defenses, they had been a feature of the European theater for decades, and they could not be blamed for threatening to destabilize the theater nuclear balance, the ultimate reason for the negotiations.[76]

Nitze also insisted that the United States would never negotiate an agreement that compensated the Soviet Union for the existence of U.K. and French missiles. The United States' reasons were manifold, and effectively making this point was one of the most important aspects of Reagan administration arms control policy. The United States did not have the right to negotiate away weapons that were not its own; this was a matter of basic sovereignty. In addition, these missiles were strategic weapons in yield, range, and delivery vehicle. They were meant to be a last line of defense to protect a country's existence and their force levels were consistent with the minimum necessary to do so. These weapons were clearly not a means of manipulating the balance of power in the region or an attempt to control the escalatory framework of a potential conflict in order to gain political concessions. In effect, the Soviet Union's argument asserted a right to a number of nuclear weapons that was equal to or greater than the sum of the weapons of the other four declared nuclear powers on the assumption that all of these weapons were directed at them. Nitze and other U.S. officials derided these arguments by claiming that Soviet calls for "equal security" in practice meant total security for the Soviet Union and total insecurity for the rest of the world.[77]

As for the temporary freeze proposal, Nitze repeated the U.S. line that it was a sham concession intended to lock the Soviet Union into its existing state of dominance. To call for a freeze in theater deployments in 1982 was akin to the United States calling for a freeze on ICBM construction in 1964. From the U.S. perspective, the freeze proposal was intended for Western European public consumption: it positioned the Soviet Union as the party that was trying to stop the arms competition and helped establish the narrative that the proposed NATO missile deployments were the true reckless escalation. By dismissing the proposal as a media stunt, however, many U.S. policymakers may have missed the insight it provided into Soviet thinking: it revealed a deep resistance to allowing any portion of the NATO missile deployment to proceed.[78]

Despite a sharp exchange of views, Nitze returned home from the first round relatively upbeat. He managed to keep the Soviet delegation off balance for much of the round and had denied them any propaganda victories. Outside the top-level positions, the two delegations had made substantial progress on other issues, such as agreed definitions and other protocols to be included in a final agreement. This level of cooperation seemed promising to Nitze.[79]

However, what Nitze failed to realize was that he was increasingly out of step with his Washington colleagues. When he returned in January, Nitze found himself at the center of several bruising interagency fights, for the most part on the losing side. Nitze stayed out of the initial fights over the form of the zero option, believing that events at the negotiating table would render detailed instructions about the zero option moot anyway. Several details in the U.S. negotiating position remained unresolved, however. The most notable of these pitted Nitze against his former protégé, Assistant Secretary of Defense Richard Perle. At issue was the familiar question of whether the treaty should ban only nuclear-equipped cruise missiles or whether the likely difficulty of verifying such a prohibition justified banning all land-based cruise missiles within a given range. The JCS decided that they would not need a conventional land-launched cruise missile and therefore would not object, and the Department of State and ACDA concurred. Perle, however, overruled the JCS and did everything possible to make sure that if by chance any agreement came to pass, it controlled as little as possible. National Security Advisor William Clark and President Reagan agreed with Perle on this issue, breaking the interagency deadlock. Nitze was able to twist the actual instructions given him into a deferral of the issue by classifying it as a verification problem. Hard-liners such as Perle insisted verification issues could not be settled until the rest of the terms of the agreement had been settled. The incident was instructive for Nitze, however. It illustrated Perle's considerable power and growing gap between them.[80]

Nitze's drift from the administration continued after the second round. In March, after expressing cautious optimism at a White House press conference, Rostow very publicly contradicted Nitze's rosy assessment, saying that the talks to date had been a disappointment and attacking the Soviet negotiators' seriousness. Nitze's forays into discussions of aircraft limitations also came back to haunt him when the relevant interagency groups began to draft much stricter instructions for the third round. In this case, Perle uncharacteristically intervened, restoring some autonomy to Nitze's instructions, but Nitze's influence seemed to be slipping. Hard-liners within the administration such as began openly questioning whether Nitze had gone soft or if his famous problem-solving mindset would lead him astray. While Nitze was very effective at the negotiating table and in NATO capitals, hard-liners began to worry that given enough time he would feel compelled to arrive at an agreement, any agreement, an outcome that at least some in the administration wished to avoid.[81]

In addition to day-to-day negotiating, one of Nitze's main jobs in Europe was to brief and consult with other NATO governments to keep them apprised of the status of the talks and the prospects for an agreement. Nitze found increasing cause for concern in the capitals of these countries, as these cities were racked by anti-nuclear, anti-INF protests that threatened to topple several governments, including West Germany's. Nitze was especially sensitive to these events. He believed that Washington's distance from Europe meant that U.S. policy makers did not appreciate how strained the NATO alliance was. Across the entire Reagan administration, Nitze was the most concerned with the political unpopularity of the deployments and the threat this unpopularity posed to

European governments and to NATO at large. Even if NATO managed to survive the deployments, without an agreement the Soviets seemed likely to walk out of the negotiations entirely, a perhaps more frightening prospect. As a child, Nitze had been on tour in Europe when the First World War erupted. The experience of hurriedly evacuating with his family from a continent on the brink of self-destruction left a lasting impression, Over the next eighteen months before the NATO missile deployments began, Nitze grew increasingly concerned that he was once again witness to the kind of civilizational unraveling that preceded a cataclysm.[82]

While Nitze was ruminating, Kvitsinsky unwittingly threw him a lifeline. The Soviet delegate's hints about Brezhnev's desires implied he had level of political connectedness that was unusual for the head of a Soviet delegation. At the start of the fourth round, Kvitsinsky warned Nitze off the record that the Politburo was planning a major review of its INF positions in the summer. According to him, the likely outcome of this review meeting would be a decision to stay the course with current Soviet positions, intensify the propaganda war, and continue to threaten to abandon talks if the United States deployed missiles. Given the timing of the review and the NATO deployment schedule starting in November 1983, there would likely not be another review before deployment. In other words, if something major did not change soon, the fate of the negotiations might be sealed by the end of the summer. Recognizing Kvitsinsky's position, Nitze asked if his counterpart would be able to communicate a backchannel proposal directly to Foreign Minister Gromyko if the proposal was serious enough. After taking time to coordinate with Moscow, Kvitsinsky confirmed that he had Gromyko's ear.[83]

Fearful of the political instabilities developing within NATO and recognizing the chaotic nature of the Reagan administration foreign policy process, Nitze faced several difficult questions. He was not opposed in theory to backchannel negotiations, even after he had observed the negative impact of Kissinger's backchannel dealings during the SALT I negotiations. And he believed that the zero option still made sense "as a basis for continuing negotiations."[84] But what if those negotiations had a limited shelf life after which there might be no hope for an agreement, or worse, there might no longer be a united West to defend? Nitze, who had railed against politically convenient arms control, found himself wondering which was worse: the threat that NATO would fracture or the possibility that the United States would sign a flawed accord featuring painful compromises and a reduced degree of verifiability. A well-fashioned compromise proposal, if presented in the right context to both sides, might avert the coming crisis. Informing only his superior and old friend Eugene Rostow, Nitze and Kvitsinsky drove into the mountains, down an old logging road, with the intent to create just such a compromise. The delegations were to be left in the dark, and when the agreed draft was set, each would present it to their superiors as the suggestion of the other. The final compromise package would be a take-it-or-leave-it deal. Both agreed that picking and choosing among the concessions would be a de facto rejection of the whole.[85]

The deal was mostly Nitze's creation, with essential input from Kvitsinsky. Together the two created a delicate mix of compromises around the issues that were most sensitive to each side. Under its terms, both parties would be subject to a limit of 225 medium-range systems (note the nomenclature) of any type in "Europe." To ensure that the Soviet Union did not just pull its SS-20s behind the Ural Mountains, an area that was still in range of NATO countries, Nitze declared the boundary of "Europe" to be the 80° east meridian, deep within the Soviet interior. Within the approved region, the superpowers were permitted 75 missile launchers of a single type only: the SS-20 for the Soviets and the Tomahawk cruise missile by the United States. This trade-off was Nitze's idea, and it was critical: the United States lost the quick-strike ability the Pershing II had provided, assuaging Soviet fears of a decapitating first strike, but it gained an advantage of 33 percent in the number of warheads, since each cruise missile launcher unit had four single-warhead missiles, whereas each SS-20 had three warheads. Beyond 80° east, a second regional ceiling permitted a total of 90 SS-20s, the number then in operation, to deter China. The absolute ceiling incorporated aircraft as well as missiles, but the package defined medium-range aircraft narrowly (for the United States, only the F/FB-111; for the Soviets, the Backfire and several older, uncontroversial Soviet bombers) and set the ceiling at about the level of aircraft then in operation.

In July 1982, Nitze and Kvitsinsky returned to their capitals to present the package. Kvitsinsky promised to have one of his contacts in the Soviet embassy inform Nitze of his success or failure convincing Gromyko. The package required both sides to swallow several bitter pills, and it was highly uncertain if Nitze's "walk in the woods" would work.[86]

Beyond SALT

While Nitze was in Geneva during most of the first half of 1982, the rest of the Reagan administration was trying to hash out a coherent position on talks to reduce central strategic systems. In the November 1981 speech where he announced the zero option, Reagan also said that his administration would negotiate on central strategic systems, although in this case the U.S. goal was substantial reductions narrowly focused on the most destabilizing systems. Reagan dubbed this initiative the Strategic Arms Reduction Talks, or START.[87]

Whereas the administration had developed an INF policy largely in response to pressure from Western Europe, the impetus for START was primarily domestic. By early 1982 Congress and public opinion had both begun to turn against the Reagan administration's rearmament policies with regard to nuclear weapons. The nuclear freeze movement had gained the support of groups ranging from the Church of Jesus Christ of Latter-Day Saints and the Conference of Catholic Bishops to Greenpeace and Patty Reagan, the president's daughter.

Polling showed that the public was opposed to the general idea of nuclear weapons, although on specific questions about the topic the results were less clear. By 1982, support for a freeze on production of new nuclear weapons had reached as high as 79 percent in some polls, though 71 percent of that group stated that they would oppose such an agreement if the Soviet Union could cheat without being detected.[88] Although these results created some room for the Reagan administration to maneuver, the nuclear freeze movement was highly visible and was a serious problem for the administration. On June 12, 1982, 750,000 people marched through Central Park in New York City to protest Reagan's nuclear policies, among the largest political demonstrations in U.S. history to that time.[89]

The movement's power was such that for a time, even stalwart defenders in Congress of Reagan's other policies ran for cover when it came to central elements of the nuclear modernization plan. Even though Reagan had changed the Carter administration's plans for basing the MX in 1981, gaining funding for the missile was an annual struggle, particularly as Reagan's approval ratings sagged in 1982 and 1983. Public opposition to the missile peaked in November 1982: over 58 percent of those surveyed were opposed and only 35 percent were in favor.[90] Only the promise to appoint a bipartisan blue-ribbon commission to reexamine the nuclear triad (and the place of the MX in it) and the promise to reopen arms control talks on central strategic systems was enough to temporarily placate Congressional opposition.[91] The administration was never opposed to restarting negotiations, and indeed most members assumed that it would happen eventually, but the rising tide of anti-nuclear sentiment motivated the often-sclerotic foreign policy apparatus to develop and implement START. Even so, the administration still moved at its own pace. When Reagan announced the concept in November 1981, Haig thought talks could begin by March 1982. Instead, the first NSC meeting dedicated to the topic did not occur until April and the administration did not finalize a position until the end of June. Talks began in July.[92]

Assistant Secretary of State Richard Burt and the Department of State developed an approach to strategic arms reduction that held out some hope of securing an agreement before Reagan's first term was over. Most Reagan appointees opposed the concept of negotiability because they believed that it was a form of self-censorship that gave too much weight to Soviet preferences. But Burt wanted to avoid a repeat of the zero option; he worried that the negotiations would stall and that the United States would seem intractable. Burt preferred a principle of "plausibility" that would allow the United States to stake out a unique position without precluding an agreement.[93]

Burt and Assistant Secretary of Defense Richard Perle co-chaired the interagency panel that developed potential U.S. negotiating positions. They almost immediately butted heads. Perle believed that Burt's emphasis on plausibility meant that his plan too closely resembled the SALT II framework. Burt's package focused first on reducing the total number of warheads on ballistic missiles(both ICBMs and SLBMs) by about one-third to 5,000; of these, land-based ICBMs could have no more than 2,500 warheads. Burt's proposal further limited the total combined number of SLBMs and ICBMs to about 1,200, a reduction of almost 400 for the United States and almost 1,100 for the Soviet Union. Perle saw in Burt's limits and sub-limits a return to the *matryoshka*-doll structure of SALT II. He argued through Secretary of Defense Weinberger that the U.S. position should not have any limit on the number of launchers but should instead focus solely on the metrics that he thought mattered most: warhead count and throw weight.[94]

Burt and Perle remained at loggerheads for several months as they tried to sell their competing plans. The question of what metrics ought to be controlled by any given agreement became known as "units of account," Preferences for specific unites of account became one of the defining differences between the major positions within the administration. Deputy National Security Advisor Robert McFarlane stepped in to break the impasse. He had come into this role after Reagan asked for Richard Allen's resignation in January 1982 as a result of a bribery scandal and a spate of bad press orchestrated by White House insiders who were interested in forcing him out. William Clark, a retired judge who had worked with Reagan as far back as his days as governor of California, replaced Allen. Clark brought McFarlane in as his deputy, in part to compensate for inexperience in foreign affairs. McFarlane, who had recently retired from the Marine Corps, had distinguished himself as a staff officer. He turned his skills to fixing the START policy process with alacrity. Many of McFarlane's efforts over the next two years focused on helping the arms control process along, covertly undermining the influence of Perle and Weinberger in the process. In 1982, McFarlane worked behind the scenes to help structure the NSC's consideration of START positions in a way that would help Burt's position.[95]

In March of 1982, McFarlane announced that the interagency team had only a few months to develop a coherent position and identified five principles to guide the discussion. These "terms of reference" proved enormously helpful, not just for structuring consideration of the options but also for helping the administration develop a common understanding of START's main goals and objectives. McFarlane stated that any agreement 1) had to have a basis in equality; 2) had to focus on fostering stability; 3) had to aim for significant reductions; 4) had to be developed with an eye toward ease of comprehensibility of the units of account (and therefore be easier to defend to the public); and 5) had to be adequately verifiable. These terms were not static, and administration officials occasionally added new terms of reference, but they were an orderly highpoint in an often disorderly process.[96]

When the National Security Council finally met to discuss START in April 1982, whether and how to include throw weight as a unit of account had become the essential question. Burt, who had consulted with Kissinger-era SALT veterans, knew well that throw-weight limitations were both nearly unverifiable and likely not negotiable. He stuck to his plan for combined warhead/launcher limits, delivering an extended presentation to the NSC, showing how his plan would still result in significant reductions in Soviet throw weight, especially for the most dangerous and supposedly destabilizing systems, the SS-19 and SS-18. Burt argued that it was better to use throw weight as a measure of an agreement's success rather than a unit of account. To that end, he presented throw-weight reductions as one of the main benefits of his plan and his warheads-and-launchers approach as one of the most practical ways of improving stability.[97]

Perle's plan had the virtue of making throw-weight limitations explicit, a position that he believed was both the received wisdom after listening to a decade of critiques of arms control and a legislative mandate that dated back to the 1972 Jackson amendment to SALT I, which Jackson later stated would have required throw weight to be explicitly equalized in any future agreement. The fact that Perle was arguing that a nonbinding Congressional resolution seriously probably seemed out of place in the executive branch, but his ability to invoke Jackson's legacy provided a powerful counterargument to Burt's pragmatism. Weinberger, predictably, backed Perle, although he did not seem to fully understand that Perle's plan still contained other metrics. Reagan, despite Haig's protests, seemed to be leaning Weinberger's way.[98]

A year earlier, this support would have been enough to make Perle's proposal the official negotiating position, but a critical defection forced a compromise. The Joint Chiefs of Staff chafed under Perle's dictatorial style and had priorities of their own. They worked out a deal with Burt: they would support Burt's package but only if it contained a substantially lower limit on ballistic missiles of 850 rather than 1,200. The reasons for this change were twofold: the JCS was responsible for implement U.S. nuclear war plans known as the Single Integrated Operational Plan (SIOP), which NSDD 13 had greatly impacted. Lower numbers of launchers created fewer targets, which made it easier to implement the SIOP's requirements. Keeping the warhead limit static while decreasing the number of launchers would mean that the only force structure that could accommodate this mission was one with substantial numbers of MIRV-equipped MX and Trident missiles. With the support of the Joint Chiefs, and continued subtle help from McFarlane, Burt was able to draw support away from the package Perle had proposed. The consensus START package Reagan approved involved a proposed a first phase of reductions centered on Burt's ceilings followed by a second phase in which direct limitations on throw weight came into play. Perle won concessions on a variety of other more minor issues in the package, but for the first time he failed to stymie Burt and the Department of State on the most important aspects of a major arms control package.[99]

The START package was a deeply flawed position. When he heard about the updated launcher limits the Joint Chiefs had proposed in a NSC meeting in May, Rostow nearly lost his composure, noting that the new package actually *increased* incentives to convert missiles to their MIRV variants and would likely produce a net decrease in strategic stability.[100] The proposed cuts were steep and would have fallen disproportionately on the Soviets' favorite systems while postponing U.S. reductions for years. Unlike the zero option, the START position also failed the test of sustainability. After barely more than a year of negotiations, the administration turned to an outside commission to produce new options, largely in response to withering criticism from Congress that had grown so severe it threatened the MX program.[101]

The sustainability test was important, particularly as it became clear that both the United States and the Soviet Union did not want to see much progress in the START talks before the INF talks bore fruit. INF deployments were the most contentious and potentially destabilizing aspect of the nuclear balance; it also was the arena in which the most important political gains could be won. These facts pointed to the wisdom of locking down medium-range nuclear levels before making a broader agreement. Personnel choices reflected these priorities. Reagan appointed retired general Ed Rowny to lead the START delegation. While Rowny was effective at managing the negotiations, at heart he was a hard-liner with very little interest in an agreement. In addition, the Soviets had very little regard for him. The head of the Soviet delegation, Victor Karpov, was a less weighty figure than Kvitsinsky. Karpov was a career diplomat and a veteran of previous SALT negotiations who was assumed to have close political ties in Moscow. U.S. delegates reached this last conclusion because Karpov was at best a functioning alcoholic and his embarrassing off-duty escapades left few other explanations for his continued employment.[102]

The U.S. START position included details relating to the treatment of bombers, the Backfire, cruise missiles, and more. Perle's objections notwithstanding, it was a definitive break with SALT. The U.S. position in the INF talks had important roots in the SALT negotiations and recentered some of the most important issues that had been discussed in those talks. But the U.S. START position abandoned the missile launcher as the primary unit of account and the idea of a combined ceiling for missiles and bombers. Its emphasis on warheads and throw weight implied a vision of nuclear competition that differed from the offense-defense dynamics that underpinned SALT I or from the technological determinism of SALT II. Although the precepts and patterns that had defined the SALT negotiations lived on in the INF talks, the Reagan administration dispensed with them permanently with its vision for START.

The Walk in the Woods Goes to Washington

When he returned to Washington, Nitze delivered a series of briefings that informed the relevant executive branch officials of the nature of his overtures and just how much he had managed to negotiate. This culminated in Nitze presenting to a secret, limited meeting of the NSC in August 1982. Nitze benefited from two notable absences from this meeting. Richard Perle was on a working vacation with his family in Colorado. Reagan had nominated Burt as assistant secretary of state for European affairs in May, but his nomination hit a snag as when Senate conservatives questioned the rumors about Burt's supposed zeal for an agreement. Incoming secretary of state George Shultz decided to limit Burt's exposure to arms control issues until his confirmation was assured, and thus he was absent from this meeting. The absence of these two individuals helped ensure a fairer hearing for the proposal, as neither could attempt to drag Nitze's proposal into the ongoing Perle/Burt turf wars.[103]

The initial response to Nitze's proposal was cautious but receptive. Even Undersecretary of State for Policy Fred Iklé, Perle's boss and no stranger to arms control, seemed impressed by Nitze's accomplishment. The former director of ACDA appreciated the elegance of Nitze's proposal and the thinking that underpinned its trade-offs. Shultz, a labor economist by training and a veteran of many contentious union-management negotiations, was less concerned with the substance of the package than with the fact that the Soviet leadership saw fit to make a private overture: in his experience, this meant that the other side was serious about seeking a compromise settlement.[104]

Reagan expressed some reservations but was definitely intrigued. He agreed with Shultz that the private approach was a good sign, speaking from his own experience as the head of the Screen Actors' Guild, but giving up the Pershing II seemed problematic, especially considering how often he had heard from the NSC how critical it was to the defense of NATO. Some of the seeds of this doubt had been planted by McFarlane, who had briefed him earlier.[105] While McFarlane generally favored the pro–arms control side of the administration and tried to help where he could, he was also a retired Marine commander with deep respect for the chain of command. Nitze had gone rogue and acted without authority. McFarlane was trying to bring a sense of order the national security process of the administration, and he believed that this kind of behavior should not be encouraged.[106]

Over the following weeks, the administration's enthusiasm waned but did not take a decisive turn against the package.[107] Perle returned from vacation and immediately began a campaign against the agreement Nitze had hammered out with Kvitsinsky. He believed that Nitze had endangered all of assurances the United States had given allies that the zero option was the only negotiating position the United States had and the pledge that if there were others it would consult with those allies first. Furthermore, the Nitze plan retreated from two of the central principles upon which the U.S. position was predicated: equality and global limits. Perle argued that equality was not just a quantitative feature; it also meant equality of rights, specifically, the right to deploy intermediate-range ballistic missiles, which the Soviet Union would retain and the United States would not in the Nitze-Kvitsinsky proposal. Perle made sure that, when the NSC reconvened, Weinberger provided a full-throated articulation of these objections in response to Nitze's presentation.[108]

The NSC met again to discuss Nitze's proposal in September. At this meeting, Reagan tended to agree with Weinberger that giving up the Pershing II went too far and that that fact needed to be communicated to the Soviet leadership, but not in such a way as to indicate that the United States was totally unwilling to privately explore more creative solutions to the INF impasse. Shultz was present, but in view of the president's feelings decided not to try to drive himself between Weinberger and Reagan. Shultz had only been in office a few months and was at the time focused on Middle East issues. He was also disinclined to think about the minutiae of specific packages, preferring to focus primarily on process. Since Reagan's instructions emphasized keeping the channel open, Shultz had less basis to object to what Reagan was recommending. Reagan thought Nitze's plan had a number of redeeming qualities, but he found it difficult to believe that a better outcome to the United States would not appear if the United States held out just a bit longer. Here Shultz tended to agree with Reagan as well. a better outcome would come about if the United States held out a bit longer, an analysis that Shultz tended to agree with. When Nitze restated his final pitch and asked what he was supposed to tell his counterpart, Reagan replied, "Well, Paul, you just tell the Soviets that you're working for one tough son-of-a-bitch."[109]

Nitze was crestfallen, but by mid-September there was already reason for him to doubt whether his package could have succeeded. He never heard from Kvitsinsky's embassy contact, an ominous sign. Shultz and Gromyko were due to meet before the INF talks reconvened, and the administration decided to discuss the U.S. reaction to the walk-in-the-woods package only if Gromyko mentioned it. Gromyko did not do so; Shultz was only able to obliquely refer to the U.S. hope that *all* channels of communication could be kept open.[110]

Only when Nitze returned to Geneva in the fall did he receive the full story from Kvitsinsky. Far from a provisional or qualified "no," the Soviet response was a total rejection of the formula and its most basic elements. Whatever the status of the Soviet leadership's review of INF policy, the walk in the woods proposal barely registered. Kvitsinsky returned with instructions to identify more strongly than ever the absolute prerequisites for Soviet acceptance: "full compensation" for British and French systems, no limits on INF systems outside Europe, and most importantly, no deployment of Pershing II or Tomahawk GLCMs within Western Europe. According to Kvitsinsky, the existing state of INF negotiations served Soviet interests already because it drove wedges between NATO members, fueled anti-nuclear activism, and pressured allied governments to break with the United States. The walk-in-the-woods package would mean the Soviets had sanctioned the U.S. deployment of INF systems to NATO countries, and thus mitigate these trends favorable to Soviet power. Finally, Kvitsinsky informed Nitze that his superiors were no longer interested in any more private discussions unless Nitze could speak with the full authority of the secretary of state. The backchannel was effectively closed.[111]

The fallout from the walk-in-the-woods episode at first was minimal. The Reagan administration did a remarkable job of keeping the exercise a secret, even from the allies. Simmering resentments remained, however. First the National Security Council rebuked both Nitze and Rostow for acting without instructions. Nitze was too much a legend in too important a role to fire, however, and in any event Shultz seemed willing to rely on him more after his first few months. Rostow was a different story; he had rubbed administration officials the wrong way from the moment he arrived by spouting off on topics unrelated to arms control,[112] claiming authority that was not his, and employing a combative, professorial style that most found grating. In January 1983, in an interview, Rostow revealed some crucial identifying details (another bad habit) about what had transpired the previous summer.[113] This interview was the last straw and Reagan almost immediately requested Rostow's resignation, making him the only casualty of Nitze's unauthorized endeavor.[114]

As more details about the proposal came to light, the walk-in-the-woods episode captured the imagination of many, inspiring much commentary and even an off-Broadway play. In most of this commentary, Reagan was blamed for the failure of the initiative. (His "one tough son-of-a-bitch" comment certainly did not help.) The Reagan administration hardly slammed the door on the proposal, however, especially as compared to the Soviet response. Subsequent Soviet accounts have shown the degree to which the Soviet leadership recoiled from the dual-track decision on principle and that they refused to accept that the propaganda dynamics of nuclear arms and arms control were shifting underneath their feet. Instead, they chose to dig in around a set of increasingly unrealistic positions in the period 1981–1983.[115] Because Soviet leaders had become so divorced from changes in the world around them, the process of finalizing an agreement was bound to be more difficult and acrimonious.

A common view among advocates of arms control at the time tried to absolve the Soviet government of its inflexibility by depicting the Soviet system as a hopelessly paralyzed bureaucracy. In this view, only initiative on the part of the United States could prompt the Soviets to reach an agreement on arms control issues. Thus when an agreement failed to materialize it was due to President Reagan's supposed intransigence on the issue of arms control. The Reagan administration explicitly disavowed this assumption, however. Perhaps the best illustration of the gulf between Reagan's intransigence and Soviet paralysis can be found in the instructions Reagan gave to Nitze before he left again for Geneva following the rejection of the walk-in-the-woods proposal. Nitze was to indicate that the provision that prohibited U.S. intermediate-range ballistic missiles was unequal from the U.S. perspective but that the United States wished to keep the channel open and to continue discussions in this vein. While the zero-zero approach was "best," according to the instructions, if the Soviet negotiators continued to oppose it, Nitze was to invite them "to propose alternatives for equitably reducing the total missile force structure."[116] The Reagan administration was signaling flexibility to the Soviet Union, but it was not willing to eat crow and abandon the zero option publicly before it found an alternative position to which both sides could agree.

Indeed, the barest hint of flexibility from the Soviet Union would likely have helped tip the scales in favor of the walk-in-the-woods plan if it had been received before the September NSC meeting. When many Reagan officials discussed the plan's rejection after the fact, they admitted that they probably could have lived with the package if it had been a final outcome, but it was the absolute outside limit of acceptability. Most administration officials feared that the Soviet leadership would engage in its longtime practice of pocketing concessions linked to a package while returning to its original position. Of course, because of this fear the Reagan administration did something similar: it selected the one aspect of the package it found unacceptable and tried to keep the compromise otherwise undisturbed. The United States did not try to hold the Soviets to all of their potential concessions in the package from then on, however. It was a sign of how far apart the superpowers were that the Soviets did not use the tactic themselves but instead rejected the package outright.[117]

The rejection of the walk-in-the-woods proposal was a key turning point from several perspectives. It was the high-water mark for the influence that individuals such as Perle and Weinberger had over arms control policymaking. Once Shultz settled into his role, he realized that negotiating with Weinberger was useless as he would never move from his opening position; it was better to avoid dealing with him in advance and thus previewing of State's arguments. Instead, Shultz adopted a strategy of slowly cutting the least cooperative people in the Department of Defense and the NSC out of the loop by gaining direct access to the president and helping frame issues before Weinberger had a chance to make them into matters of all-encompassing principle.[118]

Nitze was less fortunate. Now tainted with the scent of dovish defeatism, he found himself in a position within the administration not unlike that of Henry Kissinger a decade earlier: a pragmatist suddenly surrounded by hard-liners who questioned his commitment. Nitze doggedly implemented his instructions after this point but never gave up on identifying areas or approaches that might help bring the parties closer to an agreement. Though he put a hawkish face on his analysis, Nitze's pessimism went into overdrive in 1983, until he was far and away the least optimistic person in the Reagan administration about NATO's prospects and the likelihood that the West German government would survive the looming deployment vote.[119]

Final Moves

The year 1983 put both superpowers to the test. Public opinion in Western Europe continued to view the NATO deployments sourly and began to take a turn against them. The Schmidt government of West Germany fell as his left wing broke away, and while the more conservative government of Christian Democrat Helmut Kohl seemed slightly more resilient, Bonn continued to delay the authorization vote for the first deployments. Both the heads of state of the superpowers and their delegations began an intricate dance, each trying to demonstrate more flexibility than the other without abandoning their essential positions and using their positions as markers they could point to if the worst happened when the deployments went forward. The Soviet negotiators began making clearer threats about walking out of the negotiations and about the "military countermeasures" that would be necessary if the deployments went forward. U.S. negotiators would not publicly accept that a walkout was inevitable and continued to push for a compromise so long as the Soviet delegation remained. The goal of this position was to make a decision to walk away as costly as possible for the Soviet Union.[120]

Brezhnev's death in November 1982 did not seem to register much in Geneva, but his successor, Yuri Andropov, increasingly sought to use his bully pulpit to influence public opinion and shape perceptions of the two sides' negotiating stances. In December, Andropov publicly announced a new proposal that modified the existing Soviet stance of dual Soviet/NATO ceilings of 300 medium-range systems in the European theater. In addition to these ceilings, Andropov promised a ceiling on ballistic missiles of all kinds that would "match" the U.K. and French systems and indicated a willingness to consider warheads as the unit of account instead of missiles. This provision cleverly laid a trap for the allies that would be difficult to explain to the voting public. By linking warheads across SS-20s and British and French submarine forces, he could effectively quash plans that were already in process to upgrade these SLBMs to modern MIRV configurations.[121]

A growing chorus inside and outside the Reagan administration called for moving away from the zero option and countering Andropov's offers with a specific proposal that ensured equality of rights and some semblance of global limits. Unfortunately, most in this chorus were individuals who had opposed the zero option in the first place, such as Burt and Deputy Secretary of State Lawrence Eagleburger. By early 1983, both Helmut Kohl and Margaret Thatcher had begun hinting in public (and expressing themselves more clearly in private) that the United States had to demonstrate some level of flexibility in response to the new Soviet positions or risk placing both West Germany and the United Kingdom in an untenable position.[122]

Reagan himself likely sensed that the time was right for a change in tone. During a private meeting, Shultz indicated that the existing U.S. position was at risk of growing stale and that some efforts to augment it would probably be necessary during the coming year in order to keep the deployments on track. The president agreed and said he had been thinking the same thing. Timing would be critical: the West German elections were coming up and the United States needed to avoid the impression that it was deliberately trying to manipulate electoral outcomes. But it also needed to keep its change in position from feeling too sudden once the elections had concluded.[123]

Nothing could be certain until the rest of the executive branch weighed in. On January 13, 1983, the National Security Council met to discuss whether changes in the U.S. position on intermediate-range nuclear forces were necessary. Shultz began the meeting by making the case that some change was needed, but he sought to organize the discussion in terms of several discrete principles.

Zero-zero, he said, was important only because it kept the anti-nuclear movement at bay, framed the issue of the deployments as an undesirable but exigent
necessity, and established a moral differential between NATO and Soviet missiles. Abandoning zero-zero as the desired outcome undercut all of these efforts.
Therefore, any change in position had to be explained as "being on the way to
zero-zero." The next most important principle was equality: "we could say to
the Soviets that here is what we think equality means. If you (the Soviets)are
interested in equality but not zero-zero, what are you interested in?" The official
Department of State position going into this meeting was U.S. and Soviet ceilings of 300 weapons each, but Shultz immediately disclaimed this paper, saying
that his position was to avoid numbers and specific packages but instead to try
to frame the negotiation according to the principles had just articulated and put
the onus on the Soviet negotiators to provide specific numbers.[124]

Weinberger disagreed with the idea that flexibility was needed. Any attempt
to demonstrate flexibility was dangerous and implied that the United States was
abandoning zero-zero. None of the underlying reasons for adopting zero-zero
had changed, and therefore the time to move away from the current position
would be after deployment began. Weinberger concluded, "We are in the best
position now. We should not show flexibility." The JCS and director of central
intelligence endorsed Weinberger's comments.[125]

Reagan then spoke. After he asked a few questions about specific levels and
types on each side, he said, "We must deploy missiles. . . . But if we sit there with
zero-zero in our negotiating position, and they then propose some ridiculous
scheme, we have to respond. Why not go along with an interim reduction of the
forces while continuing the negotiations for zero-zero?" At first cross-talk dominated, as Reagan seemed to disagree with almost everyone at the table except
Shultz (and Ed Meese, who was hardly an authority on security issues). Weinberger stated that this position might be acceptable, but only after deployments
began: "As soon as we move away from zero-zero it is gone forever." Reagan disagreed, saying that "the only way there would be no deployment is if we achieve
zero-zero. We should deploy on schedule." Then he argued that negotiating for
an interim figure would meet with allied approval.[126]

Further discussion in follow-up meetings produced a return to Schultz's
approach to flexibility by setting out broad principles. In a speech to the American Legion on February 22, Reagan stated that the zero-zero approach was not a
"take it or leave it" position (borrowing language from Margaret Thatcher on the
subject) and that the United States would explore and take seriously any position
that met four criteria: 1) "equality of rights and limits"; 2) no compensation for
or accounting of U.K. and French forces; 3) provisions for adequate verifiability;
and 4) restrictions on Soviet forces in Asia as well as Europe. This final point was

crucial, as it represented an almost totally unnoticed retreat from the original U.S. position, which required "global limits" on the weapons without regard to geography. Now the U.S. requirement was a negative one: the final agreement could not shift the theater nuclear forces problem from one continent to another, a much lower standard.[127]

On March 30, after consultations with the allies, Reagan announced the new position. Short of accepting a total elimination of intermediate-range missiles, the United States was now willing to consider "interim" positions between 0 and 576 that the Soviet Union would find acceptable while negotiations continued toward total elimination. The Department of State, largely at Burt's prodding, wanted to propose a specific package, but the Department of Defense and Richard Perle, fighting a rearguard action against any concessions, argued against that, instead saying that the interim proposal should be predicated on Soviet acceptance of zero intermediate-range missiles as the ultimate goal. Reagan overruled both, and the middle-ground package he developed with National Security Advisor Clark bore a striking resemblance to Shultz and Reagan's first musings about the idea in January.[128]

For the rest of the year, each side worked around the edges of their dominant proposals, but each concession triggered more acrimonious rejection from the other side. Nitze made sure not to allow the negotiations to idle, making multiple proposals in each negotiating round on issues both great and small. When talks resumed in May, Nitze proposed a draft treaty based on the idea of interim reductions, but Kvitsinsky rejected it as the "stillborn twin brother" of the zero-zero draft the United States had proposed the year before. A month later, Nitze proposed nine separate interim packages, increasing by increments of 50 missiles between 50 and 450, only to receive a slightly less morbid rejection from the Soviet delegates.[129]

Andropov and the Soviet delegation would not allow themselves to be outdone. In May, Andropov gave another speech in which he formally offered to regard warheads as the units of account, endorsing equality in this figure while taking into account the UK and French systems. U.S. negotiators countered that this change was inconsistent with their criteria for an agreement and changed only the arithmetic of the Soviet position and nothing else. In August, Andropov modified his existing proposal, committing to "liquidate" or destroy all Soviet missiles withdrawn from Europe instead of reassigning them to the Asian theater.[130]

Reagan insisted on a response to Andropov's proposal, but events nearly derailed the process. On September 1, 1983, a Soviet fighter shot down Korean Airlines Flight 007, which had wandered off course into Soviet airspace. All 243 passengers on board, including a U.S. congressman, died. It seemed a virtual certainty that the INF and other arms-control talks would be canceled, at least for a time, especially as the Soviet response descended from denial to bumbling antagonism. Shultz and Reagan both agreed from an early point that terminating the arms talks would be counterproductive, giving the Soviets a chance to act aggrieved and the ability to complain that the talks were being politicized. A U.S. decision to halt the talks then would rescue the Soviet leadership from having to make good on their ultimatum to walk out if the U.S. missiles ever deployed.[131]

The delegations reconvened in Geneva shortly afterward and continued to exchange ever-more-unlikely proposals and counterproposals in an increasingly toxic atmosphere. In an embarrassing and bizarre effort, the Soviet Union made a last-ditch effort to derail a series of upcoming parliamentary votes in NATO countries in November. These votes would grant final authorization for the arrival of the U.S. missiles. In an off-the-record meeting, Kvitsinsky stated in simple terms that Nitze should propose a package of "equal reductions," whereby the Soviets would remove as many SS-20s as were equivalent to 576 NATO missiles on a warhead-for-warhead basis. That would leave the Soviet Union with about 120 missiles, fewer than ever before proposed. All the United States would have to do was cancel the deployments. Crucially, such a formulation said nothing explicit about third-country systems. Nitze knew that the proposal would go nowhere, as it met none of the four criteria he had helped establish earlier that year. But with all of the Soviet threats regarding walkouts and countermeasures, Nitze feared that the Soviets wanted a clear-cut U.S. rejection of a proposal to be the last official exchange before the November deployment deadline, thus making themselves look like the aggrieved party when they boycotted the negotiations. Instead of flatly rejecting the proposal, Nitze remained noncommittal and reported the exchange back to Washington.[132]

In his reporting cable, Nitze shared his concern that the Soviet delegation was trying to maneuver the United States into the position of rejecting a proposal before the deadline. He recommended that the United States develop a counterproposal based on superficially similar figures in lieu of a rejection. Nitze set to work developing a counteroffer based on a global warhead ceiling that would produce roughly the same number of leftover SS-20s but would also permit an equal number of U.S. missiles to remain in NATO.[133]

Nitze need not have bothered. On November 17, 1983, less than a week before the critical vote in the Bundestag on the deployment of the Pershing II, the Soviet embassy delivered a message to the West German government that claimed that Nitze had proposed an equal reductions scheme to the Soviet delegation but that when the Soviets had responded favorably, the U.S. government had withdrawn the offer. Similar notes were delivered to the rest of the NATO capitals the next day. The Soviet message seemed to imply that a repeat of the walk in the woods had taken place but that this time the United States had been the bad actor block-ing a deal. Alternatively, they may have been trying to imply that the United States had made an offer expecting it to be rejected, but had backtracked when it was accepted because of its fervent commitment to the NATO deployments. Both interpretations seem designed to influence the upcoming parliamentary votes, inflame West European public opinion, and derail at least some component of the deployment, thus introducing a delay or collapse of the plan.[134]

If Nitze had not immediately reported to Washington about his conversation with Kvitsinsky and his plan for a counterproposal, the Soviet trick might have worked. Instead, the process of generating the counterproposal entailed inform-ing the allies of the original offer. Leaders in NATO capitals thus knew the gulf between what had happened and what the Soviets claimed had happened. Most of them reacted with indignation at the idea that the Soviet government thought they would be that gullible. The Soviet plan had backfired badly, and the final weeks of the negotiation were dominated by the Soviet delegation's protestations that they were not guilty of attempting an underhanded ploy that threatened to poison the talks.[135]

On November 14, the first Tomahawk missiles arrived in England. Despite Soviet threats that they would walk out when that happened, the talks did not terminate. Over the following week, missiles were deployed in Italy as well, again with no change in the Soviet position. It became clear that the Soviet leadership was waiting for the Bundestag vote on November 22, after which the first Persh-ing IIs would arrive in West Germany. There had always been some debate about whether the Soviets saw the Pershing II as a greater threat than the hundreds more Tomahawk missiles, and the delegation's stalling tactics seemed to confirm that they did.[136] The Kohl government won the vote by 286 to 226 after a raucous two-day debate, with the Pershing IIs to arrive within days. On November 23rd, the INF delegations met in Geneva. Kvitsinsky read out a brief statement that declared the negotiations "discontinued" and refused to set any date for resump-tion. On December 8th, the Soviet delegation walked out of the START nego-tiations as well.[137] For the first time since 1969, there were no nuclear arms negotiations under way, and it was not apparent that they would ever resume.

Conclusion

A NATO foreign ministers' meeting followed soon after the Soviets walked out. Shultz attended, as did Nitze. On the return flight, their plane had to stop at Shan-non Airfield in Ireland to refuel. Nitze knew the site well; most of the diplomatic flights he'd taken for the last several decades had stopped there. As the plane took off, he looked out at the countryside. As Shultz recounted it, Nitze said, "In the days when Shannon first opened, we had to spend quite a few hours here; there was time to get out and wet a line, kill a salmon or two." Shultz thought Nitze was reminiscing, but it was more likely he was mourning the end of this phase of his life.[138] His wife was suffering from end-stage emphysema, and even if the talks resumed quickly, it was unlikely that he would be able to be away from her for months at a time.[139] Although Nitze would remain deeply involved in arms control issues through Shultz for the next six years, his days as the tip of the diplomatic spear were over. He had spent nearly as much time campaigning against SALT as he had working for it. Now one of the most influential phases of his life would come to a close with it.

SALT indeed ended with the collapse of the talks. If the SALT process represented an approach to nuclear arms negotiations that featured a relatively static strategic balance, a focus on offensive forces, and weak or passive means of verification, then the collapse of INF talks in 1983 was the final nail in its coffin. As much as members of the Reagan administration claimed to disapprove of SALT, it cannot be said that the majority of them actually sought the outcome they faced in 1983. The Reagan administration came into office determined to upset the settled expectations with regard to arms control, specifically the expectation that U.S. negotiators had to preemptively accommodate Soviet concerns or face political consequences. They further sought to upset the expectation that some form of arms control was necessary to provide political cover for deployments of or investments in strategic weapons. While the Reagan administration rejected these expectations, it was not opposed to arms control on principle.

Reagan intuitively understood what it meant to try to upset these expectations while still pursuing an agreement, but precious few of his appointees did. He seemed content to allow dual visions of arms control that were incompatible with his own to dominate the early years of his administration. In one vision, represented by Haig and Burt, a basically tougher form of the SALT process was needed so that important strategic deployments could occur without triggering mass public rejection or an uncontrolled arms race. This vision included the characteristics of domestic condominium that defined previous SALT negotiations, including the use of the arms control process to insulate the president from the political consequences of continued competition, and to aggrandize the president's role in foreign and domestic aspects of nuclear policymaking. The other vision, represented by Perle and Weinberger, was characterized by a moral absolutism that required little engagement with strategic minutiae but sought to avoid stoking the fires of public opinion such that a president might be tempted to sign a suboptimal agreement for political benefit. Nitze and Rostow came close to approximating Reagan's world view, but their backgrounds and their weighing of the risks and opportunities the United States faced were too distinct from Reagan's perspectives to gain traction. While both were excellent strategic thinkers, neither was able to read public opinion well enough to do anything but fear it; both failed to understand the power of public opinion once it was harnessed. Both were also far more concerned about the fragility of NATO than, in retrospect, seems warranted.

It was not until George Shultz arrived on the scene that policy makers were able to channel these conflicts into something closer to Reagan's poorly articulated vision and establish an administration line firm enough to survive the storm of protest following the Soviet walkout. It is worth noting that Shultz was far less concerned with the consequences of a Soviet walkout than most of the rest of the administration. Certainly individuals such as Perle looked forward to it in the hope that it might be permanent, but Shultz seemed relatively confident that it would not last.[140]

In his memoir, Shultz recounts one of the formative experiences of his political career. It happened when he was secretary of labor under Nixon. In late 1968 and early 1969, a massive dockworkers' strike occurred that shut down almost all shipping on the Atlantic and Gulf coasts. President Johnson had already declared the strike a national emergency and had invoked the Taft-Hartley Act to bring the dockworkers back to work and back to the bargaining table. This expired after 80 days, and the strike resumed just as Nixon took office. Nixon's options for dealing with the strike had nearly run out. Shultz told him that his best option was to do nothing. "Let the pressures produced by the strike cause the union and management" to come back to the bargaining table and work out their differences, he counseled. "There will be no dire emergency," he assured Nixon, "and in the end the pressures will work to bring about a private settlement." Sure enough, six weeks later the dockworkers returned to work under an agreement both sides found acceptable. The lesson Shultz took from the episode was that "the key to a successful policy is often to get the right process going. While the economist is accustomed to the concept of lags, the politician likes instant results."[141] Shultz did not take it upon himself to understand all of the technical issues underlying the U.S. position. Instead, he worked to ensure that the United States would be positioned within the process to take maximum advantage regardless of what happened. Managing the process in this way would ensure that any Soviet walkout would be temporary, as the same pressures that had brought the two sides together in the first place would only increase, but to the Soviets' disadvantage.[142]

As a former union negotiator himself, Reagan likely intuited the outlines of the negotiating process in a similar way. He likely realized that oftentimes union negotiators find themselves with a terrible hand and feel pressured to strike, even if there is no likelihood of it securing a better agreement. This situation arises because the alternative is to accept the deal without fighting it and then having to fend off allegations that a better deal could have been secured if only the leader had been willing to strike, an impossible counterfactual. It would not be easy for Soviet negotiators to accept a change to the settled expectations for nuclear arms control, especially one that made clear that the nuclear balance was not static and that the United States was just as capable of upgrading its forces as the Soviet Union. Once the United States demonstrated the political and diplomatic wherewithal to do so, however, it would become a reality to which the Soviets would have to accommodate themselves.

The Soviet leadership, unfortunately, entered the 1981–1983 period with the impression that time and politics were on their side. To them, the first two years of the INF negotiations represented an acceleration of trends that had been present from the outset of SALT. Content to rely on the precedent of the neutron bomb and taking note of the massive protests in Europe and Reagan's disappointing poll numbers, the Soviets doubled down on a strategy of turning the negotiations into an opportunity to subvert NATO and win a permanent victory on forward-based systems that they hoped would carry over into START. While playing on short-term political pressures to improve their position in SALT I and II had worked, the Soviet leadership neglected the fact that, in the long term, they needed arms control more than the United States did. The Soviet arms buildup had created enormous strains on their economy, and because of their increasing international isolation after détente failed to integrate them fully into the world system.

The realization of their position came to the Soviet leadership gradually over the course of 1984. Throughout this year, both in public and in private, the Reagan administration repeated overtures to the Soviet Union to reengage on arms control. The absence of an agreement produced some political problems for the Reagan administration. Any attempt to make political points on the back of the Soviet walkout would highlight what many believed to be an administration failing. Despite this, Reagan's reelection prospects gradually improved to the point of being almost certain, and the Soviet leadership felt compelled to abandon its freeze in relations. Traditionally, credit for this shift is given to Gorbachev and the generational shift in outlook that followed his ascent. While Gorbachev did a great deal to accelerate the arms control process, the return to negotiations in fact occurred under his ostensibly hard-line predecessor, Konstantin Chernenko. In June 1984, Chernenko proposed convening arms control talks that autumn on the "militarization of space," a reference to long-simmering concerns about anti-satellite weaponry. The phrase increasingly became a favored euphemism for restraints on the Reagan administration's Strategic Defense Initiative, which had begun in March 1983. All of the terms and commitments for a return to negotiation grew out of this initiative and were set before Gorbachev took office in March 1985.[143]

Chernenko's proposal put the United States in a favorable position. The Reagan administration highlighted the inconsistency of starting a new set of talks when the Soviet leadership had already declared three existing sets to be intolerable in the current atmosphere. (The Soviet delegation had also declined to set a date to reconvene the Mutual and Balanced Force Reduction talks shortly after the INF and START walkouts.) During his mini-summit with Gromyko in September 1984, Reagan indicated a willingness to engage on space weapons and missile defenses if the Soviets would resume discussions of offensive nuclear arms.[144]

These early discussions led to a meeting between Shultz and Gromyko in January 1985 in which they agreed to fold the three dominant questions into a trinity of arms control talks on intermediate-range nuclear forces, strategic offenses, and space systems.[145] These Nuclear and Space Talks were a "new" negotiation process that allowed the Soviets to save face and make good on their promise not to return to the INF and START negotiations. Negotiators would address these topics in parallel talks, all under a single umbrella. In their format and the contents of their negotiations, the Nuclear and Space Talks definitively broke with the defining characteristics of SALT and inaugurated a new process that was informed by but not controlled by the legacies of SALT.

THE CONSEQUENCES OF CONTROL

Delegates from the superpowers reconvened under the banner of the Nuclear and Space Talks in 1985. They found that although negotiations remained difficult and time-consuming, several possible areas of agreement glimmered on the horizon. Gorbachev, who had come to power in part because of his ability to cater to Western public opinion, emulated the zero option by undercutting U.S. concessions in a bid for moral superiority, usually with the caveat that the United States abandon the Strategic Defense Initiative. Whereas previous Soviet leaders had flirted with expanded means of verification, Gorbachev, with U.S. prodding, accepted the concept of intrusive onsite inspections, abandoned demands for compensation for the UK and French systems, and agreed to eliminate a vastly expanded set of missiles with ranges from 500 to 5,500 kilometers. The resulting Intermediate-Range Nuclear Forces Treaty, signed in 1987, remains one of the most successful arms control treaties of the modern era. Haggling over central strategic systems took longer, especially as detailed procedures for inspections had to be worked out. The parties reached an agreement in 1991 that is still the basic framework for bilateral nuclear arms control today.

The Nuclear and Space Talks and subsequent negotiations benefited from a number of tailwinds that SALT did not experience. Gorbachev was motivated by the fear of total national collapse, as the stagnant Soviet economy struggled to maintain the burden of military spending. For the United States, investments in strategic weapons finally began to affect the strategic balance. The MX entered service in 1986, the same year as the B-1 bomber. In 1987, the first test flight of the Trident II missile occurred, the first SLBM that was accurate enough to make it a potential counterforce weapon. In view of these changes, in 1986 the Reagan administration announced its intention to exceed some of the numerical limits SALT II required, even though the agreement had expired a year earlier. Combined with U.S. investments in missile defense technology, the strategic balance was more dynamic than it had been for decades.

From 1983 to 1989, Nitze served as senior advisor to Secretary of State Shultz on arms control issues. While Shultz never became the dominant figure in the Reagan administration, his influence on U.S.-Soviet policy continued to grow in all but a few areas. With Nitze's help, Shultz was able to steer Reagan through four major meetings with Gorbachev that made great strides in resolving the basic tensions in the U.S.-Soviet relationship and made the first steps toward winding down the Cold War. Nitze was also critical in managing the administration's positions on the Strategic Defense Initiative in such a way that it did not derail existing arms negotiations and could eventually be traded in exchange for deep reductions, despite the best efforts of many of the program's boosters. Shultz resigned at the end of the Reagan administration. President Bush decided to bring in new leadership to his cabinet agencies and conduct a top-to-bottom review of nuclear and arms control policy. Without Shultz as a patron, Nitze was offered only a position as ambassador at large emeritus with no clear powers or responsibilities. Nitze took the hint and resigned. It was a frustrating end to a remarkable career. At 82 years of age, he retired to the Johns Hopkins School for Advanced International Studies, which he had co-founded and which now bears his name.[1]

Perhaps SALT's gravest flaw was that it froze the strategic balance in a suboptimal state. Like a broken bone not properly set, it began to heal around a partially dysfunctional system of technologies and doctrines. Slowing but not halting or reversing the most negative trends in the balance, it allowed these problems to fester while inhibiting the minimal level of dynamism that was needed to grow beyond the era's problems. To be fair, dysfunction is preferable to anarchy, and it is not clear that in the absence of SALT either side would have moved toward judicious, limited deployments of new technologies designed to promote stability as the highest goal. Once SALT was established, it helped ensure that a return to unrestrained competition was highly unlikely, even if the particular framework of SALT exited the scene.

One of the main factors that kept the SALT process going, even as its limited potential became clear, was its ability to channel public discontent about nuclear annihilation into a framework that national elites could control. That framework was still limited and likely lacked the flexibility to actually end or meaningfully reduce the arms competition. Barring major changes in the underlying roots of the Cold War, breaking out of the SALT dynamic would have to be painful and politically costly in the short term.

The unwillingness of administrations to challenge the basic dynamics of SALT illustrates its utility for presidents in charge of negotiations. Nixon and Kissinger inaugurated the process, realizing the threat that the arms race and domestic discontent could pose to their vision for global condominium. In many ways, Nixon's job was the easiest, as SALT I operated with a limited scope and could focus on what seemed like the most pressing problems of the present, rather than attempting to stop or slow down developments a decade or more in the future. Despite these advantages, the Nixon administration made plenty of mistakes. Kissinger operated too autonomously, seriously harming the process when he made mistakes, as he did with the SLBM episode. In his zeal to take credit for the agreement's achievements, Kissinger also made the critical error of overcommitting himself and his credibility in the follow-on negotiations. As they stagnated, so did his influence.

Ford, who inherited the process, accepted its terms almost uncritically. Under Ford, the tendency toward domestic condominium in SALT began to emerge. Explicitly linking progress in arms control to prospects for moving defense expenditures through Congress, the SALT process by 1976 had conveniently placed the president at the nexus of decision making on the most controversial foreign policy issues of the day, but it also provided the tools necessary to insulate the occupant of that office from the controversy and resistance these policies produced. So uncritically did Ford and Kissinger accept the legitimacy of this transformation that they expressed surprise and indignation at the idea that the military would reject an agreement on the basis of its substance alone.

Carter stands out as the president who best understood the details of the SALT negotiations. Indeed, if one is willing to give the Carter administration a pass on the March 1977 summit fiasco, his arms control diplomacy had arguably the best technical execution. Yet his administration lacked a comprehensive vision and allowed the pursuit of SALT II to become a substitute for a strategy. Carter briefly tried to break out of the SALT paradigm, but the Soviet backlash and the perception that his administration had wasted precious time were too much for him to bear. Concerned about his legacy as a peacemaker, sensitive to criticism, and later fighting to preserve his claims to toughness, Carter found in the SALT process an unprecedented means of shaping the U.S. strategic outlook, both operationally and financially. But the range of outcomes that were achievable through negotiation was so limited that the end result left many to wonder whether SALT II had achieved anything significant at all.

Carter put a kinder face on Ford and Kissinger's use of SALT to manipulate domestic interests, opening the process to any constituency that took an interest in it. Unlike Kissinger, who wanted to use SALT to maintain his power, Carter thought that he could use the SALT process to further his ambition to be all things to all people. This strategy could have succeeded only if all parties remained convinced that SALT was the only means by which they could achieve their goals. The breakdown of détente, the instability imputed to Soviet activities in 1979 and 1980, and the emerging political movement for expanded defense spending all undermined this assumption and the SALT II agreement became a dead letter.

It was only with the Reagan administration that U.S. arms control policy reoriented itself in such a way as to find the prospect of a cessation of SALT-formatted talks acceptable. Unfortunately, administration officials in the first term could barely manage to put together a coherent negotiating position on time, let alone develop consensus on long-term strategies such as whether a Soviet walkout was a storm worth weathering.

The Reagan administration's indiscipline redounded to its benefit in unexpected ways. Nixon, Kissinger, and even Ford famously relied on secrecy to conduct their diplomacy, convinced that leaks would only create domestic political complications that risked undercutting their efforts. Seeking to please Soviet negotiators and thus get a better deal, the Carter administration also acceded to the Soviet preference for keeping most of the details of the negotiating table in confidence. Carter administration officials were not above leaking details about the U.S. position, but such releases rarely extended beyond that and were almost always done deliberately. In contrast, the Reagan administration leaked like a sieve. Unlike the administration-coordinated leaks under Carter, these were almost always individual leaks, sometimes made in pursuit of personal advantage and other times made to derail administration efforts with which the leaker disapproved. Had the U.S.-Soviet relationship not been so burdened with other issues, Soviet negotiators would likely have complained quite loudly about the U.S. tendency to violate their confidence.

This lack of control over information meant that the Reagan administration had to conduct its diplomacy essentially in the open. In the realm of INF issues there largely ceased to be a distinction between private and public diplomacy. This environment forced Reagan administration officials to consider the impact of public opinion and the political pressures generated by their positions far more often than they otherwise might have. Considering these factors required a different concept of public opinion, not as something that can belatedly be manipulated or calmly reasoned with, but as a force of nature that can never be discounted as a potential spoiler. Accepting that public opinion could be not be ignored, insulated against, or predicted, the Reagan administration spent much more time ensuring that it was properly positioned to navigate these currents and to ride out whatever storms might hit it, or at least weather them better than the Soviets could. The continuous awareness of these pressures enabled Reagan administration officials to avoid overreaction or to be painted into a corner as Carter found himself after the Soviet invasion of Afghanistan. Though famous for its gaffes and intemperate rhetoric, the Reagan administration's responses during clutch moments such as the downing of KAL 007, Kvitsinsky's walk-in-the-park feint, and the Soviet walkout were measured, considered, and did not limit U.S. negotiating flexibility in the future.

The deleterious effects of excessive secrecy appeared in other realms as well, ultimately hampering the SALT process. The treatment of verification, for instance, worked against the success of SALT over the long run. Satellite surveillance was adequate to verify fixed ground silos, and fortuitous design choices made it possible to verify the count of MIRV-equipped missiles. As the process grew more expansive, negotiators considered broader margins of error because of their reliance on national technical means. As long as these margins remained below the threshold of "military significance," presidential administrations did not regard them as a problem. But because they relied so heavily on highly classified intelligence systems, policymakers hobbled their ability to provide assurances that a given agreement could achieve its aims, thus undercutting a significant objective of the SALT process. Holding information about these capabilities so close to the vest added further complications as administration officials found themselves having to report on compliance with old agreements while trying to develop and defend verification protocols for subsequent agreements.

Across each of these administrations, developments in the realm of nuclear doctrine facilitated the arms control process, though neither counterforce warfighters nor classical deterrence theorists were willing to admit it. After SALT I was completed, a cohort of military planners and strategic thinkers began to emphasize the need for a more sophisticated, scalable approach to nuclear war. The advent of MIRVs and the limits SALT imposed on delivery vehicles bypassed the original stumbling block that prevented McNamara from adopting a counterforce strategy: now both sides could increase the number of weapons while keeping the number of targets the same.

One of the great ironies of classical deterrence theory is that it makes nuclear weapons a source of security. The SALT process encouraged this vision by highlighting it as the platonic ideal of strategic stability. This theory ran into complications in situations of extended deterrence or asymmetric escalatory capabilities, but it had a powerful appeal because it linked stability and security. Each iteration of the major counterforce policies helped introduce a critical level of instability into the nuclear competition without threatening the entire system. NSDM 242 forced planners to consider not just the global strategic balance but also the regional balance. The only way to dominate at a purely local level is to place the opponent's warfighting potential at the same level at risk. Considering how to counteract the unique characteristics of the Soviet arsenal, as PD 59 did, applied the objective of holding Soviet warfighting capacity at risk to global-scale arsenals. And the idea of integrating targeting selection, warfighting, and military acquisition, as NSDD 13 entertained, affirmed these policies by putting money behind them.

Arms control discussions of the early 1980s illustrated the degree to which many of these assumptions had been normalized, for instance as each side compared warhead counts in START or spoke of the theater nuclear balance in Europe and Asia. Even European peace protesters implicitly accepted this framework by opposing NATO's deployments of U.S. intermediate-range missiles on the basis that each missile would create a new target for a Soviet missile. By this point a critical transformation had occurred wherein both sides assumed that one of the main missions of each superpower's nuclear arsenal was to put the other side's nuclear weapons at risk. Unlike classical deterrence, this situation made clear that each nuclear weapon had actually become a source of insecurity in itself because each weapon was on some level a target for the nuclear weapons of the other side. Even if the threat to stability these weapons posed could be controlled, the fact that deterrents had become a source of insecurity created powerful incentives for both sides to reduce their numbers and thus the number of possible targets. While counterforce doctrines originally seemed aimed at the underpinnings of SALT, their cumulative effect was ultimately beneficial for the strategic balance and for reductions. However, this would not have been the case if the framework and parameters the SALT treaties imposed had not been in place.

As SALT passed, so too did détente and the associated concept of linkage. In many ways, the Reagan administration was the first post-linkage presidency. While some officials flirted with coercive strains of the linkage policy, a retrospective examination of Reagan's foreign policy shows that its many Soviet policy issues were usually neither linked nor explicitly delinked. Kissinger saw interconnectedness as a way to advance his many initiatives. Carter felt the need to wall off certain issues such as arms control, only to discover the reality that no issue could be effectively contained in the context of an overall relationship that had turned toxic. Only with Reagan did foreign policy seem to advance beyond linkage in practice. The Reagan administration pushed the Soviet Union on a variety of fronts, including human rights, trade, withdrawal from Afghanistan, and strategic weapons. Recognizing interconnectedness but usually refusing to use that as leverage, the Reagan administration made that it could not guarantee that a sufficient disruption in relations could overwhelm their ability to act on any given initiative. This balance proved crucial to keeping the United States engaged in the process even as the talks broke down or as U.S. criticism of Soviet human rights policies triggered threatening histrionics from Soviet diplomats.

While SALT proved to be a deeply flawed process, it is unlikely that the situation that would have developed in its absence would have been more stable or desirable. Even as its scope grew far beyond all expectations and it seemed to reinforce rather than reduce the strategic arms competition, SALT left durable and important legacies for the control of nuclear armaments. That said, it remains critical that historians acknowledge the unique contributions events and specific individuals made to these negotiations and that they recognize that the factors that shaped these agreements were often highly contingent. It is only in view of these contingencies that historians can describe why these agreements took shape as they did and how SALT failed to overcome its own contradictions.

Notes

INTRODUCTION: THE PROMISE OF CONTROL

1. Document 84, "Memorandum from the President's Deputy Assistant for National Security Affairs (Scowcroft) to President Ford," October 27, 1974, in *Foreign Relations of the United States, 1969–1976*, vol. 33, *SALT II, 1972–1980*, edited by Erin R. Mahan (Washington, DC: U.S. Government Printing Office: 2013), 371; Document 73, "Memorandum of Conversation," October 26, 1974, in *Foreign Relations of the United States, 1969–1976*, vol. 16, *Soviet Union, August 1974—December 1976*, edited by David C. Geyer (Washington, DC: U.S. Government Printing Office: 2012, 253, 254.

1. ARMS CONTROL

1. Richard Fanning, *Peace and Disarmament* (Lexington: University Press of Kentucky, 1995), 25.

2. Laurence Freedman, *The Evolution of Nuclear Strategy* (New York: Palgrave-MacMillan, 2003), 183–195.

3. Stanford Arms Control Group, *International Arms Control: Issues and Agreements* (Stanford, CA: Stanford University Press, 1984), 84–93.

4. See, for example: Michael Mandelbaum, *The Nuclear Revolution: International Politics Before and After Hiroshima* (New York: Cambridge University Press, 1981), 83–116; Fred Kaplan, *The Wizards of Armageddon* (Palo Alto, CA: Stanford University Press, 1991), 65–67. The term "security dilemma" was coined by political scientist John H. Herz in *Political Realism and Political Idealism: A Study in Theories and Realities* (Chicago: University of Chicago Press, 1951). The concept was soon extended to arms races, most prominently in Samuel Huntington, "Arms Races: Prerequisites and Results," *Public Policy* 8, no. 41 (1958): 41–86.

5. Robert J. Watson, *History of the Office of the Secretary of Defense*, vol. 4, *Into the Missile Age* (Washington, DC: Government Printing Office, 1987), 697, 699–700.

6. Freedman, *The Evolution of Nuclear Strategy*, 186.

7. Watson, *History of the Office of the Secretary of Defense*, 4:697–698.

8. Ibid., 704–705.

9. Ibid., 705; Robert A. Divine, *Blowing on the Wind: The Nuclear Test Ban Debate, 1954–1960* (Oxford: Oxford University Press, 1978), 302, 317.

10. April Carter, *Success and Failure in Arms Control Negotiations* (Oxford: Oxford University Press, 1989), 53.

11. Ibid., 53–56.

12. Robert E. Williams and Paul R. Viotti, *Arms Control: History, Theory, and Policy* (Santa Barbara, CA: ABC-CLIO, 2012), 207–208.

13. Divine, *Blowing on the Wind*, 268; Carter, *Success and Failure in Arms Control Negotiations*, 73–74.

14. Freedman, *The Evolution of Nuclear Strategy*, 186–187.

15. Watson, *History of the Office of the Secretary of Defense*, 4:727–728.

16. Gerard C. Smith, "The Arms Control and Disarmament Agency: An Unfinished History," *Bulletin of the Atomic Scientists* 40, no. 4 (1984): 13–17.

17. Kaplan, *The Wizards of Armageddon*, 330–332.

18. Freedman, *The Evolution of Nuclear Strategy*, 183–184.

19. Ibid., 182–183.

20. Ibid., 184.

21. Kaplan, *The Wizards of Armageddon*, 250–251.

22. Walter S. Poole, *History of Acquisition in the Department of Defense*, vol. 2, *Adapting to Flexible Response, 1960–1968* (Washington, DC: Government Printing Office, 2013), 3–5.

23. Kaplan, *The Wizards of Armageddon*, 268–270.

24. Ibid., 271–272.

25. Freedman, *The Evolution of Nuclear Strategy*, 221–228.

26. Ibid., 236; Kaplan, *The Wizards of Armageddon*, 321.

27. Kaplan, *The Wizards of Armageddon*, 321–322; Thomas W. Wolfe, John D. Steinbruner, and Ernest May, *History of the Strategic Arms Competition, 1945–1972* (Washington, DC: Office of the Secretary of Defense Historical Office, 1981), 453–454.

28. Strobe Talbott, *The Master of the Game: Paul Nitze and the Nuclear Peace* (New York: Vintage Books, 1988), 89–91; Kaplan, *The Wizards of Armageddon*, 347.

29. Kaplan, *The Wizards of Armageddon*, 321–322.

30. Ibid., 317–318. See also Wolfe, Steinbruner, and May, *History of the Strategic Arms Competition*, 522–525.

31. Wolfe, Steinbruner, and May, *History of the Strategic Arms Competition*, 535, 800.

32. Kaplan, *The Wizards of Armageddon*, 319–320.

33. Lawrence S. Kaplan, *History of the Office of the Secretary of Defense*, vol. 5, *The McNamara Ascendancy, 1961–1965* (Washington, DC: Government Printing Office), 319; Freedman, *The Evolution of Nuclear Strategy*, 223, 230; Kaplan, *The Wizards of Armageddon*, 319, 325.

34. Freedman, *The Evolution of Nuclear Strategy*, 240; Talbott, *The Master of the Game*, 95.

35. Talbott, *The Master of the Game*, 94–95.

36. Freedman, *The Evolution of Nuclear Strategy*, 239–240.

37. Poole, *History of Acquisition in the Department of Defense*, 2:274–276.

38. Carter, *Success and Failure in Arms Control Negotiations*, 106–107.

39. Robert S. McNamara, *Blundering into Disaster: Surveying the First Century of the Nuclear Age* (New York: Pantheon, 1986), 57.

40. Freedman, *The Evolution of Nuclear Strategy*, 240; Jeffrey W. Knopf, *Domestic Society and International Cooperation: The Impact of Protest on U.S. Arms Control Policy* (Cambridge, UK: Cambridge University Press, 1998), 168–170.

41. Carter, *Success and Failure in Arms Control Negotiations*, 106.

42. Alexsandr′ Savel′yev and Nikolay Detinov, *The Big Five: Arms Control Decision-Making in the Soviet Union* (Westport, CT: Prager, 1995), 2.

43. Ibid., 2–10.

44. Carter, *Success and Failure in Arms Control Negotiations*, 107.

2. NEGOTIATION

1. No single treaty or agreement has the title "Strategic Arms Limitation Treaty." This term and its acronym have been used to refer to the results of the Strategic Arms Limitation Talks (also abbreviated SALT) from 1968 to 1972. These talks resulted in a series of accords, including the Anti-Ballistic Missile Treaty, the Interim Agreement and Protocol, the "Accidents Agreement" regarding accidental uses of nuclear weapons, and the Revised Hot Line Agreement. I will refer to these agreements as SALT I.

2. Thomas W. Graham, "The Politics of Failure: Strategic Nuclear Arms Control, Public Opinion, and Domestic Politics in the United States, 1945–1980" (PhD diss., Massachusetts Institute of Technology, 1989), 15.

3. Bruce Russett, "Doves, Hawks, and U.S. Public Opinion," *Political Science Quarterly* 105, no. 4 (1990): 519–520.

4. Graham, "The Politics of Failure," 283–285, Appendix 8.

5. Richard Nixon: "Address Accepting the Presidential Nomination at the Republican National Convention in Miami Beach, Florida," August 8, 1968. Online by Gerhard Peters and John T. Woolley, *The American Presidency Project.* http://www.presidency.ucsb.edu/ws/?pid=25968.

6. Henry Kissinger, *The White House Years* (Boston: Little, Brown and Company, 1979), 148.

7. Document 5, "Minutes of a National Security Council Meeting," February 19, 1969, in *Foreign Relations of the United States, 1969–1976*, vol. 32, *SALT I: 1969–1972*, edited by Erin R. Mahan (Washington, DC: U.S. Government Printing Office, 2010), 12–13.

8. Kissinger, *The White House Years*, 148.

9. Document 60, "Report by President Nixon to the Congress," February 18, 1970, and Document 68, "Press Conference by President Nixon," July 30, 1970, both in *Foreign Relations of the United States, 1969–1976*, vol. 1, *Foundations of Foreign Policy, 1969–1972*, edited by Louis J. Smith and David H. Herschler (Washington, DC: U.S. Government Printing Office, 2003), 195–203 and 228, respectively.

10. Document 26, "Letter from President Nixon to the Director of the Arms Control and Disarmament Agency," July 21, 1969, in *Foreign Relations of the United States, 1969–1976*, 1:89–91.

11. Kissinger, *The White House Years*, 127.

12. Document 17, "Minutes of a Review Group Meeting," June 12, 1969, in *Foreign Relations of the United States, 1969–1976*, 32:61.

13. Ibid., 60.

14. Document 10, "Letter from President Nixon to Secretary of State Rogers," February 4, 1969, in *Foreign Relations of the United States, 1969–1976, Soviet Union, 1969–1970*, vol. 12, *South Asia Crisis, 1971*, edited by Louis J. Smith (Washington, DC: U.S. Government Printing Office, 2005), 27. Secretary Laird received a copy as well.

15. Document 4, "Essay by Henry A. Kissinger," 1969, in *Foreign Relations of the United States, 1969–1976*, 1:21–48.

16. Kissinger, *The White House Years*, 129.

17. Gerard Smith, *Doubletalk: The Story of SALT I* (Lanham, MD: University Press of America, 1985), 26.

18. Ibid., 8.

19. George Bunn, *Arms Control by Committee: Managing Negotiations with the Russians* (Stanford, CA: Stanford University Press, 1992), 127.

20. Document 5, "Minutes of a National Security Council Meeting," February 19, 1969, 12.

21. Smith, *Doubletalk*, 28.

22. Strobe Talbott, *The Master of the Game: Paul Nitze and the Nuclear Peace* (New York: Vintage Books, 1989), 95–96.

23. Ibid., 111.

24. Ibid., 112–113.

25. Document 2, "Paper Prepared in the Department of Defense," n.d., in *Foreign Relations of the United States, 1969–1976*, 32:2.

26. See Chapter 1.

27. Document 31, "Memorandum from the Chairman of the Joint Chiefs of Staff (Wheeler) to Secretary of Defense Laird," August 1, 1969, in *Foreign Relations of the United States, 1969–1976*, 32:126.

28. Document 2, "Paper Prepared in the Department of Defense," 3.

29. Kissinger, *The White House Years*, 197.

30. Document 2, "Paper Prepared in the Department of Defense," 2–3.

31. Talbott, *The Master of the Game*, 90.

32. Graham, "The Politics of Failure," 266–267.

33. Ibid., 267–270.

34. Warren Weaver Jr., "Nixon Missile Plan Wins in Senate by a 51–50 Vote," *The New York Times*, August 7, 1969.

35. Talbott, *The Master of the Game*, 93.

36. McGeorge Bundy, *Danger and Survival: Choices about the Bomb in the First Fifty Years* (New York: Vintage Books, 1990), 551.

37. Talbott, *The Master of the Game*, 103.

38. Document 14, "Paper Prepared by the Interagency SALT Steering Committee," n.d., in *Foreign Relations of the United States, 1969–1976*, 32:32.

39. John Prados, *Keepers of the Keys: A History of the National Security Council from Truman to Bush* (New York: William Morrow and Company, 1991), 27.

40. Ibid., 261.

41. For Kissinger's backchannel with Dobrynin, see Jussi Hanhimaki, *The Flawed Architect: Henry Kissinger and American Foreign Policy* (Oxford: Oxford University Press, 2004), 31–32.

42. Document 3, "Paper Prepared by the National Security Council Staff," n.d., in *Foreign Relations of the United States, 1969–1976*, 32:8.

43. Kissinger, *The White House Years*, 127.

44. Document 14, "Paper Prepared by the Interagency SALT Steering Committee," n.d., in *Foreign Relations of the United States, 1969–1976*, 32:37.

45. Document 16, "Paper Prepared in the Arms Control and Disarmament Agency," June 11, 1969, in *Foreign Relations of the United States, 1969–1976*, 32:41.

46. Document 17. "Minutes of a Review Group Meeting," June 12, 1969, in *Foreign Relations of the United States, 1969–1976*, 32:56.

47. Document 17, "Paper Prepared by the National Security Council Staff," n.d., in *Foreign Relations of the United States, 1969–1976*, 32:148.

48. Document 33, "Paper Prepared by the National Security Council Staff," n.d., in *Foreign Relations of the United States, 1969–1976*, 32:129.

49. Document 34, "Minutes of a National Security Council Meeting," October 8, 1969, *Foreign Relations of the United States, 1969–1976*, 32:132.

50. Kissinger, *The White House Years*, 149.

51. Document 27, "Summary of Response to National Security Study Memorandum 62," n.d., in *Foreign Relations of the United States, 1969–1976*, 32:115.

52. Document 65, "Memorandum of Conversation," April 8, 1970, in *Foreign Relations of the United States, 1969–1976*, 32:221. See also Document 56, "Memorandum from Laurence Lynn of the National Security Council Staff to the President's Assistant for National Security Affairs (Kissinger)," March 18, 1970, in *Foreign Relations of the United States, 1969–1976*, 32:195.

53. Document 42, "Memorandum from Helmut Sonnenfeldt of the National Security Council Staff to the President's Assistant for National Security Affairs (Kissinger)," December 3, 1969, in *Foreign Relations of the United States, 1969–1976*, 32:165; Document 39, "Minutes of a National Security Council Meeting," November 10, 1969, in *Foreign Relations of the United States, 1969–1976*, 32:158.

54. See Talbott, *The Master of the Game*, 103.

55. Document 39, "Minutes of a National Security Council Meeting," November 10, 1969, 32:158.

56. Paul Nitze, "The Merits and Demerits of a SALT II Agreement," in *The Fateful Ends and Shades of SALT: Past, Present, and Yet to Come?* edited by Frank R. Barnett (New York: Crane Russak & Company, Inc., 1979), 40.

57. Robert Semple, "Nixon Considers MIRV Test Move," *The New York Times*, June 20, 1969.

58. Document 29, "Memorandum from Frank Perez of the Bureau of Intelligence and Research to the President's Assistant for National Security Affairs (Kissinger)," July 23, 1969, in *Foreign Relations of the United States, 1969–1976*, 32:123.

59. Document 77, "Memorandum from Helmut Sonnenfeldt of the National Security Council Staff to the President's Assistant for National Security Affairs (Kissinger)," May 20, 1970, in *Foreign Relations of the United States, 1969–1976*, 32:266.

60. Document 14, "Paper Prepared by the Interagency SALT Steering Committee," n.d., in *Foreign Relations of the United States, 1969–1976*, 32:32.

61. Document 39, "Minutes of a National Security Council Meeting," 158.

62. Smith, *Doubletalk*, 465.

63. Document 26, "Letter from President Nixon to the Director of the Arms Control and Disarmament Agency (Smith)," 107.

64. Editorial Note, in *Foreign Relations of the United States, 1969–1976*, 32:163–164.

65. Document 53, "Special National Intelligence Estimate, 'Soviet Attitudes Toward SALT,'" February 19, 1970, in *Foreign Relations of the United States, 1969–1976*, 32:190.

66. Document 80, "Memorandum from Helmut Sonnenfeldt of the National Security Council Staff to the President's Assistant for National Security Affairs (Kissinger)," June 6, 1970, in *Foreign Relations of the United States, 1969–1976*, 32:281

67. Document 94, "National Security Decision Memorandum 69," July 9, 1970, in *Foreign Relations of the United States, 1969–1976*, 32:312.

68. Lawrence Freedman, *The Evolution of Nuclear Strategy* (New York: Palgrave-MacMillan, 2003), 402.

69. Tactical nuclear weapons are those typically reserved for battlefield use, and are usually less powerful than other nuclear weapons. Theater nuclear weapons are generally more powerful weapons stockpiled and maintained in-theater, but with somewhat more flexibility in their intended uses.

70. Ibid., 401–402.

71. Document 42, "Memorandum from Helmut Sonnenfeldt of the National Security Council Staff to the President's Assistant for National Security Affairs (Kissinger)," 164–166.

72. Document 77, "Memorandum from Helmut Sonnenfeldt to Henry Kissinger," May 20, 1970, 266.

73. Document 169, "Minutes of a National Security Council Meeting," June 30, 1971, in *Foreign Relations of the United States, 1969–1976*, 32:526.

74. Talbott, *The Master of the Game*, 129.

75. Paul Nitze, *From Hiroshima to Glasnost* (New York: Grove Weidenfeld, 1989), 317–318.

76. Talbott, *The Master of the Game*, 131; Nitze, *From Hiroshima to Glasnost*, 321.

77. Document 130, "Memorandum of Conversation," January 28, 1971, in *Foreign Relations of the United States, 1969–1976*, 32:399.

78. Document 132, "Memorandum of Conversation," February 10, 1971, in *Foreign Relations of the United States, 1969–1976*, 32:401.

79. Smith, *Doubletalk*, 228.

80. Document 262, "Memorandum of Conversation," April 22, 1972, in *Foreign Relations of the United States, 1969–1976*, 32:776.

81. Smith, *Doubletalk*, 372.

82. Ibid., 424.

83. Ibid., 436.

84. Document 322, "Minutes of a Verification Panel Meeting," June 7, 1972; Document 323, "Paper Prepared by the Verification Panel Working Group," June 7, 1972; Document 325, "Paper Prepared by the National Security Council Staff for the Soviet Government," n.d. All in *Foreign Relations of the United States, 1969–1976*, 32:932–940, 940–941, and 943–944, respectively.

85. Robert G. Kaufman, *Henry M. Jackson: A Life in Politics* (Seattle: University of Washington Press, 2000).

86. Document 310, "Backchannel Message from the President's Deputy Assistant for National Security Affairs (Haig) to the President's Assistant for National Security Affairs (Kissinger)," May 25, 1972, in *Foreign Relations of the United States, 1969–1976*, 32:895.

87. Document 320, "Backchannel Message from the President's Assistant for National Security Affairs (Kissinger) to the President's Deputy Assistant for National Security Affairs (Haig)," May 27, 1972, in *Foreign Relations of the United States, 1969–1976*, 32:924.

88. Document 321, "Conversation among President Nixon, the President's Assistant for National Security Affairs (Kissinger), and Assistant to the President (Haldeman)," June 2, 1972, in *Foreign Relations of the United States, 1969–1976*, 32:926.

89. Smith, *Doubletalk*, 442–443.

90. Nitze, *From Hiroshima to Glasnost*, 341.

91. Document 343, "Memorandum of Conversation," October 4, 1972, in *Foreign Relations of the United States, 1969–1976*, 32:984.

92. Smith, *Doubletalk*, 459–460.

93. Ibid., 464.

94. Raymond Garthoff, "SALT I: An Evaluation," *World Politics* 31, no. 1 (1978): 7.

95. Thomas Wolfe, *The SALT Experience: Its Impact on U.S. and Soviet Strategic Policy and Decisionmaking* (Santa Monica, CA: Project RAND, 1975), 120–121.

96. Ibid., 232.

3. AFTERMATH AND ADAPTATION

1. Gerard Smith, *Doubletalk: The Story of SALT I* (Lanham, MD: University Press of America, 1985), 8.

2. President Nixon to the Director of the Arms Control and Disarmament Agency, July 21, 1969, in *Foreign Relations of the United States, 1969–1976*, vol. 1, *Foundations of Foreign Policy, 1969–1972* (Washington, DC: Government Printing Office, 2010), 89–91.

3. Background Memorandum, "The Strategic Arms Limitation Agreements and National Security," June 13, 1972, 3, folder SALT Misc. Post-Summit, 1972, in *The Richard M. Nixon National Security Files, 1969–1974: Strategic Arms Limitation Talks*, edited by Christian James and Daniel Lewis (Bethesda, Md.: LexisNexis, 2007), Reel 10 (hereafter *Richard M. Nixon National Security Files*).

4. Document 166: "Memorandum of Conversation," 25 March 1974, in *Foreign Relations of the United States, 1969–1976*, vol. 15, *Soviet Union, June 1972–August 1974*, edited by Douglas E. Selvage and Melissa Jane Taylor (Washington, DC: Government Printing Office, 2010), 722.

5. Background Memorandum, "The Strategic Arms Limitation Agreements and National Security."

6. See Chapter 2.

7. McGeorge Bundy, *Danger and Survival: Choices about the Bomb in the First Fifty Years* (New York: Vintage Books, 1990), 551.

8. Document 190, "Memorandum of Conversation," June 30, 1974, in *Foreign Relations of the United States, 1969–1974*, 15:904.

9. "Secretary Kissinger's Talking Points, NSC Meeting on SALT," 21 Mar 1974, 1, folder SALT Two-1: Geneva (Jan. '74–Apr. '74), in *Richard M. Nixon National Security Files*, Reel 13.

10. Paul Nitze, "The Merits and Demerits of a SALT II Agreement," in *The Fateful Ends and Shades of SALT: Past, Present, and Yet to Come?* edited by Frank R. Barnett (New York: Crane Russak & Company, 1979), 40.

11. See Brent Scowcroft, memorandum to Jan Lodal, April 24, 1974, 1, folder SALT Two-1: Geneva (Jan. '74–Apr. '74), in *Richard M. Nixon National Security Files*, Reel 13.

12. Document 39, "Memorandum of Conversation," September 12, 1972, in *Foreign Relations of the United States, 1969–1974*, 15:141.

13. Anne Hessing Cahn, *Killing Détente: The Right Attacks the CIA* (University Park: Pennsylvania State University Press, 1998), 150.

14. Phil Odeen, memorandum to Henry Kissinger, September 22, 1973, 1, folder SALT Two-1: Geneva (Aug. 1973–Dec. 1973), in *Richard M. Nixon National Security Files*, Reel 12.

15. Document 343, "Memorandum of Conversation," October 4, 1972, in *Foreign Relations of the United States, 1969–1976*, vol. 32, *Salt I, 1969–1972*, edited by Erin R. Mahan (Washington, DC: U.S. Government Printing Office, 2010), 984.

16. Henry Kissinger, *Years of Upheaval* (Boston: Little, Brown and Co., 1982), 984.

17. Helmut Sonnenfeldt, memorandum to Henry Kissinger, "Sen. Jackson's SALT Questions to Alex Johnson and Fred Iklé," September 18, 1973, folder SALT Two-1: Geneva (Aug. 1973–Dec. 1973), in *Richard M. Nixon National Security Files*, Reel 12.

18. Paul Nitze, *From Hiroshima to Glasnost: At the Center of Decision* (New York: Grove Weidenfeld, 1989), 334.

19. Kissinger, *Years of Upheaval*, 1162.

20. Document 17, "Minutes of a Review Group Meeting," June 12, 1969, in *Foreign Relations of the United States, 1969–1976*, 32:56. See also Henry Kissinger, memorandum to Richard Nixon, "MIRV and SALT," April 3, 1973, 5, folder SALT Two-1: Geneva (Mar. 1973–Aug. 1973), in *Richard M. Nixon National Security Files*, Reel 12.

21. Phil Odeen, memorandum to Henry Kissinger, September 22, 1973, 1.

22. Phil Odeen, memorandum to Henry Kissinger, "Fred Iklé's Remarks at Jackson's Subcommittee Session," September 12, 1973, folder SALT Two-1: Geneva (Aug. 1973–Dec. 1973), in *Richard M. Nixon National Security Files*, Reel 12.

23. Raymond Garthoff, *Détente and Confrontation* (Washington, DC: The Brookings Institution, 1994), 471.

24. Jan Lodal, memorandum to Brent Scowcroft, March 4, 1974, folder SALT Two-1: Geneva (Jan. '74–Apr. '74), in *Richard M. Nixon National Security Files*, Reel 13.

25. Nitze, *From Hiroshima to Glasnost*, 334.

26. Document 80, "Memorandum from Helmut Sonnenfeldt of the National Security Council Staff to the President's Assistant for National Security Affairs (Kissinger)," June 6, 1970, in *Foreign Relations of the United States, 1969–1976*, 32:281.

27. Helmut Sonnenfeldt, memorandum to Henry Kissinger, "Further Thoughts on the SALT II Proposals," November 3, 1972, 1, folder SALT Two-1: Geneva (November 21, 1972–March 1973), in *Richard M. Nixon National Security Files*, Reel 11.

28. Peter Swiers, memorandum to Senior Watch Officer, Operations Center, "Distribution of SALT Statement," November 17, 1973, 4, folder SALT Two-1: Geneva (Aug. 1973–Dec. 1973), in *Richard M. Nixon National Security Files*, Reel 12.

29. Document 165, "Memorandum of Conversation," March 25, 1974, in *Foreign Relations of the United States*, vol. 15, *Soviet Union, June 1972–August 1974*, edited by Douglas E. Selvage and Melissa Jane Taylor (Washington, DC: U.S. Government Printing Office, 2011), 706.

30. James D. Forrow, "Electoral and Congressional Incentives and Arms Control," *Journal of Conflict Resolution* 35, no. 2 (1991): 245.

31. Draft National Security Decision Memorandum, February 19, 1974, 1–2, folder SALT Two-1: Geneva (Jan. '74–Apr. '74), in *Richard M. Nixon National Security Files*, Reel 13.

32. SALT II Delegation Minutes, February 22, 1974, 1–2, folder SALT Two-1: Geneva (Jan. '74–Apr. '74), in *Richard M. Nixon National Security Files*, Reel 13.

33. Smith, *Doubletalk*, 396.

34. Document 34, "Minutes of a Meeting of the Verification Panel," August 15, 1973, in *Foreign Relations of the United States, 1969–1976*, vol. 33, *SALT II, 1972–1980*, edited by Erin R. Mahan (Washington, DC: U.S. Government Printing Office: 2013), 102.

35. Steven J. Zaloga, *The Kremlin's Nuclear Sword: The Rise and Fall of Russia's Strategic Nuclear Forces, 1945–2000* (Washington, DC: Smithsonian Institution Press, 2002), 140–141; Thomas W. Wolfe, John D. Steinbruner, and Ernest May, *History of the Strategic Arms Competition, 1945–1972* (Washington, DC: Office of the Secretary of Defense Historical Office, 1981), 710.

36. Document 34, "Minutes of a Meeting of the Verification Panel," August 15, 1973, 104.

37. Ibid., 107.

38. Ibid., 108.

39. Document 45, "Minutes of a Meeting of the Verification Panel," December 28, 1973, in *Foreign Relations of the United States 1969–1976*, 33:145.

40. Kissinger, *Years of Upheaval*, 1012.

41. Document 68, "Minutes of a Meeting of the National Security Council," June 20, 1974, in *Foreign Relations of the United States 1969–1976*, 33:271; Document 66, "Memorandum of Conversation," April 29, 1974, in *Foreign Relations of the United States 1969–1976*, 33:259.

42. Document 72, "Memorandum of Conversation," July 1, 1974, in *Foreign Relations of the United States 1969–1976*, 33:291.

43. Kissinger, *Years of Upheaval*, 1010–1011.

44. Ibid., 1173.

45. Ibid., 1175.

46. Strobe Talbott, *The Master of the Game: Paul Nitze and the Nuclear Peace* (New York: Vintage Books, 1989), 138.

47. Nitze, *From Hiroshima to Glasnost*, 338–339.

48. Ibid., 341.

49. "Crisis stability" here refers to the condition of the nuclear balance forcing both powers to have an interest in de-escalating major international crises, such as the Cuban Missile Crisis or the 1973 Yom Kippur War.

50. Paul Nitze, "The Strategic Balance between Hope and Skepticism," *Foreign Policy* 17 (1974–1975): 138.

51. Ibid., 144.

52. Ibid., 146.

53. Paul Nitze, "The Vladivostok Accord and SALT II," *Review of Politics* 37, no. 2 (1975): 158.

54. Document 74, "Minutes of a Meeting of the National Security Council," September 14, 1974, in *Foreign Relations of the United States 1969–1976*, 33:307.

55. Document 82, "Memorandum from the President's Deputy Assistant for National Security Affairs (Scowcroft) to President Ford," October 25, 1974, in *Foreign Relations of the United States 1969–1976*, 33:367.

56. Document 83, "Memorandum from the President's Deputy Assistant for National Security Affairs (Scowcroft) to President Ford," October 25, 1974, in *Foreign Relations of the United States 1969–1976*, 33:371.

57. Document 91, "Aide-Memoire," December 10, 1974, in *Foreign Relations of the United States 1969–1976*, 33:402.

58. Document 92, "Memorandum from the President's Assistant for National Security Affairs (Scowcroft) to Vice President Rockefeller," January 29, 1975, in *Foreign Relations of the United States 1969–1976*, 33:404.

59. Henry Kissinger, *Years of Renewal* (New York: Touchstone, 1999), 848.

60. Document 100, "Memorandum from the President's Assistant for National Security Affairs (Kissinger) to President Ford," n.d., in *Foreign Relations of the United States 1969–1972*, 33:432.

61. Document 112, "Memorandum from the President's Assistant for National Security Affairs (Scowcroft) to Secretary of State Kissinger," n.d., in *Foreign Relations of the United States, 1969–1975*, 33:496.

62. Document 119, "Minutes of a Meeting of the National Security Council," January 21, 1976, in *Foreign Relations of the United States, 1969–1976*, 33:559–561.

63. Document 120, "Message from the President's Assistant for National Security Affairs (Scowcroft) to Secretary of State Kissinger," January 22, 1976, in *Foreign Relations of the United States, 1969–1976*, 33:572.

64. Terry Terriff, *The Nixon Administration and the Making of U.S. Nuclear Policy* (Ithaca, NY: Cornell University Press, 1995), 53.

65. Jan Lodal and Helmut Sonnenfeldt, memorandum to Henry Kissinger, January 29, 1974, 4, folder SALT Two-1: Geneva (Jan. '74–Apr. '74), in *Richard M. Nixon National Security Files*, Reel 13.

66. "National Security Decision Memorandum 242," January 17, 1974, *National Security Archive*, Electronic Briefing Book No. 173, http://www.gwu.edu/~nsarchiv/NSAEBB/NSAEBB173/SIOP-24b.pdf, retrieved February 12, 2012.

67. Eric Mlyn, *The State, Society, and Limited Nuclear War* (Albany: State University of New York Press, 1995), 99; Terriff, *The Nixon Administration and the Making of U.S. Nuclear Policy*, 4.

68. Terriff, *The Nixon Administration and the Making of U.S. Nuclear Policy*, 4."

69. Lawrence Freedman, *The Evolution of Nuclear Strategy* (New York: Palgrave-MacMillan, 2003), 404–405.

70. Ibid., 228.

71. Winston Lord, memorandum to Henry Kissinger, December 3, 1973, *National Security Archive*, Electronic Briefing Book No. 173, http://www.gwu.edu/~nsarchiv/NSAEBB/NSAEBB173/SIOP-23.pdf, retrieved February 12, 2012.

72. Garthoff, *Détente and Confrontation*, 466–467.

73. Kissinger, *Years of Renewal*, 181.

74. Albert Wohlstetter, "Is There a Strategic Arms Race?" *Foreign Policy* 15 (Summer 1974): 13–14.

75. Ibid., 13–14.

76. Cahn, *Killing Détente*, 120–122.

77. Richard Pipes, "Team B: The Reality Behind the Myth," *Commentary*, October 1, 1986, 31.

78. Cahn, *Killing Détente*, 141–146.

79. Ibid., 165–167.

80. U.S. Central Intelligence Agency, "Intelligence Community Experiment in Competitive Analysis, Soviet Strategic Objectives an Alternative View, Report of Team 'B,'" December 1976, 9, *National Security Archive*, Electronic Briefing Book No. 139, http://www.gwu.edu/~nsarchiv/NSAEBB/NSAEBB139/nitze10.pdf, accessed February 12, 2012.

81. Ibid., 6.

82. Nitze, *From Hiroshima to Glasnost*, 352–353.

83. Smith, *Doubletalk*, 459–460.

84. "Schlesinger Defends Pentagon Budget," *Washington Post*, March 4, 1974.

4. "IN GOOD FAITH"

1. For an overview of Carter's campaign style and political positioning in 1976, see Julian E. Zelizer, *Jimmy Carter* (New York: Times Books, 2010).

2. Patrick Anderson, *Electing Jimmy Carter: The Campaign of 1976* (Baton Rouge: Louisiana State University Press, 1994), 76.

3. Jimmy Carter, Address at the Council on Foreign Relations, Chicago, March 15, 1976, in Carter on Foreign Policy Debate Briefing Book, folder Second Debate: Carter on Foreign Policy—Briefing Book (1), box 2, White House Special Files Unit, Gerald R. Ford Presidential Library. Also available at http://www.fordlibrarymuseum.gov/library/document/0010/1554419.pdf, retrieved January 1, 2014. See also Mary E. Stuckey, *Jimmy Carter, Human Rights, and the National Agenda* (College Station, Texas: Texas A&M University Press, 2008).

4. The Helsinki Final Act, signed August 1, 1975, was the final act of the Conference on Security and Cooperation in Europe, a diplomatic forum convened to address a variety of European security issues, some of which dated to World War II. While non-binding, the Final Act committed all of the major powers in Europe, as well as the United States and Canada to a set of principles including the inviolability of borders and the peaceful settlement of interstate conflicts. Not all of these principles were perfectly aligned, and in many ways the document appeared to legitimate the Soviet annexation of the Baltic States and its domination over Eastern Europe. However, the Act in turn required those exercising such influence to respect and uphold the human rights of subordinate peoples.

5. Ibid. For Carter's position on defense cuts and NATO, see Donald Rothberg, "Foreign Policy, Defense Major Campaign Issues," *Associated Press*, October 27, 1976; and Daniel Southerland, "NATO Today Is in Better Shape—in Some Ways—Than Ever Before," *Christian Science Monitor*, December 13, 1976.

6. Strobe Talbott, *Endgame: The Inside Story of SALT II* (New York: Harper Colophon Books, 1980), 141.

7. Paul Nitze, Notes, "Meeting with President Elect Carter," January 13, 1977, box 1:143, folder Transition, 1976–1978, Paul H. Nitze Papers, Library of Congress.

8. Department of State Summit Briefing Book on Arms Control, May 1979, NLC-12-56-8-1-8, CIA Records Search Tool (Hereinafter CREST), Jimmy Carter Presidential Library, Atlanta, GA.

9. Jimmy Carter to Paul Nitze, October 25, 1976, box 1:143, folder Foreign and Defense Policy Task Force, 1976–1977, Paul H. Nitze Papers.

10. "Notes on the Discussion of Defense Policy," July 26, 1976, 3, box 9, folder Defense, 7/27/76–8/76, Jimmy Carter Papers (Pre-Presidential) Jimmy Carter Presidential Library, Atlanta, Ga.

11. See Russell Murray II, Office of the Secretary of Defense, cover memorandum for Paul Nitze, August 25, 1977, box 1:70, folder Committee on the Present Danger, Meetings 1976–1984, Paul H. Nitze Papers. See also Rowland Evans and Robert Novak, "A Touchy Carter: Shades of Former Presidents?" *Washington Post*, August 13, 1977.

12. Ronald L. Easley, System Planning Corporation, to Jerrold K. Milsted, Office of the Principal Deputy Secretary of Defense for International Security Affairs, November 22, 1977, box 1: Presidential Campaigns, folder 71: Committee on the Present Danger: Press, Paul H. Nitze Papers.

13. Jimmy Carter, "Acceptance Speech," July 15, 1976, *Jimmy Carter Presidential Library & Museum*, http://www.jimmycarterlibrary.gov/documents/speeches/acceptance_speech.pdf, accessed January 5, 2014.

14. Burton Ira Kaufman, *The Carter Years* (New York: Infobase Publishing, 2009), 494–498; Talbott, *Endgame*, 51.

15. Talbott, *Endgame*, 41.

16. Kaufman, *The Carter Years*, 77–80; Talbott, *Endgame*, 49–50. For discussion of Brzezinski's early work, see Raymond Garthoff, *Détente and Confrontation: American-Soviet Relations from Nixon to Reagan*, rev. ed. (Washington, DC: Brookings Institution, 1994), 123.

17. For Soviet impressions of the split, see Talbott, *Endgame*, 121. For the bipolar foreign policy that Vance eventually lost, see Garthoff, *Détente and Confrontation*, 1152.

18. For example, see Document 210, "Memorandum of Conversation, Subject: SALT," September 2, 1978, in *Foreign Relations of the United States, 1969–1976*, vol. 33, *SALT II, 1972–1980*, edited by Erin R. Mahan (Washington, DC: Government Printing Office: 2013), 870–871. See also Zbigniew Brzezinski, *Power and Principle: Memoirs of the National Security Advisor, 1977–1981* (New York: Farrar, Strauss, Giroux, 1983), 320.

19. Walter Isaacson, *Kissinger: A Biography* (New York: Simon and Schuster, 2013), 80.

20. Talbott *Endgame*, 44–45, 51; Brzezinski, *Power and Principle*, 74–75.

21. Talbott, *Endgame*, 50.

22. Ibid., 40–41.

23. Michael T. Kaufman, "Paul Warnke, a Leading Dove in the Vietnam Era, Dies," *New York Times*, November 1, 2001.

24. Paul C. Warnke, "Apes on a Treadmill," *Foreign Policy* 18 (Spring 1975): 12–29.

25. "An Act to Establish a United States Arms Control and Disarmament Agency," September 26, 1961, P.L. 87–297, in *United States Statutes at Large*, vol. 75, 1961 (Washington, DC: U.S. Government Printing Office, 1961), 631–639.

26. See Dean Rusk to Paul Nitze, February 14, 1977, box 1:168, folder Warnke, Paul, nomination, 1977–1979, Paul H. Nitze Papers.

27. Senate Armed Services Committee, *Nomination of Mr. Paul C. Warnke to Be Director of the U.S. Arms Control and Disarmament Agency and Ambassador, First Session, 95th Congress* (Washington, DC: Government Printing Office, 1977), 183. For the Rostow letter, see, 263–266; for the Jackson statement, see 16–18; for the Nunn statement, see 38–40.

28. Strobe Talbott, *The Master of the Game: Paul Nitze and the Nuclear Peace* (New York: Vintage Books, 1989), 90.

29. Paul Nitze, *From Hiroshima to Glasnost: At the Center of Decision* (New York: Grove Weidenfeld, 1989), 354–355; Talbott, *Endgame*, 56–57.

30. Document 89, "Memorandum from Jan Lodal of National Security Council Staff to Secretary of State Kissinger," November 30, 1974, in *Foreign Relations of the United States*, 33:390.

31. Document 120, "Message from the President's Assistant for National Security Affairs (Scowcroft) to Secretary of State Kissinger," January 22, 1976, in *Foreign Relations of the United States*, 33:570–571.

32. Document 151, "Letter from General Secretary Brezhnev to President Carter," n.d., in *Foreign Relations of the United States*, 33:658–659.

33. Director of Central Intelligence, *Soviet Capabilities for Strategic Nuclear Conflict through the Late 1980s*, vol. 1, *National Intelligence Summary Estimate* (Washington, DC:

Central Intelligence Agency, 1978), 26, 29, http://www.foia.cia.gov/sites/default/files/ document_conversions /89801/DOC_0000268138.pdf, accessed January 5, 2014.

34. For the Soviet position on cruise missile ranges, see Document 153, "Letter from General Secretary Brezhnev to President Carter," March 15, 1977, in *Foreign Relations of the United States*, 33:664. For attitudes within NATO, see Arthur Hartman, Leslie Gelb, and Anthony Lake, action memorandum to Secretary of State Cyrus Vance (with annotations), "European Theater Nuclear Problems: Arms Control, Cruise Missiles and Allied Perceptions," February 3, 1977, box 2, folder TL 2/1–15/77 (sic), Records of Anthony Lake, 1977–1981, NN3-059-02-003. National Archives and Records Administration, College Park, Maryland. See also Talbott, *Endgame*, 46, 141–142.

35. Talbott, *Endgame*, 104–107.

36. Document 151, "Letter from General Secretary Brezhnev to President Carter," n.d., in *Foreign Relations of the United States*, 33:660. See also Document 217, "Memorandum to the President's Assistant for National Security Affairs (Brzezinski) to President Carter), September 29, 1978, in *Foreign Relations of the United States*, 33:887.

37. Cyrus Vance, *Hard Choices: Critical Years in America's Foreign Policy* (New York: Simon and Schuster, 1983), 48.

38. Talbott, *Endgame*, 51.

39. Ibid.

40. Paul Warnke and Cyrus Vance, memorandum to President Carter, March 18, 1977, NLC-7-55-4-11-8, CIA Records Search Tool (Hereinafter CREST), Jimmy Carter Presidential Library, Atlanta, GA. See also Vance, *Hard Choices*, 48–49.

41. See, for example, Document 147, "Presidential Review Memorandum/NSC 2)," January 24, 1977, in *Foreign Relations of the United States*, 33:649; and Document 148, "Memorandum of Conversation," February 1, 1977, in *Foreign Relations of the United States*, 33:650.

42. Document 155, "Memorandum of Conversation of a Meeting of the National Security Council," March 22, 1977, in *Foreign Relations of the United States*, 33:678.

43. Ibid., 673–674, 680. See also Document 181, "National Intelligence Memorandum NIM 77–025," September 19, 1977, in *Foreign Relations of the United States*, 33:759.

44. Document 148, "Memorandum of Conversation," February 1, 1977, in *Foreign Relations of the United States*, 33:650–651.

45. Garthoff, *Détente and Confrontation*, 518.

46. See U.S. Central Intelligence Agency, "Intelligence Community Experiment in Competitive Analysis: Soviet Strategic Objectives an Alternative View: Report of Team 'B,'" December 1976, 9, *National Security Archive*, http://www.gwu.edu/~nsarchiv/NSAEBB/ NSAEBB139/nitze10.pdf, accessed January 4, 2014.

47. See Document 153, "Letter from General Secretary Brezhnev to President Carter," March 15, 1977, in *Foreign Relations of the United States*, 33:665. See also Brzezinski, *Power and Principle*, 155.

48. For informal names, see Talbott, *Endgame*, 46. For plan details, see Document 154, "Memorandum from the President's Assistant for National Security Affairs (Brzezinski) to President Carter," March 18, 1977, in *Foreign Relations of the United States*, 33:666.

49. Document 154, "Memorandum from the President's Assistant for National Security Affairs (Brzezinski) to President Carter," March 18, 1977, 666–671.

50. Talbott, *Endgame*, 47.

51. Document 100, "Memorandum from the President's Assistant for National Security Affairs (Kissinger) to President Ford," n.d., in *Foreign Relations of the United States*, 33:426.

52. Document 155, "Memorandum of Conversation of a Meeting of the National Security Council," March 22, 1977, 677.

53. Document 152, "Minutes of a Meeting of the Special Coordination Committee," February 25, 1977, in *Foreign Relations of the United States*, 33:662. See also Paul Warnke and Cyrus Vance, memorandum to President Carter, March 18, 1977. For Brzezinski's thoughts, see Document 154, "Memorandum from the President's Assistant for National Security Affairs (Brzezinski) to President Carter," March 18, 1977, 667.

54. Document 154, "Memorandum from the President's Assistant for National Security Affairs (Brzezinski) to President Carter," March 18, 1977, 665–667.

55. Ibid., 669–670. For Brown's contributions to the idea, see Talbott, *Endgame*, 54–55.

56. Office of Sen. Jackson, "Memorandum for the President on SALT," February 15, 1977, box 52, folder SALT 1–2/77, Subject File: National Security Affairs: Brzezinski Material, Presidential Papers of Jimmy Carter, Jimmy Carter Presidential Library, Atlanta, Ga.

57. Interview with Jimmy Carter, November 29, 1982, 59–60, Carter Presidency Project, *Miller Center*, http://web1.millercenter.org/poh/transcripts/ohp_1982_1129_carter.pdf, accessed January 5, 2014.

58. Office of Sen. Jackson, "Memorandum for the President on SALT," February 15, 1977, 1–4, 7, 10; Document 68, "Minutes of a Meeting of the National Security Council," June 20, 1974, in *Foreign Relations of the United States*, 33:269; Talbott, *Endgame*, 102–103; and Garthoff, *Détente and Confrontation*, 887.

59. Office of Sen. Jackson, "Memorandum for the President on SALT," February 15, 1977, 10.

60. Ibid., attached handwritten note.

61. Talbott, *Endgame*, 53–54.

62. Document 154, "Memorandum from the President's Assistant for National Security Affairs (Brzezinski) to President Carter," March 18, 1977, 670.

63. Talbott, *Endgame*, 48.

64. Document 156, "Presidential Directive/NSC–7," March 23, 1977, in *Foreign Relations of the United States*, 33:684–686.

65. For Vance and Warnke's concerns, see Talbott, *Endgame*, 62–63. For negotiating instructions, see Document 156, "Presidential Directive/NSC–7," March 23, 1977, 684–686.

66. Document 109, "Memorandum from Secretary of State Kissinger to President Ford," September 25, 1975, in *Foreign Relations of the United States*, 33:489.

67. Talbott, *Endgame*, 64–65, 67.

68. President Jimmy Carter, "Peace, Arms Control, World Economic Progress, Human Rights: Basic Priorities of U.S. Foreign Policy," *Department of State Bulletin*, vol. 76, no. 1972 (April 11, 1977): 328–331; President Jimmy Carter, "President Carter's New Conference of March 24," *Department of State Bulletin*, vol. 76, no. 1973 (April 18, 1977): 362.

69. Talbott, *Endgame*, 64–65.

70. Garthoff, *Détente and Confrontation*, 626.

71. Document 157, "Editorial Note," in *Foreign Relations of the United States*, 33:687; and Talbott, *Endgame*, 70.

72. Document 157, "Editorial Note," 688–690.

73. Ibid., 689.

74. *Department of State Bulletin*, 25 Apr 1977 (Washington, DC, Government Printing Office), 399–400.

75. Ibid., 389–408.

76. Document 157, "Editorial Note," 689.

77. President Jimmy Carter, "President Carter Discusses Strategic Arms Limitation Proposals," *Department of State Bulletin*, vol. 76, no. 1974 (April 25, 1977: 411–413.

78. Talbott, *Endgame*, 75

79. Ibid., 76.

80. Ibid., 74–75.

81. Ibid., 252.

82. Stephen Kotkin, *Armageddon Averted: Soviet Collapse, 1970–2000* (Oxford: Oxford University Press, 2008), 8.

83. Alexsandr' Savel'yev and Nikolay Detinov, *The Big Five: Arms Control Decision-Making in the Soviet Union* (Westport, CT: Praeger, 1995), 52.

5. "THINKING OUT LOUD"

1. Strobe Talbott, *Endgame: The Inside Story of SALT II* (New York: Harper Colophon, 1979), 45.

2. Special Coordinating Committee (SCC) Meeting Summary of Conclusions, "SALT and Other Arms Control Issues Addressed in Moscow," April 7, 1977, NLC-7-55-11-7, CIA Records Search Tool (hereafter CREST), Jimmy Carter Presidential Library, Atlanta, Georgia. Jimmy Carter Presidential Library, Atlanta, GA.

3. SCC Meeting Summary of Conclusions, April 7, 1977. NLC-7-55-11-7. CREST. See also Document 158, "Memorandum from the President's Assistant for National Security Affairs (Brzezinski), Subject: SALT and Other Arms Control Issues Addressed in Moscow," n.d., in *Foreign Relations of the United States, 1969–1976*, vol. 33, *SALT II, 1972–1980*, edited by Erin R. Mahan (Washington, DC: Government Printing Office: 2013), 689. For Carter-Brzezinski meetings, see Document 160, "Memorandum from the President's Assistant for National Security Affairs (Brzezinski), Subject: Follow-Up to Dobrynin," April 12, 1977, in *Foreign Relations of the United States, 1969–1976*, 33:692–693; and Document 164, "Memorandum from Secretary of State Vance and the Director of the Arms Control and Disarmament Agency (Warnke) to President Carter," April 27, 1977, in *Foreign Relations of the United States, 1969–1976*, 33:701.

4. Document 163, "Memorandum of a Meeting," April 15, 1977, in *Foreign Relations of the United States, 1969–1976*, 33:699–700.

5. Document 164, "Memorandum from Secretary of State Vance and the Director of the Arms Control and Disarmament Agency (Warnke) to President Carter," April 27, 1977, in *Foreign Relations of the United States, 1969–1976*, 33:701–704.

6. Memorandum, "Status of Exploratory Discussions with Ambassador Dobrynin on SALT (Prepared by Paul Warnke)," May 3, 1977. NLC-4-3-3-7-4, CREST.

7. For Vance's summary of the first day of talks, see Department of State Cable SECTO 4113, "From Secretary Vance, Subj: May 18 Meeting with Gromyko," May 18, 1977, NLC-4-42-1-6-4, CREST. For Brzezinski's summary of the meeting, see Situation Room Flash Report, SECTO [illegible], "From: Zbigniew Brzezinski, Summary of SALT Talks," May 22, 1977, NLC-4-33-1-25-3, CREST.

8. Document 167, "Editorial Note," in *Foreign Relations of the United States, 1969–1976*, 33:715.

9. "For the President, from Zbigniew Brzezinski, Subject: Summary Report for Your Information and Reaction of the Special Coordinating Committee Meeting, June 7, 1977," NLC-17-4-2-3-4, CREST. See also Cyrus Vance, *Hard Choices: Critical Years in America's Foreign Policy* (New York: Simon and Schuster, 1983), 58–59.

10. William Hyland, memorandum to Zbigniew Brzezinski, "Assessment of CIA Memo on SALT," June 6, 1977, NLC-33-17-17-2-7, CREST. For the original CIA report, see Director of Central Intelligence Stansfield Turner, memorandum to President Carter, "An Assessment of the Soviet Perceptions on SALT—May 1977," n.d., NLC-17-75-3-16-1 CREST. Handwritten notes on the memo indicate that copies were distributed to the NSC, Vance, and Warnke.

11. Document 173, "Summary of Conclusions of a Special Coordination Committee Meeting," July 11, 1977, in *Foreign Relations of the United States, 1969–1976*, 33:735.

12. Talbott, *Endgame*, 102; Roger Molander, memorandum to David Aaron, Subject: SALT Tutorial, May 19, 1978, NLC-7-53-3-4-9, CREST.

13. Document 188, "Memorandum from the President's Assistant for National Security Affairs (Brzezinski) to President Carter," November 4, 1977, in *Foreign Relations of the United States, 1969–1976*, 33:791.

14. Document 165, "Paper Prepared by the National Security Council Staff: 'Assessment of the New SALT Two Concept,'" n.d., in *Foreign Relations of the United States, 1969–1976*, 33:704–706.

15. Document 175, "Memorandum from Secretary of State Vance and the Director of the Arms Control and Disarmament Agency (Warnke) to President Carter," August 30, 1977, in *Foreign Relations of the United States, 1969–1976*, 33:745.

16. Document 180, "Memorandum from President Carter to Secretary of State Vance and the Director of the Arms Control and Disarmament Agency (Warnke): Instructions for SALT Discussions with the Soviets," n.d., in *Foreign Relations of the United States, 1969–1976*, 33:758.

17. See, for example, Richard Burt, "Major Concessions by U.S. and Soviets on Arms Reported," *New York Times*, October 11, 1977; Talbott, *Endgame*, 133.

18. Document 182, "Memorandum of Conversation," September 22, 1977, in *Foreign Relations of the United States, 1969–1976*, 33:182–183; "Revised Draft," attachment to memorandum, Walter Slocombe to SALT Working Group, "Backfire: 'Legally Binding,'" n.d., NLC-17-7-8-11-6, CREST.

19. Document 183, "Memorandum of Conversation," September 27, 1977, in *Foreign Relations of the United States, 1969–1976*, 33:765–773; Document 184, "Memorandum of Conversation," September 27, 1977, in *Foreign Relations of the United States, 1969–1976*, 33:774–783; Document 185, "Memorandum from the President's Assistant for National Security Affairs (Brzezinski) to President Carter, Subject: Vance-Gromyko SALT Discussion, September 30," n.d., in *Foreign Relations of the United States, 1969–1976*, 33:784.

20. Talbott, *Endgame*, 124–126.

21. Document 185, "Memorandum from the President's Assistant for National Security Affairs (Brzezinski) to President Carter," n.d., in *Foreign Relations of the United States, 1969–1976*, 33:784.

22. Talbott, *Endgame*, 127.

23. Jimmy Carter, *Keeping Faith: Memoirs of a President* (New York: Bantam Books, 1982), 154–158. See also Zbigniew Brzezinski, Presidential Review Memorandum, NSC-1, January 21, 1977, *Jimmy Carter Presidential Library & Museum*, http://www.jimmycarterlibrary.gov/documents/prmemorandums/prm01.pdf, accessed March 8, 2014.

24. Vance, *Hard Choices*, 140–141, 143, 145.

25. James R. Dickenson, "Reagan's Foreign Policy Attack is Working" *Washington Star*, May 2, 1976.

26. Carter, *Keeping Faith*, 108.

27. Vance, *Hard Choices*, 145.

28. NSC Staff, memorandum to Zbigniew Brzezinski, "Evening Report," March 17, 1978, NLC 10-9-7-11-2, CREST.

29. Carter, *Keeping Faith*, 80–83.

30. See, "Carter's Big Decision: Down Goes the B-1, Here Comes the Cruise Missile," *Time*, July 11, 1977. "Enamored" quote in Stephen I. Schwartz, ed., *Atomic Audit: The Costs and Consequences of U.S. Nuclear Weapons since 1940* (Washington, DC: Brookings Institution, 1998), 119. See also Jimmy Carter, *White House Diary* (New York: Farrar, Strauss, and Giroux, 2010), 61, 63.

31. Brezhnev's original ALCM-MIRV proposal called for the B-52 to be treated as one MIRV, but the B-1 as three. Document 124, "Memorandum from the President's Assistant

for National Security Affairs (Scowcroft) to President Ford," January 22, 1976, in *Foreign Relations of the United States, 1969–1976*, 33:577. For anti-communist criticism, see Colin S. Gray and Jeffrey Barlow, "Inexcusable Restraint: The Decline of American Military Power in the 1970s" *International Security* 10, no. 2 (1985): 27–69.

32. "Carter Clarifies Position on Stealth Aircraft Leaks," *Aviation Week & Space Technology*, September 15, 1980, 23.

33. For the criticisms of Perle and Jackson, see Talbott, *Endgame*, 136–137. See also Rowland Evans and Robert Novak, "The Counterattack for SALT II," *Washington Post*, November 11, 1977. For the Nitze press conference briefing, see Paul Nitze, "Current SALT II Negotiating Posture," November 1, 1977, box I:72, folder Committee on the Present Danger: Press Conferences 1 Nov. 1977 Briefing Materials, Paul H. Nitze Papers, Library of Congress.

34. For reporters' reactions, see Talbott, *Endgame*, 137. For the suspicions of Carter and Brown suspicions, see Carter, *White House Diary*, 133.

35. For congressional inquiries, see Ronald L. Easley to Jerrold K. Milsted, November 22, 1977, box I:72, folder Committee on the Present Danger: Press Conferences 1 Nov. 1977 Congressional Inquiries, Paul H. Nitze Papers. For the editorial that supported Nitze, see, "Leaking SALT," *Wall Street Journal*, November 9, 1977. See also Mail Merge address sheet in box I:72, folder Committee on the Present Danger: Press Conferences 1 Nov. 1977 Miscellaneous Correspondence, Paul H. Nitze Papers.

36. See Robert Kimmitt and Roger Molander, memorandum to Zbigniew Brzezinski, "Richard Burt Article on Top Secret SALT Compliance Report," November 5, 1979, NLC-17-84-1-13-6, CREST.

37. Walter Pincus, "Neutron Killer Warhead Buried in ERDA Budget," *Washington Post*, June 6, 1977.

38. Robert Ehrlich, *Waging Nuclear Peace* (Albany: State University Press of New York, 1984), 157.

39. Michael Acquino, *The Neutron Bomb* (University of California Santa Barbara Doctoral Dissertation, 1980), 20.

40. Arthur Hartman, Leslie Gelb, and Anthony Lake, Department of State action memorandum to Secretary of State Cyrus Vance, "European Theater Nuclear Problems: Arms Control, Cruise Missiles and Allied Perceptions," February 3, 1977, box 2, folder TL 5/1–5/15/77, Records of Anthony Lake, 1977–1981, NN3-059-02-003, National Archives and Records Administration, College Park, MD

41. George Kistiakowsky, "The Folly of the Neutron Bomb," *Bulletin of the Atomic Scientists* 34, no 7 (1978): 27.

42. John Harris and André Gsponer, "Armour Defuses the Neutron Bomb," *New Scientist* 109, no. 1499 (March 13, 1986): 44.

43. Thomas W. Graham, "The Politics of Failure: Strategic Nuclear Arms Control, Public Opinion, and Domestic Politics in the United States, 1945–1980" (PhD diss., Massachusetts Institute of Technology, 1989), 306–307.

44. "Public Likes Carter, Survey Finds, More for His Style Than Programs," *New York Times*, July 29, 1977.

45. Walter Pincus, "Senate Refuses, 58–38, to Kill Neutron Bomb Funding," *Washington Post*, July 14, 1977.

46. Lawrence S. Wittner, *The Struggle Against the Bomb*, vol. 3 (Palo Alto, CA: Stanford University Press, 2003), 22, 49.

47. Ibid., 42, 149.

48. For West German views on the question of production versus deployment, see "NSC Evening Report," November 11, 1977, NLC -1-4-4-18-3, CREST. For the U.S. position, see

Zbigniew Brzezinski, memorandum to President Carter, "Enhanced Radiation Warheads," November 16, 1978, NLC-SAFE-4C-17-6-1-2; Vance, *Hard Choices*, 69.

49. Raymond Garthoff, *Détente and Confrontation: American-Soviet Relations from Nixon to Reagan* (Washington, DC: Brookings, 1994), 939. See also Vance, *Hard Choices*, 69, 93; and Brzezinski, *Power and Principle*, 302.

50. For a discussion of possible options that could be explored with allies during this period, see NSC Staff Paper, "Next Steps with the ER Issue," February 11, 1978, NLC-31-174-3-2-0, CREST.

51. Vance *Hard Choices*, 96–97.

52. Ibid., 97; See also Brzezinski, *Power and Principle*, 305.

53. Situation Room Staff, memorandum to Zbigniew Brzezinski, "Evening Notes," NLC 1-5-7-33-2, CREST.

54. American Embassy, NATO, to Secretary of State, "Canadian Views on Soviet Foreign Policy," March 24, 1978, Department of State Cable E.O. 11652, NLC-17-130-3-8-8.

55. "Long-Range Theater Nuclear Capabilities and Arms Control," June 22, 1978, Presidential Review Memorandum/NSC-38, *Jimmy Carter Presidential Library & Museum*, http://www.jimmycarterlibrary.gov/documents/prmemorandums/prm38.pdf, accessed March 9, 2014.

56. Duncan Lennox, "RS-10 (SS-11 'Sego' and UR-100/8K84/15A20)," *Jane's Weapons: Strategic*, October 13, 2011. For basing and missions, see Raymond Garthoff, "Estimating Soviet Military Intentions and Capabilities," in *Watching the Bear: Essays on the CIA's Analysis of the Soviet Union*, edited by Gerald K. Haines and Robert E. Legget (Washington, DC: Government Printing Office, 2003), 149.

57. Technical details from Lennox, "RSD-10 (SS-20 'Saber' and Pioner, 15Zh45/15Zh53)." For a discussion of the strategic and bureaucratic implications of an SS-11/SS-20 link, see Thomas W. Wolfe, John D. Steinbruner, and Ernest May, *History of the Strategic Arms Competition, 1945–1972* (Washington, DC: Office of the Secretary of Defense Historical Office, 1981), 645, 703, 747, 806–807, 816–817.

58. "Dmitry Fedorovich Ustinov," Central Intelligence Agency Office of Central Reference Biography, n.d., NLC-17-70-7-4-5, CREST.

59. For the comments of General Makhmut A. Gareev and A. S. Kalashnikov, see John G. Hines, Ellis M. Mishulovich, and John F. Shull, *Soviet Intentions 1965–1985*, vols. 1 and 2 (Washington, DC: Office of Net Assessment, 1995), 1:60–63, 2:85, 92. For a competing hypothesis for the number of SS-20s produced, see Raymond Garthoff, "The Soviet SS-20 Decision," *Survival* 25, no. 3 (1983): 110–119.

60. Document 34, "Minutes of a Meeting of the Verification Panel," August 15, 1973, in *Foreign Relations of the United States, 1969–1976*, 33:102.

61. Document 54, Minutes of a Meeting of the Verification Panel," February 15, 1974, in *Foreign Relations of the United States, 1969–1976*, 33:200.

62. Whether the smaller SS-17 replacement for the SS-11 also fit this rubric was an open question until well into the Carter administration and was the source of most such consternation. Document 47, "Minutes of a Meeting of the National Security Council," January 24, 1974, in *Foreign Relations of the United States, 1969–1976*, 33:166.

63. Document 170, "Memorandum from the President's Assistant for National Security Affairs (Brzezinski) to President Carter," n.d., in *Foreign Relations of the United States, 1969–1976*, 33:725.

64. Document 186, "Memorandum from the President's Assistant for National Security Affairs (Brzezinski) to the Chief of the Delegation to the Strategic Arms Limitation Talks (Warnke)," October 4, 1977, in *Foreign Relations of the United States, 1969–1976*, 33:785.

65. Melvin Laird, "Arms Control: The Russians Are Cheating!" *Reader's Digest*, December 1977, 97–101. For an explanation of why Kissinger's statements on the definition of a heavy missile were at variance with the language of SALT I, see Garthoff, *Détente and Confrontation*, 195. For congressional reaction, see Talbott, *Endgame*, 143–145.

66. Talbott, *Endgame*, 136.

67. Ibid., 137.

68. Zbigniew Brzezinski, memorandum to President Carter, "Information Items," March 31, 1978, NLC-1-5-6-67-6, CREST; Zbigniew Brzezinski, memorandum to President Carter, "Public Acknowledgement of the 'Fact of' Photoreconnaissance Satellites," September 21, 1978, NLC-133-216-3-16-4, CREST; and Memorandum [Redacted], Acting Chief Special Security Center to [Redacted], "Presidential Policy Decision," September 26, 1978, NLC-21-54-7-3-9, CREST.

69. SCC Meeting Summary of Conclusions, June 20, 1977, NLC-15-113-9-11-9, CREST.

70. Vance, *Hard Choices*, 87, 99–101; Zbigniew Brzezinski, memorandum to President Carter, "The Soviet Union and Ethiopia: Implications for U.S.-Soviet Relations," March 3, 1978, NLC-132-184-7-1-3, CREST.

71. William Odom, memorandum to Zbigniew Brzezinski, "Evening Report," February 28, 1978, NLC-12-21-5-15-4, CREST.

72. Document 200, "Telegram from Secretary of State Vance to the Department of State," April 20, 1978, in *Foreign Relations of the United States, 1969–1976*, 33:825.

73. Document 171, "Summary of Conclusions of a Special Coordination Committee Meeting," June 20, 1977, in *Foreign Relations of the United States, 1969–1976*, 33:729.

74. Memorandum for the President, "Significant Actions, Secretary and Deputy Secretary of Defense," November 18, 1977, NLC-8-4-5-22-0, CREST.

75. Vance, *Hard Choices*, 100; Talbott, *Endgame*, 149–150.

76. Document 200, "Telegram from Secretary of State Vance to the Department of State," April 20, 1978, in *Foreign Relations of the United States, 1969–1976*, 33:825.

77. Vance, *Hard Choices*, 102–104.

78. Document 174, "Memorandum from President Carter to Vice President Mondale, Secretary of State Vance, and Secretary of Defense Brown," n.d., in *Foreign Relations of the United States, 1969–1976*, 33:825; and David Aaron, memorandum to President Carter, "SALT Guidance on New Types of Ballistic Missiles," May 23, 1978, NLC-7-53-3-4-9, CREST.

79. Department of State Cable SECTO 8019, Secretary of State Vance to Situation Room, July 12, 1978, quoted in Document 208, "Editorial Note," in *Foreign Relations of the United States, 1969–1976*, 33:856.

80. See National Security Council Issue Brief, "Cruise Missile Definition Issue," June 1977, NLC-31-191-6-3-7, CREST; and SCC Meeting Summary of Conclusions, "SALT," June 20, 1977, NLC-15-113-9-11-9. See also Roger Molander and Reginald Bartholomew, memorandum to Zbigniew Brzezinski, "SCC Meeting on SALT—March 6, 1978," March 3, 1978, NLC-17-8-9-1-5, CREST.

81. Document 218, "Memorandum of Conversation," September 30, 1978, *Foreign Relations of the United States, 1969–1976*, 33:893.

82. Ibid., 897.

83. Document 211, "Memorandum from the President's Assistant for National Security Affairs (Brzezinski) to Vice President Mondale, Secretary of State Vance, and Secretary of Defense Brown," n.d., in *Foreign Relations of the United States, 1969–1976*, 33:874

84. SCC Meeting Summary of Conclusions, May 12, 1978, NLC-31-176-2-6-5, CREST.

85. "Revised Draft," attachment to Walter Slocombe, memorandum to SALT Working Group, "Backfire: 'Legally Binding," n.d., NLC-17-7-8-11-6, CREST.

86. Document 220, "Memorandum from Secretary of Defense Brown to President Carter," October 23, 1978, in *Foreign Relations of the United States, 1969–1976*, 33:903–905.

87. Document 216, "Memorandum from the President's Assistant for National Security Affairs (Brzezinski) to President Carter," September 29, 1978, in *Foreign Relations of the United States, 1969–1976*, 33:883.

88. For Mondale and Brzezinski's influence, see Talbott, *Endgame*, 225. See also Document 234, "U.S. Oral Message to the Soviet Leadership," February 1, 1979, in *Foreign Relations of the United States, 1969–1976*, 33:931.

89. John D. Macartney, "John, How Should We Explain MASINT?" in *Intelligence and the National Security Strategist: Enduring Issues and Challenges*, edited by Roger Z. George and Robert D. Kline (New York: Rowman and Littlefield, 2006), 169–180.

90. Arms Control and Disarmament Agency SALT Working Group Memorandum, "Intelligence Community Paper: 'The Telemetry Encryption Issue in SALT' (22 October 1977)," November 11, 1977, NLC-31-90-6-13-8.

91. Department of State, Treaty between the United States of America and the Union of Soviet Socialist Republics on the Limitation of Strategic Offensive Arms (SALT II), Article XV, Section 3, *U.S. Department of State*, http://www.state.gov/t/isn/5195.htm#treaty, accessed March 9, 2014.

92. Document 155, "Memorandum of Conversation of a Meeting of the National Security Council," March 22, 1977, in *Foreign Relations of the United States, 1969–1976*, 33:673.

93. Document 232, "Summary of Conclusions of a Meeting of the Special Coordinating Committee," January 12, 1979, in *Foreign Relations of the United States, 1969–1976*, 33:925. For the involvement of Sen. Glenn, see National Security Council Memorandum for the Record, "Meeting with Senator John Glenn (D., Ohio), 19 June 1979," June 19, 1979, NLC-52-9-22-1-0.

94. For the concession Warnke extracted, see Talbott, *Endgame*, 197. For concerns about missile tests, see Document 232, "Summary of Conclusions of a Meeting of the Special Coordination Committee," January 12, 1979, in *Foreign Relations of the United States, 1969–1976*, 33:926.

95. See Talbott, *Endgame*, 256–259; and Document 233, "Memorandum from the President's Assistant for National Security Affairs (Brzezinski) to President Carter," January 20, 1979, in *Foreign Relations of the United States, 1969–1976*, 33:928.

96. Vance, *Hard Choices*, 100.

97. Document 218, "Memorandum of Conversation," September 30, 1978, 893.

98. Ibid., 894–895.

99. Talbott, *Endgame*, 222. See also David Aaron to President Carter, "SALT," October 23, 1978, Department of State Cable, SECTO 7212, NLC-7-53-6-3-7.

100. Document 227, "Letter from President Carter to Secretary of State Vance," December 20, 1978, in *Foreign Relations of the United States, 1969–1976*, 33:916.

101. Document 239, "Telegram from Secretary of State Vance to President Carter," December 22, 1978, in *Foreign Relations of the United States, 1969–1976*, 33:918–919.

102. Vance only mentions assigning the paper to Ralph Earle, but Talbott attributes the document to Timbie, Earle's resident verification expert. See Vance, *Hard Choices*, 109–110; and Talbott, *Endgame*, 238.

103. Vance, *Hard Choices*, 112.

104. Brzezinski, *Power and Principle*, 330; Talbott, *Endgame*, 242–243; Vance, *Hard Choices*, 111–113.

105. Document 230, "Telegram from Secretary of State Vance to the White House," December 24, 1978, in *Foreign Relations of the United States, 1969–1976*, 33:921.

106. Talbott, *Endgame*, 252.

107. Document 231, "Telegram from Secretary of State Vance to the White House," December 24, 1978, in *Foreign Relations of the United States, 1969–1976*, 33:922; Brzezinski, *Power and Principle* 330–331; Garthoff, *Détente and Confrontation*, 799.

108. SCC Meeting Summary of Conclusions, "SALT Decisions," January 15, 1979, NLC-17-35-4-8-3, CREST. See also David Aaron, memorandum to President Carter, "Telemetry Encryption," March 7, 1979, NLC-15-79-4-6-9, CREST.

109. Talbott, *Endgame*, 259; Zbigniew Brzezinski, memorandum to President Carter, "Letter to President Brezhnev," March 27, 1979, NLC-15-79-4-8-7; Document 237, "Letter from President Carter to Soviet General Secretary Brezhnev," March 27, 1979, in *Foreign Relations of the United States, 1969–1976*, 33:940.

110. Notburga K. Calvo-Goller and Michael A. Calvo, *The SALT Agreements: Content, Application, Verification* (Dodrecht: Martinus Nijhoff Publishers, 1987), 67; Talbott, *Endgame*, 262–263.

111. Document 233, "Memorandum from the President's Assistant for National Security Affairs (Brzezinski) to President Carter," January 20, 1979, in *Foreign Relations of the United States, 1969–1976*, 33:927; Document 232, "Summary of Conclusions of a Meeting of the Special Coordination Committee," January 12, 1979, in *Foreign Relations of the United States, 1969–1976*, 33:925. Talbott, *Endgame*, 276.

112. Document 239, "Memorandum of Conversation," June 16, 1979, in *Foreign Relations of the United States, 1969–1976*, 33:943.

113. See "Treaty between the United States of America and the Union of Soviet Socialist Republics on the Limitation of Strategic Offensive Arms, Together with Agreed Statements and Common Understandings Regarding the Treaty," June 18, 1979, *U.S. Department of State*, http://www.state.gov/t/isn/5195.htm#treaty, accessed March 9, 2014.

114. Document 191, "Memorandum from Secretary of Defense Brown to President Carter," January 6, 1978, in *Foreign Relations of the United States, 1969–1976*, 33:802.

115. Document 239, "Memorandum of Conversation," June 16, 1979, 944–945.

116. Department of State Briefing Memorandum, "Soviet Assurances on Backfire Capabilities," n.d., NLC-132-92-5-3-5; Department of State Summit Background Memorandum, "Backfire," March 1, 1978, NLC-31-89-3-4-5.

117. Jimmy Carter: "Vienna Summit Meeting Remarks of President Brezhnev and President Carter on Signing the Treaty on the Limitation of Strategic Offensive Arms," June 18, 1979, *The American Presidency Project*, http://www.presidency.ucsb.edu/ws/?pid=32496.

118. "Significant Actions, Secretary and Deputy Secretary of Defense," November 18, 1977, NLC-8-4-5-22-0, CREST. Document 233, "Memorandum from the President's Assistant for National Security Affairs (Brzezinski) to President Carter," January 20, 1979, in *Foreign Relations of the United States, 1969–1976*, 33:927.

119. See Department of State, Bureau of Intelligence and Research Analysis, "Soviet Report on NATO Theater Nuclear Forces Discussions," September 15, 1978, NLC-6-54-3-15-7, CREST.

6. "SUMMARY—BLEAK"

1. "Vienna Summit Meeting Remarks of President Brezhnev and President Carter on Signing the Treaty on the Limitation of Strategic Offensive Arms," June 18, 1979, *The American Presidency Project*, http://www.presidency.ucsb.edu/ws/?pid=32496.

2. Jimmy Carter, "Address Delivered Before a Joint Session of the Congress on the Vienna Summit Meeting," June 18, 1979, *The American Presidency Project*, http://www.presidency.ucsb.edu/ws/?pid=32498.

3. Ibid.

4. Kenneth H. Bacon, "Carter Says SALT Pact Will Make World a Safer Place and Bolster U.S. Security," *Wall Street Journal*, June 19, 1979.

5. Strobe Talbott, *Endgame: The Inside Story of SALT II* (New York: Harper Colophon, 1979), 284; Robert G. Kaiser, "Lawyer Appointed to Aid SALT Sale," *Washington Post*, June 29, 1979.

6. U.S. Congress, Senate, Committee on Foreign Relations, *The SALT II Treaty: Hearings before the Committee on Foreign Relations of the Senate*, Part 1 (Washington, DC: U.S. Government Printing Office, 1979), 88–96 (Vance statement), 97–119 (Brown statement), 132–136 (McGovern statement), 216–220 (Muskie statement). See also Robert G. Kaiser, "SALT Hearings Under Way: Brown, Vance Defend Treaty as Debate on SALT II Begins," *Washington Post*, July 10, 1979.

7. U.S. Congress, Senate, Committee on Foreign Relations, *The SALT II Treaty*, Part 1, 136–138.

8. U.S. Congress, Senate, Committee on Foreign Relations, *The SALT II Treaty: Hearings Before the Committee on Foreign Relations of the Senate*. 96th Cong. 1, Part 2 (Washington, DC: Government Printing Office, 1979), 2–86 (Smith, Warnke, Earle, and Johnson statements and responses to questions), 87–143 (Jeremy Stone statement and questions); Clayton Fritchey, "Common Sense on SALT," *Washington Post*, July 23, 1979.

9. U.S. Congress, Senate, Committee on Foreign Relations, *The SALT II Treaty*, Part 1, 435–439. Nitze's position on verification can be found throughout his work, but it is most succinctly stated when he was discussing the INF Treaty. See U.S. Congress, Senate, Committee on Foreign Relations, *The INF Treaty: Hearings before the Committee on Foreign Relations, United States Senate, One Hundredth Congress, Second Session, on the Treaty between the United States of America and the Union of Soviet Socialist Republics on the Elimination of Their Intermediate-Range and Shorter-Range Missiles. Part 1, January 25, 26, 27, and 28, 1988* (Washington, DC: U.S. Government Printing Office, 1988), 301.

10. U.S. Congress, Senate, Committee on Foreign Relations, *The SALT II Treaty*, Part 1 438, 450.

11. Ibid., 448–449, 482. See also Paul Nitze, "The ALPS Concept," June 22, 1978, box 132, folder Missiles: Multiple Aimpoint System/Alternative Launchpoint System (MAP/ALPS) Concept, 1978, Paul H. Nitze Papers, Library of Congress; Strobe Talbott, *The Master of the Game: Paul Nitze and the Nuclear Peace* (New York: Vintage Books, 1988), 156.

12. U.S. Congress, Senate, Committee on Foreign Relations, *The SALT II Treaty*, Part 1 549–550. See also Talbott, *Endgame*, 140; Walter Pincus, "Ex-Negotiator on SALT Details Split with Joint Chiefs," *Washington Post*, August 2, 1979.

13. U.S. Congress, Senate, Committee on Foreign Relations, *The SALT II Treaty*, Part I 575, 594; Document 42, "Memorandum from Helmut Sonnenfeldt of the National Security Council Staff to Secretary of State Kissinger," October 23, 1973, in *Foreign Relations of the United States, 1969–1976*, vol. 33, *SALT II, 1972–1980*, edited by Erin R. Mahan (Washington, DC: U.S. Government Printing Office: 2013), 126.

14. For receptivity to Rowny's arguments, see Rowland Evans and Robert Novak, "SALT-Selling Generals," *Washington Post*, August 22, 1979.

15. U.S. Congress, Senate, Committee on Foreign Relations, *The SALT II Treaty*, 88–90 (Vance), 101–102 (Brown). For testimony before the Armed Services Committee, see U.S. Congress, Senate, Committee on Armed Services, *Military Implications of the Treaty on the Limitation of Strategic Offensive Arms and Protocol Thereto (SALT II Treaty): Hearings Before the Committee on Armed Services of the United States Senate, Part 1* (Washington, DC: U.S. Government Printing Office, 1979), 10–21.

16. U.S. Congress, Senate, Committee on Armed Services, *Military Implications of the Treaty on the Limitation of Strategic Offensive Arms and Protocol Thereto (SALT II Treaty)*, 30.

17. U.S. Congress, Senate, Committee on Foreign Relations, *The SALT II Treaty*, Part 1, 374, 401; U.S. Congress, Senate, Committee on Armed Services, *Military Implications of the Treaty on the Limitation of Strategic Offensive Arms and Protocol Thereto (SALT II Treaty)*, Part 1, 170. Reaction to Jackson's remarks can also be found in Robert G. Kaiser, "Sen. Jackson Suggests Joint Chiefs Hedged on SALT," *Washington Post*, July 25, 1979.

18. U.S. Congress, Senate, Committee on Foreign Relations, *The SALT II Treaty*, Part 3, 160.

19. U.S. Congress, Senate, Committee on Armed Services, *Military Implications of the Treaty on the Limitation of Strategic Offensive Arms and Protocol Thereto (SALT II Treaty)*, Part 1, 59–61, 284–286; "Nunn Wants Military Outlays Increased as a Condition for His Support of SALT," *Wall Street Journal*, July 26, 1979; Robert G. Kaiser, "Nunn Ties Vote on SALT to More Defense Spending," *Washington Post*, July 25, 1979; Joanne Omang, "Carter Won't Boost Arms Outlays for SALT Votes," *Washington Post*, July 29, 1979; George C. Wilson and Walter Pincus, "Embarrassment of Riches for The Pentagon," *Washington Post*, August 3, 1979.

20. Edward L. Rowny, "Let's Get Back to the Merits of SALT II," *Wall Street Journal*, October 3, 1979; and Robert G. Kaiser, "SALT Prospects Enhanced by Hearings, Both Sides Feel," *Washington Post*, August 3, 1979.

21. Gloria Duffy, "Crisis Mangling and the Cuban Brigade," *International Security* 8, no. 1 (1983): 67–87. See also Talbott, *Endgame*, 284–285.

22. William Branigin, "U.S. Loses Iran Sites: U.S. Listening Sites Lost on Iran-Soviet Border," *Washington Post*, March 1, 1979.

23. Briefing Memo, "Status of Negotiations to Obtain U2R [*sic*] Overflight Rights," n.d., NLC-43-110-1-7-4, CIA Records Search Tool (Hereinafter CREST), Jimmy Carter Presidential Library, Atlanta, GA; Memorandum for the Record, "Meeting with Senator John Glenn," June 19, 1979, NLC-52-9-22-1-0, CREST.

24. Murrey Marder, "Monitoring: Not-So-Secret Secret: U.S. Tried to Keep Lid on Two Listening Posts in China," *Washington Post*, June 19, 1981.

25. U.S. Congress, Senate, Select Committee on Intelligence, *Principal Findings on the Capabilities of the United States to Monitor the SALT II Treaty: Report of the Senate Select Committee on Intelligence* (Washington, D.C.: U.S. Government Printing Office, 1979), 5.

26. Ibid., 4–5.

27. Richard Burt, "Poll Says Few Back Soviet Arms Treaty," *New York Times*, March 18, 1979.

28. "Panel Rejects 2 Baker SALT Changes," *Los Angeles Times*, October 25, 1979; Robert G. Kaiser, "Bid to Amend SALT Beaten in Senate Panel by 9–6 Vote," *Washington Post*, October 18, 1979.

29. "Senate Panel Approves SALT by Vote of 9 to 6," *Chicago Tribune*, November 10, 1979.

30. Ibid.; Talbott, *Endgame*, 287. See also David Aaron, memorandum to Zbigniew Brzezinski, "SALT Ratification," December 11, 1979. NLC-126-19-21-1-7, CREST.

31. Zbigniew Brzezinski, memorandum to Jimmy Carter, "Estimated Soviet Defense Spending: Trends and Prospects," n.d., NLC-6-79-7-15-6, CREST.

32. Noel E. Firth and James H. Noren, *Soviet Defense Spending: A History of CIA Estimates, 1950–1990* (College Station: Texas A&M University Press, 1998), 145; and [Redacted], "Analyzing Soviet Defense Programs, 1951–1990," *Studies in Intelligence* 42, no. 3 (1998): 5. See also Fred Iklé, "Preparing for Industrial Mobilization: The First Step toward Full Strength," in *The Politics of National Security Strategy*, edited by Marcus Raskin (New York: Transaction Publishers, 1979), 57–60; and U.S. Congress, Senate Committee on Armed Services, *Military Implications of the Treaty on the Limitation of Strategic Offensive Arms and Protocol Thereto (SALT II Treaty): Hearings Before the Committee on Armed*

Services of the United States Senate (Washington, DC: U.S. Government Printing Office, 1979), 114–119.

33. "Long-Range Theater Nuclear Capabilities and Arms Control," June 22, 1978, Presidential Review Memorandum/NSC-38, *Jimmy Carter Presidential Library & Museum*, http://www.jimmycarterlibrary.gov/documents/prmemorandums/prm38.pdf, accessed May 9, 2014. See also Vance, *Hard Choices*, 96–97.

34. Vance, *Hard Choices*, 392; "Special Meeting of Foreign and Defence Ministers," press release, December 12, 1979, *North Atlantic Treaty Organization*, http://www.nato.int/cps/en/natolive/official_texts_27040.htm, accessed May 9, 2014.

35. "Warnke Resigns Job as Arms Negotiator," *Associated Press Dispatch*, October 10, 1978. See also William W. Ross, Seventh Interview with Paul C. Warnke, April 12, 2001, Oral History Project of the Historical Society of the District of Columbia Circuit, 124, http://dcchs.org/PaulCWarnke/041201.pdf, accessed June 21, 2017.

36. "Comprehensive Net Assessment and Military Force Posture Review," February 18, 1977, Presidential Review Memorandum/NSC-10, *Jimmy Carter Presidential Library & Museum*, http://www.jimmycarterlibrary.gov/documents/prmemorandums/prm10.pdf, accessed May 9, 2014.

37. Harold Brown, memorandum to Zbigniew Brzezinski, "Single Integrated Operational Plan (SIOP) Targeting Philosophy," April 25, 1977, 1, *National Archives*, http://www.archives.gov/declassification/iscap/pdf/2010-082-doc1.pdf.Accessed August 10, 2017.

38. "U.S. National Strategy," August 26, 1977, Presidential Directive/NSC-18, https://www.jimmycarterlibrary.gov/assets/documents/directives/pd18.pdf, retrieved August 10, 2017; "Nuclear Weapons Employment Policy," July 25, 1980, Presidential Directive/NSC-59, *Jimmy Carter Presidential Library & Museum*, https://www.jimmycarterlibrary.gov/assets/documents/directives/pd59.pdf. Accessed August 10, 2017.

39. *Nuclear Targeting Policy Review: Phase II Report* (Washington, DC: Office of the Secretary of Defense, 1978), 35, 37, in National Security Archive Electronic Briefing Book No. 390, "Jimmy Carter's Controversial Nuclear Targeting Directive PD-59 Declassified," ed. William Burrhttp://nsarchive.gwu.edu/nukevault/ebb390/docs/11-1-78%20policy%20review%20summary.pdf, accessed August 10, 2017.

40. William Odom and Jasper Welch, memorandum to Zbigniew Brzezinski, "Draft PD on Nuclear Employment Policy," April 17, 1980, 7–8, http://nsarchive.gwu.edu/nukevault/ebb390/docs/4-17-80%20Odom%20and%20Welch%20on%20Brown%20memo.pdf, accessed August 10, 2017.

41. National Security Council, Minutes of Special Coordination Committee Meeting, April 4, 1979, 4, http://nsarchive.gwu.edu/nukevault/ebb390/docs/4-4-79%20SCC%20mtg.pdf, accessed August 10, 2017.

42. Harold Brown, "A Countervailing View," *National Security: The Foreign Policy Blog*, September 24, 2012, http://www.foreignpolicy.com/articles/2012/09/24/a_countervailing_view, accessed May 10, 2014.

43. Elinor Camille Sloan, *The Revolution in Military Affairs* (Toronto: McGill-Queen's Press, 2002), 25.

44. Secretary of Defense, memorandum to Chairman, Joint Chiefs of Staff, "Implementation of the Nuclear Targeting Study," January 29, 1979, 6, 11, *National Archives*, http://www.archives.gov/declassification/iscap/pdf/2011-002-doc2.pdf.

45. Brown, "A Countervailing View."

46. Thomas W. Wolfe, John D. Steinbruner, and Ernest May, *History of the Strategic Arms Competition* (Washington, DC: Office of the Secretary of Defense), 718.

47. For Muskie's reaction, see "Pentagon Says State Was Informed of Shift in A-War Strategy," *Washington Post*, August 11, 1980; Reginald Bartholomew, memorandum to Secretary of State Muskie, "U.S. Strategic Targeting Policy," August 6, 1980, http://

nsarchive2.gwu.edu/nukevault/ebb390/docs/8-6-80%20Bartholomew%20memo.pdf, accessed May 10, 2014; Zbigniew Brzezinski, memorandum to Harold Brown, March 26, 1980, http://nsarchive2.gwu.edu/nukevault/ebb390/docs/3-26-80%20Odom-Welch.pdf, accessed May 10, 2014.

48. Marshall Shulman, memorandum to Secretary of State Muskie, "PD-59," September 2, 1980, http://nsarchive2.gwu.edu/nukevault/ebb390/docs/9-2-80%20Shulman%20 critique.pdf, accessed May 10, 2014; "Nuclear Targeting Policy Review: Phase II Report," November 1, 1978, *National Archives*, http://www.archives.gov/declassification/iscap/ pdf/2010-079-doc1.pdf, accessed May 10, 2014.

49. Richard Burt, "Muskie Rebuffs Soviet on Nuclear Strategy Criticism," *New York Times*, September 17, 1980; Anthony Austin, "Soviet Calls the U.S. Strategy Shift on Nuclear War an 'Ominous' Sign," *New York Times*, August 8, 1980; Richard Burt, "The World: A New Order of Debate on Atomic War," *New York Times*, August 17, 1980; Tom Wicker, "A Lethal Delusion," *New York Times*, August 10, 1980.

50. Gen. Richard Ellis, Joint Strategic Target Planning Staff, to Harold Brown, February 8, 1980, 4–5, *National Archives*, http://www.archives.gov/declassification/iscap/pdf/2011-002-doc2.pdf. Accessed August 12, 2017.

51. Perhaps the best account of these debates and the interservice interests that informed them is Fred Kaplan, *The Wizards of Armageddon* (Palo Alto, CA: Stanford University Press, 1991).

52. Odd Arne Westad, *The Global Cold War* (Cambridge: Cambridge University Press, 2007), 299–330.

53. Document 254, "Minutes of a Meeting of the National Security Council, 2 Jan 1980," in *Foreign Relations of the United States, 1969–1976*, 33:972.

54. Vance, *Hard Choices*, 99–103; Brzezinski, *Power and Principle*, 518–519.

55. Talbott, *Endgame*, 290.

56. Document 246, "Letter from President Carter to Senator Byrd," January 3, 1980, in *Foreign Relations of the United States, 1969–1976*, 33:974–975.

57. Document 250, "Summary of Conclusions of a Meeting of the Special Coordination Committee," June 6, 1980, in *Foreign Relations of the United States, 1969–1976*, 33:985–986.

58. Document 248, "Memorandum from Roger Molander and Madeleine Albright of the National Security Council Staff to the President's Assistant for National Security Affairs (Brzezinski) and the President's Deputy Assistant for National Security Affairs (Aaron)," January 16, 1980, in *Foreign Relations of the United States, 1969–1976*, 33:976–978.

59. Document 250, "Summary of Conclusions of a Meeting of the Special Coordination Committee," June 6, 1980, 985–986.

60. Document 251, "Memorandum from Roger Molander of the National Security Council Staff to the President's Assistant for National Security Affairs (Brzezinski and Special Counsel and Consultant to the President Lloyd Cutler," June 6, 1980, in *Foreign Relations of the United States, 1969–1976*, 33:987–988.

61. "The Carter-Reagan Debate Transcript," October 28, 1980, Commission on Presidential Debates, *Commission on Presidential Debates*, http://www.debates.org/index. php?page=october-28-1980-debate-transcript, accessed June 11, 2017.

62. Early theories of deterrence developed as a result of the atomic bomb's existence. See Bernard Brodie, *The Absolute Weapon* (Freeport, NY: Books for Libraries Press, 1946).

63. Document 248, "Memorandum from Roger Molander and Madeleine Albright of the National Security Council Staff to the President's Assistant for National Security Affairs (Brzezinski) and the President's Deputy Assistant for National Security Affairs (Aaron)," January 16, 1980, 979.

64. Brzezinski, *Power and Principle*, 529; Vance, *Hard Choices*, 393, 417.

65. Garthoff, *Détente and Confrontation,* 912.

66. Pavel Podvig, "The Window of Vulnerability That Wasn't: Soviet Military Buildup in the 1970s—A Research Note," *International Security* 33, no. 1 (2008): 118–138.

67. Anne Hessing Kahn, *Killing Détente: The Right Attacks the CIA* (University Park: Pennsylvania State University Press, 1998).

68. Talbott, *Endgame,* 279

69. Talbott, *The Master of the Game,* 159.

7. INF

1. See Rowland Evans and Robert Novak, *The Reagan Revolution: An Inside Look at the Transformation of the U.S. Government* (New York: E. P. Dutton, 1981); Martin Anderson, *Revolution: The Reagan Legacy* (Stanford, CA: Hoover Institute Press, 1990). For a more balanced view, see Lou Cannon, *President Reagan: The Role of a Lifetime* (New York: Public Affairs, 2000).

2. "The Carter-Reagan Debate Transcript," October 28, 1980, *Commission on Presidential Debates,* http://www.debates.org/index.php?page=october-28-1980-debate-transcript, accessed June 11, 2017.

3. See, for example, Norman Podhoretz, "The Culture of Appeasement," *Harper's Magazine* 255, no. 1529 (1977): 25; Theodore Draper, "Détente," *Commentary* 57, no. 6 (1974): 25.

4. See Paul Nitze, *From Hiroshima to Glasnost* (New York: Grove Weidenfeld, 1989), xxi.

5. John M. Whiteley, "A World of Clear and Present Danger," interview with Eugene V. Rostow, 1985, *The Quest for Peace,* http://www.lib.uci.edu/sites/questforpeace/index.php?page=rostow, accessed August 17, 2014.

6. Richard Perle, "An Arms Control Treaty Built on American Illusions," *Washington Post,* October 7, 1979.

7. "Zumwalt: Secretary Lacks Faith in Americans: Why Kissinger Concedes to Soviets," *Human Events* 36, no. 15 (1976): 1.

8. R. M. Wharton, "Finlandization: Neutering of a Nation." *Human Events* 38, no. 15 (1978): 8. "Finlandization" is a pejorative term that refers to the process of an ostensibly sovereign and democratic country gradually accommodating or even siding with the Soviet Union in economic and foreign policy disputes due to the immediate military threat that the Soviet Union posed, as Finland was accused of doing in the post-1945 period.

9. Karol C. Thaler, "Spreading Case of Hollanditis," *Chicago Tribune,* September 30, 1981.

10. This quote is repeatedly attributed to Reagan, yet he seems not to have ever gone on record with it. See Stephen F. Hayward, *The Age of Reagan: The Conservative Counter-Revolution, 1980–1989* (New York: Crown Publishing Group, 2009), 252; and Peggy Noonan, *What I Saw at the Revolution: A Political Life in the Reagan Era* (New York: Random House Publishing, 2003), 100.

11. "Haig's Demonstration Bomb," *Chicago Tribune,* November 7, 1981; Godfrey Sperling, "Reagan Moves to Counter Aides' Gaffes," *Christian Science Monitor,* November 16, 1981; Bernard Gwertzman, "Reagan Clarifies His Statements on Nuclear War," *New York Times,* October 22, 1981.

12. Alexander Haig, *Caveat: Realism, Reagan, and Foreign Policy* (New York: MacMillan Publishing, 1984), 2–3.

13. Haig claims that this tactic was not his idea, but plentiful coverage of the incident suggests it was no accident. Haig took some pride in the event either way. Ibid., 101–102.

14. Interview with Richard Allen, May 28, 2002, 34, 54, Ronald Reagan Oral History Project, Miller Center of Public Affairs, *Miller Center,* http://web1.millercenter.org/poh/transcripts/ohp_2002_0528_allen.pdf, accessed August 18, 2014.

15. Richard Allen, "When Reagan Was Shot, Who Was 'In Control' at the White House?" *Washington Post*, March 25, 2011.

16. Frances FitzGerald, *Way Out There in the Blue: Reagan, Star Wars, and the End of the Cold War* (New York: Simon and Schuster, 2001), 158–161.

17. George Shultz, *Turmoil and Triumph: Diplomacy, Power, and the Victory of the American Ideal* (New York: Macmillan Publishing Company, 1993), 144; Strobe Talbott, *Deadly Gambits: The Reagan Administration and the Stalemate in Nuclear Arms Control* (New York: Vintage Books, 1985), 46.

18. Talbott, *Deadly Gambits*, 15–16.

19. Ibid., 48, 60, 135.

20. Michael Getler, "Rostow Accepts Top Post at Arms Control Agency," *Washington Post*, March 26, 1981.

21. Eugene Rostow to William Clark, January 15, 1982, box 3, folder Rostow File (01/01/1982–01/15/1982), Robert McFarlane Files, Ronald Reagan Presidential Library, Simi Valley, CA; Eugene Rostow, "Talking Points," January 16, 1982, box 3, folder Rostow File (01/16/1982–09/30/1982)" Robert McFarlane Files, Ronald Reagan Library; Robert G. Kaiser, "Arms Control Agency Asserts It Has Policy Role, Not State," *Washington Post*, September 5, 1981; Talbott, *Deadly Gambits*, 266; Shultz, *Turmoil and Triumph*, 161.

22. Talbott, *Deadly Gambits*, 41–42.

23. "Navy Aide: SALT Not Binding," *Washington Post*, March 4, 1981; Talbott, *Deadly Gambits*, 225.

24. Thomas Graham, *Disarmament Sketches: Three Decades of Arms Control and International Law* (Seattle: University of Washington Press, 2012), 103; Talbott, *Deadly Gambits*, 224.

25. "The President's News Conference of January 29, 1981," January 29, 1981, box 90556, folder NATO-TNF Arms Control—TNF May–June 1981, Sven Kraemer Files, Ronald Reagan Library. See also Raymond Garthoff, *The Great Transition: American-Soviet Relations and the End of the Cold War* (Washington, DC: Brookings Institution Press, 2000), 523.

26. Shultz, *Turmoil and Triumph*, 717.

27. Richard Allen, memorandum to Ronald Reagan, "SCC Postponement," March 17, 1981, box 34, folder Soviet Union-SALT EE 1/2," Jack Matlock Files, Ronald Reagan Library; Talbott, *Deadly Gambits*, 228–229. See also Richard Allen, memorandum to Ronald Reagan, "TASS Sees U.S. 'Linkage' Policy as 'Confrontation,'" February 17, 1981, box 34, folder Soviet Union-SALT EE 1/2, Jack Matlock Files, Ronald Reagan Library.

28. Oswald Johnston, "Weinberger Opposes Arms Talks until Soviets Pull Back Troops around Poland," *Los Angeles Times*, April 15, 1981. For similar language about arms control, see "President's Meeting with Paul Nitze," January 7, 1982, box 71, folder Nuclear-Intermediate Range Nuclear Forces (INF) (1/6/82–1/27/82), NSC Executive Secretariat Files, Ronald Reagan Library.

29. Richard Allen, memorandum to Carnes Lord, "Interim Policy on SALT and Arms Control," February 17, 1981, box 34, folder Soviet Union-SALT EE 1/2, Jack Matlock Files, Ronald Reagan Library; "Basic Considerations for SALT Policy," August 13, 1981, box 34, folder Soviet Union-SALT EE 2/2, Jack Matlock Files, Ronald Reagan Library.

30. Haig, *Caveat*, 227; Nitze, *From Hiroshima to Glasnost*, 367; Talbott, *Deadly Gambits*, 178–179.

31. Nitze, *From Hiroshima to Glasnost*, 369; Talbott, *Deadly Gambits*, 66–67.

32. Frank Carlucci, memorandum to Richard Allen, "TNF Negotiations," May 1, 1981, box 91282, folder NSC 000008 30 Apr 81 (2/3), NSC Executive Secretariat Meeting Files, Ronald Reagan Library; Ronald Reagan, "Presidential Directive," May 1, 1981, box 91282,

folder NSC 000008 30 Apr 81 (2/3), NSC Executive Secretariat Meeting Files, Ronald Reagan Library.

33. National Security Council Minutes of Meeting, October 13, 1981, 6, box 91282, folder NSC 00022 13 Oct 81, NSC Executive Secretariat Meeting Files, Ronald Reagan Library.

34. Steven Zaloga, *The Kremlin's Nuclear Sword: The Rise and Fall of Russia's Strategic Nuclear Forces, 1945–2000* (London: Smithsonian Institute Press, 2002), 198–199.

35. Intermediate Range Nuclear Missiles (Warheads): European Theater, April 24, 1981, box 91282, folder NSC 000008 30 Apr 81 (3/3), NSC Executive Secretariat Meeting Files, Ronald Reagan Library.

36. Alexander Haig, memorandum to Ronald Reagan, "The Atlantic Alliance," April 29, 1981, 3, box 91282, folder NSC 000008 30 Apr 81 (3/3), NSC Executive Secretariat Meeting Files, Ronald Reagan Library; Note from unknown NSC deputy to Richard Allen, October 15, 1981, box 91356, folder Arms Control and Disarmament Agency (7/8/81–12/23/81), NSC Executive Secretariat Meeting Files, Ronald Reagan Library; "NSPG Meeting 13 Jan 1983," January 13, 1983, 5, box 91603, folder NSPG 0050 13 Jan 1983 [Arms Control/INF], NSC Executive Secretariat National Security Planning Group Records, Ronald Reagan Library.

37. See Talbott, *Deadly Gambits*, 132.

38. Strobe Talbott, "Behind Closed Doors," *Time*, December 5, 1983, 29.

39. Alexander Haig, memorandum to Ronald Reagan "The Atlantic Alliance," April 29, 1981, 3.

40. Talbott, *Deadly Gambits*, 50–51; Haig, *Caveat*, 227.

41. Talbott, *Deadly Gambits*, 59–60. See also National Security Council Minutes of Meeting, November 12, 1981, 4, box 91283, folder NSC 00025 [Theater Nuclear Forces, NATO, Strategic Forces] 12 Nov 1981, NSC Executive Secretariat Meeting Files, Ronald Reagan Library; National Security Council Minutes of Meeting, October 13, 1981, 5.

42. National Security Council Minutes of Meeting, November 12, 1981, 3.

43. OSD Paper, "Timing of TNF Arms Control with the Soviets," April 28, 1981, box 91282, folder NSC 000008 30 Apr 81 (1/3), NSC Executive Secretariat Meeting Files, Ronald Reagan Library.

44. Haig, *Caveat*, 230–231.

45. Don Oberdorfer, "Haig, Gromyko Talk 4 Hours, Set Arms Statement," *Washington Post*, September 24, 1981.

46. Richard Allen, memorandum to Ronald Reagan, "National Security Council Meeting Thursday, November 12, 1981, 4:00PM," November 11, 1981, box 91283, folder NSC 00025 [Theater Nuclear Forces, NATO, Strategic Forces] 12 Nov 1981, NSC Executive Secretariat Meeting Files, Ronald Reagan Library.

47. National Security Council Minutes of Meeting, November 12, 1981, 2. See also the marginalia in "Intermediate Range Nuclear Missiles (Warheads): European Theater," April 24, 1981, box 91282, folder NSC 000008 30 Apr 81 (3/3), NSC Executive Secretariat Meeting Files, Ronald Reagan Library. For Perle intimidating the JCS, see Talbott, *Deadly Gambits*, 144.

48. This premise underpinned the Vladivostok accord, in which the United States abandoned the pursuit of controls on heavy missiles in exchange for the Soviet Union dropping attempts to control U.S. forward-based systems (see Chapter 2).

49. Ronald Reagan, "Remarks to Members of the National Press Club on Arms Reduction and Nuclear Weapons," November 18, 1981, *The American Presidency Project*, http://www.presidency.ucsb.edu/ws/?pid=43264, accessed June 11, 2017.

50. "West European Public Opinion on INF," n.d., box 3, folder NSDD-56 15 September 1982 (3), NSC Executive Secretariat NSDD Files, Ronald Reagan Library.

51. Talbott, *Deadly Gambits*, 52; Nitze, *From Hiroshima to Glasnost*, 369; Haig, *Caveat*, 231.

52. Leslie Gelb, "Reagan Orders Production of 2 Types of Neutron Arms for Stockpiling in US," *New York Times*, August 9, 1981; Richard Halloran, "Weinberger Says Neutron Weapons are Being Built," *New York Times*, August 11, 1981; National Security Decision Directive 7, "[Redacted] Weapons," August 6, 1981, *Federation of American Scientists Intelligence Resource Program*, https://fas.org/irp/offdocs/nsdd/nsdd-7.pdf, accessed June 11, 2017.

53. Rudy Abramson, "Reagan to Approve MX, B-1," *Los Angeles Times*, September 30, 1981; Clara Germani, "Former Defense Chief Raps B-1 Bomber Plan," *Christian Science Monitor*, September 21, 1981.

54. "NSC Meeting 11/18/82: MX," November 18, 1982, 2, box 91285, folder NSC 00066 18 Nov 1982 (2/2), NSC Executive Secretariat Meeting Files, Ronald Reagan Library.

55. Richard Halloran, "Reagan Drops Mobile MX Plan, Urges Basing Missiles in Silos," *New York Times*, October 3, 1981.

56. "Mormon Church Opposes Placing MX Missile in Utah and Nevada," *New York Times*, May 6, 1981; William E. Schmidt, "Political Leaders in Utah and Nevada Applaud Decision on the MX," *New York Times*, October 3, 1981.

57. Robert McFarlane, "NSPG Meeting on Soviet Noncompliance with Arms Control Agreements," n.d., box 91306, folder NSPG 0081 20 Dec 1983 [Compliance] (1 of 3), NSC Executive Secretariat National Security Planning Group Records, Ronald Reagan Library; Rowland Evans and Robert Novak, "Helms vs. Novak," *Washington Post*, April 20, 1981.

58. "Soviet Compliance with the Confidence-Building Measures of the Helsinki Final Act," December 15, 1983, box 91306, folder NSPG 0081 20 Dec 1983 [Compliance] (1 of 3), NSC Executive Secretariat National Security Planning Group Records, Ronald Reagan Library; Leslie Gelb, "U.S. Tells Soviets Any Arms Pacts Must Include On-Site Verification," *New York Times*, September 2, 1981; and Minutes, National Security Council Meeting, April 21, 1982, 6, box 91284, folder NSC 00046 21 Apr 1982 (2/5), NSC Executive Secretariat Meeting Files, Ronald Reagan Library.

59. Talbott, *Deadly Gambits*, 315; William Clark, memorandum to administration principals, "Establishment of an Arms Control Verification Committee," November 10, 1982, box 3, folder NSDD-56 15 September 1982 (3), NSC Executive Secretariat NSDD Files, Ronald Reagan Library.

60. Shultz, *Turmoil and Triumph*, 464–465, 567.

61. National Security Decision Directive 13, "Nuclear Weapons Employment Policy," October 19, 1981, Federation of American Scientists Intelligence Resource Program, *Federation of American Scientists*, https://fas.org/irp/offdocs/nsdd/nsdd-13.pdf, accessed June 11, 2017.

62. Joint Chiefs of Staff, Joint Secretariat, Historical Division, *A Historical Study of Strategic Connectivity, 1950–1981* (Washington, DC: Joint Chiefs of Staff, 1982), *U.S. Department of Defense*, http://www.dod.mil/pubs/foi/Reading_Room/Joint_Staff/92-A-0781_A_Historical_Study_of_Strategic_Command_1950-1981.pdf, accessed June 11, 2017.

63. Jeffrey Richelson, "PD-59, NSDD-13 and the Reagan Strategic Modernization Program," *Journal of Strategic Studies* 6 no. 2 (1983): 125.

64. National Security Decision Directive 13, "Nuclear Weapons Employment Policy," 1, 5.

65. "Weinberger Said to Offer Reagan Plan to Regain Atomic Superiority," *New York Times*, August 14, 1981; Gwertzman, "Reagan Clarifies His Statements on Nuclear War."

66. Mary McGrory, "Reagan Aide Offers Laid-Back Description of Nuclear War," *Washington Post*, March 2, 1982; Lawrence Freedman, *The Evolution of Nuclear Strategy* (New York: Palgrave MacMillan, 2003), 388–392.

67. Nitze, *From Hiroshima to Glasnost*, 372–373.

68. Ibid., 371; Talbott, *Deadly Gambits*, 94.

69. Nitze, *From Hiroshima to Glasnost*, 370; Sven Kraemer, memorandum to Richard Allen, "National Security Council Meeting Thursday, November 12, 1981, 4:00PM," November 11, 1981, box 91283, folder NSC 00025 [Theater Nuclear Forces, NATO, Strategic Forces] 12 Nov 1981, NSC Executive Secretariat Meeting Files, Ronald Reagan Library.

70. See also Alexsandr' Savel'yev and Nikolay Detinov, *The Big Five: Arms Control Decision-Making in the Soviet Union* (Westport, CT: Prager, 1995), xii–xiii.

71. Ibid., 57–58; Oberdorfer, "Haig, Gromyko Talk 4 Hours, Set Arms Statement."

72. Talbott, *Deadly Gambits*, 87–89. For the SS-20 deployment rate, see Haig, *Caveat*, 225.

73. Raymond Garthoff, *Détente and Confrontation: American-Soviet Relations from Nixon to Reagan* (Washington, DC: Brookings, 1994), 960; Talbott, *Deadly Gambits*, 90.

74. Talbott, *Deadly Gambits*, 88.

75. Cable, Paul Nitze to Alexander Haig, "Ambassador Nitze's Private Discussion with Ambassador Kvitsinsky," May 28, 1982, box 71, folder Nuclear-Intermediate Range Nuclear Forces (INF) September 1982, NSC Executive Secretariat Files, Ronald Reagan Library. NSC staff, likely Sven Kraemer or Richard Boverie, wrote comments in the margins of this cable that read "Read this: who gave Nitze clearance for this?"

76. Agency Views on START Negotiation Position, n.d., box 91284, folder NSC 00046 21 Apr 1982 (3/5), NSC Executive Secretariat Meeting Files, Ronald Reagan Library; Talbott, *Deadly Gambits*, 105.

77. Lawrence Eagleburger, "Why We Don't Count the French and British Missiles," *Washington Post*, May 8, 1982; "Exclusion of British and French Forces from INF Negotiations," n.d., box 91043, folder INF-United Kingdom/France Systems—CRS (Congressional Research Service) Study (1983), Sven Kraemer Files, Ronald Reagan Library; R. Craig Nation, *Black Earth, Red Star: A History of Soviet Security Policy* (Ithaca, NY: Cornell University Press, 1992), ix.

78. Haig, *Caveat*, 233.

79. Eagleburger, "Why We Don't Count the French and British Missiles"; Talbott, *Deadly Gambits*, 97.

80. Eugene Rostow, memorandum to William Clark, "The GLCM-INF Controversy," January 21, 1982, box 71, folder Nuclear-Intermediate Range Nuclear Forces (INF) (1/6/82–1/27/82), NSC Executive Secretariat Files, Ronald Reagan Library; Talbott, *Deadly Gambits*, 100–101.

81. Talbott, *Deadly Gambits*, 107; Caspar Weinberger, *Fighting for Peace: Seven Critical Years in the Pentagon* (New York: Warner Books, 1991), 320–321.

82. Talbott describes Nitze's point of view as close to panic beginning in 1982, although few sources confirm this degree of anxiety. Talbott, *Deadly Gambits*, 163–164. See also Nitze, *From Hiroshima to Glasnost*, 374.

83. Nitze, *From Hiroshima to Glasnost*, 374–375.

84. Talbott, *Deadly Gambits*, 82.

85. Nitze, *From Hiroshima to Glasnost*, 375–376.

86. Paul Nitze, memorandum to William Clark, "Memorandum of Conversation—July 16, 1982," *The Reagan Files*, http://www.thereaganfiles.com/nitze-walk-in-the-wood.pdf, accessed August 20, 2014.

87. Reagan, "Remarks to Members of the National Press Club on Arms Reduction and Nuclear Weapons."

88. Thomas W. Graham, "The Politics of Failure: Strategic Nuclear Arms Control, Public Opinion, and Domestic Politics in the United States, 1945–1980" (PhD diss., Massachusetts Institute of Technology, 1989), 413.

89. Paul L. Montgomery, "Throngs Fill Manhattan to Protest Nuclear Weapons," *New York Times*, June 13, 1982.

90. George C. Edwards III, *Predicting the Presidency: The Potential of Persuasive Leadership* (Princeton, NJ: Princeton University Press, 2016), 100.

91. Talbott, *Deadly Gambits*, 302–303.

92. Don Oberdorfer and Michael Getler, "Haig Says New Arms Talks with Soviets Could Start in February," *Washington Post*, November 5, 1981; Minutes, National Security Council Meeting, April 21, 1982, 1, box 91284, folder NSC 00046 21 Apr 1982 (2/5), NSC Executive Secretariat Meeting Files, Ronald Reagan Library; "START Criteria," n.d., box 91284, folder NSC 00046 21 Apr 1982 (2/5), NSC Executive Secretariat Meeting Files, Ronald Reagan Library.

93. Talbott, *Deadly Gambits*, 237.

94. "State Department Views," n.d., box 91284, folder NSC 00045 16 Apr 1982 (1), NSC Executive Secretariat Meeting files, Ronald Reagan Library; minutes, National Security Council Meeting, April 21, 1982, 4, box 91284, folder NSC 00046 21 Apr 1982 (2/5), NSC Executive Secretariat Meeting Files, Ronald Reagan Library.

95. Talbott, *Deadly Gambits*, 346–247. McFarlane's activities here were part of a broader pattern within the field of U.S.-Soviet relations. See Shultz, *Turmoil and Triumph*, 268, 466.

96. "START Criteria."

97. Slide Presentation, "Framework for a U.S. Negotiating Approach," n.d., box 91284, folder NSC 00046 21 Apr 1982 (2/5), NSC Executive Secretariat Meeting Files, Ronald Reagan Library.

98. Minutes, National Security Council Meeting, April 21, 1982, 4, 6, box 91284, folder NSC 00046 21 Apr 1982 (2/5), NSC Executive Secretariat Meeting Files, Ronald Reagan Library; Talbott, *Deadly Gambits*, 236.

99. "JCS Assessment of Units of Account," May 1, 1982, box 91284, folder NSC 00046 21 Apr 1982 (3/5), NSC Executive Secretariat Meeting Files, Ronald Reagan Library; William Clark, memorandum to NSC principals, "Preparations for START," box 91284, folder NSC 00046 21 Apr 1982 (3/5), NSC Executive Secretariat Meeting Files, Ronald Reagan Library; "Review of START Policy Issues," May 2, 1982, 12, box 91284, folder NSC 00049 3 May 1982 (1/2), NSC Executive Secretariat Meeting Files, Ronald Reagan Library; "Draft START Instructions," June 21, 1982, box 91284, "folder NSC 00052 25 Jun 1982 (1/2)," NSC Executive Secretariat Meeting Files, Ronald Reagan Library;

100. Minutes, "NSC 5/3/82 START," May 3, 1982, 3, box 91284, folder NSC 00049 3 May 1982 (1/2), NSC Executive Secretariat Meeting Files, Ronald Reagan Library. See also Talbott, *Deadly Gambits*, 266.

101. Freedman, *The Evolution of Nuclear Strategy*, 411–413.

102. See Edward L. Rowny, *It Takes One to Tango* (New York: Brassey's, 1992). See also Charles Stuart Kennedy, interview with Ambassador Max Kampelman, June 24, 2003, 115, *Association for Diplomatic Studies and Training, Foreign Affairs Oral History Project*, http://www.adst.org/OH%20TOCs/Kampelman,%20Max.toc.pdf, accessed June 21, 2017; Talbott, *Deadly Gambits*, 277–278.

103. Talbott, *Deadly Gambits*, 133.

104. Shultz, *Turmoil and Triumph*, 120; Talbott, *Deadly Gambits*, 134.

105. Talbott, *Deadly Gambits*, 143.

106. A memo to Clark by an unknown NSC member was likely penned by McFarlane; at the very least it reflected his views. See Memorandum for William Clark, "Rostow/Nitze Initiative on INF Talks," July 29, 1982, *The Reagan Files*, http://www.thereaganfiles.com/82729.pdf, accessed August 21, 2014.

107. William Clark, draft talking points on new INF package, July 30, 1982, *The Reagan Files*, http://www.thereaganfiles.com/july-31-draft-tps.pdf, accessed August 21, 2014.

108. Graham, *Disarmament Sketches*, 115; Talbott, *Deadly Gambits*, 141.

109. Talbott, *Deadly Gambits*, 144; Graham, *Disarmament Sketches*, 115.

110. Shultz, *Turmoil and Triumph*, 123.

111. Nitze, *From Hiroshima to Glasnost*, 388–389.

112. Graham, *Disarmament Sketches*, 116.

113. Michael Getler, "The Arms Control Debate Goes into a New Phase," *Washington Post*, December 23, 1982.

114. Talbott, *Deadly Gambits*, 168.

115. Savel'yev and Detinov, *The Big Five*, 65–66.

116. National Security Decision Directive 56, "Private INF Exchange," September 15, 1982, *Federation of American Scientists Intelligence Resource Program*, https://fas.org/irp/offdocs/nsdd/nsdd-056.htm, accessed June 11, 2017.

117. Shultz, *Turmoil and Triumph*, 120; Talbott, *Deadly Gambits*, 144.

118. Shultz, *Turmoil and Triumph*, 144.

119. "INF Update," November 19, 1983, box 73, folder Nuclear-Intermediate Range Nuclear Forces (INF) (11/01/83–11/21/83), NSC Executive Secretariat Files, Ronald Reagan Library.

120. "West European Public Opinion on INF"; Talbott, *Deadly Gambits*, 158.

121. "Excerpts from Speech by Andropov on Medium-Range Nuclear Missiles," *New York Times*, December 22, 1982; Talbott, *Deadly Gambits*, 162.

122. Joint Press Conference with West German Chancellor (Helmut Kohl), February 4, 1983, *Margaret Thatcher Foundation*, http://www.margaretthatcher.org/document/105249, retrieved August 21, 2014; Ronald Reagan, "Draft Message to Kohl, Thatcher, Fanfani, Mitterrand, Lubbers, and Mars tens," n.d., box 71, folder Nuclear-Intermediate Range Nuclear Forces (INF) (2/1/83–2/24/83), NSC Executive Secretariat Files, Ronald Reagan Library; John Poindexter, memorandum to Dan Fortier et al., "Secretary Shultz's Evening Report of Feb 18," February 18, 1983, box 71, folder Nuclear-Intermediate Range Nuclear Forces (INF) 2/22/83 American Legion Speech (2/1/83–2/24/83), NSC Executive Secretariat Files, Ronald Reagan Library.

123. Shultz, *Turmoil and Triumph*, 351.

124. "NSPG Meeting 13 Jan 1983," January 13, 1983, 1, box 91603, folder NSPG 0050 13 Jan 1983 [Arms Control/INF], NSC Executive Secretariat National Security Planning Group Records, Ronald Reagan Library.

125. Ibid., 2–3.

126. Ibid., 4–8.

127. Ronald Reagan, "Remarks at the Annual Washington Conference of the American Legion," February 22, 1983, *Ronald Reagan Presidential Library*, http://www.reagan.utexas.edu/archives/speeches/1983/22283b.htm, accessed August 21, 2014.

128. "Reagan: 'We Are Prepared to Negotiate an Interim Agreement,'" *Washington Post*, March 31, 1983; Talbott, *Deadly Gambits*, 180.

129. William Staples, memorandum to Robert Kimmit, "Chronologies of U.S. and Soviet Initiatives in INF," January 17, 1984, 3, box 73, folder Nuclear-Intermediate Range Nuclear Forces (INF) 12/11/83–January 1984, NSC Executive Secretariat Subject Files, Ronald Reagan Library.

130. Ibid., 6.

131. Shultz, *Turmoil and Triumph*, 364–365.

132. Nitze, *From Hiroshima to Glasnost*, 391–393.

133. Talbott, *Deadly Gambits*, 203.

134. George Shultz to all NATO capitals and Tokyo, "INF: Presidential Message," November 19, 1983, box 73, folder Nuclear-Intermediate Range Nuclear Forces (INF) (11/01/83–11/21/83), NSC Executive Secretariat Files, Ronald Reagan Library.

135. Nitze, *From Hiroshima to Glasnost*, 396–398; Talbott, *Deadly Gambits*, 205.

136. "INF Update," November 19, 1983.

137. Shultz, *Turmoil and Triumph*, 375.

138. Ibid., 376.

139. Strobe Talbott, *The Master of the Game: Paul Nitze and the Nuclear Peace* (New York: Vintage Books, 1989), 66, 340.

140. Shultz, *Turmoil and Triumph*, 377.

141. Ibid., 30–31.

142. Ibid.

143. Ibid., 477.

144. Ibid., 484.

145. Ibid., 519.

CONCLUSION: THE CONSEQUENCES OF CONTROL

1. Michael R. Gordon, "Reagan Arms Adviser Says Bush Is Wrong on Short-Range Missiles," *New York Times*, May 3, 1989; Marilyn Berger, "Paul Nitze, Cold War Strategist, Dies at 97," *New York Times*, October 20, 2004; Strobe Talbott, *The Master of the Game: Paul Nitze and the Nuclear Peace* (New York: Random House, 1988), 383–394.

Bibliography

ARCHIVAL COLLECTIONS

Gerald R. Ford Presidential Library
  White House Special Files Unit
Jimmy Carter Presidential Library
  1976 Presidential Campaign Issues Office Files
  National Security Affairs: Brzezinski Material—Subject Files
Library of Congress
  Paul H. Nitze Papers
Ronald Reagan Presidential Library
  Jack Matlock Files
  National Security Council Executive Secretariat—Meeting Files
  National Security Council Executive Secretariat—Subject Files
  Robert McFarlane Files
  Sven Kraemer Files
U.S. Central Intelligence Agency. CIA Records Search Tool (CREST).
U.S. National Archives and Records Administration. General Records of the Department
  of State (RG 59)

INTERVIEWS

Interview with Jimmy Carter, November 29, 1982. Carter Presidency Project, Miller
    Center of Public Affairs. http://web1.millercenter.org/poh/transcripts/
    ohp_1982_1129_carter.pdf. Accessed January 5, 2014.
Interview with Richard Allen, May 28, 2002. Ronald Reagan Oral History Project,
    Miller Center of Public Affairs. http://web1.millercenter.org/poh/transcripts/
    ohp_2002_0528_allen.pdf. Accessed August 18, 2014.
Kennedy, Charles Stuart. Interview with Ambassador Max Kampelman, June 24, 2003.
    Association for Diplomatic Studies and Training, Foreign Affairs Oral History
    Project. http://www.adst.org/OH%20TOCs/Kampelman,%20Max.toc.pdf.
    Accessed June 21, 2017.
Ross, William W. Seventh interview with Paul C. Warnke. April 12, 2001. Oral History
    Project of the Historical Society of the District of Columbia Circuit. http://
    dcchs.org/PaulCWarnke/041201.pdf. Accessed June 21, 2017.
Whiteley, John M. "A World of Clear and Present Danger." Interview with Eugene V.
    Rostow, 1985. The Quest for Peace. http://www.lib.uci.edu/sites/questforpeace/
    index.php?page=rostow. Accessed August 17, 2014.

PUBLISHED SOURCES

Acquino, Michael. "The Neutron Bomb." PhD diss., University of California Santa
    Barbara, 1980.
Anderson, Martin. Revolution: The Reagan Legacy. Stanford, CA: Hoover Institute
    Press, 1990.

Anderson, Patrick. *Electing Jimmy Carter: The Campaign of 1976.* Baton Rouge: Louisiana State University Press, 1994.

Brodie, Bernard. *The Absolute Weapon.* Freeport, NY: Books for Libraries Press, 1946.

Brzezinski, Zbigniew. *Power and Principle: Memoirs of the National Security Advisor, 1977–1981.* New York: Farrar, Strauss, Giroux, 1983.

Bundy, McGeorge. *Danger and Survival: Choices about the Bomb in the First Fifty Years.* New York: Vintage Books, 1990.

Bunn, George. *Arms Control by Committee: Managing Negotiations with the Russians.* Stanford, CA: Stanford University Press, 1992.

Cahn, Anne Hessing. *Killing Détente: The Right Attacks the CIA.* University Park: Pennsylvania State University Press, 1998.

Calvo-Goller, Notburga K., and Michael A. Calvo. *The SALT Agreements: Content, Application, Verification.* Dodrecht, The Netherlands: Martinus Nijhoff Publishers, 1987.

Cannon, Lou. *President Reagan: The Role of a Lifetime.* New York: Public Affairs, 2000.

Carter, April. *Success and Failure in Arms Control Negotiations.* Oxford: Oxford University Press, 1989.

Carter, Jimmy. *Keeping Faith: Memoirs of a President.* New York: Bantam Books, 1982.

———. *White House Diary.* New York: Farrar, Strauss, and Giroux, 2010.

"Carter Clarifies Position on Stealth Aircraft Leaks." *Aviation Week & Space Technology,* September 15, 1980, 23.

Director of Central Intelligence. *Soviet Capabilities for Strategic Nuclear Conflict through the Late 1980s.* Vol. 1, *National Intelligence Summary Estimate.* Washington, DC: Central Intelligence Agency, 1978. http://www.foia.cia.gov/sites/default/files/document_conversions/89801/DOC_0000268138.pdf. Accessed January 5, 2014.

Divine, Robert A. *Blowing on the Wind: The Nuclear Test Ban Debate, 1954–1960.* Oxford: Oxford University Press, 1978.

Draper, Theodore. "Détente." *Commentary* 57, no. 6 (1974): 25–47.

Duffy, Gloria. "Crisis Mangling and the Cuban Brigade." *International Security* 8 (1983): 67–87.

Edwards, George C., III. *Predicting the Presidency: The Potential of Persuasive Leadership.* Princeton, NJ: Princeton University Press, 2016.

Ehrlich, Robert. *Waging Nuclear Peace.* Albany: State University Press of New York, 1984.

Ehrman, John. *The Rise of Neoconservatism: Intellectuals and Foreign Affairs, 1945–1994.* New Haven, CT: Yale University Press, 1995.

Fanning, Richard. *Peace and Disarmament.* Lexington: University Press of Kentucky, 1995.

Firth, Noel E., and James H. Noren. *Soviet Defense Spending: A History of CIA Estimates, 1950–1990.* College Station: Texas A&M University Press, 1998

FitzGerald, Frances. *Way Out There in the Blue: Reagan, Star Wars, and the End of the Cold War.* New York: Simon and Schuster, 2000.

Forrow, James D. "Electoral and Congressional Incentives and Arms Control." *Journal of Conflict Resolution* 35, no. 2 (1991): 245–265.

Freedman, Lawrence. *The Evolution of Nuclear Strategy.* New York: Palgrave-MacMillan, 2003.

Garthoff, Raymond. *Détente and Confrontation.* Washington, DC: The Brookings Institution, 1994.

———. "Estimating Soviet Military Intentions and Capabilities." In *Watching the Bear: Essays on the CIA's Analysis of the Soviet Union,* edited by Gerald K. Haines and Robert E. Legget, 135–186. Washington, DC: Government Printing Office, 2003.

——. *The Great Transition: American-Soviet Relations and the End of the Cold War.* Washington, DC: Brookings Institution Press, 2000.

——. "SALT I: An Evaluation." *World Politics* 31, no. 1 (1978): 1–25.

——. "The Soviet SS-20 Decision." *Survival* 25 (May–June 1983): 110–119.

Graham, Thomas. *Disarmament Sketches: Three Decades of Arms Control and International Law.* Seattle: University of Washington Press, 2012.

Graham, Thomas W. "The Politics of Failure: Strategic Nuclear Arms Control, Public Opinion, and Domestic Politics in the United States, 1945–1980." PhD diss., Massachusetts Institute of Technology, 1989.

Gray, Colin S., and Jeffrey Barlow. "Inexcusable Restraint: The Decline of American Military Power in the 1970s." *International Security* 10 (Fall 1985): 27–69.

Haig, Alexander. *Caveat: Realism, Reagan, and Foreign Policy.* New York: MacMillan Publishing, 1984.

Hanhimaki, Jussi. *The Flawed Architect: Henry Kissinger and American Foreign Policy.* Oxford: Oxford University Press, 2004.

Harris, John, and Andre Gsponer. "Armour Defuses the Neutron Bomb." *New Scientist* 109 (March 1986): 44–49.

Hayward, Stephen F. *The Age of Reagan: The Conservative Counter-Revolution, 1980–1989.* New York: Crown Publishing Group, 2009.

Herz, John H. *Political Realism and Political Idealism: A Study in Theories and Realities.* Chicago: University of Chicago Press, 1951.

Hines, John G., Ellis M. Mishulovich, and John F. Shull. *Soviet Intentions 1965–1985.* Vols. 1 and 2. Washington, DC: Office of Net Assessment, 1995.

Hirschfeld, Thomas J., ed. *Intelligence and Arms Control: A Marriage of Convenience.* Austin: Texas Monthly Press, 1987.

Horrocks, David, and Helmi Raaska, eds. *The Vladivostok Summit Meeting on Arms Control, November 23–24, 1974.* Gerald R. Ford Presidential Digital Library. https://www.fordlibrarymuseum.gov/library/exhibits/vladivostok/vladivostok.asp. Accessed October 2, 2013.

Huntington, Samuel. "Arms Races: Prerequisites and Results." *Public Policy* 8, no. 41 (1958): 41–86.

Iklé, Fred. "Preparing for Industrial Mobilization: The First Step toward Full Strength." In *The Politics of National Security Strategy*, edited by Marcus Raskin, 57–60. New York: Transaction Publishers, 1979.

Isaacson, Walter. *Kissinger: A Biography.* New York: Simon and Schuster, 2013.

James, Christian, and Daniel Lewis, eds. *The Richard M. Nixon National Security Files, 1969–1974: Strategic Arms Limitation Talks*: Bethesda, MD: LexisNexis, 2007.

Joint Chiefs of Staff. Joint Secretariat. Historical Division. *Joint Chiefs of Staff Special Historical Study, A Historical Study of Strategic Connectivity, 1950–1981.* Washington, DC: Joint Chiefs of Staff, 1982. http://www.dod.mil/pubs/foi/Reading_Room/Joint_Staff/92-A-0781_A_Historical_Study_of_Strategic_Command_1950-1981.pdf. Accessed June 11, 2017.

Kahn, Anne Hessing. *Killing Détente: The Right Attacks the CIA.* University Park: Pennsylvania State University Press, 1998.

Kaplan, Fred. *The Wizards of Armageddon.* New York: Simon and Schuster, 1983.

Kaplan, Lawrence S., Ronald D. Landa, and Edward J. Drea. *History of the Office of the Secretary of Defense.* Vol. 5, *The McNamara Ascendancy, 1961–1965.* Washington, DC: Government Printing Office.

Kaufman, Burton Ira. *The Carter Years.* New York: Infobase Publishing, 2009.

Kaufman, Robert G. *Henry M. Jackson: A Life in Politics.* Seattle: University of Washington Press, 2000.

Kissinger, Henry. *The White House Years*. Boston: Little, Brown and Company, 1979.
——. *Years of Renewal*. New York: Touchstone, 1999.
——. *Years of Upheaval*. Boston: Little, Brown and Co., 1982.
Kistiakowsky, George. "The Folly of the Neutron Bomb." *Bulletin of the Atomic Scientists* 34 (Spring 1978): 25–29.
Knopf, Jeffrey W. *Domestic Society and International Cooperation: The Impact of Protest on U.S. Arms Control Policy*. Cambridge, UK: Cambridge University Press, 1998.
Kotkin, Stephen. *Armageddon Averted: The Soviet Collapse, 1970–2000*. Oxford: Oxford University Press, 2008.
Laird, Melvin. "Arms Control: The Russians Are Cheating!" *Reader's Digest*, December 1977, 97–101.
Macartney, John D. "John, How Should We Explain MASINT?" In *Intelligence and the National Security Strategist: Enduring Issues and Challenges*, edited by Roger Z. George and Robert D. Kline, 169–180. New York: Rowman and Littlefield, 2006.
Mahan, Erin R., ed. *Foreign Relations of the United States, 1969–1976*. Vol. 32, *Salt I, 1969–1972*. Washington, DC: U.S. Government Printing Office, 2010.
——. *Foreign Relations of the United States, 1969–1976*. Vol. 33, *SALT II, 1972–1980*. Washington, DC: U.S. Government Printing Office: 2013.
Mandelbaum, Michael. *The Nuclear Question: The United States and Nuclear Weapons*. Cambridge: Cambridge University Press, 1979.
McGwire, Michael. *Military Objectives in Soviet Foreign Policy*. Washington, DC: Brookings Institute Press, 1987.
McNamara, Robert S. *Blundering into Disaster: Surveying the First Century of the Nuclear Age*. New York: Pantheon, 1986.
Mlyn, Eric. *The State, Society, and Limited Nuclear War*. Albany: State University of New York Press, 1995.
Mueller, Richard. *Physics for Future Presidents*. New York: W.W. Norton and Co., 2008.
Myer, David S. *A Winter of Discontent: The Nuclear Freeze and American Politics*. New York: ABC-CLIO, 1990.
Nation, R. Craig. *Black Earth, Red Star: A History of Soviet Security Policy*. Ithaca, NY: Cornell University Press, 1992.
Newhouse, John. *Cold Dawn: The Story of SALT*. Washington: Pergamon-Brassey's, 1989.
Nitze, Paul. *From Hiroshima to Glasnost: At the Center of Decision*. New York: Grove Weidenfeld, 1989.
——. "The Merits and Demerits of a SALT II Agreement." In *The Fateful Ends and Shades of SALT: Past, Present, and Yet to Come?* edited by Frank R. Barnett, 3–20. New York: Crane, Russak & Company, 1979.
——. "The Strategic Balance between Hope and Skepticism." *Foreign Policy* 17 (Winter 1974–1975): 136–156.
——. "The Vladivostok Accord and SALT II." *The Review of Politics* 37, no. 2 (1975): 147–160.
Noonan, Peggy. *What I Saw at the Revolution: A Political Life in the Reagan Era*. New York: Random House Publishing, 2003.
Novak, Robert. *The Reagan Revolution: An Inside Look at the Transformation of the U.S. Government*. New York: E. P. Dutton, 1981.
Nuclear Targeting Policy Review: Phase II Report. Washington, DC: Office of the Secretary of Defense, 1978. http://www2.gwu.edu/~nsarchiv/nukevault/ebb390/docs/11-1-78percent20policypercent20reviewpercent20summary.pdf. Accessed May 10, 2014.
Pipes, R. "Team B: The Reality behind the Myth." *Commentary*, October 1986: 25–40.

Podhoretz, Norman. "The Culture of Appeasement." *Harper's Magazine* 255, no. 1529 (1977): 25–32.

Podvig, Pavel. "The Window of Vulnerability That Wasn't: Soviet Military Buildup in the 1970s—A Research Note," *International Security* 33, no. 1 (2008): 118–138.

Poole, Walter S. *History of Acquisition in the Department of Defense.* Vol. 2, *Adapting to Flexible Response, 1960–1968.* Washington, DC: Government Printing Office, 2013.

Prados, John. *Keepers of the Keys: A History of the National Security Council from Truman to Bush.* New York: William Morrow and Company, 1991.

Reagan, Ronald. "Remarks at the Annual Washington Conference of the American Legion." February 22, 1983. *Ronald Reagan Presidential Library.* http://www.reagan.utexas.edu/archives/speeches/1983/22283b.htm. Accessed August 21, 2014.

——. "Remarks to Members of the National Press Club on Arms Reduction and Nuclear Weapons." November 18, 1981. *The American Presidency Project.* http://www.presidency.ucsb.edu/ws/?pid=43264. Accessed June 11, 2017.

Richelson, Jeffrey. "PD-59, NSDD-13 and the Reagan Strategic Modernization Program." *Journal of Strategic Studies* 6 no. 2 (1983): 125–146.

Rowny, Edward L. *It Takes One to Tango.* New York: Brassey's, 1992.

Russett, Bruce. "Doves, Hawks, and U.S. Public Opinion." *Political Science Quarterly* 105, no. 4 (1990): 515–538.

Saval'yev, Alexsandr', and Nikolay Detinov. *The Big Five: Arms Control Decision-Making in the Soviet Union.* Westport, CT: Prager, 1995.

Schwartz, Stephen I., ed. *Atomic Audit: The Costs and Consequences of U.S. Nuclear Weapons since 1940.* Washington, DC: Brookings Institution, 1998.

Seaborg, Glen, with Samuel Loeb. *Stemming the Tide: Arms Control in the Johnson Years.* Lanham, MD: Lexington Books, 1987.

Selvage, Douglas E., and Melissa Jane Taylor, eds. *Foreign Relations of the United States.* Vol. 15, *Soviet Union, June 1972–August 1974.* Washington, DC: U.S. Government Printing Office, 2011.

Senate Armed Services Committee. *Nomination of Mr. Paul C. Warnke to Be Director of the U.S. Arms Control and Disarmament Agency and Ambassador, First Session, 95th Congress.* Washington, DC: Government Printing Office, 1977.

Shultz, George. *Turmoil and Triumph: My Years as Secretary of State.* New York: Charles Scribner's Sons, 1993.

Sloan, Elinor Camille. *The Revolution in Military Affairs.* Toronto: McGill-Queen's Press, 2002.

Smith, Gerard. "The Arms Control and Disarmament Agency: An Unfinished History." *Bulletin of the Atomic Scientists* 40, no. 4 (1984): 13–17.

——. *Doubletalk: The Story of SALT I.* Lanham, MD: University Press of America, 1985.

Smith, Louis J., and David H. Herschler, eds. *Foreign Relations of the United States, 1969–1976.* Vol. 1, *Foundations of Foreign Policy, 1969–1972.* Washington, DC: U.S. Government Printing Office, 2003.

Stanford Arms Control Group. *International Arms Control: Issues and Agreements.* Stanford, CA: Stanford University Press, 1984.

Stuckey, Mary E. *Jimmy Carter, Human Rights, and the National Agenda.* College Station: Texas A&M University Press, 2008.

Suri, Jeremi. *Power and Protest: Global Revolution and the Rise of Detente.* Cambridge, MA: Harvard University Press, 2005.

Talbott, Strobe. "Behind Closed Doors." *Time,* December 5, 1983.

——. *Deadly Gambits: The Reagan Administration and the Stalemate in Nuclear Arms Control.* New York: Vintage Books, 1985.

——. *Endgame: The Inside Story of SALT II.* New York: Harper Colophon Books, 1980.

——. *The Master of the Game: Paul Nitze and the Nuclear Peace.* New York: Vintage Books, 1989.

Teriff, Terry. *The Nixon Administration and the Making of U.S. Nuclear Strategy.* Ithaca, NY: Cornell University Press, 1995.

Thornton, Richard C. *The Nixon-Kissinger Years: Reshaping America's Foreign Policy.* New York: Paragon House, 1989.

U.S. Central Intelligence Agency. "Intelligence Community Experiment in Competitive Analysis, Soviet Strategic Objectives an Alternative View, Report of Team 'B.'" December 1976. National Security Archive, Electronic Briefing Book No. 139. http://www.gwu.edu/~nsarchiv/NSAEBB/NSAEBB139/nitze10.pdf. Accessed February 12, 2012.

U.S. Congress. Senate. Committee on Armed Services. *Military Implications of the Treaty on the Limitation of Strategic Offensive Arms and Protocol Thereto (SALT II Treaty): Hearings Before the Committee on Armed Services of the United States Senate.* Washington, DC: U.S. Government Printing Office, 1979.

U.S. Congress. Senate. Committee on Foreign Relations. *The INF Treaty: Hearings before the Committee on Foreign Relations, United States Senate, One Hundredth Congress, Second Session, on the Treaty between the United States of America and the Union of Soviet Socialist Republics on the Elimination of Their Intermediate-Range and Shorter-Range Missiles. Part 1, January 25, 26, 27, and 28.* Washington, DC: U.S. Government Printing Office, 1988.

——. *The SALT II Treaty: Hearings Before the Committee on Foreign Relations of the Senate.* Washington, DC: U.S. Government Printing Office, 1979.

U.S. Congress. Senate. Select Committee on Intelligence. *Principle Findings on the Capabilities of the United States to Monitor the SALT II Treaty: Report of the Senate Select Committee on Intelligence.* Washington, DC: U.S. Government Printing Office, 1979.

Vance, Cyrus. *Hard Choices: Critical Years in America's Foreign Policy.* New York: Simon and Schuster, 1983.

Warnke, Paul C. "Apes on a Treadmill." *Foreign Policy* 18 (Spring 1975): 12–29.

Watson, Robert J. *History of the Office of the Secretary of Defense.* Vol. 4, *Into the Missile Age.* Washington, DC: Government Printing Office, 1987.

Weinberger, Caspar. *Fighting for Peace: Seven Critical Years in the Pentagon.* New York: Warner Books, 1991.

Westad, Odd Arne. *The Global Cold War.* Cambridge: Cambridge University Press, 2007.

Wharton, R. M. "Finlandization: Neutering of a Nation." *Human Events* 38, no. 15 (1978): 296–308.

Williams, Robert E., and Paul R. Viotti. *Arms Control: History, Theory, and Policy.* Santa Barbara, CA: ABC-CLIO, 2012.

Wittner, Lawrence S. *The Struggle Against the Bomb.* Vol. 3. Palo Alto, CA: Stanford University Press, 2003.

Wohlstetter, Albert. "Is There a Strategic Arms Race?" *Foreign Policy* 15 (Summer 1974): 3–20.

Wolfe, Thomas. *The SALT Experience: Its Impact on U.S. and Soviet Strategic Policy and Decisionmaking.* Santa Monica, CA: Project RAND, 1975.

Wolfe, Thomas W., John D. Steinbruner, and Ernest May. *History of the Strategic Arms Competition.* Washington, DC: Office of the Secretary of Defense, 1981.

Zaloga, Steven. *The Kremlin's Nuclear Sword: The Rise and Fall of Russia's Strategic Nuclear Forces, 1945–2000.* London: Smithsonian Institute Press, 2002.

Zelizer, Julian E. *Jimmy Carter.* New York: Times Books, 2010.

"Zumwalt: Secretary Lacks Faith in Americans: Why Kissinger Concedes to Soviets." *Human Events* 36, no. 15 (1976): 1–7.

Index

CPSIA information can be obtained
at www.ICGtesting.com
Printed in the USA
BVOW09*1045060318
509417BV00001B/5/P